EQUAL JUSTICE

EQUAL JUSTICE

A HISTORY OF THE
LEGAL AID SOCIETY OF MILWAUKEE

By

THOMAS G. CANNON

MARQUETTE
UNIVERSITY
PRESS

LIBRARY OF CONGRESS CATALOGING-IN-PUBLICATION DATA

Cannon, Thomas G. (Thomas Gildea), 1946-
Equal justice : a history of the legal aid society of Milwaukee / by Thomas G. Cannon.
    p. cm.
Includes bibliographical references and index.
ISBN-13: 978-0-87462-067-2 (hardcover : alk. paper)
ISBN-10: 0-87462-067-8 (hardcover : alk. paper)
1. Justice, Administration of—Milwaukee—History. 2. Milwaukee Legal Aid Society. I. Title.
KFW2908.C36 2010
347.775'95—dc22

                                                        2011009449

Association of American
University Presses

MARQUETTE UNIVERSITY PRESS
MILWAUKEE

The Association of Jesuit University Presses

DEDICATION

To the poor of Milwaukee —
whom it has been
the Legal Aid Society's great privilege to represent
for nearly a century.

CONTENTS

PREFACE

The centennial anniversary of Professor John R. Commons' visionary proposal in 1910 to establish a free legal aid program in Milwaukee offers a unique opportunity to reflect back on the past hundred years as we contemplate going forward into a second century of service. Reviewing the rich and colorful history of the Legal Aid Society of Milwaukee conjures up an overwhelming sense of gratitude to all those who have gone before us in the ongoing struggle to achieve our mission of equal justice for the poor.

Academics tend to treat the national legal aid movement as a subsidiary development of the Progressive Reform Era (1890-1920) in American history.[1] That view, however, obscures the movement's earlier origins in the Freedmen's Bureau (1865) and in New York's German immigrant organization (1876). Although the history of legal aid in the United States has been relatively little studied, it is more complex than some have previously suggested. As this book shows, in Milwaukee at least, it was informed by multiple impulses that included religious values, Anglo-American constitutional principles, the legal profession's ethical norms, Wisconsin's populist constitution and nineteenth-century jurisprudence, a sense of noblesse oblige among the well off, good government reforms of the Progressive Era, the Wisconsin Idea, and Milwaukee's unique brand of urban socialism. For comparative purposes, accounts of some of the larger individual legal aid programs around the country may be usefully consulted, notably those in New York, Chicago, Boston, and Cleveland.[2] Nonetheless, the emergence of the legal aid movement, both locally and nationally, remains a virtual footnote in American legal history.

By way of contrast, selected aspects of Wisconsin's legal history have been well served by scholars over the years. To mention just a few of the outstanding books in this fecund tradition, we have benefit of an important study on the state's constitutional conventions, a narrative history of the Wisconsin Supreme Court, a biography of one of the state's most influential jurists, a legal history of a vital state industry, two recent accounts of the state's most controversial litigation, a chronicle of the state's largest private law firm, an album of the state's historic county courthouses, a biographical directory of early women lawyers in Wisconsin, and a comprehensive analysis of the development of the state's legal system.[3] To this impressive list, we can now add a study of Wisconsin's oldest public-interest law firm: the Legal Aid Society of Milwaukee.

This monograph had its origin in a talk that Tom Zander invited me to give at an LAS staff retreat in 1991 marking the 75th anniversary of the founding of the Society. Five years later, for the 80th anniversary, I conducted some independent research on the 1910-16 period, which is described herein as the birth struggle that led to creation of the Legal Aid Society of Milwaukee. When asked to return to the staff in 2005, one of my goals was to write a comprehensive history of the organization that has served Milwaukee's poor so admirably throughout the past century. Knowing the fragility of records and memories, I wanted to ensure that LAS's story would be preserved for the future.[4]

This book is not a formal academic study. Rather, it is intended to tell the story of the Legal Aid Society for the general reader in an accessible format through a combination of narratives, biographical notices, chronology, newspaper clippings, photographs, digest of noteworthy cases, and personnel rosters. Compiling a list of these early trailblazers, it might be noted, turned out to be the most challenging research aspect of this effort. Therefore, if any reader is aware of an individual who has been inadvertently overlooked, kindly contact the Legal Aid Society with his or her name.

For scholars, though, who recognize the value of allowing the sources to speak for themselves, a series of forty-five key historical documents recounting the origin and development of legal services to the poor in Milwaukee should prove of great interest. These revealing windows to the past provide insight into the philosophical outlook of, and particular issues facing, the Society's leadership during the past century. Many constitute a snapshot of LAS at various stages of its evolution. Given LAS's chronically precarious funding, it is fitting that the last two documents reflect threats to the Society's work in two important areas. As this book goes to press, both issues were unresolved.

The historical documents are buttressed by more than 400 source references and legal citations. These materials are generally embedded in the text; however, where elaboration was deemed necessary, such references have been relegated to chapter endnotes. Taken together, the broad range of materials collected here forms the raw database for a full academic study in the future. The goals of this more modest effort are to preserve the Society's valuable heritage, to acknowledge the enduring contributions of past staff, board, and supporters, and to provide some larger context within which to understand the organization's development.

In putting together this retrospective look, I have carefully examined the Society's minute books, annual reports, Superintendent's reports, and considerable archives. I have also perused the annual city directories, newspaper clippings file, and microfilmed local newspaper collection at the Milwaukee Public Library. Vital records in the Milwaukee County Register of Deeds Office were helpful. The microfilmed local newspaper clippings files at the Milwaukee County Historical Society and the City of Milwaukee Legislative Reference Library were extremely helpful as well. Marquette University Law Library's complete set of publications by the Milwaukee Bar Association (*Gavel, Messenger*) and State Bar of Wisconsin (*Proceedings of the SBAW, Wisconsin Bar Bulletin, Wisconsin Lawyer*) were quite useful. Much of the biographical information on the founders of LAS was gleaned from sources collected in that most rewarding of research compendia: the 23-volume *Subject Catalogue of the Library of the State Historical Society of Wisconsin* (Westport, CT: Greenwood Publishing Corp. 1971).

No history of an individual legal aid society can be fully told without access to four record sources that chronicle the early years of the national legal aid movement. Thus, I am grateful to Julia Jaet of the Marquette University Law Library for making available its full run of the *Legal Aid Brief Case*. Keith Buckley at Indiana University Law Library made that institution's comprehensive holdings of the *Legal Aid Review* accessible to me. Staff at the Duke University Law Library allowed me to read through their complete collection of the *Proceedings of the National Association of Legal Aid Organizations*. Finally, particular thanks are due to Thomas F. Harkins and Eleanor Mills at the Duke University Archives; they facilitated my review of the extremely valuable John S. Bradway Papers in the Perkins Library Special Collections. Bradway was a formative figure in the national legal aid organization for more than two decades.

Patrick B. Lavey and Amanda Patterson of the Social Law Library in Boston, keeper of the Reginald Heber Smith papers; Anne Mar, project archivist at the National Equal Justice Library at Georgetown University Law Center; and the staff of the Urban Archives at Temple University's Paley Library searched for, and retrieved, documents from their respective collections. The early papers of United Way of Greater Milwaukee and those of the City Club, both archived at the Milwaukee Area Research Center in the Golda Meir Library at the University of Wisconsin-Milwaukee, shed additional light on LAS's history. Steve Daily at the Milwaukee County Historical Society kindly provided access to the useful Victor Berger correspondence and Socialist Party records in his keeping. Daily, together with Lisa R. Marine at the Wisconsin Historical Society and Michele Sweetser at the Marquette University Archives, also made a generous selection of photographs available from their munificent collections.

In addition, I wish to record my gratitude to the following individuals and institutions: Tony Anderson at the *Wisconsin Law Journal*; Jeff Brown at the State Bar of Wisconsin; Dave Erne at Reinhart Boerner Van Deuren S.C.; Jerry Felsecker at the St. Vincent de Paul Society; Anthony Gad at the Wisconsin Legislative Reference Bureau; Professor Ramon A. Klitzke at Marquette University Law School; David M. Lucey at Foley & Lardner LLP; Gail McCarthy at United Way of Greater Milwaukee; Ann M. Murphy of Quarles & Brady LLP; Jane Ribadeneyra at National Legal Aid & Defender Association; and Jim Temmer at the Milwaukee Bar Association.

Many people have generously helped out in various ways on this project. Patrick Devitt, Laura Emerson, Michael P. Gallagher, Marie Rohde, the Honorable Julia Vosper, and Joseph R. Wall all freely gave of their time and insights. Student interns Lucy Kelly, Sam Levine, Marie Lynch, and Alexandra Porteshawver tracked down obscure references at my request. Katie Haensel, daughter-in-law of Alma C.

Schlesinger, John Dolan, son of Julia Dolan McClelland, and Barbara Berman, widow of Dave, patiently answered numerous biographical queries.

Two LAS colleagues, Pete Koneazny and Amy Quester, very kindly read a preliminary draft of the text and offered many helpful comments. Chief Staff Attorney Shelia Hill-Roberts assisted in compiling the historical roster of LAS social workers. My predecessors as Executive Director, Tom Zander, Carole Wenerowicz, and Jim Walrath, provided useful insights as well. Two other staff members, Jack Corbin and Brian Kemper, helped make possible the large and interesting collection of photographs. Finally, Paulette Wymbs and Mary Burks, my wonderful legal assistants, solved all my word-processor problems with their characteristic competence and patience.

Special thanks, of course, are owed to Governor Jim Doyle and Chief Justice Shirley S. Abrahamson for taking time out of their busy schedules to contribute the Foreword and Introduction respectively. Copyright holders of the *The Daily Reporter*, *Legal Aid Brief Case*, *MBA Gavel*, *Milwaukee Journal Sentinel*, *Wisconsin Law Review*, and *Wisconsin Law Journal*, kindly granted permission to reprint several items of historical interest. Particular acknowledgement must also be made of the resources and helpful staff in the Frank P. Zeidler Humanities Room at the Milwaukee Public Library.

Professor Dan Blinka of Marquette Law School, himself a noted American legal historian, generously read an early draft of the manuscript and supplied many valuable suggestions. His constant encouragement makes him the godfather of this book. Julia Jaet, reference librarian at Marquette Law School, kindly assisted in obtaining several rare items on inter-library loan. Professor Andy Tallon and Maureen Kondrick of Marquette University Press smoothed the transition from electronic text to finished book in splendid fashion. Of course, any remaining errors or omissions in this work are entirely my own responsibility.

TGC

---

1. See especially Phillip L. Merkel, "At the Crossroads of Reform: The First Fifty Years of American Legal Aid, 1876-1926" in *Houston Law Review* 27 (1990) 1-44; Earl Johnson, Jr., *Justice and Reform: The Formative Years of the American Legal Services Program* (New Brunswick: Transaction Books,

1978) 3-19; Reginald Heber Smith, *Justice and the Poor* (New York: Carnegie Foundation, 1919).

2. For individual programs, see John MacArthur Maguire, *The Lance of Justice:
A Semi-Centennial History of the Legal Aid Society, 1876-1926* (Harvard
University Press, 1928); Harrison Tweed, *The Legal Aid Society of New York
City, 1876-1951* (New York Legal Aid Society, 1954); Jack Katz, *Poor Peo-
ple's Lawyers in Transition* (Rutgers University Press, 1982), a study of the
Chicago Legal Aid Society; Mark Spiegel, "The Boston Legal Aid Society:
1900-1925" in *Massachusetts Legal History* 9 (2003) 7-48; and Carol Poh
Miller, *A Passion for Justice: A History of the Legal Aid Society of Cleveland,
1905-2005* (Legal Aid Society of Cleveland, 2006).

3. Milo M. Quaife, ed. *The Struggle Over Ratification, 1846-47* (Madison:
State Historical Society of Wisconsin, 1920); John B. Winslow, *The Story
of a Great Court* (Chicago: T.H. Flood, 1912); Alfons J. Beitzinger, *Edward
G. Ryan: Lion of the Law* (Madison: State Historical Society of Wiscon-
sin, 1960); James Willard Hurst, *Law and Economic Growth: The Legal
History of the Lumber Industry in Wisconsin, 1836-1915* (Cambridge, MA:
Belknap Press, 1964); Robert H. Baker, *The Rescue of Joshua Glover: A
Fugitive Slave, the Constitution, and the Coming of the Civil War* (Ohio Uni-
versity Press, 2006); Ruby West Jackson and Walter T. McDonald, *Find-
ing Freedom: The Untold Story of Joshua Glover, Runaway Slave* (Madison:
Wisconsin Historical Society Press, 2007); Ellen Langill, *Foley & Lardner,
Attorneys at Law, 1842-1992* (Madison: State Historical Society of Wis-
consin, 1992); *Pioneers in the Law: The First 150 Women* (Madison: State
Bar of Wisconsin, 1998); L. Roger Turner and Marv Balousek, *Wisconsin's
Historic Courthouses* (Oregon, WI: Badger Books, 1998); and Joseph A.
Ranney, *Trusting Nothing to Providence: A History of Wisconsin's Legal Sys-
tem* (Madison: University of Wisconsin Law School, 1999).

4. Water and smoke damage from a 1985 fire in the building that housed
the headquarters of the Legal Aid Society destroyed some valuable historical materials. Among the items lost were two wonderful photographs:
one of Milwaukee's City Hall with signage welcoming a convention of the
national legal aid organization in 1942, the other of an LAS float carrying a
replica of the Statue of Liberty in the Community Fund parade *circa* 1950.
Cf. this description: "Perhaps the most massive float is the one representing the Legal Aid Society with a row of law books up to 16 ft. high" in
"Bulky Parade Floats Await Tinsel Touches," *Milwaukee Journal* (September 25, 1951). Some news clippings from the 1940s and 1950s were also
destroyed by the fire.

FOREWORD

The Legal Aid Society of Milwaukee is a unique treasure of statewide significance. Each year since 1916 it has provided powerful advocacy on behalf of Wisconsin's most vulnerable residents in a broad array of state and federal forums, including administrative tribunals, trial and appellate courts, and legislative halls. In this way, the Society has ensured that the voices of the marginalized and dispossessed are heard in the councils of power.

1. Wisconsin Governor Jim Doyle. *Courtesy of the Office of the Governor.*

The Legal Aid Society of Milwaukee has also spearheaded a number of innovative initiatives to improve the administration of justice in Wisconsin: the first small claims court, the first public defender program, the first discrete children's court, and the first anti-discrimination project for persons living with HIV/AIDS, to name just a few. In addition, the Society's record of published cases and legislative advocacy has created an impressive body of jurisprudence and statutory law that protects the constitutional and civil rights of all Wisconsinites. The result is a state that is a more equitable place to live and raise our families.

In reading this fascinating history, I have been struck by the numerous connections between my gubernatorial predecessors and the Legal Aid Society of Milwaukee. Former Governors Emanuel L. Philipp and Francis E. McGovern both served on the Society's Advisory Board in the 1920s; Judge John W. Reynolds, another former Governor, was a member of the Society's Board of Directors in the late 1960s and early 1970s. In 1972, the Governor's Task Force on Judicial Reorganization (established by Governor Patrick Lucey) obtained valuable input from the Society's staff.

More recently, Legal Aid Society attorneys worked closely with my own administration on efforts to protect Wisconsin consumers from predatory lenders, fight mortgage foreclosure fraud, and encourage state funding for civil legal services to the poor. How appropriate, then, that the national legal aid movement was founded in 1876 by Edward Salomon, who served as Governor of Wisconsin during the Civil War.

I have a deep personal interest in the work of the Legal Aid Society of Milwaukee, which stems from the proud fact that my sister Catey serves as Chief Staff Attorney of its Civil Division. Moreover, after graduating from Harvard Law School, I worked as a staff attorney at DNA People's Legal Services representing members of the Navajo Nation in Chinle, Arizona. My experience there taught me the value, indeed the necessity, of having a strong advocate to represent the poor against entrenched corporate interests. See, for example, *Little Redhouse v. Quality Ford Sales, Inc.*, 523 F.2d 1 (10th Cir. 1976).

On behalf of the people of our state, I thank the dedicated staff, board, and volunteers of the Legal Aid Society of Milwaukee – a bright jewel in the state's legal crown – for their exemplary public service. I wish them much continued success as they look forward to a second century of compelling advocacy on behalf of Wisconsin's poor.

Jim Doyle
Governor of Wisconsin

INTRODUCTION

Many years ago my uncle Max, who like many Jews had fled to South America to escape Nazi persecution, came from his adopted country of Chile to visit my folk in New York. On the way, he stopped to see the famed Miami. While driving his rented car, he was picked up for a traffic violation and found himself in court.

2. Chief Justice Shirley S. Abrahamson. *Courtesy of Wisconsin Supreme Court.*

Now, Max spoke many languages: the Polish of his native country, as well as some German and Russian he picked up while living in Poland; a little French and Italian he learned after fleeing Poland; and the Spanish of his new homeland. But he did not speak English, and thus could not understand the proceedings of the court. Finding no one in the courtroom who spoke any of the other languages he knew, and fearing anti-Semitism, Max reluctantly admitted that he spoke Yiddish as well. To his surprise and relief, so did the judge – and the clerk, the court reporter, and many others in the courtroom. Yiddish became the court language. Max got a warning and a welcome to the USA, and was soon back in the car. "Only in America," my uncle always said when retelling this story.

Like many who become involved in legal proceedings, my uncle found himself in a situation in which he was unable to understand or participate in the process. Luckily for him, the confusion was temporary; once he and the judicial system found a common language, his case could be resolved. But even when everyone involved in court proceedings speaks English, those who are unfamiliar with the "language" of the legal system are at a great disadvantage if they cannot afford an attorney to "interpret" for them and guide them through the process. Providing legal assistance to the poor is thus critical in ensuring that the court system can provide justice for all. Milwaukee has been fortunate to have its Legal Aid Society engaged in that vital mission for nearly 100 years.

Executive Director Thomas Cannon has put together an impressive array of materials from a variety of sources to tell the story of the Legal Aid Society of Milwaukee, one of the nation's oldest, continuously operating organizations committed to providing legal assistance to the poor. The Society's incorporation in Milwaukee followed closely the reinvigoration of the Boston Legal Aid Society in 1914, directed by Reginald Heber Smith, which is often viewed as starting the modern period of legal assistance to the poor.

The story Tom Cannon tells through his fine selection of historical documents begins in 1910, before the Society's incorporation, as the brainchild of University of Wisconsin Professor John R. Commons, and continues through to documents reflecting the organization's advocacy of children and the mentally ill in 2010.

The story of the Milwaukee Legal Aid Society, "a poor man's lawyer," is one of co-operation, collaboration, and alliances (and sometimes disagreements) with numerous organizations and individuals, including the State Bar of Wisconsin, the Milwaukee Bar Association, Marquette University Law School, University of Wisconsin Law School, Legal Action of Wisconsin, State Public Defender, national organizations and their affiliates, individual lawyers committed to pro bono representation, and volunteer non-lawyers such as lawyers' wives (now referred to as lawyers' spouses).

The Society's story is one of an organization changing directions and changing emphasis in providing legal services for the poor, from social services to servicing individual cases and impact cases, from criminal and civil cases to only civil cases (including juveniles and the elderly), and finally to comprehensive advocacy for the poor before legislative, executive, and judicial tribunals. The Society's staff has taken numerous roles over the years: social worker, community organizer, law reformer, lobbyist, and litigator.

Although the Society's activities and emphases may have changed, "its fundamental purpose" has remained unchanged – namely "to see that persons who are poor and oppressed shall obtain justice according to law." Throughout its history, the Legal Aid Society of Milwaukee has struggled to achieve equal justice for the poor. And it has performed its assigned task admirably.

The number of indigent persons needing legal assistance in Milwaukee is striking. The State Bar of Wisconsin's 2007 study, entitled *Bridging the Gap: Wisconsin's Unmet Legal Needs*, estimates that more than half a million people in Wisconsin face significant legal problems without legal assistance. The single biggest barrier to obtaining legal assistance is poverty.

In recent years, the Society has provided legal services to more than 8,000 persons a year with a diverse spectrum of problems such as parental rights, housing, civil commitments, bankruptcies, foreclosures, employment, and government benefits. Despite the Society's efforts, many Milwaukee residents do not have access to legal services. Tom Cannon characterizes the problems now facing the poor as a crisis. Many cannot be served by the Society, and many do not even know of the existence of the Society.

Throughout its history, the Society has suffered from what it calls malnourishment, a lack of adequate funding to provide attorneys to all indigents who need lawyers.

There are no easy answers to the question of how all people can be guaranteed access to an attorney. As I have written elsewhere, solutions can be found only through the efforts of many, including the legal profession, the law schools, the courts, the legislature, non-governmental entities, and dedicated individuals.

We in Wisconsin are working to improve access to justice.

The Wisconsin legislature has for the first time appropriated funds (one million dollars) to support civil legal services for low-income persons.

Legal assistance for the indigent is being funded by the Interest on Lawyers' Trust Accounts (IOLTA).

The Wisconsin Supreme Court has imposed an assessment on attorneys and judges of fifty dollars a year to create additional funds for civil legal services to low-income persons.

The Wisconsin bar has a proud history of providing pro bono representation, in keeping with the Code of Professional Responsibility.

The Wisconsin court system has a program to address language barriers and has worked to help the self-represented. We have a Website with interactive forms, self-help centers in courthouses, volunteers in the courthouses, and a public library initiative to foster communication between local courts and public libraries to meet the legal information needs of self-represented litigants. Judges are teaching judges how to manage cases involving self-represented litigants.

The University of Wisconsin Law School hosted the second Wisconsin Equal Justice Conference in 2009 to develop additional programs for improving access to justice. The first conference was held at Marquette University in 2007. The Equal Justice Fund continues to sponsor an annual Howard B. Eisenberg Memorial Dinner to raise funds and honor the late Marquette University Law School dean and Legal Aid Society of Milwaukee board member, who was dedicated to providing pro bono legal services.

Even with these programs, we are not able to guarantee counsel to the poor of Wisconsin. Yet there is hope in each successive generation that new answers to this age-old problem will be found. Change comes about through the dedication of legal professionals and others who embrace the principle of every person's basic right to justice. The history of the Legal Aid Society of Milwaukee is a history of accomplishments and successes. For nearly a century, it has addressed the needs of the poor, performing an invaluable service in the public interest. We're fortunate that the story of the Society has now been captured in print and that this long-established 20th-century organization will continue to evolve and to work in the 21st century toward equal justice for the poor.

Shirley S. Abrahamson
Chief Justice
Wisconsin Supreme Court

1
THE LEGAL AID SOCIETY TODAY

The Legal Aid Society of Milwaukee is one of America's oldest public-interest law firms. When it vigorously celebrated a recent anniversary, one local newspaper reported the event by describing the Society as Milwaukee's "venerable public interest law firm." ("Celebrating 90 Years" in *Shepherd Express*, August 31–September 6, 2006). Another paper characterized the organization's work as "heroic." ("Legal Aid Society celebrates 90 years in Milwaukee" in *Wisconsin Law Journal*, August 30, 2006).

Each year, the Legal Aid Society provides free legal services to more than 8,000 of Milwaukee's most vulnerable residents: abused and neglected children, developmentally disabled adults, persons living with HIV/AIDS, battered women, the mentally ill, the physically impaired, immigrants, prisoners, consumers, the elderly, the homeless, and the unemployed – all of whom are too poor to hire legal counsel on their own.

Clients often face catastrophic events during which representation by an attorney is essential. These include termination of parental rights, eviction, bankruptcy, foreclosure, custody disputes, domestic violence, wage garnishment, repossession of household goods, civil mental commitment, housing code violations, identity theft, protective placement, loss of employment, civil forfeitures, tax liens, denial of government benefits to which the client is entitled by law, Municipal Court warrants, consumer problems, and discrimination based on race, gender, age, religious affiliation, or health status.

In addition to representing families and individuals, the Legal Aid Society also challenges patterns and practices of abusive behavior by large corporations and governmental entities. Staff lawyers act in these matters as private attorneys general by vindicating constitutional rights or advancing important public interests on behalf of the poor.

The Legal Aid Society provides a full range of civil legal representation in all state and federal forums, including administrative agencies, legislative halls, and all trial and appellate courts. The Society's long tradition of legislative advocacy continues robustly today. In just the past state legislative session, LAS staff worked on various bills to restrict certain payday lending practices in the state, to fund civil legal services to the poor, to abolish the statute of limitations for victims of childhood sexual abuse, to regulate mortgage reconveyances and consultants, to protect elderly patients in nursing homes with code violations, to protect children's right to receive competent medical treatment, and to require mediation in foreclosure cases. See, for example, "Legislature wrestles with ways to rein in payday lending" in *Milwaukee Journal Sentinel* March 18, 2010); "Assembly panel urged to slow foreclosures" in *Milwaukee Journal Sentinel* (February 12, 2009).

It is sometimes erroneously assumed that the Legal Aid Society of Milwaukee's work is purely local in character. However, this assumption ignores a substantial statewide dimension to the Society's advocacy in four distinct areas. First, LAS currently maintains four class action cases on behalf of more than 155,000 clients who reside in all 72 counties of Wisconsin. Second, the Society's legislative advocacy affects the state's entire poverty population of nearly 600,000 residents in every county. Third, LAS's appellate advocacy has produced nearly 150 published state and federal court opinions that serve as statewide legal precedents. And finally, the Society conducts continuing legal education and judicial education seminars in all parts of the state to train judges and lawyers in areas of the law that affect Wisconsin's large poverty community. As Governor Doyle notes in his Foreword to this history: "The Legal Aid Society of Milwaukee is a unique treasure of statewide significance."

To increase access to free legal services, the Legal Aid Society opened two neighborhood offices in 1966. Funding cutbacks forced their closure three years later. Today, however, staff attorneys meet with clients at ten locations throughout Milwaukee County, including LAS's convenient Downtown office, its quarters in the Vel R. Phillips Juvenile Justice Center, and at the Milwaukee County Mental Health Center. Staff attorneys also conduct regular outreach sessions at St. Benedict's

Community Meal, The Gathering Meal Program at St. James Church, Christian Faith Fellowship Church, Gary Dobbs Family Resource Center, Sixteenth Street Community Health Center, Martin Luther King Heritage Health Clinic, and Sojourner Family Peace Center. The Legal Aid Society continues multiple efforts on other fronts to expand access to legal counsel. For example, in conjunction with Marquette University Law School, LAS helped establish the Coalition for Access to Legal Resources (CALR), an internet-based initiative designed to connect low-income clients with legal services providers. The Society also sponsors Milwaukee's 2-1-1 Community Resource Specialists referral hotline. In addition, the Legal Aid Society helped organize the Milwaukee Justice Center, an effort to assist *pro se* litigants at the Milwaukee County Courthouse. All three initiatives are widely used by residents of the city's poverty community to participate in legal and other social service programs.

The work of our staff continues to cover an amazingly diverse range. Within just the past few years, for example, Jim Brennan led the effort to provide free legal services to Hurricane Katrina refugees forced to flee to Milwaukee. Mike Vruno filed a response to a petition for certiorari in the United States Supreme Court in a case involving application of the Indian Child Welfare Act. Paula Lorant organized the Social Security Intervention Network, a novel consortium of district managers, congressional liaisons, and disability advocates working together to reduce lengthy administrative backlogs. Jenny Ortiz was appointed to serve as a guardian ad litem by the United States District Court in a case involving the Hague Convention on Civil Aspects of International Child Abduction. Christie Christie and Pete Koncazny taught as adjunct professors at Marquette University Law School, and Mike Vruno lectured at the University of Wisconsin-Milwaukee School of Social Welfare.

In two recent terms, Shelia Hill-Roberts, Carol Petersen, and Cindy Lepkowski each argued important children's rights cases before the Wisconsin Supreme Court. Litigation Director Pete Koneazny is currently trying a complex class action lawsuit against Milwaukee County for maintaining substandard jail conditions. "Legal Aid brings jail to justice" in *Milwaukee Journal Sentinel* (April 13, 2008). He is also representing low-income consumers in two suits against predatory financial institutions for victimizing the poor. In one of them, a single mother borrowed $800; after interest, finance charges, and insurance coverage were added, her debt ballooned 583% to $4,667. "Lawsuits accuse lender of deception" in *The Business Journal* (April 25, 2008). Both cases are ongoing.

Staff attorney Lisa Clay Foley forced Johnston Community Health Center to reverse its illegal ban on treating persons living with HIV/AIDS. Karen Dardy supervises an innovative project that assigns volunteer lawyers from Milwaukee's largest law firms to donate their services to the poor. Colleen Foley succeeded in setting aside more than $600,000 in small claims judgments procured by a landlord who fraudulently claimed to have served legal papers on tenants in hundreds of eviction cases. On behalf of a destitute widow living in a women's shelter, Phil Rosenkranz recently negotiated an extraordinary result: a tax liability in excess of $1 million was reduced down to $500. In another case, representing a widow working at a minimum-wage job, Rosenkranz knocked a $680,000 tax debt down to $150. Both sums are being repaid by the clients in manageable monthly installments. Karen Kotecki is arguing a case in the Wisconsin Court of Appeals challenging a trial court's refusal to provide a Spanish-language interpreter to translate English-language court documents for a Latino client in a mental commitment proceeding.

A contentious child custody case handled by staff attorney Janet Mueller, guardian ad litem in the Family Court, garnered national attention when a mother secreted her infant son from the court and stubbornly chose to go to jail for contempt rather than reveal the child's whereabouts to the judge. "When Motherhood Gets You Jail Time" in *TIME* (online ed. December 19, 2007); "Choosing Jail Over Joint Custody" in *Id.* Mike Vruno is currently handling a challenging international child custody case involving two wards under the protection of an English court; the case requires application of choice-of-law principles under the Uniform Child Custody Jurisdiction and Enforcement Act (Wisconsin) and the Children Act, 1989 (United Kingdom).

Legal Aid Society lawyers also make important contributions to development of the law by researching and writing articles for professional journals. Staff attorney Christie Christie edits the *Children's*

Law News, bulletin of the Children & the Law Section of the State Bar of Wisconsin. Amy Quester published an analysis of the development of eviction law in the prestigious *American Journal of Legal History* xlviii (2006) [2008] 408-52. Mike Vruno wrote an article, "Applying Chapter 54 to Minor Guardianship Cases: Fitting a Square Peg in a Round Hole" in *Children's Law News* 15, no. 3 (2007) 13. In addition, a dozen LAS staff attorneys have presented papers at continuing legal education and judicial education conferences during the past several years.

Chief Staff Attorney Catey Doyle has established a cutting-edge specialty in fighting mortgage fraud resulting from the recent collapse of the sub-prime real estate market. "Sinking in a sea of foreclosures: Legal Aid helps woman keep home" in *Wisconsin Law Journal* (April 21, 2008). Within the past year, she has put on a series of legal education seminars on mortgage foreclosure fraud for lawyers in Madison, Green Bay, Eau Claire, and Milwaukee; she also trained judges at conferences in Appleton and Waukesha on the same topic. Doyle's work raised the Society's profile to the international stage after she was featured in an investigative report aired on the British Broadcasting Corporation network (August 23, 2007) and in an interview by German Public Radio (June 2010). In 2008, she testified as an expert witness before the U.S. Senate Special Committee on Aging concerning the mortgage foreclosure crisis and its effect on elderly homeowners [see Historical Documents Section]. She also spoke on mortgage fraud to a national conference sponsored by the Federal Trade Commission in Chicago.

During the past year, Executive Director Tom Cannon was appointed to the Supreme Court Task Force, an ad hoc group of lawyers and law professors whose mission was to help prepare Senator Herb Kohl, a member of the U.S. Senate Committee on the Judiciary, for confirmation hearings involving the nominations of Judge Sonia Sotomayor (2009) and Solicitor General Elena Kagan (2010) to the U.S. Supreme Court. Members of the Task Force met with the Senator, developed lines of questioning, and prepared background memoranda for use in the nationally-televised hearings and later floor debates involving the Senate's consideration of the two nominees. Last month, Staff Attorney Nicole Penegor met in Washington, D.C. with officials of the U.S. Treasury Department to urge improvements in the Home Affordable Modification Program (HAMP).

The Legal Aid Society is blessed with an award-winning staff whose commitment to excellence has been widely recognized by its peers in the legal community. Supervising Attorney Carmen Ortiz was re-

3. Legal Aid Society staffers wave from their headquarters in the Railway Exchange Building, 2002. *Courtesy of Legal Aid Society of Milwaukee.*

cently named a Leader in the Law for her child advocacy work in the Family Court. "Attorney tackles child-custody cases" in *Wisconsin Law Journal* (Spring 2009 Supplement) 28. Catey Doyle was named Legal Professional of the Year ("Doyle dedicates her career to the underdog" in *Wisconsin Builder* [November 2007] 42). Chief Staff Attorney Shelia Hill-Roberts was honored as a Leader in the Law for her outstanding advocacy on behalf of battered, abused, and neglected children ("Protecting the Interests of Children" in *Wisconsin Law Journal,* Spring 2007 Supplement) 15.

Jim Brennan was awarded the 2006 Lawyer of the Year Award by the Milwaukee Bar Association for his client outreach efforts. Staff Attorney Paula Lorant won the State Bar of Wisconsin's Pro Bono Lawyer of the Year Award in 2007 for her exemplary work with the elderly; Beatrice Garrett was also honored that year for her work on the Society's mortgage foreclosure project. Guardian ad Litem Cindy Lepkowski was given the State Bar's Legal Services Attorney of the Year award in 2009 for her exemplary representation of abused children. Karen Dardy won the first-ever Women in the Law Award in 2009 for her significant contributions to the profession. "Late law school bloomer finds her calling in public service" in *Wisconsin Law Journal Supplement* (February 2009) 11. Also in 2009, Staff Attorney Rachel Arfa was named Up and Coming Lawyer of the Year, an award designed to recognize Milwaukee's newer generation of promising young attorneys. Legal Assistants Paulette Wymbs, Sue Mouthey, Brian Kemper, and Mary Burks were honored as Unsung Heroines and Heroes of the state's legal community by the editors of *Wisconsin Law Journal* (2007, 2008, 2010).

Our staff continues to assume leadership positions in the broader community as well. Cindy Lepkowski is President of the Wisconsin Professional Society on the Abuse of Children. Jessica Lasser serves on the Milwaukee Jewish Council for Community Relations. Catey Doyle is chair of the Milwaukee Board of Zoning Appeals and a former President of the American Civil Liberties Union of Wisconsin. Mike Vruno serves on the Children's Law Office Advisory Board of the National Association of Counsel for Children. Isa Gonzalez-Zayas is Assistant Editor of the American Bar Association's Young Lawyers Division newsletter. Social worker Diana Pitkaranta serves as Vice President of Greater Milwaukee TRIAD, an organization of law enforcement, community agencies, and elderly residents that seeks to protect vulnerable older adults from criminal victimization.

Carmen M. Ortiz was re-elected in 2009 to another term as a Governor of the State Bar of Wisconsin; she is a former co-chair of the Bar's Public Interest Law Section. Staff attorney Jessica Lasser is a director of the Wisconsin Family Assistance Center for Education, Training, and Support (WI FACETS), a leading source of support and information for disabled children and adults with special needs and their families. Lisa Clay Foley recently served as Chair of the Milwaukee County Healthwatch Consortium. Pete Koneazny sits on two committees of the Milwaukee County Community Justice Council, which coordinates services and resources to promote crime reduction, victim support, and restorative outcomes in the criminal justice system. In 2008, social worker Diana Pitkaranta was appointed to serve on the Nursing Home Workgroup, a state legislative watchdog committee investigating abuse of elderly residents in nursing homes. Other members of the staff are involved in a wide range of neighborhood, church, and charitable activities.

Last year, Staff Attorney Isa Gonzalez-Zayas noticed that many of her wards in the Children's Court have to carry their personal belongings in garbage bags when they transfer from one foster home to another because they have no suitcases. A nine-year-old girl told the lawyer that moving this way made her feel as though her life was garbage. Gonzalez-Zayas immediately organized the "We Care Luggage Drive." As soon as they heard about the project, our funding partners at Potawatomi Bingo Casino and United Way of Greater Milwaukee joined LAS to help co-sponsor this important initiative. Soon the Milwaukee County AFL-CIO and a local television station began to promote the project as well. "Children's Court lawyers take donations to give kids luggage" (FOX 6 News, October 1, 2009). The drive ultimately produced more than 1,000 suitcases, duffel bags, and backpacks for impoverished foster children.

At the request of the City of Milwaukee Election Commission, six Legal Aid staffers volunteered to serve as impartial Election Inspectors for the 2008 presidential election. Last year, the Downtown LAS staff "adopted" a family residing at the Sojourner Family Peace Center for victims of domestic violence; staffers collected nearly $400 to provide a Christmas meal, presents, and gift certificates for the family. This year, the Children's Court staff raised $1,200 at its annual bake sale for the benefit of the Child Abuse Prevention Fund. The guardian ad litem staff at Children's Court also collaborated with News Radio 620 (WTMJ) and Kapco Inc. to help launch a Christmas toy drive that produced gifts and a free McDonald's breakfast for 2,500 inner-city children during the past two years.

Legal Aid Society attorneys partner with other poverty and public interest law firms in a number of ways. This cooperation most often takes the form of client referrals, serving as co-counsel in complex litigation matters, or filing *amicus curiae* briefs in cases brought by our colleagues. In addition, staff lawyers from the American Civil Liberties Union, Catholic Charities Immigration Law Project, Disability

Rights Wisconsin, Legal Action of Wisconsin, State Public Defender Office, and other interested low-income advocates attend the Legal Aid Society's Annual Poverty Law Update conference, a free continuing legal education seminar held each October since 1997.

LAS also relies on a diligent cadre of volunteer law-student interns to assist staff attorneys in our Downtown and Children's Court offices. Interns conduct necessary legal research and factual investigation under supervision of the Society's experienced staff attorneys. During the summer of 2010, for example, LAS trained students from Harvard, Michigan, Notre Dame, Wisconsin, and Marquette law schools to work on various projects. The Society maintains ongoing relationships with the last three institutions.

Within the past year and a half, the Legal Aid Society has inaugurated five exciting collaborations with various public and private partners to address poverty issues in Milwaukee's inner city. First, the Society helped Mayor Tom Barrett create the Milwaukee Foreclosure Partnership Initiative, an innovative venture composed of city government officials, mortgage lenders, private foundations, and community housing advocates designed to deal with the record avalanche of home foreclosures. When the Mayor unveiled the project to the media, he announced it "would be spearheaded by the Legal Aid Society." See "Foreclosure plan detailed" in *Milwaukee Journal Sentinel* (February 26, 2009). The first stage was successful in obtaining a new local court rule providing mediation services in all foreclosure cases in Milwaukee County so that practical solutions could be worked out to address the city's burgeoning housing crisis. This mediation program is now being implemented statewide – more evidence of LAS's wide reach.

A second collaboration, this one a joint effort between the Legal Aid Society and the City Attorney's Office, focuses on protecting elderly low-income homeowners who are victimized through criminal activities perpetrated by their adult children or grandchildren. In many cases, younger family members have turned the homes of elderly relatives into drug houses. This joint partnership helps aged homeowners in the inner city avoid being taken advantage of for criminal purposes.

A third new venture is LAMP (Legal And Medical Partnership) for Families, a project recently developed with Children's Hospital, the Medical College of Wisconsin, Marquette University Law School, and the Legal Aid Society. It focuses on providing a full range of free legal services to families of inner-city children being treated at the pediatric clinic of Children's Hospital at the Martin Luther King Heritage Health Center. Studies have shown that poor children's health and well-being can be measurably improved when their family's legal needs are addressed in conjunction with medical issues.[1] Start-up funding has been received from the Charles D. Jacobus Family Foundation.

Another collaboration was initiated by Attorney Nicholas Toman, an Equal Justice Works Legal Fellow on the staff of the Legal Aid Society, and Sister Ann Halloran, President of the Dominican Center for Women. They assembled a broad-based coalition of nonprofit groups, local officials, and low-income residents in the Amani neighborhood on the city's North Side to focus on abandoned and foreclosed homes. Cooperation has thus far been obtained from Allied Churches Teaching Self-Empowerment (ACTS), City Attorney's Office, City Health Department, Department of City Development, District Attorney's Office (Community Prosecution Unit), Habitat for Humanity, Milwaukee Housing Authority, Milwaukee Police Department, and the Joseph Zilber Family Foundation's Brush With Kindness Program. A grant from the Housing Trust Fund will be used to create a sustained attack on neighborhood blight that will lead to stable, healthy, and safe living conditions for impoverished residents.

The Society's newest program is a partnership with the Milwaukee Bar Association to provide free legal services to 50 low-income residents of the Water Tower View Senior Citizens Housing Project in Greenfield. LAS attorneys Rachel Arfa and Paula Lorant recruited and trained volunteer lawyers to provide estate planning, powers of attorney (financial and healthcare), and burial disposition plans for elderly deaf residents. Funding provided by the State Bar of Wisconsin and the Wisconsin Department of Health Services, Division of Disability and Elder Services, is used to hire sign-language interpreters and deaf interpreters. The successful project provides clients with peace of mind and helps them overcome longstanding social isolation, cultural attitudes, and educational deficits.

These new programs are a powerful sign of the Legal Aid Society's vitality and innovation at age 94. As Milwaukee's premier advocate for the poor, LAS gives voice to the voiceless and hope to the hopeless.

The current economic crisis facing the nation, undoubtedly the worst since the Great Depression, poses many challenges today for the organization and its clients. "Grant-Making Plummeted 8.4% During 2009" in *The NonProfit Times* (April 19, 2010); "Government Cutting Back on Social Service Spending" in *The NonProfit Times* (September 14, 2009); "Fewer dollars for funding grants: foundations report drop in assets" in *Milwaukee Journal Sentinel* (May 22, 2009). As the *New York Times* recently editorialized:

> The proven national program of civil legal aid for impoverished Americans … is suffering from multiple blows in funding. While the poor are caught increasingly by foreclosure, eviction, and food-stamp fights for their daily bread, deficit-bedeviled statehouses across the country are cutting support for legal services or dropping the programs outright.
>
> Creative funding that taps lawyers' escrow accounts has evaporated because it is tied to the Fed's fading interest rate. Local governments, charities, and pro bono law firms are similarly tight-pursed. Scores of legal aid societies are cutting their staffs just as requests for help are booming.
>
> Bar associations continue to help, and even in these tough times, probably could do more. But federal funding is the ultimate hope in a dire situation. Given the tough times – underfunded programs and ever more desperate clients – more money is needed.

"Sins of Omission: The Forgotten Poor" (February 2, 2009). A similar theme was struck in an essay by a University of Southern California law professor:

> Publicly funded and private legal services for those who can't afford to pay are overwhelmed, and the need is rising dramatically as the country's economic crisis worsens. For every client whom legal services can accept, many are turned away because the number of lawyers available cannot meet the need.
>
> Every day, Americans without access to legal counsel unnecessarily lose homes, jobs, retirement benefits, healthcare, and custody of their children. This is because, in America, we have not yet recognized a right to counsel in civil cases … Indigent litigants with the law on their side often find themselves losing to well-funded opponents simply because they have no means of fighting back.

Clare Pastore, "Rescuing Legal Aid" in *Los Angeles Times* (February 23, 2009). See also "More poor need legal aid" in *Wisconsin Law Journal* (September 27, 2010).

Three years ago, the Legal Aid Society began calculating the overall annual economic impact of its services in the community. In 2007, $4,068,030 was realized in recovery of court awards, attorney fees, government benefits, and debt forgiveness on behalf of clients in the Civil Division alone. In addition, lawyers in the Family Court Guardian ad Litem project obtained $376,692 in court-ordered child support payments for our wards. Milwaukee County saved another $720,600 in corporate guardian fees by appointing volunteers from the Society's GAIN Project. Therefore, the total economic impact of the Legal Aid Society's presence in Milwaukee was $5,165,322 for the year. More recent comparable impact figures are $5,095,455 in 2008 and $5,548,365 in 2009.

The actual value of the legal services provided annually by the Legal Aid Society is about $15.3 million. In other words, if LAS were a private law firm charging prevailing market rates standard in Milwaukee's legal community, its 32 lawyers would bill an average of 35 hours per week at an average of $250 per hour; its 10 social workers would have their time charged out at the prevailing paralegal rate of $75 per hour. Thus, the actual market value of the services provided every year by the Legal Aid Society to its impoverished clients is $15.3 million. The Society provides these services on a budget that is just shy of $4 million a year – an extraordinary bargain by any measure.

Despite the current economic crisis, which pundits have dubbed the "Great Recession," LAS's staff and board continue to pursue their mission of equal justice for the poor. Today, the Legal Aid Society enthusiastically looks forward to a second century of service as the state's flagship public-interest law firm.

---

1. Mary E. Northridge, "It Takes Lawyers to Deliver Health Care" in *American Journal of Public Health* 95, no. 3 (2005) 376; Pamela Tames et al., "The Lawyer Is In: Why Some Doctors Are Prescribing Legal Remedies for Their Patients, and How the Legal Profession Can Support This Effort" in *Public Interest Law Journal* 12, nos. 2-3 (2003) 505-27.

2

EQUAL JUSTICE FOR THE POOR

The universal ideal of equal justice for the poor is preserved in one of humankind's earliest surviving legal texts, the Codex Hammurabi (compiled *circa* 1750 B.C.), which is etched in cuneiform characters on a polished black basalt stele. In the epilogue to this famous collection of juridical principles, the Babylonian king informs

4. Stele containing the Codex Hammurabi, the world's oldest surviving legal code.
Courtesy of Musée du Louvre, Paris.

subjects that he has ordered his laws published in permanent form
"that the strong may not oppress the weak and so to give justice to
the orphan and the widow ... and so to give justice to the oppressed."[1]
Hammurabi's royal proclamation was developed further as a moral
imperative in Hebrew scripture. Thus, the Book of Exodus (23:7-
8) declares emphatically: "You must not cheat any poor man of his
right at law." A similar injunction is taught in the Book of Psalms (82:
2-4): "No more mockery of justice, no more favoring the wicked! Let
the weak and the orphan have justice, be fair to the wretched and
destitute; rescue the weak and the needy, save them from the clutches
of the wicked." The Book of Isaiah (1:17) demands identical action
from its audience: "Search for justice, help the oppressed, be just to the
orphan, plead for the widow."

The religious articulation of our core principle was evoked in modern times by Judge Learned Hand's celebrated dictum, delivered on
the 75th anniversary of the Legal Aid Society of New York: "If we
are to keep our democracy, there must be one commandment: Thou
shalt not ration justice." *Legal Aid Brief Case* xi, no. 4 (1951) 3. On the
occasion of the Legal Aid Society of Milwaukee's 90th anniversary,
longtime *Milwaukeel Sentinel* columnist Bill Janz alluded to the same
wellspring of values. He restated the concept of equal justice with re-
sort to another biblical teaching: "The meek shall inherit the earth, but
only if they receive proper legal representation."

According to legal historian John H. Wigmore, it was the ecclesiastical courts in medieval Europe that "first laid down the modern principle of equality before the law; it [the Church] protected the poor
and the weak against the rich and the powerful." *A Panorama of the
World's Legal Systems*, 3 vols. (St. Paul: West Publishing Co. 1928) iii
958. Indeed, application of this ancient concept pointed to the initial
development of legal aid. St. Ives Hélory (1253-1303), *officialis* in the
ecclesiastical court of the diocese of Tréguier in Brittany, led the way.
The title *advocatus pauperum*, "lawyer for the poor," was conferred on
him by church authorities, as well as by popular opinion, because he
represented the poor free of charge and visited them in prison. Moreover, "to provide legal aid for the poor," according to one standard reference work, "he created confraternities that have spread over France,
Belgium, and Brazil, and also to Rome."[2] These medieval confraterni-

ties of canon law practitioners, idealistically offering their services to the poor without fee, mark the origin of the international legal aid movement. Not long after his death, the Vatican followed recommendations from the leading law faculties in Europe and declared St. Ives Hélory the patron saint of lawyers.

During the Middle Ages, the religious duty to make justice freely available to the poor was slowly recognized as a secular legal obligation as well. Thus, in Magna Carta (1215), it was stated: "To none will we sell, to none will we deny right or justice." The ecclesiastical courts' practice of providing free lawyers to the poor seeped into secular tribunals during the late-thirteenth and fourteenth centuries at which time "counsel were assigned to plead the causes of people too poor to pay any fees."[3] In the following century, Scotland's Parliament enacted the Poor Advocate's Statute, which provided that an impoverished litigant, whom "for default of cunning or dispense cannot or may not follow his cause, the king for the love of God shall ordain that the judge, before whom the cause should be determined, purvey and get a loyal and a wise advocate to follow such poor creature's cause." Acts of Parliament of Scotland, 2 James I, c. 45 (1424).[4]

Later in that same century, England's Parliament required justices of the King's Bench to appoint attorneys, without compensation, to represent poor plaintiffs in civil cases. Finding that "poor subjects be not of ability nor power to sue according to the laws of this land for the redress of injuries and wrongs to them daily done," Parliament directed that "if it be before the King in his Bench, the Justices there shall assign to the same poor person or persons Counsel learned by their discretions which shall give their Counsels nothing taking for the same, and in like wise the same Justices shall appoint attorney and attorneys for the same poor person and persons." 11 Henry VII, c.12 (1495), *An Act to admit such persons as are poor to sue in forma pauperis*. Modern legal scholars deem this Tudor-era statute a codification of the then-existing common law. These early Scottish and English precedents are now followed throughout much of the civilized world as a result of a landmark decision issued by the European Court of Human Rights that established the right to counsel in some civil cases.[5] *Airey v. Ireland*, 32 Eur. Ct. H.R. (ser. A), 2 E.H.R.Rep. 305 (1979). See also Earl Johnson, Jr., "Comparing Access to Justice in the United States and Other Industrial Democracies" in 24 *Fordham International Law Journal* 83 (2000).

Two separate guarantees found in the Constitution of the United States enshrine the right of access to the administration of justice. The first is the right to effective assistance of counsel established by the Sixth Amendment (1791); the second is the right to due process and equal protection of the laws preserved in the Fourteenth Amendment (1868). In addition, the Wisconsin Constitution (1848) expresses Midwestern populist values prevalent in the mid-nineteenth century by recalling the ancient language of Magna Carta: "Every person ... ought to obtain justice freely, and without being obliged to purchase it." (Art. I, sec. 9).

These sources reflect the natural law ideal that all persons, no matter how humble their station, have an innate right to be heard in the courts. That lofty ideal is incorporated into the oath taken by all federal judges and Supreme Court justices: "I will administer justice without respect to persons, and do equal right to the poor and to the rich." 28 U.S.C. § 453. Unfortunately, such noble aspirations frequently fall short in actual practice. As Irish poet Oliver Goldsmith perceptively acknowledged: "Laws grind the poor, and rich men rule the law." *The Traveller* (1764), line 386. Anatole France framed the same thesis in a more sardonic way: "The law, in its majestic equality, forbids the rich as well as the poor to sleep under bridges, to beg in the streets, and to steal bread." *The Red Lily* (1894), chap. 7.

Access to justice, of course, necessarily begins with access to a lawyer. The Wisconsin Supreme Court recognized this obvious predicate early in its history. In *Carpenter v. County of Dane*, 9 Wis. 274, 276 (1859), the court asked:

> And would it not be a little like mockery to secure to a pauper these solemn constitutional guaranties for a full and fair trial of the matters with which he is charged, and yet say to him when on trial, that he must employ his own counsel, who could alone render these guaranties of any real permanent value to him.

Sixty-three years later, the United States Supreme Court agreed: "The right to be heard would be, in many cases, of little avail if it did not comprehend the right to be heard by counsel. Even the intelligent and educated layman has small and sometimes no skill in the science of law. . . He requires the guiding hand of counsel at every step in the proceedings." *Powell v. Alabama*, 287 U.S. 45, 68 (1932). A generation later, the nation's high court reiterated this rationale by noting: "[A]ny person hailed into court, who is too poor to hire a lawyer, cannot be assured of a fair trial unless counsel is provided for him. This seems to us to be an obvious truth." *Gideon v. Wainwright*, 372 U.S. 335, 344 (1963).

While these pronouncements dealt with criminal prosecutions, the Legal Aid Society of Milwaukee has long recognized that the principle is equally applicable to civil cases. As former Attorney General Nicholas deB. Katzenbach put it: "Hopelessness and poverty do not observe neat jurisdictional lines between civil and criminal law." *The Extension of Legal Services to the Poor: Conference Proceedings* (Washington, D.C.: U.S. Government Printing Office, 1964) 10. Dr. Martin Luther King, Jr. echoed this view in his famous *Letter from Birmingham Jail* (1963): "Injustice anywhere is a threat to justice everywhere." Thus, an early mission statement of the board of directors declared:

> The concern of the Legal Aid Society of Milwaukee is with the administration of justice as it affects the poor. Our constitution has provided for the equal protection of the law to all persons regardless of nationality, color, sex, or creed. But if the individual seeking to protect himself is without money to avail himself of the judicial procedure to protect his rights, justice according to law may be practically denied him. The poor man is taught that he is entitled to justice, but he finds that to get it he must pay for legal services for which he has no money. *The fundamental purpose of the Legal Aid Society, therefore, is to see that persons who are poor and oppressed shall get justice according to law.*

Twelfth Annual Report of the Legal Aid Society of Milwaukee (1928) [see Historical Documents Section]. The role of the lawyer for the poor, then, is to serve as an equalizer before the bar of justice by giving voice to those who cannot speak on their own behalf.

Regrettably, recent studies have demonstrated that 80% or more of eligible poor still cannot obtain access to justice because of the inadequate funding of civil legal aid programs. *Bridging the Justice Gap: Wisconsin's Unmet Legal Needs* (Madison: State Bar of Wisconsin, 2007); *Documenting the Justice Gap in America* (Washington, D.C.: Legal Services Corporation, 2005). The denial of justice to more than half a million Wisconsinites each year is exacerbated by the failure of courts to place civil justice on par with criminal justice. John F. Ebbott et al., *Toward a Civil Griffin in Wisconsin: Equal Justice Under the Wisconsin Constitution* (Milwaukee: Legal Action Press, 2005). Thus, in Milwaukee County, more than 76% of all Family Court cases and nearly half of all Civil cases involve litigants struggling to represent themselves without benefit of counsel. Mary E. Triggiano and John F. Ebbott, "Gideon's New Trumpet" in *Wisconsin Lawyer* 82, no. 6 (2009) 51. Moreover, it has been estimated that, every year, 98% of

5. United States Supreme Court building in Washington, D.C.
Courtesy of U.S. Supreme Court.

the 45,000 defendants in Milwaukee County's Small Claims Court, 98.5% of the 160,000 defendants in Milwaukee's Municipal Court, and 99% of the 86,000 students suspended by the Milwaukee Public School system – virtually all of them indigent – go without any legal representation whatsoever.[6] The presence of so many *pro se* parties in the court and administrative systems increases the risk of miscarriages of justice and places heavy burdens on trial court judges, hearing examiners, and their staffs.

"Equal justice under law is not merely a caption on the façade of the [U.S.] Supreme Court building," Justice Lewis F. Powell, Jr. once said, "it is also fundamental that justice should be the same, in substance and availability, without regard to economic status." *Legal Services Corporation Revisited* (Address to the American Bar Association, 1976). This principle was stated elegantly and concisely in *Griffin v. Illinois,* 351 U.S. 12, 19 (1956): "There can be no equal justice where the kind of trial a man has depends on the amount of money he has." In civil cases, unfortunately, these inspiring principles are more often honored in the breach than applied in practice.

The founders of the Legal Aid Society of Milwaukee felt passionately about the failure to deliver on the constitutional promise of equal justice under law. One of them, Victor L. Berger, wrote the following essay on this topic:

> The Declaration of Independence is a document that is supposed to contain the cardinal principles of the American republic. The famous declaration starts with the following gem of thought: "All men are created equal." It is a phrase which did well enough in its time, but which now has become a lie. The reason? The struggle for existence has entirely changed since the days of Jefferson and Paine.
>
> "All men are created equal." But do they live equal? Do they die equal? The child of the poor is born in a hovel, surrounded by misery and poverty from his first moments. How about the child of the rich? Surrounded by all the comforts and protections which paternal love and money can furnish, he grows up in comfort and security and receives an excellent education.
>
> Are we equal before the law? There are thousands of laws passed by the legislatures every session, not to speak of Congress. There is a flood of laws. Under the protection of these laws, the steel trust, the sugar trust, the meat trust, the oil trust, and many other trusts rob the people of many millions every year. Under the protection of these laws, women and children are exploited and their life-blood coined into dollars for the capitalist class.
>
> How many of these laws are for the purpose of protecting the poor, the weak, and the helpless? Equality before the law is a phrase like so many others.
>
> Suppose a poor tramp – a workingman who has become discouraged during the present panic [1908] – is found sleeping on a bench in a park, or on a wagon in an alley. The eye of the law will soon find him, and he will be hauled up before a judge the next morning.
>
> "Why did you sleep in that alley, or on that bench in the park?" the judge will ask sternly. "Why did you not go to a hotel or a rooming house?" "I had no money, your honor," answers the hobo. "What, no

money to pay for a room! And sleeping in an alley – that is clearly disorderly behavior. It means ten dollars fine and the costs," says the judge. "But, your honor, if I had the ten dollars and the costs, I would not have been sleeping in the alley," murmurs the tramp. "That is just it – you will go to the house of correction for thirty days – and if you say another word I will make it ninety days for vagrancy. For you have no visible means of support. You are a criminal in the eyes of the law." And to the house of correction he goes.

In small things, as in big affairs, we have a class government. This shows plainly in the fact that for misdemeanors the culprits have to pay fines in money, which is simply a joke for the rich man, while it hits the poor man terribly hard. This is equality before the law!

Abridged and arranged from Victor L. Berger, *Broadsides*
(Milwaukee: Social-Democratic Publishing Co.,
2nd ed. 1912) 115-20.

The Legal Aid Society of Milwaukee has been aptly described as "one of the working symbols of American justice." See "Legal Aid Society Bolsters Faith in Democratic Ideals" in *Milwaukee Journal* (November 26, 1942). Today, the Legal Aid Society is still dedicated to its founders' mission of achieving equal justice for the poor. For nearly a century, the Legal Aid Society of Milwaukee has served as the premier guarantor of that threshold constitutional principle in our community. Liberty, Justice, Equality – without lawyers, they're mere words.

NOTES

1. G.R. Driver and John C. Miles, ed. *The Babylonian Laws*, 2 vols. (Oxford: Clarendon Press, 1952) ii 97. A French archaeological expedition discovered the stele in 1901-02 buried beneath the acropolis of Susa (in modern Iran), capital of the ancient kingdom of Elam. Today, the carved, seven-foot pillar is on display at the Musée du Louvre in Paris.

2. *The New Catholic Encyclopedia* (Washington, D.C.: Catholic University of America, 2003) vii 679; Alban Butler, *The Lives of the Saints*, ed. Herbert Thurston et al. (New York: P.J. Kenedy and Sons, 1926-38) v 242-43. "St. Ives, the Poor Man's Lawyer" in *Legal Aid Review* xxix, no. 3 (1931) 12-13.

3. William C. Bolland, "Introduction" to *Select Bills in Eyre, A.D. 1292-1333*, ed. Bolland [in 30 Selden Society Publications] (1914) xlviii. The historical background is discussed further in Note, "The Right to Counsel in Civil Litigation" in 66 *Columbia Law Review* (1966) 1322-39; and John MacAr-

thur Maguire's classic study, "Poverty and Civil Litigation" in 36 *Harvard Law Review* (1923) 361-404.

4. Spelling of both the Poor Advocate's Statute and the Statute of Henry VII has been modernized for the reader's convenience.

5. For evidence that these fifteenth-century statutes were followed in Colonial America, see John F. Ebbott et al., *Toward a Civil Griffin in Wisconsin: Equal Justice Under the Wisconsin Constitution* (Milwaukee: Legal Action Press, 2005) 114-15.

6. Thomas G. Cannon, "Barriers Faced by *Pro Se* Litigants," an unpublished paper presented to the Symposium on the Right to Counsel in Civil Cases in Wisconsin (May 5, 2010) 1-2.

3

CREATING THE LEGAL AID
SOCIETY OF MILWAUKEE
1910 – 1916

The first organized effort to provide free legal aid in the United States began in 1865, when the Freedmen's Bureau (a federal agency located within the War Department) engaged both salaried counsel and retained private attorneys to represent newly emancipated slaves on an *ad hoc* basis in civil and criminal cases in the District of Columbia and in some Southern states. Regrettably, this seminal Civil War Reconstruction program, initiated by President Abraham Lincoln a month before his assassination, lapsed after just three years. Nonetheless, the Freedmen's Bureau created a crucial prototype that has been described as "this first of all legal aid projects" in the United States. Howard C. Westwood, "Getting Justice for the Freedman" in 16 *Howard Law Review* 492-537 at 505 (1970-71).

In 1876, eight years after the demise of the Freedmen's Bureau, Edward Salomon, a Prussian-born lawyer and former Governor of Wisconsin, founded *Der Deutscher Rechts-Schutz Verein* ("German Legal Aid Society") to provide free legal assistance to German immigrants in New York City. Fourteen years later, that pioneer program evolved into the New York Legal Aid Society. John MacArthur Maguire, *The Lance of Justice: A Semi-Centennial History of the Legal Aid Society, 1876-1926* (Harvard University Press, 1928). In 1888, the Ethical Culture Society of Chicago established a Bureau of Justice, making it the first organization in the United States to offer free legal assistance to all needy individuals regardless of ethnicity, race, creed, or gender. Jack Katz, *Poor People's Lawyers in Transition* (Rutgers University

Press, 1982) 34-50. The New York and Chicago programs became the twin pillars upon which a national movement was founded.

Legal aid societies soon opened in Boston (1900), Philadelphia (1902), and Cleveland (1905). The modern era in the legal aid movement, though, is said to have begun in 1914 when Reginald Heber Smith (1889-1966) took over as General Counsel to the Boston Legal Aid Society (1914-19). Smith graduated from Harvard Law School (LL.B. 1914) and wrote the hugely influential book, *Justice and the Poor* (New York: Carnegie Foundation, 1919), which documented massive failure of the organized bar and the courts to protect legal rights of the poor in the United States. Smith argued eloquently for establishment of adequately-funded legal aid programs to meet this pressing need. He also brought in faculty from the Harvard Business

6. Wisconsin Governor Edward Salomon, founder of the nation's first legal aid society in 1876. *Courtesy of Wisconsin Historical Society (WHi-2899).*

School to manage the organization's finances. Smith went on to serve as managing partner (1921-56) of Hale and Dorr, a prominent Boston law firm. Something of an efficiency expert, he is credited with

7. Reginald Heber Smith, circa 1919, founder of the modern legal aid movement in the United States. *Courtesy of Social Law Library, Boston.*

developing the billable hour and the daily time sheet for measuring the work product of lawyers.

"Legal aid," according to one historian of the movement, "represented an important Progressive Era reform." Phillip Merkel, "At the Crossroads of Reform: The First Fifty Years of American Legal Aid, 1876-1926" in 27 *Houston Law Review* 3 (1990). In its formative stages in the United States, the movement was strictly an urban phenomenon. As of 1915, some thirty cities around the country had established offices providing legal representation to low-income residents. Further details of the movement's growth can be found in Alan W. Houseman and Linda E. Perle, *Securing Equal Justice for All: A Brief History of Civil Legal Assistance in the United States* (Washington, D.C.: Center for Law and Social Policy, 2003). By 1915, though, efforts had already been long underway in Milwaukee to form an organization that would soon join this pioneering band of first-generation legal service programs.

The origin of the Legal Aid Society of Milwaukee can be traced directly to Professor John R. Commons, the renowned University of Wisconsin economist, labor historian, and political reformer. On April 11, 1910, Commons wrote a letter to Milwaukee Alderman-at-Large Victor L. Berger, German-language-newspaper editor, head of the Socialist Party, and soon to be elected (in November of that year) to the first of several controversial terms in Congress. Sensing a local Socialist sweep in the upcoming April elections, Berger sought to establish an ambitious agenda of municipal reform. Therefore he asked the UW scholar to outline such a program in anticipation of his party's takeover of City Hall. Professor Commons responded by recommending that Milwaukee's city government conduct a municipal survey of eleven topics crucial to the community's future. Third on his list was "Legal Aid" [see Historical Documents Section].

Somewhat surprisingly, however, Commons did not look initially to the New York and Chicago programs for a model. Perhaps with a view towards Milwaukee's ethnic composition, he suggested instead that an investigation be made "with the view of working out a practicable plan for free legal aid similar to that of German cities." The German model was organized by private associations – such as labor unions, churches, and ethnic groups – that offered free legal aid as a service to their membership.[1] Commons also suggested that the proposed Legal Aid Bureau could be given responsibility for protecting the rights of immigrants. His letter provided the crucial intellectual spark for the concept of the Legal Aid Society of Milwaukee – a classic illustration of the famed Wisconsin Idea (public service by its university faculty) in action. See Jack Stark, "The Wisconsin Idea: The University's Service to the State" in *Wisconsin Blue Book 1995-96* (Madison: Wisconsin Legislature, 1995) 99-179, esp. 116-23.

It was Victor Berger, the practical politician, though, who sought to convert the abstract concept of free legal aid into reality. Berger convinced his colleague, Socialist Mayor Emil C. Seidel, to appoint Commons as head of Milwaukee's newly created Bureau of Economy and Efficiency, an entity that had been conceived by Berger. For its well-told history, see Mordecai Lee, *Bureaus of Efficiency: Reforming Local Government in the Progressive Era* (Milwaukee: Marquette University Press, 2008) 41-65, 218-21. During the spring and summer of 1911, the Bureau, with Commons at the helm, drew on the city's existing social service agencies to compile an extensive report on the need for a legal aid program in Milwaukee. Fred A. King, who was likely one of Commons' graduate students, was tasked with researching and writing the report.[2] King was a special investigator for the Bureau's social survey, but the City Directory of that year identified him as Manager of the Citizens Employment Office; shortly thereafter, he became Superintendent of the Wisconsin Free Employment Bureau. King had already authored a report for the Bureau that recommended establishment of a free employment agency in Milwaukee. In preparing the legal aid report under Commons' direction, King examined existing legal aid programs in New York, Chicago, Philadelphia, and Kansas City as part of his background research.

The King-Commons report documented the pressing need for creating a program of free legal services for Milwaukee's poor. It noted that parties in civil cases "must provide their own counsel, and failure to secure a competent attorney by persons of small means often results in a miscarriage of justice." The study, culled from the files of local social service agencies, detailed numerous instances of injustice suffered by Milwaukee's poor for want of legal counsel. The King-Commons report went on to conclude that the poor "should at least be able to secure their rights under law, and that as far as possible, none should find their lack of financial resources an effective barrier in obtaining these rights. Free legal service is an important means to this end." The findings of the King-Commons investigation were published in *Free Legal Aid* (Milwaukee Bureau of Economy and Efficiency, 1911), Bulletin no. 7 [reprinted below in the Historical Documents Section].

8. Professor John R. Commons, the intellectual sparkplug who, in 1910, first proposed creation of a free legal aid program in Milwaukee. *Courtesy of Wisconsin Historical Society (WHi-39217).*

The fourteen-page King-Commons report was said to support a bill then pending before the state legislature, which sought creation of a municipal bureau in Milwaukee to furnish free legal aid for persons financially unable to hire an attorney.[3] That measure, Senate Bill 253, had been introduced by Senator Gabriel Zophy (Social-Democrat of Milwaukee) on February 15, 1911.[4] The proposal authorized the Common Council to establish a "legal information bureau" with unspecified duties. Other provisions included mayoral power to appoint a bureau chief, and Common Council authority to fix compensation, determine fees to be collected and paid into the city treasury, and the power to raise additional revenue through the local property tax levy [see Historical Documents Section]. Enabling legislation was necessary because local governments at this period in Wisconsin lacked home rule authority. Although it is puzzling as to why Zophy labeled his proposed entity a "legal information bureau," Professor Commons clearly considered it to be the functional equivalent of a legal aid society.[5]

The famous 1911 legislature has been described by one modern historian as "the most productive and progressive legislature in Wisconsin history."[6] Elections the previous fall had produced a large majority of reform legislators, including twelve Socialist members of the Assembly and two in the Senate. The unquestionable leader of the state's progressive forces at this juncture was Governor Francis E. McGovern, a Milwaukee lawyer who was also a firm supporter of free legal aid to the poor. In such a heady political environment, the Socialists' legal information bureau bill should have passed with ease. It was disappointing, and indeed startling, that the measure failed even to make it to the Senate floor. On May 10, 1911, the Committee on Judiciary voted to postpone the bill indefinitely.[7] It would appear that vindictively partisan Democrats and Republicans sought to deny Socialists the political credit for sponsoring successful legislation; some legislators may also have feared that the proposal was "too socialistic."[8]

Nonetheless, Professor Commons felt the need for this type of program to be "of such prime importance" that he urged "steps be taken at once to offer free legal aid." On October 30, 1911, he wrote Mayor Seidel to recommend that his administration inaugurate a voluntary legal aid bureau [see Historical Documents Section]. The King-Commons report was touted in Socialist campaign literature the following spring. *Milwaukee Municipal Campaign Book 1912*, p. 204. Commons' proposal, unfortunately, was tabled after Seidel was defeated and the Socialists lost control of the Milwaukee Common Council in the city elections of April 1912. The Mayor, however, went on in the fall of that year to become Eugene Debs' Vice Presidential nominee on the national Socialist ticket. Lewis L. Gould, *Four Hats in the Ring: The 1912 Election and the Birth of Modern* 109, 114-15.

Looking back on the King-Commons report, J.E. Treleven, Secretary to the Bureau of Economy and Efficiency, lamented: "A plan suggested by the Bureau for giving free legal aid to indigent persons has not as yet been accepted by any organization." See "The Milwaukee Bureau of Economy and Efficiency" in *Annals of the American Academy of Political and Social Science* 41 (1912) 272. Treleven's statement jibes with Commons' view that the Socialists' "legal information bureau" was intended to be the same kind of free legal aid program available in other cities. It also implied that the programmatic concept may have been shopped around unsuccessfully to existing institutions within the city (most likely the Milwaukee Bar Association and Marquette University Law School), but the search to find or create an organizational home languished. Despite this initial disappointment, Professor Mordecai Lee credits the influential King-Commons report with helping lead directly to creation of the Legal Aid Society in Milwaukee.[9]

On January 24, 1913, Assemblyman Carl Minkley (Social-Democrat of Milwaukee) introduced a second bill in the Wisconsin Legislature to "establish a legal information bureau" (1913 AB 65).[10] This follow-up to the 1911 bill contained some modifications of Zophy's earlier effort: it looked to the Milwaukee County Board of Supervisors rather than the Mayor and Common Council to appoint staff, collect fees, and use the property tax levy to raise additional funds. The measure showed that Socialists had not been discouraged by the results of the previous legislative session or the 1912 municipal elections in Milwaukee. Unfortunately, on April 11, the Minkley bill was killed in the Committee on Municipalities, of which he was a member. Like its predecessor, it never got to the floor for a vote. In fact, Minkley was recorded as the lone dissenter to the tabling of his measure.

Two years later, on January 28, 1915, Assemblyman Edward H. Zinn (Social-Democrat of Milwaukee) made a third run at the goal by introducing a bill (1915 AB 72) that was a virtual reprise of the Minkley measure.[11] Surprisingly, on March 29, the Assembly Committee on Municipalities recommended passage of the bill. This promising development was undoubtedly due to the fact that Socialists no longer controlled the Milwaukee County Board and, thus, would not have the power to establish the new bureau. However, the Zinn bill was stillborn three weeks later when his measure was postponed indefinitely on a floor vote of 48-39. *Index to Journals of the Legislature* (1915) 566. Having gotten his bill to the floor, though, Zinn pressed for reconsideration. The Assembly agreed to reconsider the proposal on a 46-40 vote, but then again voted to table it indefinitely by a 47-35 margin. It was now abundantly clear that the small caucus of Milwaukee Socialists in the state legislature lacked the political heft to secure passage of a legal aid bill. Their failure in three successive sessions of the Legislature (1911, 1913, 1915) shifted the focus from the partisan atmosphere of the state capitol to Milwaukee's private sector.

In the fall of 1915, with the King-Commons report still serving as a useful catalyst, a joint committee was appointed by E.W. Frost, President of the Central Council of Social Agencies, and Walter D. Corrigan, Sr., President of the Milwaukee Bar Association, to revisit the issue. The committee was chaired by Attorney Walter S. Bartlett, a young, Harvard-educated member of the state's oldest and largest law firm (Miller, Mack & Fairchild). Other members were Assistant City Attorney Charles W. Babcock, Attorney Frank Mackut, Jr. (member of the Milwaukee Bar Association), Attorney Arnold C. Otto (Republican member of the Wisconsin Legislature, member of the City Club and Milwaukee Bar Association), Mrs. Susie Bruce (Superintendent of Associated Charities, which later became the Family Welfare Association), Miss Alice C. Miller (daughter of Attorney George Peckham Miller of the Miller, Mack & Fairchild law firm), and Mrs. Leonora Morse Rosing (influential Secretary of the Central Council of Social Agencies). Not surprisingly, the Bartlett Committee recommended formation of a legal aid society in Milwaukee. On December 11, 1915, the Bartlett report was endorsed by the Bar Association [see Historical Documents Section].

Five weeks later, on January 17, 1916, the Central Council of Social Agencies also signed on to the proposed establishment of a free legal services program for Milwaukee's poor [see Historical Documents Section]. Soon after, the City Club followed suit. In joining forces, the three organizations reflected an amalgam of varied motivations that included civic philanthropy, the legal profession's ethical responsibility to the needy, and the political philosophy of the city's Socialist Party. These ingredients were then added to the broader mix of biblical values, Anglo-American constitutional ideals, and Wisconsin Idea progressivism. Such varied strands were woven together to create the new organization. As legal historian Daniel D. Blinka notes: "The Legal Aid Society's founding married several elements of early twentieth-century progressivism, which used local government to remedy social ills, with older nineteenth-century ideas of voluntarism and private action."[12]

The Legal Aid Society of Milwaukee was officially incorporated on February 25, 1916. The original articles of incorporation provided a broad mandate to the fledgling Society: *The purpose of this organization shall be to furnish legal aid to those financially unable to obtain legal counsel, to promote laws and measures, and to do all things necessary for the prevention of injustice.* The mission statement's first purpose was standard in legal aid charters. The second provision, concerning the promotion of laws and measures (*i.e.* legislative advocacy), was borrowed from the charter of the New York Legal Aid Society. It appears, though, that Milwaukee's third charge was unique in the breadth of its scope "to do all things necessary for the prevention of injustice." No program in the country had such an expansive vision. The charter was also unusual in the absence of a common requirement employed elsewhere that clients first be found "worthy" before receiving services.[13] The Milwaukee founders saw access to justice as a fundamental constitutional right, not as charity to be doled out to "deserving" poor.

The initial incorporators included six members of the Bartlett Committee: Walter S. Bartlett, Charles W. Babcock, Mrs. Susie B. Bruce, Frank Mackut, Jr., Arnold C. Otto, and Leonora Morse Rosing. Six prominent Milwaukee attorneys joined them as remaining signatories of the Articles: Emmett A. Donnelly, George G. Goetz (member of the Lines, Spence & Quarles firm and the Milwaukee Bar Association), Guy D. Goff (prominent Republican and President Theodore Roosevelt's appointee as United States Attorney), William Kaumheimer, Stephen J. McMahon (law professor at Marquette University,

9. Attorney Walter S. Bartlett, chair of a joint committee of the Milwaukee Bar Association and the Council of Social Agencies that recommended creation of a legal aid society in 1915.
Courtesy of Milwaukee County Historical Society.

member of the City Club, and active Republican), Harold W. Story (member of the Quarles, Spence & Quarles law firm). The new Society began as a membership organization composed mostly of attorneys. Modest annual dues were established at $1 per member. A yearly luncheon meeting was held to nominate and elect members of the board of directors. The first board inaugurated a tradition of attracting distinguished citizens to serve as officers and directors of the Society. Attorney William Kaumheimer, a leading member of the local bar, was elected first President of the Society. Meta S. Berger, a well-known political activist (and wife of Victor), was named Vice President. Attorney Emmett A. Donnelly was elected Secretary-Treasurer. Rounding out the original board of directors were Wisconsin Supreme Court Justice John Barnes; Clara (Mrs. Emanuel D.) Adler, wife of a successful clothier and philanthropist; Neil W. Norris and Miss Alice Miller, both scions of socially prominent Milwaukee families.

The founders of the Legal Aid Society of Milwaukee had to make some important decisions at the program's outset. Their goal was to incorporate "the best features of the free legal aid societies of other cities which have been pioneers in the work of securing equal protection of the law to all, regardless of financial ability." See "Legal Aid Society Expects Many Cases of Poor" in *Milwaukee Journal* (June 4, 1916) [Historical Documents Section]. First, they had to determine an operational model. Legal aid efforts elsewhere had produced five distinct types: (i) municipal bureaus, (ii) departments of organized charities, (iii) bar association programs, (iv) law school clinics, and (v) private corporations.[14] Notwithstanding crucial involvement by the Milwaukee Bar Association, the Central Council of Social Agencies, and a faculty member from Marquette University Law School, it was decided that the new organization should be a private corporation. Chief among the advantages of that choice was that the Milwaukee program would be independent of an umbrella organization (*e.g.* a social agency, law school, or municipal bureau) that had a different mission. In addition, a private corporation would be insulated from political influence found in a municipal bureau, free to raise funds from the public, and its services would not be seen as a matter of grace.

A second choice focused on the type of service delivery model: staff attorney versus retained counsel plan. The founders of the Milwaukee program adopted a collaborative model that employed social workers as the primary client contact and factual investigator, and retained outside legal counsel to handle those matters requiring litigation. Reginald Heber Smith thought the "pooling of all experiences [legal and social work] in one office furthers the preventive work which the legal aid society can do." *Justice and the Poor*, 224. The format was undoubtedly influenced by William Kaumheimer's endorsement of assigned counsel as the best method of representing the poor in criminal cases, though it also may have been imposed by budget necessity. Nonetheless, the cross-disciplinary partnership was seen at the time as establishing a new paradigm in the emerging field of social sciences. John S. Bradway, *Law and Social Work: An Introduction to the Study of the Legal-Social Field* (University of Chicago Press, 1929).

A third decision made by the founders focused on whether to follow the lead of more established legal aid programs in New York, Chicago, Boston, Philadelphia, and Cleveland, all of which charged clients a nominal registration (retainer) fee and/or charged clients a commission on monies recovered for the client's benefit.[15] The charging of fees, it should be recalled, had been a staple of all three bills that Socialists had previously introduced in the Wisconsin Legislature. Nonetheless, the organizers of the Legal Aid Society of Milwaukee rejected that conventional provision. Instead, they opted to follow the King-Commons report and offer legal services entirely free of charge to all eligible clients. Thus, early annual reports of the Milwaukee society proclaim: "No Charge Made for Services" (1918), "No registration fee is required and no fee of any kind is charged" (1922), and "No Fee Charged, No Commission Taken" (1928). As LAS President Charles Babcock explained in 1931: "No suggestion is made to the client that he may give something to the Society. We are very punctilious about this" [see Historical Documents Section]. The thinking of the Milwaukee founders was based on three factors: (i) justice should not be administered for sale; (ii) the minimal benefits of fees and commissions were purely speculative; and (iii) private attorneys would be reluctant to contribute to the Society if they felt that clients were able to pay something toward their lawyer's fees.

From various comments, surveys, and reports presented to the National Association of Legal Aid Organizations, we can glean further particulars on the early operation of the Legal Aid Society of Milwaukee. First, the initial client contact was made with social workers who determined financial eligibility of applicants and investigated the facts of each case. Second, those who could not be represented by LAS were referred to a list of private counsel selected by the Society's retained attorney. This was a sensitive issue because, on the one hand, the organization wanted to ensure that people seeking its help were directed to competent lawyers with expertise in the client's particular legal issue; on the other hand, such referrals might open the organization to charges of favoritism. This would remain a thorny issue until the Society joined forces with the Milwaukee Bar Association in 1943 to form the Lawyer Referral Service. Third, no criminal cases were accepted because Wisconsin law and local practice allowed for assigned counsel to be paid in both felony and misdemeanor cases. See Wis. Stats. 1915, s. 4713. Fourth, the Society did accept a limited number of divorce cases, deemed by some a luxury, but only after a social service agency evaluated the family conditions and recommended divorce. Fifth, no personal injury cases were accepted because private lawyers were available to take such matters on a contingent fee basis (otherwise known as "the poor man's key to the courthouse").

It had taken Professor Commons' original idea nearly six years to bear fruit. Finally, though, on June 1, 1916, the Legal Aid Society of Milwaukee opened its doors and accepted the first of more than half-a-million clients it would ultimately represent over the course of the next century. At the time, Milwaukee's program was one of about thirty legal aid organizations in the United States, but almost half of these early efforts failed to survive the institutional stresses brought about by World War I (when many idealistic staff resigned to join the American Expeditionary Force in France) and the Great Depression (when many programs lost their precarious funding). The Legal Aid Society of Milwaukee would endure and, eventually, flourish.

NOTES

1. "The legal aid system of Germany is very largely built on group lines. There are political, religious, and class bodies or associations which provide legal

assistance for their members." Reginald Heber Smith, *Justice and the Poor* (New York: Carnegie Foundation, 1919) 171.

2. In discussing his work in the Bureau of Economy and Efficiency, Commons remarked: "I took over to Milwaukee a number of my graduate students." *Myself: The Autobiography of John R. Commons* (Madison: University of Wisconsin Press, 1964) 151.

3. Reginald Heber Smith expressed concern about placing legal aid programs within municipal government because of the danger that such programs would be corrupted by political influence. *Justice and the Poor*, 185-86.

4. Gabriel Zophy was born in 1869 at Schwanden, Canton Glarus, Switzerland. At age 10, he emigrated to Wisconsin with his parents. Zophy grew up on a farm in Green County. After moving to Milwaukee, he became a carpenter and contractor by trade. His first political experience was as a village trustee and school commissioner in suburban West Allis. Zophy was elected to a single four-year term in the State Senate in 1910. His 7th District covered most of southern Milwaukee County. *Wisconsin Blue Book 1913* (Madison: Democrat Printing Co. 1913) 640-41.

5. Reginald Heber Smith comments: "Up to this time [1900], there was no standard nomenclature; there was one Legal Aid Society, one Protective Agency, one Bureau of Justice, and one Poor Man's Lawyer. With its adoption in Boston, and later elsewhere, the term 'legal aid' grew into the standard and uniform name for this sort of organization. *Justice and the Poor* 148.

6. John D. Buenker, *The History of Wisconsin, Volume IV: The Progressive Era, 1893-1914* (Madison: State Historical Society of Wisconsin, 1998) 535.

7. See SB 253 in *Senate Journal 1911*, pp 197, 276, 644, 673. The bill's demise is also noted in Elmer Axel Beck, *The Sewer Socialists: A History of the Socialist Party of Wisconsin, 1897-1940* (Fennimore, WI: Westburg Associates, 1982) 105.

8. About the 1911 legislature, Professor Buenker comments: "On virtually every issue involving advantage-seeking among the parties ... party loyalty overwhelmed ideological conviction." Moreover, "Progressive Republicans and Democrats and Socialists frequently cooperated, but rarely on matters that were 'too socialistic.'" *The Progressive Era* 533. Another historian notes: "Milwaukee's Socialists faced ... the double enmity of the Republican and Democratic organizations. Both parties were deeply embarrassed by the Socialist victory of 1910, and they were determined not to let it happen again. As the 1912 mayoral election approached, the erstwhile opponents decided to join forces" against the Seidel administration by running a fu-

sion ticket. John Gurda, *The Making of Milwaukee* (Milwaukee County Historical Society, 1999) 218.

9. Mordecai Lee, *Bureaus of Efficiency: Reforming Local Government in the Progressive Era* (Milwaukee: Marquette University Press, 2008) 219.

10. See AB 65 in *Assembly Journal 1913*, pp 105, 652, 679. Carl Minkley (Social Democrat) was born in 1866 in Strelno, Germany. He emigrated to Milwaukee in 1893 where he worked as a painter/decorator. In 1911, Minkley was elected alderman-at-large in Milwaukee to fill the vacancy created by the election of Victor L. Berger to Congress in the previous year. Minkley was elected to the Legislature in 1912 and re-elected in 1914. He represented Milwaukee's 4th Assembly District on the city's Northside. *Wisconsin Blue Book 1915* (Madison: Democrat Printing Co. 1915) p. 521.

11. See AB 72 in *Assembly Journal 1915*, pp 122, 461, 481, 505, 517, 536, 540, 573. Edward H. Zinn (Social Democrat) represented the 7th Assembly District on the city's near Northwest Side. He was born in Milwaukee in 1877 and was employed as a mechanical engineer. Zinn was elected to the Legislature in 1912 and re-elected in 1914. *Wisconsin Blue Book 1915*, p. 522.

12. Daniel D. Blinka, *In a Public Spirit: Origins of the Milwaukee Bar Association* (MBA, 2008) 22.

13. The 1903 revision to the corporate charter of the New York Legal Aid Society stated: "The purpose of this Society shall be to render legal aid, gratuitously if necessary, to all who may appear worthy thereof and who are unable to procure assistance elsewhere, and to promote measures for their protection." John MacArthur Maguire, *The Lance of Justice: A Semi-Centennial History of the Legal Aid Society, 1876-1926* (Harvard University Press, 1928) 112. The Boston Legal Aid Society adopted the New York statement verbatim. St. Louis and Cleveland pledged "to render legal assistance gratuitously or for a moderate charge to deserving persons not otherwise able to obtain the services of competent attorneys." Forrest C. Donnell, "St. Louis Municipal Legal Aid Bureau" in *Annals of the American Academy of Political and Social Science* 124 (1926) 49; Carol Poh Miller, *A Passion for Justice: A History of the Legal Aid Society of Cleveland, 1905-2005*, p. 5.

14. Smith, *Justice and the Poor*, 169-86.

15. Smith, *Justice and the Poor*, 165-68.

4

SPONSORING ORGANIZATIONS

The founding of the Legal Aid Society here was sponsored by three of the city's principal private-sector organizations: Milwaukee Bar Association, Central Council of Social Agencies, and City Club. Each realized the need in the community for what an early LAS annual report (1922) called "A Poor Man's Lawyer."[1] Their combined efforts proved what public-spirited leadership was capable of achieving, even without public funding. Like a relay race, they accepted the equal justice baton from the Socialists whose valiant first efforts failed in the Wisconsin Legislature.

The Milwaukee Bar Association, established in 1858, is one of just five antebellum bar associations in the country. Its founders addressed the great constitutional challenges leading up to the Civil War, thus beginning a tradition of making the legal profession an integral component of America's democratic infrastructure. Since inception, this public-spirited organization has successfully advocated for local and state practice standards, codes of ethics and lawyer discipline, and continuation of Wisconsin's unique diploma privilege. Among its greatest accomplishments are the establishment of the Milwaukee Law School (forerunner of Marquette University Law School) and the founding of the Legal Aid Society of Milwaukee. MBA President Walter D. Corrigan, Sr., committee chair Walter S. Bartlett, and a dedicated band of other attorneys were behind the push to establish the Society. Once LAS was up and running, relations between it and the Bar Association were described as amicable [see Historical Documents Section].

Today, the MBA has a voluntary membership of more than 2,600 lawyers, annually organizes more than 100 continuing legal education seminars, and works through 26 committees to improve the professionalism of its members. Each year, its Lawyer Referral & Information Service (co-founded by the Legal Aid Society) makes 8,300 client referrals and provides information to another 40,000 callers. The MBA and the Legal Aid Society are currently collaborating on two ventures: development of the Milwaukee Justice Center at the Milwaukee County Courthouse to assist *pro se* litigants in the legal process and a *pro bono* program to provide legal services to elderly deaf residents at the Water Tower View Senior Housing Project in Greenfield. The MBA Foundation continues to be a valued funding source for the Legal Aid Society's mission. Indeed, the organization's historian, Professor Daniel D. Blinka, concluded that one of the "Milwaukee Bar Association's most enduring and significant accomplishments has been its consistent support for the Legal Aid Society of Milwaukee."[2] Apropos of the organization's continuing involvement in legal services to the poor, eighteen former presidents of the Milwaukee Bar Association have served on the LAS board of directors; two more presidents were members of the Society's Advisory Board.[3]

The Central Council of Social Agencies was founded in Milwaukee in 1909 as the Central Council of Philanthropies. CCP was the product of a study conducted by Francis H. McLean, under the auspices of the Russell Sage Foundation, which urged coordination of social

10. Logo of the Milwaukee Bar Association. *Courtesy of MBA.*

services in the city. Over the years, this umbrella organization underwent several name changes (Community Fund, United Community Services, United Fund) – eventually becoming United Way of Greater Milwaukee. In November 1916, CCSA organized the city's first combined charity fundraising campaign, known as the Centralized Budget of Philanthropies. That initial effort enlisted just under 3,000 donors and raised $97,709 for the original 22 organizations, the newest of which was the Legal Aid Society of Milwaukee. The fundraising arm was also known by several names throughout the twentieth century, *e.g.* Centralized Budget of Social Agencies, Centralized Budget of Philanthropies, Community Chest, and the Red Feather Campaign. Chief backers of the Legal Aid Society at CCSA were President E.W. Frost, and two of his key board members, Edessa K. Lines and Leonora Morse Rosing. Their support set a template that has continued down to the present. In fact, United Way and its predecessor organizations have been the Legal Aid Society's most steadfast supporter – giving every year for 94 consecutive years – through World War I, the Great Depression, World War II, and all the way into the 21st century. In recent decades, United Way pioneered the concept of outcome measures to assess the effectiveness of social service programs in the community. Today, United Way of Greater Milwaukee enlists an army of 2,500 campaign volunteers and raises $45 million a year from 72,000 donors on behalf of 160 charitable programs. The agencies it funds serve 425,000 clients a year. United Way and its delivery partners impact individuals throughout the entire life cycle and across all ethnic, racial, and religious backgrounds.

The City Club was formed in 1908 to study municipal affairs and to promote effective ways to improve social, civic, and economic conditions in the community. Its motto, "For the betterment of civic life," was proudly emblazoned on its letterhead. One historian noted that the organization's membership represented a smorgasbord of "diverse reform interests: Progressive Republicanism, liberal Democracy, Socialism, and the Social Gospel, as well as nonpartisan movements." Roger Roy Keeran, *Milwaukee Reformers in the Progressive Era: The City Club of Milwaukee, 1908-22* (University of Wisconsin-Madison: M.A. thesis, 1969) 23. Certain figures instrumental in founding the Legal Aid Society were also members of the City Club: Victor L. Berger,

11. Logo of United Way of Greater Milwaukee. *Courtesy of UWGM.*

Professor John R. Commons, and Attorneys William Kaumheimer, Charles W. Babcock, and Walter S. Bartlett. Alma C. Schlesinger, the Society's first Superintendent, and Meta S. Berger, a founding director of LAS, were among the earliest women to be admitted as members of the Club. Undoubtedly, the Legal Aid Society also had the support of the Club's President, Fred S. Hunt, and Civic Secretary, Hornell Hart.

The City Club supported numerous good government initiatives such as non-partisan elections, pay-as-you-go financing of public works, transparency and accountability in public office, and expansion of civil service. The watchdog organization also sponsored an extensive list of conferences, reports, and speakers on municipal projects, transportation, housing, education, capital improvements to public infrastructure, daylight savings time, and efficient waste disposal. Between 1912 and 1917, the City Club "became the most important reform group in the city in both membership and influence." Keeran, *Milwaukee Reformers* 16. Unfortunately, the organization's size and vitality declined greatly in later years, especially throughout the 1960s. The Club dissolved in 1975, shortly after the death of its longtime Secretary, Leo Tiefenthaler. Its fundamental work, though, continues today under the aegis of the Public Policy Forum, formerly known as the Citizen's Governmental Research Bureau.

Long after its founding, the Legal Aid Society still considered United Way and the Bar Association as its primary funding constituencies. This view can be seen most clearly below in the Historical Documents Section, particularly in Agnes Campbell Kiewert's replies to an NALAO survey (1926) concerning relations with social agencies and in

12. Logo of City Club. *Courtesy of Golda Meir Library at the University of Wisconsin-Milwaukee.*

Charles W. Babcock's comments on relations with the local bar (1931). And for nearly half a century, the Legal Aid Society regularly held its lunchtime board meetings and annual corporate meetings at the City Club's various Downtown venues. Without the vision of these three organizations and their committed leaders, it is doubtful that the Legal Aid Society of Milwaukee would ever have come into existence as early as it did.

NOTES

1. The phrase is almost a term of art since it originated as the title of an English-model legal aid program developed at the Mansfield Settlement House in London during the nineteenth century. See Smith, *Justice and the Poor*, 138; Maguire, *Lance of Justice* 24-25, 215-17.
2. Daniel D. Blinka, *In a Public Spirit: Origins of the Milwaukee Bar Association* (MBA, 2008) 22.
3. The eighteen MBA presidents who served on the LAS board are: Robert R. Freeman, William Kaumheimer, Walter H. Bender, Edmund B. Shea, Albert B. Houghton, Reginald J. Kenney, John F. Baker, Charles L. Goldberg, John A. Kluwin, Patrick W. Cotter, Laurence C. Hammond, Jr., Wayne E. Babler, Jr., David J. Cannon, David A. Erne, David R. Olson, Arthur J. Harrington, Daniel D. Blinka, and Margaret W. Hickey. Two more MBA presidents, Christian Doerfler and Francis E. McGovern, served on the Society's Advisory Board. In addition, two former LAS staff attorneys, William A. Jennaro and Hannah C. Dugan, have been elected President of the MBA.

5
THE FOUNDING GENERATION

The Legal Aid Society of Milwaukee was founded by a group of remarkable men and women whose pioneering efforts are not as well known today as they deserve to be. The founders came from diverse backgrounds and represented varied constituencies including Stalwarts and Socialists, suffragettes and socialites. And although they have long since departed from the community, their actions continue to reverberate in the annals of the Society down to the present era.

John Rogers Commons, the visionary reformer who originated the idea of the Legal Aid Society of Milwaukee, was born in 1862 at Hollandsburg, Ohio, and educated at Oberlin College (B.A. 1888; M.A. 1890) and Johns Hopkins University. Commons taught at Wesleyan University, Oberlin, and Syracuse University. In 1904, he began a long and productive tenure as professor of economics at the University of Wisconsin. Commons served at various times as President of three influential national organizations: National Consumers' League, American Economic Association, and National Monetary Association. He was deemed the foremost exponent of the Wisconsin Idea, the unique concept that the public service obligations of the University of Wisconsin should reach beyond the classroom to advance the broader political, economic, and social interests of the entire state.

A modern historian rightly describes Professor Commons as one "whose name should head any list of professional scholars who shaped legislation and its administration in the progressive era."[1] Commons was a close policy advisor to Wisconsin Governor Robert M. La Follette and Milwaukee Mayor Emil C. Seidel. The latter appointed Commons as Director of the Bureau of Economy and Efficiency, a short-lived (18 months) city department that created a blueprint for

sound municipal governance through the issuance of eighteen visionary reports designed to improve the quality of urban life. One of these
white papers recommended establishment of a legal aid society in Milwaukee. That report became a plank in the Socialist campaign plat-
form of 1912.

Commons was a strong advocate of civil service laws, collective bar-
gaining, public utility regulation, and labor democracy. He helped establish the Wisconsin Industrial Commission and also played a leading role in developing the Wisconsin Idea in public policy formulation.
Commons is considered by many scholars to be the father of two landmark pieces of Wisconsin economic legislation: worker's compensation (1911) and unemployment compensation (1931); the state was
the first in the nation to enact each of these measures. The intellectual
told the story of his life in *Myself: The Autobiography of John R. Commons* (New York: Macmillan, 1938). See also La Fayette G. Harter, Jr.,
John R. Commons: His Assault on Laissez-Faire (Oregon State University Press, 1962). Commons died in 1945 at the age of 83. He lived
long enough, though, to see one of his best ideas grow and flourish: the
Legal Aid Society of Milwaukee.

Victor L. Berger was born in 1860 at Nieder Rehbach, Austria.
After studying at the University of Budapest and the University of
Vienna, he emigrated to the United States with his family. The Berg-
ers settled in Milwaukee in 1881. Victor edited and published several
newspapers including the German-language *Wisconsin Vorwaerts* and
the English-language *Milwaukee Leader*. He also became head of Milwaukee's Socialist Party and was elected to Congress in 1910 – the
first Socialist ever to serve in that legislative body. Berger has been perceptively described by a historian of the Socialist Party as "ambitious,
sometimes domineering, aggressive, but above all an astute politician,
a skilled organizer, and an able editor ... no one questioned his ability
and no one who challenged his authority within the party survived."[2]

Berger's pacifism and outspoken opposition to American entry into
World War I put him at the center of two famous cases in the United
States Supreme Court. In 1917, the Wilson administration revoked
mailing privileges for the *Milwaukee Leader*. Since newspapers were
delivered as second-class mail at that time, the Post Office ruling seriously threatened the economic viability of the *Leader*. Berger chal-

13.   Victor L. Berger, Congressman, newspaper editor, and co-founder of the Legal Aid Society of Milwaukee. *Courtesy of Milwaukee County Historical Society.*

lenged the ban in federal court, but the Supreme Court (with Justices Holmes and Brandeis dissenting) upheld the edict. *Milwaukee Social Democratic Publishing Co. v. Burleson,* 255 U.S. 407 (1921).

   In 1918, Berger was indicted under the Espionage Act of 1917 for repeatedly denouncing American entry into World War I. He was found guilty by a jury, and sentenced to 20 years in federal prison. Berger challenged the impartiality of the trial judge, Kenesaw Mountain Landis, who shortly afterward resigned to become the first Commissioner of Baseball. The Supreme Court held that Landis had improperly presided over Berger's case; as a result, the justices set aside the publisher's conviction. *Berger et al. v. United States,* 255 U.S. 22 (1921).

Despite being under indictment in 1918, Berger was reelected to Congress in the Fifth District on the city's North Side. In the following year, though, Congress refused to seat him on the grounds that a convicted felon could not serve. The House of Representatives declared the seat vacant, but Berger won a special election to succeed himself. In 1920, Congress again refused to admit Berger and again declared his seat vacant. Victor was reelected in 1922 and finally allowed to serve because, by that time, his felony conviction had been overturned by the Supreme Court.

Berger served two more terms in Congress and continued publishing the *Leader*. In 1926, he succeeded his longtime friend and political ally, Eugene V. Debs, as National Chairman of the Socialist Party. Berger was killed in a streetcar accident in 1929. His political views were collected and published in Victor L. Berger, *Broadsides* (Milwaukee: Social-Democratic Publishing Co., 2nd ed. 1912); *The Voice and Pen of Victor L. Berger: Congressional Speeches and Editorials* (Milwaukee Leader, 1929). For his biography, see Sally M. Miller, *Victor Berger and the Promise of Constructive Socialism, 1910-1920* (Westport, CT: Greenwood Press, 1973).

Walter S. Bartlett, just two years out of law school, chaired a joint committee of the Milwaukee Bar Association and the Central Council of Social Agencies. In the fall of 1915, his committee recommended formation of a legal aid society. The son of a socially prominent physician, he was born in Milwaukee in 1888. Bartlett was educated at the University of Wisconsin (B.A. 1910) and Harvard Law School (LL.B. 1913). Walter soon joined the Miller, Mack & Fairchild law firm (today's Foley & Lardner LLP) where he specialized in corporate law.

After his seminal report provided the necessary green light for founding the Legal Aid Society, the young attorney became an incorporator and initial director of the nascent organization in 1916.

Bartlett resigned from his law firm the following year to accept a lieutenant's commission in the U.S. Army. He served with the American Expeditionary Force in France during World War I. Following his discharge, Bartlett returned to Milwaukee to begin his own law firm. He was involved in many community organizations, including service as President of the Juvenile Protective Association and Secretary of the exclusive Country Day School. He was also an active member of the Republican Party. Bartlett married Ruth Fitch, daughter of a prominent Milwaukee banking family. In 1923, the LAS board appointed him an alternate delegate to the organizing conference of the National Association of Legal Aid Organizations. Shortly thereafter, he and his wife moved to New York where he became President of Brooklyn Cooperage Company, a subsidiary of the American Sugar Refining Company. Bartlett died in New York in 1934 at the age of 46.

The Legal Aid Society of Milwaukee was most fortunate in attracting William Kaumheimer to serve as its founding President. This gifted lawyer, the son of German immigrants, was born in Houston, Texas, in 1869. After his family moved to Milwaukee, young Kaumheimer began taking night classes at the old Milwaukee Law School. He was admitted to the bar here in 1894 and opened a law practice in the Wells Building on East Wisconsin Avenue. Although specializing in corporate and commercial law, he was deeply committed to the concept of equal justice for the poor. In 1919, he entered into a successful law partnership with Reginald Kenney that became known as Kaumheimer & Kenney.

Kaumheimer helped found the Legal Aid Society of Milwaukee in 1916 and served as President of its board during the first thirteen years of the organization's existence. He took an almost proprietary interest in the Society and was a founding member of the National Association of Legal Aid Organizations in 1923. In the following year, he authored a NALAO committee report urging adoption of a Model Law on Collection of Wages [see Historical Documents Section]. In 1925, he was named first chair of the Standing Committee on Legal Aid of the Wisconsin State Bar Association. A year later, he drafted a proposal for appointed defense counsel in criminal prosecutions. Kaumheimer was elected President of NALAO in 1928-29. He also served as Chairman of the Trustees of the Milwaukee Public Library,

14. Attorney William Kaumheimer, President of the Legal Aid Society of Milwaukee, 1916-29. *Courtesy of Duke University Archives.*

President of the Milwaukee Bar Association, and Director of the Milwaukee Auditorium. His law partner, Reginald Kenney, served as a director of the Legal Aid Society of Milwaukee, as well. Today, their firm employs more than a hundred attorneys and is known as Reinhart Boerner Van Deuren S.C.

One wonders how he found the time, much less the energy, to be active on so many fronts, both locally and nationally. By 1928, however, a long bout with Parkinson's disease began to take its progressive toll on Kaumheimer's health and vitality. He was unable to attend the NALAO conference in 1929, even though he was outgoing President of the organization. In the same year, he was replaced as LAS board president. Kaumheimer died on August 31, 1932, just a little over a year after the Wisconsin Legislature enacted the Wage Collection Act that his seminal report had recommended in 1924. Passage of the law served as a fitting testament to Kaumheimer's sustained advocacy.

His son and law partner, Leon, later made two bequests of $10,000 each to the Legal Aid Society to help continue his father's legacy. After his death, John S. Bradway, longtime Secretary of the National Association of Legal Aid Organizations saluted Kaumheimer as "a tower of strength in our National work," and noted that "his keen mind added immeasurably to our work." Letter to Charles W. Babcock (Duke University Archives, September 17, 1932). Bradway also established a memorial endowment in Kaumheimer's name to continue the Milwaukee lawyer's legacy of energetic leadership at the national level.

Meta Schlichting Berger served as the initial Vice President of the Legal Aid Society. She was born to German immigrant parents in Milwaukee in 1873. Meta received a teaching degree from Milwaukee State Normal School in 1894. Three years later, she married Victor L. Berger. That marital partnership launched Meta on her own career as a political and social activist. In 1909, she became one of the first women ever elected to public office in Wisconsin when she won a seat on the Milwaukee School Board. Six years later, Meta was named President of the Board and continued to hold office as an elected board member for thirty years. She also served as a Regent of the University of Wisconsin and later ran for Congress after the death of her husband.

Meta was a radical suffragette, a vigorous opponent of American entry into World War I, and a leader in the local and national Socialist Party. She was undoubtedly the force behind the Legal Aid Society's decision to offer draft counseling free of charge to young men in 1917-18. Berger resigned from the Socialist Party in 1940 after naively concluding that Communism offered the best alternative to fascism. She

15. Meta S. Berger, Vice President of the Legal Aid Society of Milwaukee, 1916-17.
Courtesy of Milwaukee County Historical Society.

died in 1944 in Milwaukee. Her autobiography was published posthumously. Kimberly Swanson, ed. *A Milwaukee Woman's Life on the
Left* (Madison: State Historical Society of Wisconsin, 2001). See also
Michael E. Stevens, ed. *The Family Letters of Victor and Meta Berger,
1894-1929* (Madison: State Historical Society of Wisconsin, 1995).
Professor Genevieve G. McBride sums up the significance of her career: "Meta Berger left us many useful lessons on how to win against
the odds and obstacles and how to transform a city, a state, even a

Constitution ... she evolved a new role as a leader among women in Socialist Party politics and – although belatedly and briefly – among Wisconsin women in suffragist politics."[3]

Wisconsin Supreme Court Justice John Barnes was another member of the original LAS board of directors. Barnes was born on a farm in Manitowoc County in 1858. He was the son of immigrants from County Kilkenny, Ireland. After graduating from the University of Wisconsin Law School in 1885, Barnes went on to a successful career as a lawyer, school board president, and Municipal Court judge in Rhinelander. Although a staunch Democrat, Governor Robert M. LaFollette appointed him to serve as Chairman of the Wisconsin Railroad Commission in 1906. Two years later, Barnes was elected to the Wisconsin Supreme Court. He resigned from that post in 1916 to become Chief Counsel to Northwestern Mutual Life Insurance Co. Barnes became Vice President of the Legal Aid Society after the resignation of Meta Berger. He died unexpectedly at the age of 59 in 1919. Chief Justice John B. Winslow described Barnes as "unquestionably in the very first rank of Wisconsin's great lawyers and statesmen." 169 Wis. at lxii (1919).

Alice Chapman Miller was a daughter of George Peckham Miller, senior partner in the Miller, Mack & Fairchild law firm; on her mother's side, she was an heiress to the Chapman's Department Store. Alice was born in Milwaukee in 1893 and graduated from Bryn Mawr College in 1914. A year later, she founded the Junior League in Milwaukee to provide young women from socially prominent families with an opportunity to contribute to local charities. Also in 1915, Alice served on the Bartlett Committee and then became an original member of the Legal Aid Society board. Shortly after she married Lt. William Merrill Chester of the U.S. Army Air Corps in 1917, her husband shipped overseas with the American Expeditionary Force. Deciding to do her part in the war effort as well, Alice resigned from the LAS board and booked passage to France where, for the next two years, she drove an ambulance for a hospital serving wounded soldiers. She returned to Milwaukee after the armistice and became Secretary of the National League of Women Voters affiliate here during the final push for women's suffrage (Wisconsin became the first state to ratify the Nineteenth Amendment in 1919). In 1921, she founded the first

16. Wisconsin Supreme Court Justice John Barnes, member of the Legal Aid Society of Milwaukee's board of directors, 1916-19. Courtesy of Wisconsin Supreme Court.

Girl Scouts Council in Milwaukee and later served on that organization's national board. Alice Miller Chester died in Milwaukee in 1972 after an active life filled with many contributions to the community. The Girl Scouts' Camp Alice Chester in East Troy was named in her memory.

Daniel Wells Norris was another member of the original LAS board of directors. His maternal grandfather, Daniel Wells, Jr. (1808-1902) had been prominent in the city's early history as a judge, congressman, and magnate of railroad, lumber, and real estate interests; in fact, at his death he was said to be the wealthiest individual in Wisconsin. One of the city's principal thoroughfares (Wells Street) and one of its major downtown high rises (Wells Building) are named after him. His grandson and namesake, known as Neil, was born in Milwaukee in 1886. Neil used his inheritance to become a philanthropist and child welfare advocate. He founded the Norris Farm for Boys, an institution that provided structure and practical job training for wayward boys aged 10 to 18. It had a print shop, carpentry shop, barber shop, store, and small farm along the Fox River in Mukwonago that taught young boys a trade and kept them out of trouble. Juvenile authorities and sociologists came from all over the world to study the successful record of the Norris Farm's programs. Neil Norris died in Milwaukee in 1948. His legacy continues today on its original site as the Norris Adolescent Center.

Clara H. Adler was the wife of Emanuel D. Adler, a prominent clothier, philanthropist, and pillar of Milwaukee's Jewish community. Her husband served as a Trustee of Northwestern Mutual Life Insurance Co. and as Vice President of Mount Sinai Hospital. Clara balanced her LAS board duties with her responsibility for raising the couple's four children.[4] The final member of the original board was Attorney Emmett A. Donnelly, son of Chief Judge Joseph G. Donnelly (a native of Ireland and former President of the Milwaukee Bar Association). Donnelly, who had also served as a member of the Bartlett Committee, was elected first Secretary-Treasurer of the Legal Aid Society in 1916.

William Frawley Hannan was the first Counsel to the Legal Aid Society.[5] He was born into a pioneer Milwaukee family in 1866 in the city's historic Third Ward. Both his parents had immigrated here from their home in County Limerick, Ireland. Hannan was educated at the University of Wisconsin (B.A. 1908) and the University of Wisconsin Law School (LL.B. 1912). He was admitted to the bar in 1912 and soon after formed a law partnership in Milwaukee with James A. Johnson and William J. Goldschmidt. The firm located in the Majestic

Building on Grand (now 233 West Wisconsin) Avenue and developed
a thriving practice in labor law and civil litigation. A long-time legal
counsel for the Milwaukee Teachers Association and the Wisconsin
Teachers Association, Hannan worked closely with Meta Berger to
protect the rights of teachers in public schools.

As the son of Irish immigrants and senior partner in his own law
firm, Hannan supported the principle of equal access to justice for the
poor, so much so that he volunteered the services of Hannan, Johnson & Goldschmidt to the Legal Aid Society as its outside retained
counsel. By virtue of his official position as Counsel to the Society, he
was the first Legal Aid lawyer in Milwaukee. A biographical notice described Hannan's principled approach to the law: "The more difficult
the situation, the more arduously he applies himself to the mastery of
the question before him ... and all respect him for his firm and unwav-
ering stand in support of any principle or measure which he deems
right." William G. Bruce, *History of Milwaukee City and County*, 3 vols.
(Chicago: S.J. Clarke Publishing Co. 1922) ii 613. Hannan died unexpectedly at the young age of 53. "W.F. Hannan, Attorney for Teachers,
Dies" in *Milwaukee Sentinel* (December 27, 1939). Nonetheless, he left
behind an enduring legacy in the community, one that has been faithfully carried out through the work of nearly 200 Legal Aid Society
lawyers who followed in his path-breaking footsteps.

Looking back in later years, the founding generation took great
pride in recounting its role in organizing the Legal Aid Society of Milwaukee as an effective advocate for the city's poor. They considered
the Society one of their principal lifetime achievements – something
worthy of mention in biographical notices and obituaries.[6]

NOTES

1 Robert C. Nesbit, *Wisconsin:A History* (Madison: University of Wisconsin
Press, rev ed. by William F. Thompson, 1989) 426.

2. Frederick I. Olson, "Milwaukee's Socialist Mayors: End of an Era and Its
Beginning" in *Historical Messenger* (March 1960), reprinted in *Milwaukee
Stories*, ed. Thomas J. Jablonsky (Marquette University Press, 2005) 432.

3. McBride, "Foreword" to *A Milwaukee Woman's Life on the Left* viii.

4. Biographical information on Alice C. Miller and Neil W. Norris was
gleaned from John G. Gregory, *History of Milwaukee, Wisconsin*, 4 vols.
(Chicago: Clarke Publishing Co. 1931) iii 81-86 and 534-36; for their

obituaries, see "Girl Scout Patron, Mrs. Chester, Dies" in the *Milwaukee Journal* (July 13, 1972); and "Neil Norris Is Dead at 62" in *Milwaukee Journal* (November 21, 1948). For Clara H. Adler, see William George Bruce, *History of Milwaukee City and County*, 3 vols. (Chicago: S.J. Clarke Publishing Co. 1922) iii 12-15. For Daniel Wells, Jr., see Carl Baehr, *Milwaukee Streets: The Stories Behind Their Names* (Milwaukee: Cream City Press, 1995) 278; *Dictionary of Wisconsin Biography* (Madison: State Historical Society of Wisconsin, 1960) 369.

5. In the days before legal aid societies shifted to a staff attorney model of service delivery, it was common to refer to outside retained attorneys by this title. Reginald Heber Smith, for example, held the post of Counsel (later General Counsel) to the Boston Legal Aid Society.

6. See, for example, Bruce, *History of Milwaukee*: Walter S. Bartlett (ii 483) and William Kaumheimer (iii 353). See also Gregory, *History of Milwaukee*: Edessa K. Lines (iii 211) and Arnold C. Otto (iii 502); Fred L. Holmes, ed. *Wisconsin Stability Progress Beauty*, 5 vols. (Chicago: Lewis Publishing Co. 1946) re Charles B. Quarles (3:226). See further the *Milwaukee Journal* obituaries of Lenora Morse Rosing (February 29, 1948) and Edessa K. Lines (October 23, 1962).

6

NATIONAL LEGAL AID &
DEFENDER ASSOCIATION

The proliferation of legal aid societies during the first two decades of the twentieth century created the natural desire to form a central clearinghouse of information. Consequently, the National Alliance of Legal Aid Societies was established in 1911. The Legal Aid Society of Milwaukee joined the organization in 1916, but did not send a delegate to its national convention that fall in Cincinnati. Like many locally-based programs, however, NALAS became defunct during World War I. In fact, the number of legal aid programs in the United States dropped from 60 in 1917 to 33 in 1923. The Columbus, Ohio, program, for example, was also founded in 1916, but it folded the following year. In 1923, those legal aid offices that did survive the Great War determined to band together once again, this time in an entirely new and permanent organization. These individual programs, among which was the Milwaukee society, met in Cleveland in 1923 to form the National Association of Legal Aid Organizations. President William Kaumheimer signed the original charter on behalf of the Legal Aid Society of Milwaukee [see Historical Documents Section].[1]

From the outset, the Milwaukee society played an active role in the new national organization. Kaumheimer was named to the body's Executive Committee in 1924, he was elected President of the National Association in 1928. Each year he led a relatively large delegation from Milwaukee to the national conference; in 1924, for example, the Society sent Kaumheimer, Director William A. Klatte, Director Perry J. Stearns, and Superintendent Agnes Campbell Kiewert at a time when total conference attendance generally numbered little more than two dozen persons. Somewhat surprising, though, is the fact that no attorneys from the Hannan law firm ever attended a single NALAO conference.

Until serious health problems disabled him in 1929, Kaumheimer's sharp legal mind, incisive manner, confident speaking style on all manner of subjects relating to legal aid, and boundless energy marked him as a genuine national leader. When he got up to leave one early NALAO conference, the remaining delegates gave him a spontaneous ovation. He chaired a committee on accounting that issued a report recommending stringent guidelines for handling all funds collected "because," as he put it, "we are dealing with money which is not our own." *Proceedings of NALAO* (1923-24) 114. A year later, Kaumheimer proposed a model law making it possible for workers to collect their back wages in an efficient manner from defaulting employers. *Proc. NALAO* (1924-25) 105-20. A decade after his death, he was eulogized at a national conference:

> William Kaumheimer, as President of the Milwaukee Society and later as President of the National Association, combined rare qualities of common sense and idealism and endeared himself to those of us who worked with him by his keenness of vision and forcefulness of expression.
>
> *Proc. NALAO* (1942) A-136.

Charles W. Babcock, Kaumheimer's successor as President of the Legal Aid Society of Milwaukee, also participated actively in the affairs of the National Association. Babcock became a member of the Executive Committee in 1930-31, and Superintendent Margery Heck was named to the same body in 1936. Milwaukee attendance fell off

17. National Legal Aid & Defender Association logo. *Courtesy of NLADA.*

for the next three years, but then revived upon the arrival of Julia Dolan as Superintendent. In 1940, the Society sent Babcock, Dolan, and Edessa Lines (a Director) to the national conference as delegates. Babcock was elected Vice President of NALAO in 1941 and 1942. In the latter year, Milwaukee hosted the organization's national conference. Julia Dolan worked on a number of NALAO committees in the early 1940s. She conducted a national survey on lawyer referral practices in 1942; two years later, she chaired a committee on post-war planning designed to address issues facing returning veterans, especially those dealing with family disruption. She was elected to the Executive Committee during 1946-49. In 1961, the organization, by then known as the National Legal Aid & Defender Association, awarded Dolan its highest honor, the Reginald Heber Smith Gold Medal. In later years, Judge F. Ryan Duffy, President of the Legal Aid Society of Milwaukee, served as a Director of NLADA 1958-64. Margadette Demet, Deputy Director of the Society's Milwaukee Plan Legal Services project, also won election to the NLADA board of directors in 1966-69.

Looking back on its first half-century of service, NLADA recognized William Kaumheimer of Milwaukee as one of its most significant and influential leaders during the organizaton's formative years. *Legal Aid Brief Case* xix, no. 5 (1961) 139. The Society's role in the national organization has diminished in recent years, largely because of NLADA's phenomenal growth, a development that was precipitated by creation of the federal legal services program and repeated constitutional mandates from the U.S. Supreme Court to provide counsel in criminal and juvenile proceedings. Nonetheless, the Legal Aid Society of Milwaukee co-hosted another national conference of NLADA in Milwaukee in 2002 – thus re-emphasizing the Society's co-founder status within the national umbrella organization.

Today, the National Legal Aid & Defender Association is the most prominent advocate for equal justice in the United States It serves as an invaluable resource for more than 2,000 civil legal aid and public defender offices around the country.[2] NLADA also provides a leading voice in public policy formulation and legislative debates on numerous issues facing the nation's poverty community. It is the oldest and largest such organization in America.

NOTES

1. The story of the 1923 Cleveland conference that gave birth to the National Association of Legal Aid Organizations is told by Reginald Heber Smith, "The First Twelve Critical Years" in *Legal Aid Brief Case* xix, no. 5 (1961) 128-35, 171-76. See also Mark W. Acheson, "An Historical Sketch of the Organization of Legal Aid in the United States" in *Legal Aid Review* xxxii, no. 2 (1934) 1-4.

2. *The Directory of Legal Aid & Defender Offices and Resources in the United States and Territories, 2009-10* (Washington, D.C.: National Legal Aid & Defender Association).

7

THE LAWYER'S ROLE

[*Note*: The Legal Aid Society of Milwaukee has a long tradition of representing some individuals who have proven unpopular with the general public. The following op-ed article was written more than thirty years ago to help explain the Society's role in defending such clients.]

On the evening of March 5, 1770, an angry, taunting mob attacked a garrison of British soldiers in Boston. In the ensuing melee, five people were killed. Nine soldiers were prosecuted for murder. Colonial sentiment ran high against the soldiers, who quickly became the symbol of British oppression. The authorities worried that they might not be able to protect the soldiers long enough to bring them to trial.

Into this highly charged atmosphere, one courageous man stepped forward to offer his legal services as defense counsel to the soldiers. He was quickly condemned for betraying his fellow countrymen and accused of approving British tyranny for the price of the Crown's retainer. This singular act of courage in an unpopular cause jeopardized his political and legal career and very nearly ruined his health.

The defense lawyer was, of course, John Adams, signatory of the Declaration of Independence and second president of the United States.

A recent attack on the criminal defense bar, published in this column, served to underscore that Adams was merely one of a long line of advocates, past and present, who are part of the great tradition of Anglo-American jurisprudence that holds no citizen, however humble his station or unpopular his cause, can be denied counsel in a criminal proceeding.

Other notable examples that might be cited range from Andrew Hamilton's famous defense of John Peter Zenger in 1735, a case that established the principle of freedom of the press in America, to the fictional Atticus Finch, who represented an African American man falsely accused of raping a white woman in a small Alabama town in Harper Lee's celebrated novel, *To Kill A Mockingbird* (1960).

It is important to note that undertaking the defense of one accused of murder or rape does not imply the attorney's condonation of such crimes. A lawyer who represents an accused should not be disparaged for accepting an unpopular cause. It is the jury, not the defense counsel, who determines guilt or innocence. Were attorneys to prejudge their client's cases, the cause of the poor or the despised might go unrepresented. This is why all lawyers, upon admission to the bar of the Wisconsin Supreme Court, take a solemn oath that includes this promise: "I will never reject, from any consideration personal to myself, the cause of the defenseless or oppressed."

It is the function of the criminal defense lawyer to represent that historic principle enshrined in Magna Carta (1215): "No free man shall be taken or imprisoned ... unless by the lawful judgment of his peers, or by the law of the land." In short, the lawyer's obligation is to

18.   Old Milwaukee County Courthouse (1873-1931) where the first Legal Aid Society cases were tried. *Courtesy of Milwaukee County Historical Society.*

ensure that no citizen is deprived of the ancient right to personal liberty absent carefully proscribed circumstances.

In this way, the lawyer acts as guarantor of the Bill of Rights by interposing himself or herself as a shield between the individual citizen and the awesome power of the State in order that that power not be abused. Scurrilous attacks on the criminal defense bar are, in essence, an assault on the very Rule of Law itself.

The majesty of the law has perhaps never been more eloquently stated than in a magnificent colloquy from Robert Bolt's acclaimed play, *A Man For All Seasons* (1960). Sir Thomas More, the leading lawyer of England who was beheaded in 1535 for defending the principle of liberty of conscience, speaks to his son-in-law, Will Roper:

More: The law, Roper, the law. I know what's legal, not what's right. And I'll stick to what's legal.

Roper: Then you set man's law above God's.

More: No, far below, but let me draw your attention to a fact – I am not God. The currents and eddies of right and wrong, which you find such plain sailing, I can't navigate. I'm no voyager. But in the thickets of the law, oh, there I'm a forester. I doubt if there is a man alive who could follow me there, thank God ... and go (there) he should, if he was the Devil himself, until he broke the law!

Roper: So now you give the Devil benefit of law!

More: Yes. What would you do? Cut a great road through the law to get after the Devil?

Roper: I'd cut down every law in England to do that!

More: Oh? And when the last law was down, and the Devil turned round on you – where would you hide, Roper, the laws all being flat? This country's planted thick with laws from coast to coast – man's laws not God's – and if you cut them down – and you're just the man to do it – do you really think you could stand upright in the winds that would blow then? Yes, I'd give the Devil benefit of the law, for my own safety's sake ... and whoever hunts for me, Roper, God or Devil, will find me hiding in the thickets of the law.

More's view that the "thickets of the law" must necessarily serve as protection for the guilty as well as the innocent has not, unfortunately, gained universal acceptance, as a column on this page so recently demonstrated.[1]

NOTE

1. This op-ed article was written by the Society's Executive Director and first appeared under the title, "A strong legal defense for people accused of crime guarantees every citizen the right to rule of law," in the *Milwaukee Journal* (December 24, 1979). It was penned in response to an earlier essay by a prominent labor leader who had urged imprisoning the defense lawyer every time a criminal defendant-client is convicted by a jury.

8

THE GUARDIAN AD LITEM ROLE

The founders of the Legal Aid Society of Milwaukee maintained a profound interest in child welfare issues. Thus, Walter Bartlett became President of the Juvenile Protective Association; Metal Berger served on the Milwaukee School Board for thirty years; and Neil Norris founded the Norris Farm for Boys. Nonetheless, virtually all of LAS's clients during its first quarter-century of service were adults. As Superintendent Agnes Campbell Kiewert reported in 1926, issues concerning neglected children were referred to child welfare authorities. That situation changed in 1941 when representatives of social agencies focusing on the needs of minors asked LAS "to safeguard the interests of children involved in applications for adoption."[1]

Since that year, lawyers from the Legal Aid Society have served regularly as guardians ad litem for Milwaukee County's most vulnerable residents. In 1944, the District Attorney's Office and Family Court judges requested that the Society expand its child advocacy practice by representing minor wards in paternity cases.[2] The original case-by-case arrangement, provided free of charge to the courts, was eventually formalized into a separately-staffed office at the Children's Court Center, with its own budget and an annual contract, to represent juveniles in delinquency, dependency, and neglect proceedings in 1970.[3] LAS's representation was expanded to include children in Family Court in 1981.[4] Today, the Society deploys a staff of eighteen lawyers, ably assisted by ten social workers and four legal assistants, to serve as advocates on behalf of more than 5,000 minor or incompetent wards each year in Children's Court, Family Court, and Probate Court. In addition, Family Court judges appoint LAS's staff to protect the interests of active-duty members of the armed forces under the Soldiers and Sailors Civil Relief Act.

The role of the guardian ad litem, who is required by law to be a licensed attorney with specialized training, carries some significant distinctions from the role of counsel in conventional litigation. Of crucial importance is the requirement that "the guardian ad litem shall function independently, in the same manner as an attorney for a party to the action, and shall consider, but shall not be bound by, the wishes of the minor child or the positions of others as to the best interests of the minor child." Wis. Stats. secs. 48.235 (3)(a), 54.40(3), and 767.407 (4). See generally Joan N. Alschuler et al., ed. *The Guardian ad Litem Handbook* (Madison: State Bar of Wisconsin, 3rd ed. 2007).

When a minor or incompetent person is made party to a legal matter, that individual becomes a ward of the court. It is the duty of the judge to see that his or her interests are protected. Under such circumstances, the court appoints a guardian ad litem to advocate the best interests (not necessarily the wishes) of fragile persons who cannot speak on their own behalf. The Wisconsin Supreme Court has defined this unique role by holding that "the guardian ad litem's duty is not only to be an advocate for the minor [or incompetent ward], but also to assist the court in its governmental function of seeing to it that justice is done to minors and others who are the objects of the special concern of government." *In Matter of Estate of Trotalli*, 123 Wis.2d 340, 355, 366 N.W.2d 879 (1985). Because the guardian ad litem discharges an office of special trust and confidence, and must provide the court with independent judgment, s/he is cloaked with absolute quasi-judicial immunity in the performance of his or her many challenging duties.

Representing children is a highly complex task that has evolved into a distinct specialty of the law. Guardians ad litem must be well versed in a broad array of substantive and procedural laws, trial and appellate advocacy skills, acquisition of community services and resources for children and their families, alternative dispute resolution techniques, recognition of child maltreatment and failure-to-thrive signs, drug and alcohol treatment issues, family dynamics, child development (both physical and psychological), cultural competency in the various ethnic and racial groups from which our wards come, and the special requirements of confidentiality relating to records involving children. To help ensure maintenance of high professional standards, the Legal Aid Society's board of directors has adopted the *Best Practices Guide-*

lines for Organizational Legal Representation of Children in Abuse, Neglect, and Dependency Cases (Denver: National Association of Counsel for Children, 2006).

The Society's Guardian ad Litem office argues an average of a dozen appellate matters each year in the Wisconsin Court of Appeals and Wisconsin Supreme Court. Among the significant issues litigated by the Society on behalf of its minor wards over the years have been the right to a probable cause hearing within 24 hours of detention (*State ex rel. Morrow*), the right to release from detention within five days of final adjudication (*State ex rel. Harris*), a class action suit against the Child and Adolescent Treatment Center establishing the right to least restrictive treatment of troubled juveniles (*State ex rel. R.T.*), and a challenge to systemic foster care neglect resulting in a state takeover of Milwaukee County's foster home program (*Jeanine B.*). The office is currently handling a case of first impression in Milwaukee County: an adoption petition filed by a same-sex couple (*In re Matthew Safehaven*). And recently, Guardian ad Litem Deanna Weiss filed a motion to hold the Bureau of Milwaukee Child Welfare in contempt of court for its failure to provide statutorily-required services to a nine-year-old girl. *In the Interest of Nicole H.*, case no. 10JC000430.

The Legal Aid Society's guardians ad litem serve under difficult circumstances. They and their social workers are called upon to make home visits, frequently in the evening, to some of the most dangerous neighborhoods in Milwaukee, places where lethal weapons and crimes of violence are commonplace. The highly-charged context of child custody battles, with its volatile mix of vindictive family members and caregivers who may have a criminal record, drug abuse, or mental illness in their past, adds to the danger of the work. Almost everyone on the staff has been threatened or cursed on more than one occasion during their career at the Legal Aid Society. Within the past few years, Guardian ad Litem Antonique Williams was punched by an angry parent. In another case, police were called in to protect Supervising Attorney Carmen Ortiz as she monitored the handoff of a child for visitation. A home-visit inspection was delayed some months ago when gunfire erupted as social worker Julie Rozek-Brady was getting out of her car in an inner city neighborhood. Some years ago, Chief Staff Attorney Shelia Hill-Roberts went into labor after sheriff deputies restrained an angry parent from physically attacking her inside a courtroom at the Children's Court Center; other guardians ad litem have also had to be personally escorted away from hostile courtroom confrontations.

Notwithstanding the physical dangers of their position, the Legal Aid Society's guardians ad litem have built a distinguished record of fearless advocacy for the voiceless. Their work includes researching arcane choice-of-law issues in such foreign jurisdictions as India, Mexico, England, and Jordan, trying an average of twelve jury trials a year, litigating a significant appellate caseload each term, and advocating legislation designed to safeguard the best interests of their vulnerable wards: children in need of protection or services, elderly adults in a protective placement, or innocent youngsters caught up in bitter custody disputes between competing parents. The following story offers a unique window on the work of LAS's Guardian ad Litem staff.[5]

* * *

Family Court GALs protect children's interests in divorce, paternity, guardianship, and child abuse injunction cases, devoting most of

19. Guardian ad Litem Debra N. Fohr advises a young boy in the offices of the Legal Aid Society. *Courtesy of Legal Aid Society of Milwaukee.*

their work to contentious child custody disputes. It is the guardian ad
litem's responsibility first to investigate, and then to make a custody
and placement recommendation, to Circuit Court Judges and Family
Court Commissioners. Using a "best interest of the child" standard,
the guardian ad litem recommends who should make major decisions
for the child and how the child's time should be divided between parents – extremely sensitive questions for both parents and children.

GALs gather information from the parents and the child, and then
investigate parent and child circumstances by contacting collateral
sources, usually physicians, school personnel, social workers, and probation officers. The Legal Aid Society's staff of social workers provides
invaluable assistance in conducting these investigations.

Because GALs are appointed only when parents cannot reach agreement on legal custody and physical placement, they often carry out
their duties in an emotionally charged environment. A recent article
on this subject noted: "This kind of work isn't for the faint-hearted. To
deal with people at this level of combativeness [requires] a clear framework and a sense of larger purpose." ("Custody Wars" in *Psychotherapy
Networker*, January-February, 2003). The following recent paternity
case provides an actual example.

The Family Court appointed LAS to serve as guardian ad litem for
ten-year-old "Monique." Monique's parents were constantly arguing
with each other, and frequently brought their battles into the courtroom. While their boyfriend-girlfriend relationship had ended over
three years before the custody dispute came to court, and both had
found new partners, their animosity for each other remained strong.
The father frequently failed to show up for scheduled visits, left hostile telephone messages for the mother, and videotaped Monique's
transfers from one parent to the other. The mother tape-recorded all
of Monique's phone conversations with her father, refused to allow
court-ordered visits solely to punish the father, and repeatedly refused
to allow the father to talk to Monique on the telephone. Regrettably,
Monique was increasingly traumatized by their ongoing battle and required psychotherapy treatment from a counselor.

Legal Aid's GAL determined that only an extremely detailed court
order would be effective in deterring the continuing battles between
parents. The GAL conducted in-depth interviews with both parents,

the child, and the child's counselor to identify how the parents' feud was affecting their child. The GAL then drafted an order for review by the Court, giving parents clear directions on what they must do, and everything they were forbidden to do. After reviewing the order, which was significantly more complex than normal, and listening to the GAL's reasoning, the Family Court gave its approval. The order directed the GAL's appointment (which usually ends with the approval of custody and placement plans) to continue for an additional year to monitor any problems that might come up. Since then, the parents have not complained to the GAL. Most importantly, neither has Monique. The parents know the rules set out by the Court, and Monique no longer bears the burden of their senseless feuding.

* * *

Guardians ad litem also look beyond individual cases to examine larger issues facing their fragile wards. One of the office's latest initiatives is the Safe Exchange and Supervised Visitation Project, a collaboration between the Legal Aid Society and Sojourner Family Peace Center. The two organizations are working together to seek funding from the Wisconsin Department of Children and Families to create a place where children can be safely exchanged and supervised visitation can take place in circumstances where domestic violence has been present. The hope is that sufficient monies will be made available to offer parenting education, batterer's treatment, anger management classes, AODA services, and other resources critically needed in the city's poverty community.

The Legal Aid Society recently opposed Senate Bill 384 (2009) in the Wisconsin Legislature [see Historical Documents Section]. That bill would have created an affirmative defense to criminal prosecutions for child abuse or child neglect where a parent or guardian has employed "the reasonable use of spiritual, prayer, or religious treatment in lieu of medical treatment." Joining LAS in opposition were the Wisconsin Medical Society, Wisconsin District Attorneys Association, and state chapters of the American Academy of Pediatrics and the National Association of Social Workers.

In the same legislative session, the Legal Aid Society supported the Child Victims Act (Senate Bill 319 and Assembly Bill 453).[6] The measure would have abolished the statute of limitations in cases of sexual abuse against children, thereby allowing victims of such heinous crimes to have their day in court. The proposal, which did not pass, faced powerful opposition, including objections raised by the Archdiocese of Milwaukee and the Wisconsin Council of Churches. Nonetheless, such legislative advocacy carries out the Society's original mandate "to promote laws and measures" on behalf of our vulnerable clients.

Those who know our work best are the Children's Court and Family Court judges who observe LAS lawyers advocating in their courts every day on behalf of vulnerable wards. Judge Mary M. Kuhnmuench, Presiding Judge of the Family Division, recently wrote:

> I have seen first hand the dedication and commitment that these fine lawyers demonstrate in each of the difficult custody and placement cases that they take on in their role as court-appointed Guardian ad Litem. Many of their cases involve parents struggling with language barriers, literacy issues, untreated mental health problems, and the difficulties of raising young children in extremely difficult circumstances. The stress level is high and the hours are long. The Legal Aid Society lawyers who do Guardian ad Litem work in the Family Courts are tenacious, careful, thoughtful, and hard-working. But above all else, they are passionate about the children they represent.
>
> As I have said on many occasions to a variety of audiences, the Legal Aid Society Guardians ad Litem do God's work in our courts, and they do it because, to them, it's a vocation, not a job. I can't imagine a finer group of lawyers doing this work, and doing it as well as the staff lawyers of the Legal Aid Society.

(Letter to Milwaukee County Board of Supervisors, March 11, 2009). Her counterpart, Mary Triggiano, Presiding Judge in the Children's Division, agreed:

> Not only do Legal Aid Society's guardians ad litem provide zealous advocacy for children, their unique attorney-social worker "team advocacy" approach assists the court in the governmental function of seeing to it that children are living in a safe environment, provided services, and obtain permanency at the earliest possible date.
>
> The Legal Aid Society's guardians ad litem have established an impressive track record in safeguarding these interests. Despite the alarmingly high number of children abused and neglected each year, the staff has remained committed to excellence. Their commitment to deliver high quality legal services to children is highly commendable. Legal Aid

Society is blessed with award-winning guardians ad litem whose passion for child welfare has been recognized by the entire legal community.

(Letter to Chair of County Board Judiciary Committee, March 9, 2009). Finally, in reviewing the value of the Society's longtime contract with Milwaukee County, Chief Judge Jeffrey A. Kremers concluded:

> Legal Aid Society has been providing high quality legal representation on behalf of children and litigants in both our Family and Children's Divisions for many years. Legal Aid clients have received exemplary service at a fair price to Milwaukee County. The Courts are assured a level of service across the board that is unmatched by any other method of appointed counsel.

(Letter to Chair of the County Board Judiciary Committee, March 10, 2009).

NOTES

1. Superintendent's Annual Report (1941).
2. LAS Board Minutes (August 8, 1944).
3. The origin and history of Milwaukee's Juvenile Court, established in 1901 and renamed Children's Court in 1949, is discussed in Karel D. Bicha, "Courts and Criminal Justice: Law Enforcement in Milwaukee County" in *Trading Post to Metropolis: Milwaukee County's First 150 Years*, ed. Ralph M. Aderman (Milwaukee County Historical Society, 1987) 145-95, especially pp 158-64.
4. After the State Public Defender took over LAS's broader role in 1979, the Society's Executive Director negotiated the first contract solely for guardian ad litem services. An agreement was reached with Milwaukee County Executive William F. O'Donnell and Clerk of Circuit Court Francis X. McCormack that resulted in the signing of a formal contract in November 1980. That agreement included LAS representation in Family Court cases as well. The first GAL appointments in Family Court were handled by lawyers from LAS's Civil Division. As the number of appointments rose, staff was added to specialize in this area. Today, five LAS lawyers work fulltime as Family Court guardians ad litem.
Rule 506 (A)(4), Milwaukee County Circuit Court Rules, now provides: "If the party raising the issue [custody, placement, visitation in Family Court] is found not to have the present ability to pay said [guardian ad litem] deposit by the judge, the Legal Aid Society of Milwaukee, Inc. shall be appointed guardian-ad-litem at county expense."

5. Reprinted from "Family Court Guardians ad Litem Help Resolve Custody Disputes One Child at a Time" in *Opening Statements* (Spring 2003) 3.

6. See letter of support for the Act (April 20, 2010) from LAS Executive Director Thomas G. Cannon to Senator Julie Lassa and Representative Joe Parisi.

9

THE SOCIAL WORKER ROLE

The Legal Aid Society of Milwaukee was originally founded on a model of collaboration between the then-emerging social work profession and the long-established legal profession. Prospective clients were first interviewed by a trained social worker to determine financial eligibility, screen out conflicts of interest, and determine case suitability. After factual investigation, if the case could not be resolved by advice, referral, or negotiation, the client would be put in contact with the Society's retained outside counsel, the Milwaukee law firm of Hannan, Johnson & Goldschmidt. Early annual reports demonstrate that social workers resolved approximately 93% of all matters; only 7% were referred over to the Hannan firm. Milwaukee was then one of just "a few legal aid societies [that] retain a social worker on the staff to give a preliminary interview to clients" according to Robert W. Kelso, "Legal Aid and Social Welfare Agencies" in *Annals of the American Academy of Political and Social Science* 124 (1926) 128. Originally, it was felt that lawyers took too narrow a view of their clients' problems; adding social workers was thought to help focus LAS on wider social, economic, and political issues, as well as to deploy more community resources to bear on developing a solution to the client's predicament. Mary Isham, "A Social Worker in a Legal Aid Society" in *Id.* 205 (1939) 134-40.

An early annual report (1918) described the Society as "one of the recognized social service agencies of the city." This self-description was echoed ten years later when another annual report noted: "There is an inevitable tendency to closer co-operation between social worker and legal aid worker for it becomes readily apparent that each needs the other." From a very early date, all LAS cases were registered with the Social Services Exchange. The head of the Family Welfare Association of Milwaukee declared at the time: "The work of the Legal Aid Society is an indispensable part of the social work of the community." The close working relationship between LAS and social service agencies in Milwaukee is further documented in a 1926 survey from the National Association of Legal Aid Organizations [see Historical Documents Section]. The Society's early outlook was also influenced by the fact that its funding was controlled by the Milwaukee Community Fund, an umbrella organization dominated by social service agencies.

The Legal Aid Society did, over time, evolve from a social service agency into a modern public interest law firm, a process that began slowly in 1930 with the appointment of the first attorney, Margery M. Heck, to serve as Superintendent. Heck's two predecessors had each been social workers. The transition may have been the product of economic necessity because it coincided with the first year of the Great Depression, which led to budget cutbacks that eliminated the staff social worker position.[1] For the first time in its fourteen-year history, LAS had no social worker on staff. Eventually, the remaining legal work moved in house when the Society hired its first staff attorney. In 1940, the Council of Social Agencies issued a report that sought to reverse LAS's identity back to that of a social service organization whose primary mission would be to provide legal services to the clients of those existing agencies [see Historical Documents Section]. By then, however, the board and its new Superintendent (Julia Dolan) had already embarked upon the process of becoming a law firm. The final phase in that evolution was accelerated by changes in law and society during the 1960s, culminating in the appointment of David S. Berman as Executive Director in 1971.

Ironically, the 1970s saw the return of social workers to the roster in order to staff the Society's Public Defender, Guardian ad Litem, and Mental Health Division projects. See, e.g. "Alternatives running out for patients" in Milwaukee Journal (December 6, 1982). Nearly a century after the Society's founding, the professional collaboration between attorneys and social workers is stronger than ever. This partnership is perhaps best personified in the career of Jocelyn Doctura Jurva. She began working with the Legal Aid Society's CASA Project in 1999 as a social worker (M.S.W., University of Michigan); after graduating from Marquette University Law School, Jocelyn then became a staff attorney in the Guardian ad Litem program. Similarly, our newest staff attorney, Rebecca A. Foley, earned a joint M.S.W.-J.D. degree at Loyola University of Chicago.

Today, the Legal Aid Society provides field placement instruction, under the tutelage of social workers Marcy Wichman and Julie Rozek-Brady, for graduate social work students from Marquette University, Concordia University, and the University of Wisconsin-Milwaukee. LAS social worker Donna Hibbler conducts professional training for employees of the Bureau of Milwaukee Child Welfare through the UW-M School of Social Work. At present, the Society has a complement of 10 social workers (nine in the Guardian ad Litem Project, one in the GAIN Project), its largest number ever. They serve as valued partners with our staff of 32 lawyers. The interdisciplinary background is examined in Lesley-Anne Cull and Jeremy Roche, ed. *The Law and Social Work: Contemporary Issues for Practice* (New York: Palgrave Publishers, 2001); Raymond Albert, *Law and Social Work Practice* (New York: Springer Publishing Co. 2000).

Judicial Court Commissioner Julia E. Vosper recently praised the effective partnership embedded in the Legal Aid Society's unusual

20. Legal Aid Society social worker Gena Clark conducts home visit for a case in Children's Court. *Courtesy of Legal Aid Society of Milwaukee.*

cross-disciplinary approach to representing its child wards in Children's Court and Family Court:

> The [Legal Aid Society's] GAL division has established a unique, efficient, and very thoughtful approach to the representation of children in child abuse and neglect cases. They provide a team to the court: a social worker, employed by Legal Aid, conducts visits with the children in their own homes (not in offices or at the Court Center, but in the home of the child so that the child can be as comfortable as possible). That social worker then assists the lawyer in devising recommendations for the Court. I personally find these independently gained reports (from a source distinct and separate from the BMCW) to be very helpful.

(Letter to Milwaukee County Board of Supervisors, March 10, 2009). What follows is one story selected out of many that could be considered representative of some cases handled by the Society's lawyer-social worker team.[2]

* * *

Soon after nine-year-old "Roberta" arrived at school with a black eye, she disclosed that her mother had hit her numerous times in the face. The abuse incident was triggered by the mother's anger over her daughter's supposed dalliance with homework. But Roberta said that this was not the first time her mother had physically injured her. After an investigation by the Bureau of Milwaukee Child Welfare (BMCW), the Children's Court issued an initial custody order placing the little girl temporarily in foster care, and appointing one of the Legal Aid Society's thirteen Children's Court staff attorneys to serve as Guardian ad Litem (GAL) to advocate for Roberta's "best interests." A petition alleging that she was a child in need of protection or services (CHIPS) was filed with the court.

The Legal Aid Society attorney and one of the Society's social workers immediately collaborated to investigate Roberta's case, a standard "team advocacy" practice in the Guardian ad Litem Office. The social worker interviewed the girl in her foster home just eight days after she had been detained. Roberta spoke freely about the abuse incident, and there was no indication that her mother had pressured her to be untruthful. She told the social worker that her mother apologized to her during their supervised visits and promised that she wouldn't hurt her again. She was no longer fearful of her mother and wanted badly to return home. The social worker also interviewed the foster mother who reported that Roberta was very depressed about the separation from her mother. She noted that Roberta exhibited no signs of chronic abuse such as aggressiveness, withdrawal, or hyper-vigilance. The social worker discussed the case with the GAL and then summarized her findings in a written report.

Within two weeks of the initial detention, the Legal Aid Society GAL conferred with the BMCW case manager, Roberta's mother, and her attorney. The mother appeared to be genuinely contrite about the incident, honest with the caseworkers, and deeply affected by the temporary loss of her daughter. The case manager and the GAL agreed that, if Roberta's mother consented to participate in a BMCW family reunification program, including anger management and parenting classes, Roberta could safely return to her mother's care with a period of monitoring. Fourteen days after Roberta's detention, following a "Service Implementation Hearing," she returned home to her mother while the BMCW provided the necessary monitoring and appropriate follow up services. The GAL then made an independent home visit to assess Roberta's circumstances and interactions with her mother.

Through a coordinated effort by the Legal Aid Society's attorney and social work staff, Roberta's circumstances were professionally and objectively evaluated. Mother and daughter were quickly reunited without extensive foster care involvement. The best interests of Roberta were well served by the responsive and concerned efforts of the Legal Aid Society's unique attorney-social worker "team advocacy" approach. According to BMCW estimates, of the more than 5,000 children represented annually at the Children's Court Center by the Legal Aid Society, approximately 70% return home within one year.

NOTES

1. In 1949, LAS requested funding from the Community Welfare Council for a social worker position to assist in handling the increasing number of domestic relations cases. CWC denied the request.
2. The foregoing story originally appeared in "Children's Court Guardian ad Litem Attorneys and Social Workers Engage in Team Advocacy" in *Opening Statements* (Spring 2003) 1.

10

MENTAL DISABILITY LAW

In 1944, Milwaukee County judges requested that the Legal Aid Society represent clients referred by the Hospital for Mental Diseases in commitment proceedings before the Lunacy Commission. The Society's board acceded to the request.[1] In 1977, LAS established a Mental Health Division after the Society litigated the *State ex rel. Memmel* case, which successfully challenged the sufficiency of civil mental commitment proceedings. Two years later, when the State Public Defender took over this responsibility in Milwaukee County, it contracted with the Legal Aid Society for several years. In large part, this arrangement was a recognition of Tom Zander's national reputation as an advocate for the mentally ill.[2] After Zander's retirement in 1995, LAS continued to accept appointments in cases that could not be handled by the SPD (conflicts of interest and non-indigents entitled to representation by statute). For the past fifteen years, LAS's services have been provided pursuant to an informal agreement with Milwaukee County and, since 2008, by contract with the State Public Defender.

Civil commitments represent just one aspect of the Society's broader advocacy for clients with mental disabilities. In 1980, for example, LAS received an anonymous grant to create the innovative AIMH (Alternatives to Involuntary Mental Hospitalization) Project. Four years later, the Society was awarded a grant from the Wisconsin Coalition for Advocacy to start an Institutional Advocacy Project. That IAP Project, later renamed PAL (Protection and Advocacy Law) Project, provided representation to mentally ill residents of state and county facilities on issues relating to abuse, neglect, and deprivation of civil rights. In 1985, Executive Director Tom Zander formed the present Mental Disability Law Division to consolidate the Society's civil commitment work with its broader advocacy work, adult guardianship representation, and protective placement initiatives. Today, the Society continues multiple responsibilities to those suffering from a wide range of mental disabilities.

The Legal Aid Society has litigated a number of important cases involving the rights of the mentally ill over the years. These include the right to the most appropriate and least restrictive mental health treatment for children (*State ex rel. R.T.*), the right to confidentiality of psychiatric records (*Guardianship of K.S.*), the right of prisoners in the Milwaukee County Jail to receive adequate mental health services (*Christensen*), the right to cross examine adverse psychologists in court proceedings (*Guardianship of R.S.*), prohibiting the practice of "hiding" patients to avoid timely hearing requirements imposed by law (*Delores M.*), and attacking municipal zoning regulations that discriminate against mentally-disabled individuals (*Oconomowoc Residential Programs*).

Today, the Society carries out its original charge to represent individuals facing civil mental commitments in the Milwaukee County Probate Court. How long this work will continue remains to be seen. The Wisconsin Department of Administration recently required the State Public Defender to bid out civil commitment cases in Milwaukee County among individual private attorneys. Nonetheless, for several cogent reasons, the Legal Aid Society has urged DOA to consider extending the existing SPD contract with the Society [see Historical Documents Section]. As this book goes to press, the issue remains unresolved.

The following client stories detail the type of cases handled by the Society's Mental Disability Law Division.

* * *

All civil commitments coming before the Probate Court must involve allegations that a person suffers from mental illness and presents a danger to themselves or others.[3] About 3,000 such cases are filed annually in Probate Court. Staff Attorney Karen Kotecki handles the bulk of cases appointed to the Legal Aid Society; she appears in the Probate Court Hearing Room at the Milwaukee County Mental Health Center on virtually a daily basis.

Legal Aid Society's statutory duty in these cases is to prevent unjustified restraints on a person's liberty – outpatient services, for example, may be more appropriate than a six-month commitment. There are other instances, as well, where a petition wrongly alleges that a person suffers from mental illness. Recently, the Society represented a 90-year-old widow facing just such a situation, where the allegations had been lodged by the woman's daughter.

The nightmare for LAS's client "Mary" began when she was taken into police custody based upon claims by her daughter that she was unable to care for herself and suffered from delusions. Police officers took her to the Mental Health Center, which involuntarily admitted her under a diagnosis of dementia with possible psychosis. The next day, LAS was appointed to represent Mary. Attorney Kotecki quickly communicated with other family members in New Jersey who raised questions about the daughter's motives.

LAS learned that the daughter had moved into her mother's home without her consent, after the daughter had lost work and welfare support in New York. It wasn't until Mary had demanded that her daughter (and the daughter's boyfriend) leave the home, that the daughter called police to say her mother was a danger to herself and mentally ill. Attorney Kotecki prevailed upon geriatric/psychiatric specialists at the Mental Health Center to conduct a more thorough evaluation, with the result that the original diagnosis of dementia was ruled out and the staff concluded that Mary was competent.

Of course, the civil commitment was then dismissed. As a follow up, other Legal Aid Society staff attorneys assisted Mary in getting a "no contact" restraining order against the daughter and her boyfriend so that Mary could return home without harassment. When further investigation revealed that the daughter was actually stealing from her mother, the police were brought in again – this time to seek theft charges against the daughter, which are now pending in Circuit Court. As Attorney Kotecki noted, sometimes it takes "a Legal Aid village" to achieve success for our clients.

* * *

Chronically disabled persons who are deemed legally incompetent, and who pose harm to themselves or others, are subject to long-term protective placement court orders.[4] Prior to 1985, some wards languished in substandard residential facilities or nursing homes without any periodic review. In other cases, wards were relegated to overly restrictive placements, even though their conditions had improved. The landmark *State ex rel. Watts* case, litigated by Legal Aid Society Executive Director Tom Zander, challenged the practice of "warehousing" such patients. In 1985, the Wisconsin Supreme Court ruled that an annual judicial review of each protective placement must be conducted to ensure that the ward is in an appropriate, least-restrictive placement. The *Watts* case changed the legal landscape for persons with chronic mental, developmental, cognitive, or physical disabilities. Over the past seventeen years, LAS attorneys have conducted court-supervised annual reviews for more than 4,000 disabled Milwaukee County residents as guardians ad litem. Many of these reviews have succeeded in obtaining new, more appropriate residential settings for wards in group homes or supervised apartments.

In one of these *Watts* cases, the Legal Aid Society was appointed to represent "Shirley," a 42-year-old woman with severe mental retardation who had been placed in a 238-bed facility in Milwaukee County.

21. Milwaukee County Hospital for Mental Diseases, circa 1940.
Courtesy of Milwaukee County Historical Society.

LAS's attorney investigated Shirley's specific conditions and discovered that her behavior had actually regressed, causing her to be rejected for participation in day programs. Instead, she was confined to a large facility that was plagued with poor staffing and filthy living conditions. In fact, when the Society's attorney first investigated, she found Shirley curled up on the facility's floor, totally non-communicative, and residing in a roach-infested unit. The attorney requested a court-ordered psychological assessment. After the psychologist reported that Shirley had lost the socialization skills she had developed at a prior placement, LAS's attorney had ample evidence to recommend a new one. The County agreed, and the Probate Court ordered that she be moved to a well-run group home in West Allis. Shirley's entire situation improved due to staff interaction on a one-to-one basis and frequent community activities. Shirley has regained her communication skills and is thriving under the group home's caring supervision. She even helps with basic group home projects. Legal Aid Staff Attorney Lisa Clay Foley represented Shirley as guardian ad litem.

* * *

One of the Legal Aid Society's most innovative programs is its GAIN Project. Social worker Diana Pitkaranta recruits and trains more than 300 lay volunteers to serve as court-appointed guardians of the person for approximately 550 adults suffering from Alzheimer's Disease, Down's Syndrome, traumatic brain injuries, mental retardation, stroke impairments, dementia, or chronic mental illness. In most cases, these fragile individuals, often elderly, have no family members to look after their best interests. Guardians must visit their wards at least once a month; they are also required to file an annual written report with the Probate Court. The GAIN Project was featured in "Helping hand: People needed to help seniors" in *Milwaukee Sentinel* (February 21, 1994).

The case of "Dorothy" might be considered typical. She is a 68-year-old nursing home resident who was referred to the GAIN Project in 2008. She is morbidly obese and suffers from a severe brain injury. Dorothy is unusual only in that she is one of the very few wards who has a volunteer guardian older than she. Pat, her guardian, is a very spry 82-year-old retired volunteer. When Pat first visited, Dorothy was bedridden and essentially nonverbal. In three short months, Pat was able to get Dorothy a reclining wheelchair, which made it more comfortable for Dorothy to get out of bed and participate in nursing home activities. Pat has successfully encouraged Dorothy to take an interest in personal hygiene. Dorothy now gets her hair and nails done on a regular basis, whereas previously she would not let the staff even comb her hair. Pat has also noticed a major increase in Dorothy's sociability. These changes, which were initiated by a volunteer guardian recruited and trained by the Legal Aid Society, have vastly improved the quality of Dorothy's life.

GAIN Project coordinator Diana Pitkaranta was recently appointed to serve on the Milwaukee County Guardianship Task Force, a collaboration that identifies 17-year-old special needs children from low-income families unable to pay for private guardianships, recruits law firms to offer pro bono legal services, and finds adults to serve as guardians (if no family member is appropriate) when the minor turns 18 years and ages out of the system. Pitkaranta also testified last year before the State Assembly's Committee on Aging and Long-Term Care in support of a measure (Assembly Bill 389) requiring disclosure of code violations to the guardians and families of nursing home residents.

The GAIN Project confers a major economic benefit on Milwaukee County taxpayers every year. The County pays a modest $15/month stipend to each volunteer guardian recruited and trained by the Legal Aid Society. If the Society had not created the GAIN Project, Milwaukee County would have to pay a corporate guardian fee of up to $425/month. It has been estimated that GAIN saves county taxpayers an average of $750,000 per year.

Through its regular Civil Division programs, the Legal Aid Society also offers services to a large number of other clients suffering from a wide range of mental disabilities. For example, it has been estimated that 80% of the city's homeless community suffers from mental illness. The Society's OATH Project provides outreach to that segment of Milwaukee's under-served population of street people. Similarly, it is estimated that over half of the disability claims litigated by the Legal Aid Society's Civil Division involve some mental disability component. LAS's commitment to advocate vigorously for this fragile sector of the community continues in full force and effect.

NOTES

1. LAS Board Minutes (March 31, 1944). For background to the County's treatment of the mentally disabled, see Steven M. Avella, "Health, Hospitals, and Welfare: Human Services in Milwaukee County" in *Trading Post to Metropolis: Milwaukee County's First 150 Years*, ed. Ralph M. Aderman (Milwaukee County Historical Society, 1987) 196-254, especially pp 211-16, 220, 235-37; "The fall of the house of anguish" in *Milwaukee Journal* (December 4, 1994).

2. For several years, Zander maintained a dual relationship with LAS (Executive Director) and the SPD (Chief Attorney of its Mental Health Division), which occasionally led to confusion over his law firm affiliation. See, *e.g. State ex rel. Lockman v. Gerhardstein*, 107 Wis.2d 325, 320 N.W.2d 27 (Ct. App. 1982), and *In Matter of Athans*, 107 Wis.2d 331, 320 N.W.2d 30 (Ct. App. 1982), where he is identified with the SPD, but in reality both cases were appealed, briefed, and decided well after September 1981, when Zander returned to the LAS staff as Executive Director.

3. This article was first published in "Staff Lawyers Challenge Commitment Abuses" in *Opening Statements* (Summer 2003)

4. This article originally appeared in "Legal Aid Pursues Court Reviews in Adult Protective Placements" in *Opening Statements* (Summer 2003) 1.

11
LEGISLATIVE ADVOCACY

As noted elsewhere in this history, from its very beginning the Legal Aid Society of Milwaukee has maintained a strong tradition of legislative advocacy. LAS's original Articles of Incorporation charged the organization "to promote laws and measures" for the benefit of the poor. This mandate has been faithfully followed throughout the past 94 years. LAS's first great achievement in the field was enactment of the Small Claims Act (1921 Wis. Laws, c. 538). In 2007, the Legal Aid Society registered as a lobbyist principal with the State Ethics Board to promote passage of a budget provision (successfully) making funds available for civil legal aid to the poor.[1] The Society's most recent legislative success was passage of a bill to regulate predatory lending in the state. While it is not possible here to cover the full historical range of this small but influential aspect of LAS's overall work, it may be worthwhile to examine in some detail the Society's productive efforts on the consumer credit issue.

As stated earlier, the Legal Aid Society has long advocated for making small loans available to the poor on equitable terms. Among LAS's earliest efforts in this area was the launching of a 1927 campaign against loan sharks and usurers who gouged the poor with exorbitant interest rates. That campaign, in cooperation with the Russell Sage Foundation, led to passage of the Small Loans Act (1927 Wis. Laws, c. 540), which imposed a rate cap of 10% on micro-credit transactions. Decades later, that law and its usury successor were abandoned in favor of "the free market," meaning that powerful financial interests could use their leverage to charge desperately poor consumers an unlimited rate of interest without any restrictions by government.[2]

Up until this year, Wisconsin remained the only state in the nation that did not regulate such transactions as payday loans or auto-title loans. Two bills were introduced into the 2009 session on this topic: Senate Bill 530 and Assembly Bill 447. Unfortunately, neither proved adequate to the task. LAS joined Wisconsinites for Responsible Lending, a broad coalition of consumer groups that included WISDOM (a faith-based group promoting economic justice), the League of Women Voters, American Association of Retired Persons, the Wisconsin Catholic Conference, the Lutheran Office of Public Policy, and the Wisconsin Public Interest Research Group. Litigation Director Pete Koneazny and Staff Attorney Andy Gehl spoke out against the bills at a public forum that was organized and sponsored by the Social Development Commission. Later, both LAS staffers offered written and oral testimony before the Senate Committee on Financial Institutions. Legal Aid client Michael Reit, a victim of auto-title lending abuses, also testified at the Senate hearing.

Andy Gehl led the charge with numerous letters to, and meetings with, legislative staffs. He also appeared on radio programs and, together with Bruce Speight of WISPRIG, co-authored an op-ed article, "Protect consumers with payday rate cap" that appeared in Madison's *Capital Times* (March 30, 2010). Gehl followed up by preparing a detailed list of consumer objections to the pending measures; these were then formulated into a memorandum that Executive Director Tom Cannon sent to members of the State Senate.[3] The memo argued that the two bills failed to offer meaningful protections to Wisconsin consumers in need of responsible loan products and, instead, disguised minimal regulation under the misleading guise of genuine "reform" legislation.

The LAS memo went on to urge support for a third proposal (Assembly Bill 392) that would have imposed a 36% rate cap on both payday loans and auto-title loans. The latter measure was co-sponsored by 43 representatives and 15 senators – just shy of a majority in both houses. However, AB 392, in turn, was opposed by well-financed lobbyists for the predatory lending industry. That industry spent $669,000 on legislative lobbying in Wisconsin during 2009, plus another $140,000 in campaign donations made to legislators during the 2008 election cycle. In addition, reform advocates were discomfited at the disclosure that the Speaker of the Assembly switched his position from supporting rate-cap legislation to opposing it after he began dating a lobbyist for the payday loan industry.[4] Eventually the Legislature passed a watered-down version of SB 530 that did not contain a rate cap. Although some minor modifications proposed by Andy Gehl and other consumer advocates were accepted, the bill was a disappointment. Not ready to give up, though, Gehl drafted a last-minute memorandum to Governor Doyle suggesting twelve line-item vetoes that would strengthen the weak legislation. The Governor implemented most of them – including the most significant one that banned auto-title loans altogether in Wisconsin.[5] Although the final version enacted into law still left much to be desired, LAS's tenacious fight resulted in better protection for the state's indigent consumers than would otherwise have been the case.

NOTES

1. In order to preserve its tax-exempt status, IRS regulations prohibit the Legal Aid Society from devoting "a substantial part of its activities [to] attempting to influence legislation." Treas. Reg. § 1.501(c)3-1(c)3(ii). Lobbying activity that is 5% or less of an organization's activity has been deemed "insubstantial." See *Seasongood v. Commissioner*, 227 F.2d 907 (6th Cir. 1955). Moreover, since a number of LAS's governmental and private-foundation funding sources prohibit any attempts to influence legislation with their grants, LAS uses a discrete fund representing the proceeds of the sale of real estate to finance such activities.

2. This writer's first case as a Legal Aid Society lawyer in 1971 resulted in dismissal of a collection lawsuit against a client on the grounds that the actual interest rate violated Wisconsin's usury statute.

3. Memorandum from Thomas G. Cannon to Members of the Wisconsin State Senate (March 16, 2010).

4. "Legislature wrestles with ways to rein in payday lending" in *Milwaukee Journal Sentinel* (March 18, 2010).

5. "Doyle used partial veto to toughen payday loan measure" in *Milwaukee Journal Sentinel* (May 19, 2010).

12

CHRONOLOGY
1910–2010

1910

In a letter to Alderman Victor L. Berger, University of Wisconsin Professor John R. Commons proposes establishment of "a practicable plan for free legal aid" in Milwaukee.

1911

State Senator Gabriel Zophy introduces a bill (SB 253) authorizing City of Milwaukee to establish a legal information bureau. Bill fails passage.

Free Legal Aid, a 14-page report prepared by Fred King under the direction of Professor Commons, recommends establishment of a free legal aid program. Milwaukee Bureau of Economy and Efficiency (Bulletin no. 7).

1913

Assemblyman Carl Minkley introduces a bill (AB 65) authorizing Milwaukee County to establish a legal information bureau. Bill fails passage.

1915

Assemblyman Edward I I. Zinn introduces a bill (AB 72) authorizing Milwaukee County to establish a legal information bureau. Bill fails passage.

E.W. Frost, President of the Central Council of Social Agencies, and Walter D. Corrigan, President of the Milwaukee Bar Association, appoint a joint committee to investigate establishment of a program of free legal aid for Milwaukee's poor. So-called Bartlett Committee urges creation of a legal aid society.

1916

The Legal Aid Society of Milwaukee is incorporated on February 25. Twelve prominent individuals sign the original Articles of Incorporation.

22. In 1916, the Legal Aid Society opened its first office on the 7th floor of the Merchants & Manufacturers Building on West Water Street, now North Plankinton Avenue. *Courtesy of Milwaukee County Historical Society.*

The Society's first office is located in rooms 707-08 of the Merchants & Manufacturers Bank Building at 214 West Water Street (later renumbered and renamed 740 North Plankinton Avenue). The first telephone number is Grand 519. The Society begins work on June 1 and accepts its first two clients on that day. Casework is performed by trained social workers under the direction of Superintendent Alma C. Schlesinger. Attorney William F. Hannan serves as the first Counsel to the Legal Aid Society.

The Society's annual budget of $2,795 is provided by the Central Council of Social Agencies and $1 membership dues paid by Milwaukee lawyers.

To keep track of funds handled, the Society opens a client trust account at the Marshall & Ilsley Bank. This customer relationship continues unbroken down to the present day.

The Society joins the National Alliance of Legal Aid Societies, but does not send a delegate to the organization's convention in Cincinnati (October 11-12). See *Proceedings of the NALAS, Third Biennial Convention* (1916) 161.

In November, the Society becomes one of the original 22 organizations to participate in the city's first combined charitable fundraising campaign. The initiative is sponsored by the newly created Centralized Budget of Philanthropies of Milwaukee.

During its first full year of operation, the Society opens more than a thousand cases and recovers a total of $1,892 on behalf of its clients.

1917

After Congress declares war against Germany, the Society decides to provide free legal services to all members of the armed forces and their dependents.

Wisconsin Governor Emanuel L. Philipp complains that private attorneys are charging exorbitant fees to counsel young men on exemptions to the Selective Service Act. The Society responds by offering draft counseling free of charge.

1918

The Society issues its first publication, *Legal Suggestions for Soldiers and Sailors and Their Dependents*, written and edited by its outside retained counsel, Attorney William J. Goldschmidt. The pamphlet is printed by the Milwaukee County Council of Defense and given to each local selectman (draftee). It explains rights under the newly enacted Soldiers and Sailors Civil Relief Act for military personnel serving during World War I and invites the selectman and his dependents to apply to LAS for free service.[1]

For the period of October 1, 1917 to September 30, 1918, the Society's caseload increases to more than 1,400 matters. Of this number, 82 are referred to the Society's retained counsel.

1919

The Society is praised as a "strong organization" in Reginald Heber Smith's seminal book, *Justice and the Poor* (New York: Carnegie Foundation, 1919) 148. Smith is recognized as the founder of the modern legal aid movement in the United States.

The Society establishes an Advisory Board of prominent citizens to encourage community support for its programs. Among the members, whose names appear on the Society's letterhead, are Governor Emanuel L. Philipp, Mayor Daniel W. Hoan, former Governor Francis E. McGovern, Wisconsin Supreme Court Justice Christian Doerfler, Archbishop Sebastian Messmer, Marquette University President Father Herbert C. Noonan, S.J., Rabbi Samuel Hirshberg,[2] Miss Paula Uihlein (of the Schlitz Brewing Co. family), and industrialists Albert Trostel, Walter Davidson, and Louis Allis.

1921

The Society plays a leading role in establishing the state's first Small Claims Court in Milwaukee. 1921 Wis. Laws, c. 538.

The Society launches an investigation of unbonded, out-of-state collection agencies dunning Milwaukee consumers for nonexistent debts. "Legal Aid Will Sift Out State Bill Collectors" in *Milwaukee Leader* (April 13, 1921).

Alma C. Schlesinger resigns as Superintendent. Her assistant, Agnes Campbell, is appointed successor.

1922

The Society's casework is featured in a detailed story, "Legal Aid Society Gets Many Wage Claims From Jobless" in *Milwaukee Leader* (January 26, 1922).

23.   Former Wisconsin Governor Francis E. McGovern served on the Legal Aid
            Society of Milwaukee's Advisory Board, 1919-44.
            Courtesy of Wisconsin Historical Society (WHi-62290).

The Society moves its headquarters to room 411 of the Pereles
Building located at 85 Oneida Street (later renumbered and renamed
259 East Wells Street).

Albert F. Bigelow, President of the National Alliance of Legal Aid Societies, appoints William Kaumheimer to serve on the Committee on Social Agencies. *Proceedings of the Fifth National Conference of Legal Aid Bureaus and Societies* (meeting in Philadelphia) 130, 133. Bigelow also serves as President of the Boston Legal Aid Society. The Society's annual report notes that one-third of its clients are immigrants who come from 33 foreign countries, most of them natives of Poland or Germany. Thirty-three clients are members of the city's nascent African American community. By gender, LAS clients are 68% male, 32% female. The Society's staff recovers a total of $11,638 for the year in funds (mostly wage claims) on behalf of clients [see Historical Documents Section].

1923

The Society reports 2,380 cases handled during the year. The total operating budget is $6,043. LAS recovers a record amount of $14,253 in funds for clients.

Milwaukee Bar Association appoints a committee "to report on the work of the Legal Aid Society with a view toward bringing about a closer relationship with the Bar Association." Report of the Committee on Legal Aid Work in *Legal Aid Review* xxi, no. 3 (1923) 10.

The Legal Aid Society of Milwaukee becomes a founding member of the National Association of Legal Aid Organizations. The Society's president, William Kaumheimer, serves as an official delegate to the NALAO Constitutional Convention in Cleveland. Former President and current Chief Justice William Howard Taft is named Honorary President of the new organization.

1924

William Kaumheimer drafts a report recommending a Model Law on Collection of Wage Claims to provide workers with an efficient method of forcing defaulting employers to meet their obligations. The Kaumheimer Report is later published in *Proc. NALAO: Reports of Committees* (1924-25) 105-20.

1925

State Bar Association of Wisconsin establishes a Standing Committee on Legal Aid in an explicit effort to duplicate the success of the

Legal Aid Society of Milwaukee in the state's other 71 counties. William Kaumheimer is named Chairman. (1925 *Proceedings of SBAW* 105-09). The group continues today as the Legal Assistance Committee of the State Bar of Wisconsin.

1926

John S. Bradway, NALAO Secretary, speaking to Wisconsin State Conference of Social Welfare in Milwaukee, says: "You have a very efficient Legal Aid Society in Milwaukee, which cares for about 4,000 cases a year." Published in "Legal Aid Work in Reference to Wisconsin" in *Legal Aid Review* xxiv, no. 4 (1926) 4.[3]

William Kaumheimer, President of the Society, publishes an article, "Assigned Counsel in Criminal Cases" in *Annals of the American Academy of Political and Social Science* 124 (1926) 81-83, ed. John S. Bradway and Reginald Heber Smith. Relying on early Wisconsin legal authorities, Kaumheimer proposes public payment of legal fees necessary to engage court-assigned private attorneys to defend indigents in criminal matters.

The Society adopts NALAO standards for financial accountability and classification of records.

At 4,121 cases for the year, the Society records nearly a 400% increase during its first decade of service to Milwaukee's poor. The Society's annual budget is $9,109, an increase of more than 300% from its first year.

1927

The Society wages a campaign against usurers who advance money on workers' salaries, also known as wage assignments – a forerunner to today's predatory payday lenders. *Proc. NALAO* (1927) 68.

The Society cooperates with the Russell Sage Foundation to secure passage of the Small Loans Act, 1927 Wis. Laws, c. 540. The measure regulates microcredit and imposes a 10% limit on the amount of interest that can be charged. It is modeled on a national uniform act of the same name.

A Milwaukee County Community Fund study recommends that the Legal Aid Society "eventually" be placed under supervision of the courts.

1928

The Society's president, William Kaumheimer, is elected President of the National Association of Legal Aid Organizations.

The Society's annual report notes that fully half of its cases are referrals from the District Attorney's Office. More than one-third of the cases involve wage claims against employers. Small claims and landlord-tenant matters are the next most common categories. The Milwaukee Community Fund provides over 98% of the Society's budget.

The Society's staff consists of one outside retained attorney (at the Hannan law firm) who is paid $100/month; 2 social workers compensated at a total of $325/month; 1 stenographer/clerk paid $115/month; and a part-time bookkeeper paid $5/month.

The state's second legal services program is inaugurated, Madison Legal Aid Bureau. Under the auspices of the Dane County Bar Association and the University of Wisconsin Law School, students work under supervision of volunteer lawyers from the bar association. Bureau later undergoes two name changes, Madison Legal Aid Society and Dane County Legal Services Center, before being succeeded by Legal Action of Wisconsin in 1977.

1929

John S. Bradway, Secretary of the National Association of Legal Aid Organizations, lauds the Legal Aid Society of Milwaukee and ranks it with the best programs in the country. "Visit Free Legal Clinic and Learn Their Rights" in *Milwaukee Journal* (August 20, 1929).

The Society's staff is downsized to one outside retained attorney at $200/month, 1 social worker compensated at $165/month, 1 stenographer/clerk paid $115/month, and 1 part-time bookkeeper at $5/month.

1930

Agnes Campbell Kiewert resigns as Superintendent. Margery M. Heck is appointed successor. "Legal Aid Changes" in *Milwaukee Journal* (April 30, 1930). Heck is the first attorney to serve as Superintendent. Her appointment inaugurates a tradition of the Society providing professional employment and career opportunities to women lawyers.

Due to the illness of William Kaumheimer, Attorney Charles B. Quarles, member of the Society's board, is named Chair of the State Bar Association of Wisconsin's Committee on Legal Aid. *Proc. SBAW* 20 (1930) 191-92.

1931

Legislature enacts measure to enforce collection of workers' wages modeled on William Kaumheimer's NALAO report. 1931 Wis Laws, c. 262.

1932

County Board announces that Society will move its quarters at year's end to rent-free space in room 502 of the new Public Safety Building located at 818 West Kilbourn Avenue. "Grant Offices to Aid Society" in *Milwaukee Sentinel* (December 17, 1932).

24. Public Safety Building was headquarters of the Legal Aid Society, 1932-50. *Courtesy of Milwaukee County Historical Society.*

1933

County Board Supervisor James P. Sheehan objects to Society's tenancy in Public Safety Building on grounds that taxpayers should not subsidize private charities. "Seek Ouster of Legal Aid" in *Milwaukee Sentinel* (January 28, 1933).

The Society's annual report reflects staff and funding cuts imposed by economic realities of the Great Depression. Total agency budget over past five years declines 35% from $8,578 in 1928 to $5,613 this year; caseload drops 57% from 4,121 in 1927 to 1,828.

1935

The Society hires its first staff counsel, Melville H. Sell, as half-time Assistant Attorney. An experienced trial and appellate counsel, he serves for seven years.

1938

The Society handles 2,691 legal matters for the year. The total agency budget is steady at $5,858.

25. Entrance to old University of Wisconsin Law School building circa 1930s.
Courtesy of Wisconsin Historical Society (WHi-57832).

1939

The Society establishes its first clinical program with two students from the University of Wisconsin Law School's office practice course. Margery M. Heck granted leave of absence as Superintendent. Attorney Bernard F. Mathiowetz named Acting Superintendent. Julia B. Dolan appointed Superintendent in November. The Society's annual caseload increases to 3,292 cases.

1940

John S. Bradway, newly elected President of the National Association of Legal Aid Organizations, addresses the annual luncheon meeting of the Legal Aid Society at the Pfister Hotel. His topic is "The Growth of Legal Aid Work in the United States."

Council of Social Agencies issues report containing suggestions to improve relations between the Society and local social service organizations.

The Society establishes a revolving fund account to allow LAS to advance court costs to clients.

Mayor Carl F. Zeidler joins the Society's Advisory Board.

Statistics of Legal Aid Work in the United States and Canada (prepared by John S. Bradway for NALAO) demonstrates that the Legal Aid Society of Milwaukee has one of the lowest operating costs of any legal aid program in the nation for a comparably sized city.

The Society's board decides to opt into providing Social Security coverage for staff members.

1941

The Society establishes a Volunteer Lawyer Panel in collaboration with the Saint Vincent de Paul Society of the Archdiocese of Milwaukee. Panel attorneys accept nineteen pro bono referrals in divorce and legal separation matters during the first year.

The Society begins accepting guardian ad litem appointments in adoption cases after representatives of social agencies serving children ask LAS "to safeguard the interests of children involved in applications for adoption."

26. Mayor Carl F. Zeidler served on the Legal Aid Society of Milwaukee's Advisory
Board for two years. He was killed in action during World War II.
Courtesy of Milwaukee County Historical Society.

Board discusses liberalizing intake rules governing acceptance of
bankruptcy cases because of the hardship suffered by clients facing
multiple wage garnishments.

Advisory Intake Committee is established to help LAS consider
applications for service in domestic relations cases. Committee has

representatives from Family Welfare Association, St. Vincent de Paul Society, Juvenile Court, and Department of Public Assistance.

1942

The Society follows its World War I precedent and offers free legal services to members of the armed forces regardless of financial ability to pay. "Advice is Free to Servicemen" in *Milwaukee Journal* (June 14, 1942).

The Society hosts the twentieth annual convention of the National Association of Legal Aid Organizations at the Schroeder Hotel in Milwaukee. Speakers include Reginald Heber Smith, John S. Bradway, Wisconsin Chief Justice Marvin B. Rosenberry, Milwaukee Mayor John L. Bohn, Dean Wilbur G. Katz of the University of Chicago Law School, Dean Lloyd K. Garrison of the University of Wisconsin Law School, and John M. Morris, President of the American Bar Association. "Tell War Job for Legal Aid" in *Milwaukee Journal* (September 25, 1942).

Conference program is published in "Twentieth Annual Conference of NALAO" in *Legal Aid Review* xl, no. 4 (1942) 3-4. Photograph of Milwaukee City Hall appears on front cover with signage proclaiming "Welcome to Legal Aid Organizations."

National Association of Legal Aid Organizations establishes a memorial endowment in William Kaumheimer's name. John S. Bradway notes that Kaumheimer "combined rare qualities of common sense and idealism, and endeared himself to those of us who worked with him by his keen vision and forcefulness of expression." *Proc. NALAO* (1942) A-136.

Attorney Elizabeth C. Leis replaces Melville H. Sell as Assistant Attorney. She serves for twelve years.

The Society compiles and publishes *Information on Legal Procedures Commonly Requested by Social Workers*. The pamphlet is disseminated to social welfare agencies in Milwaukee and throughout the state.

Internal Revenue Service issues a letter ruling recognizing the Society as a tax-exempt organization and determining that donations made to it are deductible for federal income tax purposes.

Julia Dolan reports: "We are getting an increasing number of cases involving service men and their dependents. The panels set up by the

Bar Association are used to some extent by the Red Cross, so we are sharing in this type of work. For the last fiscal year, October 1, 1941 – October 1, 1942, 177 cases involved service men or their dependents. We have made no special efforts to inform [military] camps or draft boards of our services except through press publicity, which we think has been unusually fine." *NALAO Brief Case* i, no. 2 (1942) 4.

1943

The Society's board adopts a resolution in opposition to Assembly Bill 567, which would increase the filing fee in Milwaukee County divorce cases from $8.20 to $15, on the grounds that higher fees would work a hardship on Legal Aid clients.

The Society helps establish the Lawyer Referral Plan in cooperation with the Milwaukee Bar Association and the Milwaukee Junior Bar Association. "Plan for Legal Reference Service Inaugurated" in *MBA Gavel* 5, no. 3 (1943) 12-13.

The Society ends historic practice of referring out litigation work to private counsel. Julia Dolan's title is changed to Superintendent and Counsel in recognition of fact that all of the Society's court work is now be done from the office under her supervision.

The Society handles 2,465 legal matters for the year. Total agency budget is $7,715. Both figures are still well below pre-Depression levels.

The Society serves 283 servicemen. Superintendent Dolan reports on the Society's work with armed forces personnel in *Proc. SBAW* 33 (1943) 72-77.

1944

The Society's internship program with University of Wisconsin Law School ends due to plummeting enrollments caused by military draft.

The Society works with the American Bar Association, National Association of Legal Aid Organizations, and Miller, Mack & Fairchild law firm to compile a national digest of laws relating to the legal problems of servicemen and women.

Discovery of a case of spinal meningitis elsewhere in the Public Safety Building closes the Society's office for one week as a precautionary measure.

The Society works closely with the American Bar Association Committee on War Work and the State Bar Association of Wisconsin's War Legal Services Committee to address legal needs of dependents of servicemen and women. The Society serves 348 servicemen. Superintendent Dolan reports on the Society's work with armed forces personnel in *Proc. SBAW* 34 (1944) 80-85.

The Society agrees to request by District Court Judge Harvey Neelen asking that organization represent indigent inmates of the Hospital for Mental Diseases in petitions for re-examination of their commitment by the Lunacy Commission.

Secretary of the Navy James V. Forrestal awards a Certificate of Appreciation to the Society in recognition for its providing free counsel to members of the Navy and Marine Corps and their dependents. A similar certificate is issued by Secretary of War Henry L. Stimson for services to Army personnel and their dependents.

Julia Dolan authors an article, "Legal Reference Service Plan" in *MBA Gavel* 5, no. 7 (1944) 18.

At the request of the District Attorney's Office and the Family Court, the Society also agrees to accept guardian ad litem appointments in illegitimacy proceedings where one of the parties is a minor.

1945

Superintendent Julia B. Dolan is elected to the Executive Board of the National Association of Legal Aid Organizations.

The Society's work on behalf on men and women in the armed forces is highlighted in *Proc. SBAW* 35 (1945) 74-78.

1946

Attorney George Van Dyke contributes $100 to establish a Legal Aid Society Endowment Fund.

Board adopts policy that a woman defendant in a divorce action, who has committed adultery, should not be disqualified from representation by the Society if she has been an adequate mother to her children.

Judge F. Ryan Duffy, Sr., former United States Senator and, later, Chief Judge of the United States Court of Appeals in Chicago, begins a twenty-five-year tenure on the board of directors.

1947

The Board approves suggestion of the staff that Society's offices be closed for regular business on Saturdays. The Society handles 2,768 legal matters during the year. Workload involves 66% consultation only, 11% referral and consultation, 16% other services without court work, 5% court work, and 2% partial services. Referral sources of clients include 44% referred from public and private law offices, 14% referred from social service agencies, 3% from the unemployment office; 6% are previous clients, and 33% are classed as "other." Total agency budget is $12,545. Of this sum, $11,085 comes from the Community Chest, $260 from membership fees paid by Milwaukee lawyers, and $1,200 from an in-kind contribution (free office space) by Milwaukee County. The staff consists of 1.5 attorneys, no social workers, and 2 secretaries. Source: Emery A. Brownell, *Legal Aid in the United States* (Rochester, NY: Lawyers Co-Operative Publishing Co. 1951).

1948

Tappan Gregory, President of the American Bar Association, addresses the Society's annual luncheon meeting at the City Club. He praises LAS's work as "gratifying, commendable." See "Urges Setup for Legal Aid" in *Milwaukee Journal* (March 31, 1948).

1949

Board adopts policy accepting only those divorce cases that demonstrate a social necessity. The freeing of a wife from an undesirable marriage, or making it possible for her to re-marry, would not, in itself, be classified as social necessity.

The Society unsuccessfully seeks funding from the Community Welfare Council to add a staff social worker position to assist in handling the rising caseload of domestic relations matters.

Robert W. Landry and Jack N. Eisendrath join the staff as part-time Assistant Attorneys.

Charles W. Babcock dies in office after serving a record 20 years as President. He is the last of the Society's original directors.

1950

The Society moves its quarters to 757 North Water Street, second floor.

The Society's complete endowment fund, totaling $410, is spent to purchase new office equipment.

Mrs. Arlene Kennedy is hired as a second half-time staff attorney to meet rising caseload. Having earned a degree in social work as well, she is assigned as a liaison with social agencies to focus on domestic relations and adoption matters. The Society's three women lawyers (Dolan, Leis, Kennedy) constitute Wisconsin's first all-female law firm.

1951

The Society inaugurates a clinical education program with twenty students from Marquette University Law School. Two students staff the office each afternoon.

27. Detail over entrance to Marquette University Law School.
Courtesy of Marquette University Archives.

Following previous precedents, the Society agrees to provide free legal services to armed forces personnel and their dependents for the duration of the Korean War.

1952

Roger W. Finnegan replaces Arlene Kennedy as Assistant Attorney. He serves for twenty years. The Society also contracts out work on a part-time basis to additional outside counsel (including his twin brother, Clinton J. Finnegan).

1953

The Board changes Julia B. Dolan's title from Superintendent and Counsel to Executive Attorney to bring it in line with other legal aid organizations around the country.

1954

Jack N. Eisendrath replaces Elizabeth C. Leis as full-time Assistant Attorney. He serves for four years.

The Society's work is highlighted in Julia B. Dolan, "Legal Aid in Milwaukee" in *MBA Gavel* 15, no. 4 (1954) 6-8.

1955

Julia Dolan and Richard McGuire of the Community Welfare Council of Milwaukee author an article, "The United Way," in *Legal Aid Brief Case* xiv, no. 1 (1955) 8-10. It notes that 75% of legal aid societies around the country are funded primarily by local commu-

28. YWCA Building, headquarters of the Legal Aid Society, 1957-70.
Courtesy of Milwaukee County Historical Society.

nity chests. Article also points out that, while the Legal Aid Society of
Milwaukee "has had to cut corners and make do year after year, which
has not been easy," it nonetheless receives 99% of its funding from the
Community Chest. Authors urge national support for such federated
campaigns.

1956

Report of the Public Administration Survey of Court and Legal
Services recommends that Milwaukee County establish a public defender office in felony and misdemeanor courts.

1957

The Society moves its quarters to Room 602 of the YWCA Building located at 610 North Jackson Street.

The Society establishes a Voluntary Defender Program to represent
indigent defendants accused of misdemeanor violations. Members of
the Milwaukee Junior Bar Association form a panel to provide pro
bono attorneys in District Court for the project. "Public Defender
Program to Start" in *Milwaukee Journal* (November 1, 1957). Project
is modeled in part on William Kaumheimer's 1926 proposal.

1958

Francis J. Demet replaces Jack N. Eisendrath as Assistant Attorney.
He serves for seven years.

Annual Report notes that Society handled 4,126 matters for the
year: 2,134 involved consultation only, 739 required consultation and
referral, 905 involved legal work without litigation, and 293 cases
required litigation. The largest category of issues is family law, *i.e.*
1,918 cases or 46.4% of the total workload. Clients are referred to
the Society from a variety of sources: previous clients (25%), courts
and government departments (18%), social agencies (13%), employers
and business (3%), and other sources. The Society's annual budget is
$31,312, which is raised from the Community Chest ($30,055), court
recoveries ($130), and memberships in the Society ($291).

The work of the Society's public defender program is highlighted in
Francis J. Demet, "The Voluntary Defender Plan in Milwaukee County" in *MBA Gavel* 19, no. 2 (1958) 14-24.

The Society arranges to present multiple cases of consumer fraud, which demonstrate a pattern and practice by a single business, to District Attorney's Office for possible criminal prosecution.

1959

The Society's board raises annual membership dues from $1 to $2. Increase is the first since 1916.

The Society's board directs Julia Dolan to oppose Assembly Bill 277 relating to establishment of a public defender program.

State Bar's Committee on Legal Aid reports: "In view of the splendid work being done by the Legal Aid Society of Milwaukee; in view of the prompt and efficient services being rendered under the voluntary defender plan, which has been in operation in Milwaukee for some time ... your committee is unalterably opposed to enactment into law of Bill 277." *Wis. Bar Bulletin* 32, no. 3 (1959) 62.

The Lawyers' Wives Volunteer Program is started in response to cutbacks in the United Fund's annual support. Thirty-five wives of lawyers provide volunteer typing, filing, and registering of clients, work that Julia Dolan estimates to be the equivalent of two full-time secretaries. Their work is highlighted in *Legal Aid Brief Case* xvii, no. 6 (1959) 215.

Board decides to expand the Society's family law practice by representing indigent defendants in paternity cases.

1960

To celebrate twenty years at the helm of the Society, Julia Dolan is feted by the State Bar of Wisconsin at a testimonial breakfast in the Schroeder Hotel. "Her Legal Aid to Indigent Is Basis for a Testimonial" in *Milwaukee Journal* (February 7, 1960); "Case of Julia Dolan: 20 Years of Service" in *Milwaukee Sentinel* (February 19, 1960).

Judge F. Ryan Duffy's remarks on this occasion are published in "Laurels for Legal Aiders: Julia B. Dolan" in *Legal Aid Brief Case* xviii, no. 5 (1960) 123-26.

1961

Julia Dolan is awarded the Reginald Heber Smith Gold Medal at the National Legal Aid & Defender Association convention in Chicago. "Julia Dolan Wins Legal Aid Honor" in *Milwaukee Sentinel* (October 13, 1961). Citation is published in *Proc. NLADA* (1961) 35.

1962

The Society's work is featured in two articles: Lenore Woolf, "The Legal Aid Story" in *MBA Gavel* 23, no. 1 (1962) 28; William L. Randall, "The Voluntary Defender Plan" in *MBA Gavel* 23, no. 3 (1962) 26-27.

1963

Vital contributions made by Lawyers' Wives of Greater Milwaukee are praised in "Legal Aides Lauded" in *Milwaukee Sentinel* (March 29, 1963); "Lawyers' Wives Become Friends of the Court" in *Milwaukee Journal* (March 29, 1963).

1964

Julia Dolan writes article highlighting work of attorneys in Voluntary Defender Program and the Lawyers' Wives of Greater Milwaukee. "We Honor Our Volunteers" in *Legal Aid Brief Case* xxii, no. 3 (February 1964) 130-32.

Julia Dolan is named Chair of the State Bar of Wisconsin's Committee on Legal Aid.

1965

The Society receives largest single gift in its first half-century of existence: a bequest of $10,000 from the estate of Leon E. Kaumheimer in honor of his father, William, who served as the Society's first president.

Julia Dolan attends National Conference on Poverty and the Law in Washington, D.C. [see Historical Documents Section]. Later in the year, she submits Wisconsin's first grant application for federal funding (from the U.S. Office of Economic Opportunity) for civil legal services to the poor. The Society, in conjunction with the Milwaukee Bar Association, Milwaukee Junior Bar Association, and Marquette University Law School, creates Milwaukee Plan Legal Services. For background, see E. Clinton Bamberger, "The Legal Services Program of the Office of Economic Opportunity" in *Notre Dame Lawyer* 41

(1965-66) 847-52; Edgar and Jean Cahn, "The War on Poverty: A Civilian Perspective" in *Yale Law Journal* 73 (1964) 1317-52.

Julia Dolan reports to LAS board that from June 1, 1916, through December 31, 1965, the Legal Aid Society served a total of 158,314 indigent Milwaukeeans.

1966

National Legal Aid & Defender Association advises members that "the Vietnam war will curtail any expansion of the [OEO Legal Services] program" in the coming year.

The Society celebrates its 50th anniversary with a dinner at the Milwaukee Athletic Club. "Bar's President-Elect to Address Legal Aid" in *Milwaukee Journal* (February 2, 1966). Special citations are awarded to Judge F. Ryan Duffy, Sr., Albert B. Houghton, Charles B. Quarles, and Edmund B. Shea to honor their combined 130 years of service on the Society's board of directors. Speakers include Wisconsin Chief Justice George R. Currie, American Bar Association President Orison S. Marsden, and National Legal Aid & Defender Association President William Avery. "Legal Aid Goals Told" in *Milwaukee Sentinel* (March 10, 1966); "US Bar Leader Hails Legal Help for Needy" in *Milwaukee Journal* (March 10, 1966).

Also marking the anniversary is publication of *The Law and the Palate*, ed. Mrs. Darryl K. Nevers (Milwaukee: North Shore Publishing Co. 1966), a collection of recipes compiled by the Lawyers' Wives of Greater Milwaukee.[4] Proceeds from sale of the book are donated to the Society. Among those contributing recipes are the spouses of Senator Robert F. Kennedy, Supreme Court Justice Hugo L. Black, United Nations Ambassador Arthur Goldberg, Wisconsin Governor Warren P. Knowles, and Wisconsin Chief Justice George R. Currie. The book is extensively reviewed in *Legal Aid Brief Case* xxv, no. 4 (1967) 148-49.

Funding of $139,605 is obtained by the local Board of Legal Services for initial six months from the U.S. Office of Economic Opportunity. Board contracts with the Legal Aid Society to operate Milwaukee Plan Legal Services. Julia B. Dolan is named Director, and Margadette M. Demet is appointed Deputy Director of MPLS.

Details of the MPLS project are set out in Margadette M. Demet, "Legal Services for Urban Needs: Implementation of the Economic Opportunity Act of 1964" in *MBA Gavel* 27, no. 1 (1966) 6-16. Two neighborhood storefront offices, each staffed by two attorneys and two secretaries, open in May. Letterhead and window signage describe the offices as "Legal Aid Society – Southside Branch" and "Legal Aid Society – Northside Branch" respectively. Attorney Paul T. Miller is appointed Chief Attorney of the Northside office at 2218 North 3rd Street; Attorney E.F. ("Bill") Stanelle is appointed Chief Attorney of the Southside office at 1322 South 16th Street. "Poor to Get Legal Aid in Rich Setting" in *Milwaukee Sentinel* (June 21, 1966); "Legal Aid for Poor Begins" in *Milwaukee Journal* (June 21, 1966). For the concept, see D.H. Lowenstein and M.J. Waggoner, "Neighborhood Law Offices: The New Wave in Legal Services for the Poor" in *Harvard Law Review* 80 (1967) 805-13.

1967

The Society receives its first Reginald Heber Smith Community Law Fellow, Attorney Glenn E. Carr. The African American lawyer is a recent graduate of Howard University Law School. He is assigned to work in the Society's Northside neighborhood office.

OEO income eligibility standards are $51 per week for an individual and $87 per week for "a married couple with 2 children."

The Society establishes a Law Reform Division to develop legislative proposals and to bring test cases challenging discriminatory policies and procedures. The new endeavor represents a collaboration, unique in the nation, among staff attorneys, private practice lawyers, and community activists. Staff Attorney Bettie McJunkin serves as coordinator of the Law Reform Division. The general strategy is discussed in Geoffrey C. Hazard, "Law Reforming in the Anti-Poverty Program" in *University of Chicago Law Review* 37 (1970) 242-55; Sargent Shriver, "Law Reform and the Poor" in *American Law Review* 17 (1967) 1-11.

Riots break out on city's Northside. Staff attorneys from the Society's neighborhood office provide legal counsel to dozens of Northside residents associated with the civil unrest.

The Society opens a Bail Project Services office in the Public Safety Building. Bernette Odegard is appointed Administrator. The program evaluates arrestees to determine suitability for release on their own personal recognizance. "24 Hour Legal Aid for Poor" in *Milwaukee Journal* (September 29, 1967).

The Society adopts a health insurance plan through Blue Cross/ Blue Shield for all employees. Staff members contribute $4 per month for individual coverage or $6 per month for family coverage.

The Society's Law Reform Division successfully litigates its first class action case, *Ramos v. Health & Social Services Board*, 276 F.Supp. 474 (1967), in which a three-judge panel strikes down Wisconsin's one-year residency requirement for welfare benefit eligibility. Case also represents the Society's first published decision.

Additional early successes of the Law Reform Division are highlighted by Margadette M. Demet, "Law Firms in the Legal Services Program" in *Legal Aid Brief Case* xxvi, no. 2 (1967) 84-87.

1968

The Society submits proposal for a pilot project Public Defender Office in response to a decision of U.S. Supreme Court requiring appointment of defense counsel in felony proceedings. *Gideon v. Wainwright*, 372 U.S. 335 (1963). Joint funding is sought from the National Defender Project (a collaboration between the Ford Foundation and the National Legal Aid & Defender Association) [$67,000], and Milwaukee County [$33,000]. "Improved Defender Plan Eyed" in *Milwaukee Sentinel* (June 28, 1968).

1969

United Community Services directs the Society to find new headquarters. "Committee Will Study New Legal Aid Home" in *Milwaukee Journal* (March 11, 1969).

Supreme Court cites *Ramos* case, successfully litigated by the Society, in *Shapiro v. Thompson*, 394 U.S. at 622 (1969), n. 1.

Differences concerning the delivery of legal services to the poor result in the Society's decision to end Milwaukee Plan Legal Services project and sever its ties with Office of Economic Opportunity Legal Services Program. See "2 Legal Aid Agencies May Cut Their Ties" in *Milwaukee Journal* (April 8, 1969); "Milwaukee Plan May Cut Ties With Legal Aid Group" in *Milwaukee Journal* (May 25, 1969); "Link Broken Between Legal Aid Groups" in *Milwaukee Sentinel* (June 3,

1969). Milwaukee Legal Services and Freedom Through Equality emerge on October 1 as federally-funded spin-offs of MPLS (they later recombine to form Legal Action of Wisconsin). Mark Braun, *Policies, Programs, Politics, and the Poor in Two Milwaukee Legal Service Organizations, 1966-72.* The Society continues its course independent of the OEO programs.

The Society's work is highlighted in Bettie McJunkin, "Law Reform in Milwaukee Plan Legal Services" in *MBA Gavel* 29, no. 3 (1969) 14-19.

The Society receives funding to begin a pilot project Public Defender program in the felony courts. Attorneys John H. Lauerman and Thomas P. Doherty are appointed the first public defenders. David S. Berman joins the staff soon after.

John W. Reynolds, former Governor of Wisconsin and, later, Chief Judge of the United States District Court in Milwaukee, is elected to the Society's board of directors.

Wisconsin Supreme Court adopts Code of Professional Responsibility requiring every state lawyer to support legal aid programs and other efforts to provide counsel to those unable to retain it. See Eugene L. Smith, "Canon 2: A Lawyer Should Assist the Legal Profession in Fulfilling its Duty to Make Legal Counsel Available" in *Texas Law Review* 48 (1969-70) 285-310.

1970

The Society's lawyers successfully litigate *Dickhut v. Norton* in Wisconsin Supreme Court. Decision recognizes the defense of retaliatory eviction. Dissent notes that appeal was brought by the Society's Law Reform Division, which was part of Milwaukee Plan Legal Services Project.

Success of the Society's Public Defender pilot project leads to expansion of office and full funding by Milwaukee County. "More Legal Aid Sought" in *Milwaukee Journal* (August 7, 1970); "Legal Aid Project Boosts Public Defender Concept" in *Milwaukee Journal* (November 29, 1970). A Safe Streets grant from the Law Enforcement Assistance Administration funds some positions.

In the wake of *In Re Gault*, 387 U.S. 1 (1967), Milwaukee County awards the Society a contract to begin representation of juveniles

29. Former Wisconsin Governor and Chief Judge of the U.S. District Court, John W.
Reynolds, served as a director of the Legal Aid Society of Milwaukee, 1969-73.
He was awarded the Society's Equal Justice Medal in 2001.
Courtesy of Wisconsin Historical Society (WHi-26542).

in delinquency, dependency, and neglect proceedings in Children's Court. County Board rejects rival bids submitted by Milwaukee Legal Services and Hersh & Stepke law firm.

The Society moves its central office to the Marquette University campus at 1204 West Wisconsin Avenue, second floor. Divisional offices are located in the Public Safety Building and the Children's Court Center.

National Legal Aid & Defender Association, at the behest of United Community Services of Greater Milwaukee, conducts an evaluation of legal services for the poor in Milwaukee. Report salutes the Society as "one of the pioneers in recognizing and implementing this much needed community service" and acknowledges its "elder statesman" role. It goes on to encourage UCS to increase significantly its annual financial support for LAS so that the Society can become more aggressive in pursuing law reform activities and in fulfilling its original promise.

1971

The Society establishes an Appellate Division, staffed by three lawyers, to represent indigent defendants in criminal appeals as required by *Douglas v. California*, 372 U.S. 353 (1963).

The Society and Milwaukee County agree to establish an expanded Public Defender office. The contract provides an annual budget of $141,847. Additional funding is received from the Wisconsin Council on Criminal Justice. Michael D. Guolee is named head of the Felony Division; William A. Jennaro is placed in charge of the Juvenile Division; and Anthony K. Karpowicz is appointed chief staff attorney for the Appellate Division.

Julia Dolan McClelland retires as Executive Attorney after a record tenure of thirty-one years and six months. David S. Berman is appointed successor with the title of Executive Director. "David Berman Named to Legal Post" in *Milwaukee Sentinel* (April 15, 1971).

1972

Discussion of possible merger with Milwaukee Legal Services, which was suggested by the NLADA evaluation, proves impractical. The primary impediment is that, because of conflict-of-interest rules, merger would eliminate legal representation for many eligible poor currently being served by the two-program model in Milwaukee. For example, where LAS now represents a wife and MLS represents a husband in Family Court, a single program could only represent one spouse. Similarly, where LAS now represents a child and MLS represents a parent in Children's Court, a combined program could only represent one party. Both firms agree that merger would undercut joint goal of increasing access to counsel for poor.

The Board raises annual membership dues from $5 to $10. The Board also creates a category of Law Firm membership status to increase revenue generated from dues. By year's end, the Society garners $1,100 in individual dues and $3,200 in firm dues.

Chief Staff Attorney Jordan B. Reich urges Governor's Task Force on Judicial Reorganization to include state funding for civil legal services to the poor in its recommendations to the Legislature. "Statewide Legal Aid Promoted" in *Milwaukee Journal* (April 15, 1972).

Cases litigated by the Society's Civil, Juvenile, and Appellate divisions result in ten published decisions this year.

Civil Division adds two attorneys to provide civil legal services to inmates of Wisconsin correctional institutions. Positions are funded by a federal Safe Streets grant.

The Society hires its first social worker in more than forty years, Marnie Wisniewski, through the VISTA (Volunteers In Service To America) program. She is assigned to the Juvenile Division.

1973

Judge Reynolds resigns from board of directors to avoid possibility that he might be required to rule on matters being litigated by staff attorneys in federal court.

The Society receives a second gift of $10,000 as a final distribution from the Leon E. Kaumheimer Trust in honor of his father, William, first President of LAS.

OEO invites the Society to apply for funding to become the sole provider of federal legal services in Milwaukee. After consultation with representatives of Milwaukee Legal Services and Freedom Through Equality, the Society elects not to pursue application. Later in the year, MLS and FTE announce their merger.

U.S. Supreme Court cites *Application of Ottman*, another case won by the Society, in *United States v. Kras*, 409 U.S. 434, 453n. (1973). The Society contracts with Milwaukee County to add a Misdemeanor Division in the wake of U.S. Supreme Court's decision in *Argersinger v. Hamlin*, 407 U.S. 25 (1972), which recognizes a right to counsel in such cases. Martin E. Love is appointed Chief Staff Attorney. The Society files its first petition for certiorari before the U.S. Supreme Court in *State ex rel. Akulicz v. Wolke*, a right-to-counsel case in civil contempt proceedings. *Cert. denied*, 414 U.S. 881 (1973). Justices Blackmun and Douglas vote to grant the petition.

1975

David Berman reports to the board that attorneys in the Felony Division have won ten not-guilty verdicts in their last nineteen jury trials. The Board increases annual membership dues from $10 to $15.

1976

To mark its 60th anniversary, the Society adopts a distinctive logo depicting Justitia, the Roman goddess of justice, as a blindfolded matron bearing the traditional sword of law and scales of equity.

30. Legal Aid Society's first logo.
Courtesy of Legal Aid Society of Milwaukee.

New York Times reports its first Legal Aid Society of Milwaukee case (*State ex rel. Memmel*), a successful class action writ of habeas corpus ordering the release or retrial of all patients in the Milwaukee County Mental Health Center ("75 Mental Patients Win Milwaukee

Suit," August 20). The case makes the banner headline twice in the *Milwaukee Journal* (August 5 and September 1, 1976). A second Legal Aid Society case garners national attention. "Milwaukee Man Is Hanged In Bahamas for Murder" in *New York Times* (October 20, 1976); "Bahamas hangs Milwaukee killer" in *Chicago Tribune* (October 20, 1976).

1977

President Robert Christensen and Executive Director David Berman testify before Wisconsin Legislature in favor of Senate Bill 77, which creates a statewide, trial-level public defender system.

David S. Berman resigns as Executive Director to enter private practice. Thomas G. Cannon is appointed successor. "Cannon to Head Legal Aid Society" in *Milwaukee Journal* (October 14, 1977).

1978

The Society is awarded a contract with Milwaukee County to provide representation in mental commitment proceedings as a result of its successful litigation in *State ex rel. Memmel v. Mundy*. Attorney Thomas K. Zander is named first head of the Mental Health Division.

The Society is awarded a contract from the State Public Defender Office to continue the Society's public defender program. "Legal Aid Society Backed in Handling Poverty Cases" in *Milwaukee Journal* (September 10, 1978).

Executive Director Thomas G. Cannon testifies before the Legislature's Joint Finance Committee on behalf of the State Public Defender budget.

The Society's revenue achieves all-time high when annual budget tops $1 million for the first time.

1979

LAS staff reaches record size of 32 attorneys who are deployed in five divisions (Civil, Felony, Juvenile, Mental Health, and Misdemeanor).

The Society elects not to renew its public defender contract in dispute with the State over excessive caseloads and inadequate support staff. The Society continues its representation of clients in civil cases and mental commitment proceedings.

Chief Staff Attorney Thomas K. Zander testifies before legislative committee concerning standards and procedures for civil mental commitments (now incorporated into sec. 51.20, Wis. Stats).

1980

The work of the Society is profiled in "Legal Aid needs help itself" in *Milwaukee Journal* (June 29, 1980).

The Milwaukee Foundation awards a grant of $18,500 to the Legal Aid Society to create an innovative Alternatives to Involuntary Mental Hospitalization (AIMH) Project.

The Society enters into a contract with Milwaukee County for $208,580 to provide guardian ad litem representation in Children's Court and Family Court. The initial staff consists of four attorneys, two social workers, and two secretaries in Children's Court. Family Court cases are handled by staff attorneys in the Civil Division.

The Society revises and restates its original Articles of Incorporation and Bylaws to comply with changes in the Internal Revenue Code and to avoid the potential for a hostile takeover. Revisions include transforming the Society from a membership organization to a self-perpetuating board of directors.

1981

Thomas G. Cannon resigns as Executive Director to accept an appointment as professor of constitutional law and legal ethics at Marquette University Law School. Thomas K. Zander is appointed successor. "Legal Aid Society elects director" in *Milwaukee Journal* (August 21, 1981).

1982

Milwaukee County declines to fund the Society's AIMH Project. "Legal Aid rebuffed on bid for funds" in *Milwaukee Sentinel* (December 22, 1982).

1984

The Society inaugurates an Anti-Discrimination Project to advocate for the rights of persons living with HIV/AIDS, one of the first such programs in the country.

LAS is awarded a grant from the Wisconsin Coalition for Advocacy to create an Institutional Advocacy Project (later renamed PAL: Protection and Advocacy Law Project). The program represents mentally ill persons who are institutionalized on issues relating to abuse, neglect, and civil rights violations while confined in state or county facilities.

1985

The Society establishes a Municipal Ordinance Defense (MOD) Project to defend individuals in Municipal Court prosecutions. Staff attorney Katie Walsh is appointed project supervisor.

The Mental Disability Law Division is formed to consolidate the Society's civil commitment work with services in adult guardianships and protective placements.

Fire causes extensive smoke and water damage, broken glass, and interior destruction to the Society's headquarters. "3-alarm blaze guts MU campus store" in *Milwaukee Sentinel* (February 12, 1985). Repairs take three months to complete.

The Society begins conducting annual reviews of court-ordered protective placements mandated by *State ex rel. Watts v. Combined Community Services*, a case litigated by Executive Director Thomas Zander.

1988

The new position of Litigation Director is created to expand the Society's commitment to major impact cases and assist staff in handling LAS's growing appellate practice. Prominent Milwaukee civil rights attorney, Curry First, is named to the post.

The Wisconsin Trust Account Foundation makes it first grant to the Society from the Interest on Lawyers' Trust Account Fund (Wis. SCR, chap. 13).

1989

The Society establishes a Nursing Home Residents Advocacy Project (NHRAP) with private funding.

The Society turns down a request from the State Public Defender Office to enter into a contract for representation in misdemeanor cases. LAS board concludes that amount offered ($200 per case) is insufficient to guarantee effective assistance of counsel.

1990

The Society returns to its tradition by providing legal representation to men and women in the armed forces called up for active duty in the Persian Gulf War. LAS attorneys provide counsel on rights secured by the Soldiers and Sailors Civil Relief Act, Veterans Reemployment Act, and various provisions of state law designed to protect servicemen and women.

The Society prepares an extensive memorandum of law for Milwaukee County Circuit Court Judges, which outlines the legal rights of servicemen and women in Wisconsin courts. In addition, LAS presents a statewide training seminar to assist private practice lawyers in representing armed forces personnel on a *pro bono* basis.

The Society initiates three innovative programs: OATH (Outreach and Advocacy for the Homeless Project), GAIN (Guardianship Advocacy, Instruction, and Networking Project), and CHAMP (Child Advocacy and Monitoring Project). The latter is affiliated with the national CASA (Court Appointed Special Advocates) program.

1991

The Society celebrates its 75th anniversary with a banquet at the Marc Plaza Hotel attended by more than 300 guests. Principal speaker is distinguished newspaper editor John Siegenthaler. The first Equal Justice Medals are struck to commemorate the occasion. They are presented to Julia Dolan McClelland, Helen Bader (posthumously), and Judge Janine Geske in recognition of their service to the poor.

In a landmark case litigated by the Society, Wisconsin Supreme Court strikes down Milwaukee ordinance on hindering or obstructing a police officer. "Resisting officer ordinance ruled unconstitutional" in *Milwaukee Sentinel* (March 7, 1991); "City ordinance on resisting struck down" in *Milwaukee Journal* (March 7, 1991).

1992

The Society establishes its HELP (Helping Elderly with Legal Problems) Project, a program that serves the legal needs of senior citizens.

1993

The Society and the Milwaukee Bar Association celebrate Law Day with a dinner at the Marc Plaza Hotel. Linda Greenhouse, *New York Times* correspondent for the U.S. Supreme Court, is principal speaker.

After 23 years on Marquette University campus (LAS's longest period of occupancy in any facility), severe overcrowding forces the Society to move its headquarters.

The Society purchases the Railway Exchange Building (listed on the National Register of Historic Buildings) and moves its offices to 229 East Wisconsin Avenue. "Downtown building sold to Legal Aid Society" in *Milwaukee Sentinel* (June 16, 1993).

The Society inaugurates the HOLA (Hispanic Outreach & Legal Aid) Project to assist victims of domestic violence in the Latino community. "Project targets Hispanic women" in *Milwaukee Sentinel* (September 6, 1993).

The Society receives its first gift from the Helen Bader Foundation in the amount of $150,000.

The Society reaches another revenue milestone: its first $2 million budget.

1994

Thomas K. Zander retires as Executive Director. Carole Wenerowicz is appointed successor.

Historic photograph is taken of the Society's five living executive directors, covering a span of seven decades: Dolan McClelland, Berman, Cannon, Zander, and Wenerowicz.

The Society establishes a program to review and screen citizen complaints filed with Fire and Police Commission, and, in collaboration with Milwaukee Bar Association, to train private lawyers to handle such cases on a pro bono basis. "Lawyers to offer free legal help to police complainants" in *Milwaukee Journal* (October 7, 1994).

1995

Carole Wenerowicz resigns as Executive Director to become President of the Wisconsin Council on Children and Families. James A. Walrath is appointed successor.

31. Historic Railway Exchange Building on East Wisconsin Avenue served as
headquarters of the Legal Aid Society, 1993-2005.
Courtesy of Milwaukee County Historical Society.

Executive Director Walrath reports to the Board that LAS currently has ten cases pending in the Wisconsin Supreme Court and Court
of Appeals – a record number.

1996

The Society celebrates its 80th anniversary with a dinner at the Milwaukee Hilton Hotel. Daniel Schorr, senior news analyst for National Public Radio, is principal speaker. ("Legal eagles in motion" in *Milwaukee Journal Sentinel*, May 12, 1996).

The Society inaugurates publication of a newsletter, *Opening Statements*, which is sent out (occasionally) to friends and supporters.

The Society receives a recognition award from the Episcopal Diocese of Milwaukee for the OATH Project's legal assistance to homeless persons at The Gathering Meal Program sponsored by St. James Episcopal Church.

1997

The Society initiates the ALERT (AIDS Law, Education, Representation, and Training) Project to serve the legal needs of persons living with HIV/AIDS.

The Society receives the Benedict Center's Justice Award for its MOD Project and jail-overcrowding litigation.

Associate Director Mary Gundrum organizes the Legal Aid Society's first Annual Poverty Law Update, a free continuing legal education seminar for attorneys working in the field of legal assistance to the poor.

The Society receives the J.C. Penney Golden Rule Award for the success of its CHAMP volunteer project for abused children.

1998

The Society establishes the SOLACE Project, an outreach program providing legal services to residents of the Sojourner Truth House for battered women.

Chief Staff Attorney Julia Vosper testifies before state legislative committee on duties of guardians ad litem and court-appointed special advocates (Wis. Stats. secs. 48.235 and 48.236).

1999

The Society initiates the TACS (Taxpayer Advocacy and Counseling Service) Project to represent low-income households in controversies with the Internal Revenue Service (particularly over child care credits, earned income credits, and collection issues).

The Society's payroll, board minutes, and contractual documents are held to be public records. *Cavey v. Walrath*, 229 Wis.2d 105, 598 N.W.2d 240 (Ct. App. 1999).

2001

The Society celebrates its 85th anniversary with a reception at Marquette University's Alumni Union. Wisconsin Chief Justice Shirley S. Abrahamson is principal speaker. "Legal Aid Society's Oct. 18th party celebrates 85th birthday" in *MBA Messenger* (September 2001) 1; "Legal Aid Celebrates 85th Birthday" in *MBA Messenger* (November 2001) 6.

The Society achieves another revenue milestone: its first $3 million annual budget.

The Society receives a second J.C. Penney Golden Rule Award, this time for its GAIN project.

The Society establishes the A-LINE (Advocacy for Low Income Neighborhood Equity) Project, a new anti-predatory lending initiative.

2002

The Society hosts annual convention of the National Legal Aid & Defender Association at the Hilton Hotel. *NLADA Cornerstone* 24, no. 4 (2002/03) 1, 6, 10, 22. Co-hosts are Legal Action of Wisconsin and the State Public Defender Office.

2003

The University of Notre Dame Law School establishes an annual summer clerkship at the Legal Aid Society. The position is funded by the Notre Dame Alumni Club of Milwaukee.

The Society's staff works toward passage of Wisconsin Responsible High Cost Mortgage Lending Act (Wis. Stats. sec. 428.202 et seq.). Governor presents bill-signing pen to Staff Attorney Catherine M. Doyle in recognition of her leadership on the issue.

2005

The Society sells Railway Exchange Building and moves its central headquarters to 521 North 8th Street. Mayor Tom Barrett and Wisconsin Supreme Court Justice Louis B. Butler, Jr. speak at opening reception.

Executive Director James Walrath and Litigation Director Peter Koneazny testify before State Senate Financial Institutions Committee in Madison on regulation of predatory lenders.

James A. Walrath resigns as Executive Director to accept an appointment as Federal Defender of Wisconsin. Thomas G. Cannon is appointed successor.

The Milwaukee Bar Association confers its Distinguished Service Award on the Society in recognition of its work on behalf of the poor.

To make knowledge about its services more accessible, the Society establishes a Website at www.lasmilwaukee.com.

City of Milwaukee awards the Society its first Community Development Block Grant ($50,000) to represent low-income homeowners and consumers in anti-predatory loan cases. "Legal Aid Society seeks funds from city" in *Milwaukee Journal Sentinel* (September 27, 2005).

The Society receives its first grant from the Public Interest Legal Services Fund (Wis. SCR, chap. 13).

2006

In collaboration with Marquette University Law School, the Society becomes a charter member of the Coalition for Access to Legal Resources, a Web-based consortium designed to facilitate contact between potential low-income clients and the programs that serve them. The address is www.legalhelpmilwaukee.com.

A Legal Aid Society Endowment Fund is established with the Greater Milwaukee Foundation.

The Society celebrates its 90th anniversary with a luncheon for 535 guests at the Italian Community Center. Wisconsin Governor Jim Doyle is principal speaker. Other speakers include Attorney General Peg Lautenschlager and Chief Judge Kitty K. Brennan. The event raises more than $118,000 for the Society.

The anniversary is highlighted in "To Protect and Serve: Legal Aid Society celebrates 90 years" in *The Daily Reporter* (August 24, 2006);

"Legal Aid Society celebrates 90 years of serving Milwaukee's poor" in *Milwaukee Courier* (September 2, 2006); "Agency helps the poor to fight injustice" in *Milwaukee Journal Sentinel* (September 3, 2006).

State Bar of Wisconsin awards the Society a Special Pro Bono Award in recognition of its 90th anniversary of serving the legal needs of Wisconsin's poor.

The Society unveils a new logo with the founding year embossed inside a traditional half-moon format against a blue background. The logo echoes window signage from the Society's former headquarters on both West and East Wisconsin Avenue.

The Archdiocese of Milwaukee Supporting Fund, Inc. announces a grant of $1,000,000 to the Society. The gift is the largest single donation in the Society's 90-year history. The donor requests that the Equal Justice Medal be named in honor of Thomas G. Cannon in recognition of his contributions to the Fund and to the Society.

2007

The Society helps organize the first Wisconsin Equal Justice Conference, held at Marquette University.

Chief Staff Attorney James M. Brennan retires after 31 years of service – second only to Julia Dolan in length of tenure.

The Society's board adopts the American Bar Association *Standards for the Provision of Civil Legal Aid* (revised edition 2006) for its Civil Division.

The Society's board adopts the *Best Practices Guidelines for Organizational Representation of Children in Abuse, Neglect, and Dependency Cases* promulgated by the National Association of Counsel for Children (2006) for its Guardian ad Litem Office.

The British Broadcasting Corporation airs a feature on the Legal Aid Society's fight against mortgage scams and predatory lenders. "Shrewd lenders spark US mortgage chaos" (August 23).

In light of the success of the previous year's anniversary event, the Board decides to restore the tradition of an annual luncheon to raise funds for the Society. Mayor Tom Barrett is main speaker. Other speakers include Attorney General J.B. Van Hollen and Forest County Potawatomi Chair Gus Franks. Event raises a record $148,000.

The Society registers as a lobbyist principal with State Ethics Board to promote passage of gubernatorial budget line item authorizing $1

32.   Milwaukee Mayor Tom Barrett, longtime supporter of the Legal Aid Society.
Courtesy of Mayor's Office.

million for civil legal services to the poor. Executive Director Thomas G. Cannon testifies in favor of such funding before Legislature's Joint Finance Committee. Provision is adopted. 2007 Wis. Act 20.

At year's end, the Society's Endowment Fund stands at $1,119,832.

2008

The A-LINE Project receives a $300,000 grant, payable over three years, from the Institute for Foreclosure Legal Assistance (National Association of Consumer Advocates) in Washington, D.C. The gift is designated for the fight against mortgage fraud.

State Public Defender contracts with the Society to defend subjects of involuntary civil mental commitments. Contract continues work that the Society first began performing in 1944.

The Society successfully urges Congress to amend the Americans with Disabilities Act of 1990 to include coverage for persons living with HIV/AIDS [H.R. 3195, 110th Cong. § 3406 (2008)].

Executive Director Thomas G. Cannon testifies at hearing before the State Equal Rights Division in Madison in favor of increasing Wisconsin's minimum wage from $5.90 to $7.25 per hour.

Annual luncheon features Wisconsin Chief Justice Shirley S. Abrahamson as principal speaker and attracts a record attendance of 625 guests.

The Society successfully urges the Federal Deposit Insurance Corporation to expand its coverage by insuring funds in Interest on Lawyers' Trust Accounts, which support civil legal aid programs across the nation.

2009

Chief Staff Attorney Catherine M. Doyle testifies before State Assembly Committee on Financial Institutions in Madison in favor of legislation imposing mandatory mediation requirement in mortgage foreclosure cases.

Governor signs Mortgage Foreclosure Rescue Scam Act into law (2009 Wis. Act 2, § 847 et seq.). Measure had been advocated by Chief Staff Attorney Catherine M. Doyle.

The Society urges passage of Senate Bill 61, which provides federal bankruptcy judges with authority to modify terms of mortgage loans.

The Society hosts Yudong Gao, an attorney from Beijing, China, as part of an exchange program through the auspices of the International Academy of Trial Lawyers.

The Society urges passage of Senate Bill 700 and H.R. Bill 1708 to eliminate the two-year waiting period for Social Security Disability beneficiaries to be eligible for Medicare.

U.S. Senator Herb Kohl is principal speaker at the Society's 93rd anniversary luncheon at the Italian Community Center. Other speakers include Mayor Tom Barrett and County Board Chairman Lee Holloway. Event draws a record 31 corporate and law firm sponsors.

Milwaukee County bids out guardian ad litem contract. "Milwaukee seeks bid on guardian ad litem work" in *Wisconsin Law Journal* (September 10, 2009). County rejects bids from three private law firms and awards contract to Legal Aid Society for 3 more years.

The Society also urges passage of the Protecting Consumers from Unreasonable Credit Rates Act (Senate Bill 500, H.R. Bill 1608), which, if enacted, would curb abusive practices by predatory lenders.

Executive Director Tom Cannon co-founds the Wisconsin Alliance for Equal Justice to push for increased funding for civil legal aid to the poor. Partners in the new organization are John F. Ebbott, Executive Director of Legal Action of Wisconsin, and Lynn Breedlove, Executive Director of Disability Rights Wisconsin.

The Society supports passage of Assembly Bill 389 requiring families of nursing home residents to be notified when the home is issued a serious citation by the Department of Health Services.

The Business Journal ranks the Legal Aid Society as Milwaukee's twelfth largest law firm. *Book of Lists* (2009) 158.

2010

The Society begins its LAMP (Legal and Medical Partnership) for Families project in collaboration with Children's Hospital, Medical College of Wisconsin, and Marquette University Law School. Project is designed to improve health of inner-city children by providing legal services to their families. Initial funding is provided by the Charles D. Jacobus Family Foundation.

Chief Staff Attorney Catey Doyle presents a paper on mortgage foreclosure fraud to a Federal Trade Commission conference in Chicago.

The Society opposes Senate Bill 384, which would create an affirmative defense to child abuse and child neglect prosecutions for parents and guardians who rely on spiritual or faith healing in lieu of providing medical treatment for sick children.

Governor gives signature pen to Chief Staff Attorney Catey Doyle when signing AB 471 into law. New law regulates mortgage broker activities in the interests of Wisconsin consumers.

Executive Director Tom Cannon delivers speech to Symposium on the Right to Counsel in Civil Cases in Madison on the challenges confronting *pro se* litigants in the court system.

Chief Staff Attorney Catey Doyle is interviewed by German Public Radio on involvement of Deutsche Bank in Milwaukee's mortgage crisis.

Society supports Child Victim Act, which would abolish statute of limitations for victims of childhood sexual abuse.

The Society staff ties its previous all-time high size (1978) with 32 attorneys. The staff's 10 social workers, and 9 support staff represent new records.

U.S. Court of Appeals Judge Terence T. Evans is keynote speaker at the Society's 94th anniversary luncheon. Event draws more than 600 attendees and sets a new record for number of sponsors.

The Society is honored by NeighborWorks America (Washington, D.C.) for its successful program of mortgage foreclosure legal assistance.

NOTES

1. The 38-page pamphlet was based on Reginald Heber Smith's pamphlet of the same title, which was published by the Boston Legal Aid Society. See Smith, *Justice and the Poor*, 214. Goldschmidt revised chapters v, vi, vii, and viii to bring them into accord with applicable Wisconsin law.
2. "For more than forty years," the Harvard-educated Hirshberg "was the leading voice of Reform Judaism in Milwaukee." John Gurda, *One People, Many Paths: A History of Jewish Milwaukee* (Jewish Museum Milwaukee, 2009) 78.
3. John S. Bradway (1890-1985) was second only to his friend and colleague, Reginald Heber Smith, as an early pioneer in the modern legal aid movement. Longtime Secretary (1922-40) and President (1940-42) of the National Association of Legal Aid Organizations, Bradway also served as Chief Counsel to the Philadelphia Legal Aid Society in the 1920s and, later, as director of the Legal Aid Clinic at Duke University Law School (1931-59). He and Smith co-authored *The Growth of Legal Aid Work in the United States* (Washington, D.C.: Government Printing Office, 1936). Bradway was especially interested in promoting cooperation between the legal and social work professions. His papers charting the growth of the national legal aid movement are preserved in the Duke University Archives. For further particulars on Bradway's career, see the tributes to him in *California Western Law Review* 10, no. 2 (1974), ix-xi, 219-38.
4. Perhaps the book was inspired by an earlier publication compiled in the city: Lizzie Black Kander, *The Settlement Cookbook* (Milwaukee, 1901).

13
RECURRING THEMES

Throughout nearly a century of operations, certain overarching issues surface again and again in the history of the Legal Aid Society of Milwaukee. They might not be readily apparent in the study of an isolated year, but they tend to reappear with regularity down through the decades. Some worth noting here are:

INNOVATIVE LEADERSHIP

Ever since its founding in 1916, the Legal Aid Society of Milwaukee has been a leader, both locally and nationally, on a number of fronts. During its inaugural year, the Society participated in Milwaukee's first combined charitable fundraising campaign, which was sponsored by the Central Budget of Philanthropies. In 1921, LAS led the way in helping establish the state's first Small Claims Court in Milwaukee. Two years later, the Society co-founded what today is known as the National Legal Aid & Defender Association, a powerful voice on behalf of equal justice for the poor. LAS was also instrumental in promoting passage of such reform legislation as the Small Loans Act of 1927 and the Wage Collection Act of 1931. Eight years later, in conjunction with the University of Wisconsin Law School, the Society began one of the country's first clinical legal education placements. In 1943, in partnership with the Milwaukee Bar Association, the Society established the state's first Lawyer Referral Service.

In 1948, the Society worked to help create a dedicated Children's Court in Milwaukee. In 1957, long before the United States Supreme Court recognized the right to counsel in criminal cases, the Legal Aid Society of Milwaukee began Wisconsin's first public defender program. Three years later, the Society's Executive Attorney helped draft the landmark Wisconsin Family Code. In 1980, LAS established an innovative project to explore less restrictive alternatives to involuntary mental commitment. Four years later, Legal Aid created one of the nation's first anti-discrimination projects specifically designed to protect the civil rights and civil liberties of persons living with HIV/AIDS. The innovation continues today. In 2005, LAS was among the first law firms in the country to recognize, and respond to, the legal needs of Hurricane Katrina refugees. In 2007, our leading-edge work against predatory lenders and mortgage scams was featured on a program of the British Broadcasting Corporation. In 2008, the Society attracted the attention of the United States Senate Committee on Aging, which requested testimony from its Chief Staff Attorney for background in drafting protective legislation to prevent senior citizens from being bilked out of their hard-earned home equity. In 2010, LAS formed a series of new partnerships, including its LAMP for Families project, an innovative collaboration with Children's Hospital, the Medical College of Wisconsin, and Marquette University Law School to improve the health of inner-city children by free providing legal services to their families.

INDEPENDENT COUNSEL

Within the first year of the opening of the Legal Aid Society, President Woodrow Wilson asked Congress to declare war on Germany. The nation soon found itself embroiled in World War I. That conflict presented the new organization with its first test of principle. Shortly after America entered the war, the Society decided to make its services available free of charge to members of the armed forces, thereby inaugurating a tradition that would later be followed during World War II, the Korean War, and the Persian Gulf War as well. In 1918, the Society's outside legal counsel, William J. Goldschmidt, published an important pamphlet advising servicemen and women of their rights under the recently enacted Soldiers and Sailors Civil Relief Act. See "The Military Affairs Committee and Its Work for Milwaukee" in *Civic and Commerce* 103 (January 1919) 16-17. That legacy continues today as LAS currently protects the state and federal legal rights of active-duty members of the armed forces in Family Court by judicial appointment.

Not long after the Great War began, however, Wisconsin Governor Emanuel L. Philipp complained that private attorneys were charging young men exorbitant legal fees to counsel them on exemptions to the Selective Service Act. The Legal Aid Society of Milwaukee stepped

33. Wisconsin Governor Emanuel L. Philipp prompted the Legal Aid Society of Milwaukee to offer free draft counseling to young men during World War I. After the war, Philipp served on LAS's Advisory Board. *Courtesy of Wisconsin Historical Society (WHi-32600).*

forward and offered to provide such advice free of charge. The Society's first Superintendent, Alma C. Schlesinger, worked out a referral arrangement with the Chairman of the Milwaukee County Draft Board to counsel young men facing conscription. Reginald Heber Smith, *Justice and the Poor* (New York: Carnegie Foundation, 1919) 213. One can only imagine the Society's waiting room on the seventh floor of the Merchants & Manufacturers Bank Building. On the one hand, young men who had voluntarily placed themselves in harm's way sought advice on drafting a power of attorney or making a last will and testament to protect their dependents. On the other hand, a second group of young men sought advice on utilizing exemptions to the draft as a means of avoiding military service altogether. Regardless of the individual's decision, though, it was clear from the very start that the Legal Aid Society was committed to providing counsel independently of political belief, thus charting a course for the organization that focused services on client needs rather than the prevailing winds of expediency or ideology.

Over the years, the Society has taken criticism from some quarters for its vigorous advocacy of unpopular clients. For example, even though the overwhelming majority of the Society's annual budget has long been derived from Milwaukee County government, beginning in the late 1960s, lawyers from the Legal Aid Society successfully sued the County in a series of groundbreaking cases concerning the rights of welfare recipients, children, mental patients, the homeless, the elderly, and prisoners. These cases focused on reforms in the General Assistance Program (*Denny, Clark II*), Juvenile Detention Center (*State ex rel. Morrow, State ex rel. Harris*), Mental Health Center (*State ex rel. Memmel, State ex rel. Jones, Joan S.*), Child & Adolescent Treatment Center (*State ex rel. R.T.*), foster care system (*Jeanine B.*), the adult protective placement system (*State ex rel. Watts, In Matter of Guardianship of Agnes T.*), the old County Jail (*Jackson*), and the new Criminal Justice Facility (*Christensen*).

Such actions have assisted Milwaukee County in meeting its statutory and constitutional responsibilities for the care of vulnerable populations. Nonetheless, the County has not always appreciated LAS's distinctive role. During the course of the *Memmel* case in 1976, for example, the County's Corporation Counsel explicitly threatened to terminate the Society's public defender contract (then providing 90% of the total annual LAS budget) if Legal Aid persisted in going forward with its class action writ of habeas corpus on behalf of all involuntarily committed patients at the Milwaukee County Mental Health Center. The Society did persist in the face of such threatened retaliation, eventually forcing the County to agree to the release or retrial of every member of the class. "Patients Denied Rights, County Says," in *Milwaukee Journal* (August 5, 1976).

Two years later, the Chief Judge complained that the Society's public defenders were demanding jury trials "in virtually every case" and consistently filing "every motion known to law." See "Legal Aid Lambasted By Sullivan" in *Milwaukee Sentinel* (February 16, 1978). The Society's Executive Director immediately defended his staff. "Legal Aid Director May Sue Sullivan" in *Milwaukee Journal* (February 17, 1978). The *Journal* editorial board supported the Legal Aid Society. See "Just Doing Their Job, Judge" in *Milwaukee Journal* (February 18, 1978). A day later, an editorial cartoon criticized the Chief Judge and defended the Society's staff attorneys. Eventually, the Chief Judge backed down. "Judge Sullivan Retracts Criticism" in *Milwaukee Journal* (March 13, 1978).

34. Milwaukee Journal editorial cartoon, February 19, 1978.
Courtesy of Milwaukee Journal Sentinel.

In 1992, Milwaukee County's Corporation Counsel complained to the Society's board of directors that LAS was accepting large sums of money each year to represent incompetent adults and children while at the same time maintaining multiple lawsuits against the County. Like his predecessor in 1976, he threatened to terminate the County Guardian ad Litem contract unless the Society agreed to a "no-sue" provision. The situation was exacerbated when three private attorneys appeared that year before the County Board Judiciary Committee; they volunteered to match LAS's contract bid *and* agreed not to sue Milwaukee County. Despite its competitors' position, the Society's board advised the Corporation Counsel that his threat "could constitute tortious interference with a contract or a possible violation of the Rules of Professional Conduct for Attorneys since the threat was being made to gain advantage in the lawsuits filed by LAS against the County." Eventually, the Corporation Counsel withdrew his demand and the County Board agreed to extend the Guardian ad Litem contract with the Legal Aid Society. See LAS Board Minutes, August 26, 1992 through April 1, 1993.

Also in the early 1990s, the city of Milwaukee initiated a new program aimed at preventing homeless people from congregating in the Downtown area. In particular, police officers began shooing people away from such sites as meal programs and overnight shelters. When the Legal Aid Society criticized the policy and threatened legal action to end the practice, one irate financial supporter penned an angry note to protest the Society's advocacy for the homeless: "I will never again contribute since you foolishly made our city more dangerous by standing up for the rights of beggars. Very poor judgment!"

More recently, in 2008, Legal Aid lawyers successfully prosecuted two simultaneous contempt actions against Milwaukee County. The first involved a massive failure to comply with the consent decree in the jail class action case. "Inmates can get damages for jail violations" in *Milwaukee Journal Sentinel* (January 30, 2008); "Attorneys seek fines against county" in *Milwaukee Journal Sentinel* (February 3, 2006); "County found in contempt over jail" in *Milwaukee Journal Sentinel* (January 7, 2006). The other case arose out of the County's repeated failure to conduct a court-ordered review of a protective placement for an elderly nursing home resident. *In re Protective Placement of J. B.*, case no. 2005-GN-000316.

These two cases prompted the Milwaukee County Board of Supervisors to vote 11-8 in the following year to put the Legal Aid Society's Guardian ad Litem contract out for competitive bids. "Milwaukee seeks bids on guardian ad litem work" in *Wisconsin Law Journal* (September 14, 2009). After forty years of vigorously representing children in court, several members of the Board majority argued that, "the County should not contract with an organization that asks for our money and then turns around and sues us." The County issued a Request For Proposals containing numerous restrictions that would have had the effect of destroying the statutory guarantee of independence for guardians ad litem by placing them under the thumb of the Chief Judge's office. The Legal Aid Society objected to the proposed restrictions and the County eventually withdrew them [see Historical Documents Section].

In 2010, Supervisor Patricia Jursik introduced a proposed ordinance (10-202) that would ban contractors with Milwaukee County from filing class action lawsuits against the County. "Class Dismissed: Resolution to restrict class actions against Milwaukee County draws opposition" in *Wisconsin Law Journal* (July 19, 2010). Jursik admitted that her resolution was aimed at the Legal Aid Society and said she was upset that LAS accepted a court appointment to represent prisoners in the County Jail in a class action suit against the County at the same time that the Society's lawyers served as guardians ad litem under a contract to represent children in Family Court and Children's Court. As she put it, the Legal Aid Society was "biting the hand that feeds it." The Society's Executive Director objected to the proposed ordinance; he argued that such a measure promoted bad public policy, violated several constitutional provisions, and conflicted with Supreme Court ethical mandates governing the conduct of attorneys [see Historical Documents Section].

The *Milwaukee Journal Sentinel* editorial board weighed in with a strong editorial supporting the Legal Aid Society. See "A harmful measure" (June 12, 2010). The editorial argued that the "ordinance change would seriously harm the Legal Aid Society of Milwaukee's ability to represent those most in need of legal services. The proposed change may be in violation of the state constitution, reason enough that it shouldn't go anywhere. But it's also just the wrong thing to do." The newspaper went on to note that the class-action ban was "squarely aimed at the Legal Aid Society, which filed a class action suit on behalf of prisoners in the county's Criminal Justice Facility on grounds of overcrowding, unsanitary living conditions, and failure to provide adequate mental health services to inmates." The editorial concluded by stating that "the Legal Aid Society provides an invaluable service to children and to the county at a reasonable cost. It shouldn't be hampered from doing so because it represented another group of people in need." As this book goes to press, the issue remains unresolved.

Independently and loyally serving the needs of vulnerable clients, regardless of institutional consequences, has been a tradition at LAS from the very beginning. And as long as there is a Legal Aid Society of Milwaukee, those professional principles will never be surrendered.

PARENT ORGANIZATION

A 1970 report from the National Legal Aid & Defender Association recognized the Legal Aid Society's role as "elder statesman" of Wisconsin's poverty law community. In fact, as early as 1925, the State Bar Association of Wisconsin purposefully sought to duplicate the success of the Legal Aid Society of Milwaukee by creating a Standing Committee on Legal Aid (1925 *Proceedings of SBAW* 105-09). Over time, the Society became the parent organization of the state's two largest providers of legal services to the poor.

In 1957, the Legal Aid Society established a Voluntary Defender Program with the Milwaukee Junior Bar Association – the first such program in the country. Twelve years later, through the leadership of Judge John A. Decker and Julia Dolan, respectively President and Executive Attorney, the Society obtained a Ford Foundation grant to create a full-time, staffed office of public defenders for Milwaukee County's trial courts. That program's substantial cost savings and record of success became the prototype for creation of the State Public Defender Office. See "Legal Aid Project Boosts Public Defender Concept" in *Milwaukee Journal*, November 29, 1970; "Defender Plan Shown To Be Economical" in *Milwaukee Sentinel* (January 6, 1971); "Legal Aid Charges One-third as Much" in *Milwaukee Journal*, March

2, 1972; "Legal Aid Proves a Bargain for Public" in *Milwaukee Journal,* April 18, 1976. In fact, the Society's President and Executive Director testified in favor of legislative passage of the bill (1977 Wis. Laws, c.29). After enactment, the new state agency contracted with LAS to continue its public defender program in Milwaukee County. When that relationship was relinquished in 1979 as a result of inadequate state funding, the SPD hired Legal Aid's entire public defender staff.

On the civil side, the Legal Aid Society obtained the state's first federal grant from the Office of Economic Opportunity for legal services to the poor in 1966. Julia Dolan and the board established Milwaukee Plan Legal Services, a project under the auspices and management of the Legal Aid Society [see Historical Documents Section]. Dolan was named (Executive) Director of MPLS. See Margadette M. Demet, "Legal Services for Urban Needs: Implementation of the Economic Opportunity Act of 1964" in *MBA Gavel* 27, no. 1 (1966) 6-16. Personal, philosophical, and generational differences quickly arose between adherents of the traditional individual service model and the newer law reform model that focused on systemic social change.[1] For the background, see Ted Finman, "OEO Legal Services Programs and the Pursuit of Social Change" in *Wisconsin Law Review* (1971) 1001, especially pp 1036-45, which contains a critical analysis of the Society's MPLS project [see Historical Documents Section]. Identical disagreements, it should be noted, were taking place in legal aid offices across the country. See, *e.g.* Carol Poh Miller, *A Passion for Justice: A History of the Legal Aid Society of Cleveland, 1905-2005,* pp 65-69; Katz, *Poor People's Lawyers in Transition,* pp 136-59 (Chicago Legal Aid Bureau); Mark Spiegel, "The Boston Legal Aid Society: 1900-1925" in *Massachusetts Legal History* 9 (2003) 45.

These differences led the Legal Aid Society to withdraw from the OEO Legal Services program effective October 1, 1969. "Legal Aid Groups in City to Cut Ties" in *Milwaukee Journal* (June 3, 1969). Two new organizations, Milwaukee Legal Services and Freedom Through Equality, emerged. Mark Braun, *Policies, Programs, Politics and the Poor in Two Milwaukee Legal Services Organizations, 1966-1972* (paper delivered to a conference at Marquette University on "Historical Perspectives on Milwaukee's Urban Experience" (1966)).[2] These successor programs hired the Society's MPLS staff, took over the Society's neighborhood offices, and divided what had been the Society's OEO grant between them. Four years later, the two groups merged and, in 1977, adopted a new organizational name, Legal Action of Wisconsin. John F. Ebbott, *Forty Years of Equal Justice With Legal Action of Wisconsin: A History* (LAW 2009).

Like any parent, the Legal Aid Society of Milwaukee takes great pride in the growth of its two successful progeny. We salute the important contributions of the State Public Defender and Legal Action of Wisconsin, and welcome their continuing valuable cooperation toward our common mission of equal justice for the poor.

PROMINENT ALUMNI

The 1941 Annual Report of the Legal Aid Society mentions Catherine B. Cleary as one of two University of Wisconsin Law School students who completed their office practice internship that year at LAS. Despite graduating with highest honors, Cleary found Milwaukee's private law firms unreceptive to the idea of a woman lawyer. Sidestepping the legal profession altogether, she went on to become one of America's foremost business leaders. Cleary served as Assistant Treasurer of the United States during the first year of the Eisenhower administration. In 1969, she was elected President and CEO of the First Wisconsin Trust Company. Later, she became the first woman to serve as a director on such major corporate boards as General Motors, American Telephone & Telegraph, Kraft Foods, and Northwestern Mutual Life. Cleary also served as a director of numerous charitable and philanthropic organizations, including the University of Notre Dame, Mayo Clinic Foundation, Marquette University, and the Robert Wood Johnson Foundation. In addition, she was named President of the National Association of Bank Women and served as President of the Wisconsin Alumni Research Foundation.

Service on the staff of the Legal Aid Society of Milwaukee has proven to be a judicial incubator. Twelve former LAS attorneys have gone on to become judges on the Wisconsin Supreme Court, Court of Appeals, Circuit Court, or Tribal Court. Robert W. Landry was the first. He joined the Society's staff as a part-time attorney after his graduation from the University of Wisconsin Law School in 1949. Landry was appointed a Civil Court Judge in 1954 and went on to a long and distinguished career on the bench. Other staff alumni who have served as judges include Thomas P. Doherty, Janine P. Geske, Bonnie L. Gordon, Stephan M. Grochowski, Michael D. Guolee, Paul B. Higginbotham, William A. Jennaro, Charles F. Kahn, Jr., Jess Martinez, Freder-

35.   Wisconsin Supreme Court Justice Janine P. Geske, former Chief Staff Attorney at the Legal Aid Society of Milwaukee. *Courtesy of Wisconsin Supreme Court.*

ick C. Rosa, and Russell W. Stamper. Judge Higginbotham currently serves on the Wisconsin Court of Appeals and Judge Grochowski sits on the Menominee Tribal Court in Keshena, Wisconsin; the others all served as Circuit Court judges.

Janine Geske's stellar legal career began in the Legal Aid Society's Civil Division 1975-81, the last four years of which she served as Chief Staff Attorney. She left LAS to join the faculty of Marquette University Law School where she founded the Legal Clinic for the Elderly. Geske was appointed a Circuit Court Judge in 1981 by Governor Lee S. Dreyfus; twelve years later, Governor Tommy Thompson named her a Justice of the Wisconsin Supreme Court where she served 1993-98. After leaving the high court, Janine returned to the law faculty at Marquette, serving as Dean (2002-03). She also held the office of Milwaukee County Executive on an interim basis in early 2002. Geske has taught at the National Judicial College in Reno, Nevada, and served as Dean of the Wisconsin Judicial College for five years. She currently holds a Distinguished Professor chair at Marquette Law School where she has pioneered the concept of restorative justice for victims and perpetrators of crimes. She is a national expert in alternative dispute resolution.

Another prominent alumnus is Lawrence E. Norton II, who worked as a staff attorney in the Legal Aid Society's Criminal Appeals Division during 1972-74. A graduate of Yale College (B.A. 1966) and Yale Law School (LL.B. 1969), Larry previously served a stint with the Appalachian Research and Defense Fund before coming to Milwaukee. After the Society's appellate work was taken over by the State Public Defender, he went on to a long career in various legal services programs throughout the country. Since 2004, Norton has served as Executive Director of the Community Justice Project in Harrisburg, Pennsylvania, an organization with a dozen staffers and more than a million-dollar budget. It provides statewide advocacy on issues, or for poor clients, where representation is barred by current Legal Services Corporation regulations (e.g. migrant and seasonal farm workers, undocumented aliens, prisoners, etc.). He has become a national expert on employment law, especially the Fair Labor Standards Act, and has published numerous articles in such diverse journals as the *U.C.L.A. Law Review* and the *New York Times*. Norton has also served as an

Adjunct Professor of Law at Pennsylvania State University's Dickinson School of Law.

Equally eminent among Legal Aid Society alumni is Randolph N. Stone. He was appointed a staff attorney in the Society's Felony Division after his graduation from the University of Wisconsin Law School in 1978. Stone resigned from LAS after the State Public Defender takeover the following year. He received a Reginald Heber Smith Fellowship and went on to serve as Deputy Director of the District of Columbia Public Defender Service. From there, he returned to his hometown of Chicago where he was appointed Public Defender of Cook County (1988-91), responsible for administering a budget of $32 million and supervising a staff of over 500 attorneys. For the past two decades, Randy has been Clinical Professor of Law at the University of Chicago Law School and Director of the Mandel Legal Aid Clinic there. He worked closely with faculty colleague Barack Obama to block proposed legislation in Illinois that sought to transfer large numbers of juveniles into the adult criminal court system. Stone has also served as Chair of the American Bar Association's Criminal Justice Section; he has received many awards for his distinguished career in public service.

EQUAL OPPORTUNITY EMPLOYER

An interesting feature of the Legal Aid Society's history is its leadership in providing professional opportunities for working women. During its first fifty-five years, the Society was headed exclusively by women chief executives: Alma C. Schlesinger, Agnes Campbell Kiewert, Margery M. Heck (Riffle), and Julia B. Dolan (McClelland). In addition, Attorney Ida E. Luick, the first woman graduate of Marquette Law School's evening division (class of 1917) served as an LAS director in the mid-1920s. This record is significant when one considers that LAS was founded at a time when women were not permitted by law to vote. Ironically, Campbell Kiewert thought that male attorneys would not accept a woman lawyer (Heck) to succeed her as Superintendent. In 1930, she remarked that, "women attorneys are not beloved by the Milwaukee bar" [see Historical Documents Section]. Twenty years later, however, the Society's three women lawyers (Julia B. Dolan, Elizabeth C. Leis, and Arlene Kennedy) constituted the first all-female law firm in Wisconsin. Luick, Heck, Dolan, Leis, and Dorothy K. von Briesen (who later served as a staff attorney) were all featured in *Pioneers in the Law: The First 150 Women* (Madison: State Bar of Wisconsin, 1998). Today, the Society's professional staff is still overwhelmingly female. Twenty-five of our thirty-two attorneys and nine of our ten social workers are women – thus making us the largest predominantly-female law firm in the state.

The Society's first African American lawyer, former Assistant District Attorney Paul T. Miller, was appointed Chief Attorney of the Northside Neighborhood Office in 1966. His successor as Chief Attorney, Horace Ray George, was also African American. Another former Legal Aid staff attorney, Judge Paul B. Higginbotham, is the first African American judge to sit on an appellate court in Wisconsin. In a recent interview, he recalled:

> My first professional position was as a staff attorney at the Legal Aid Society of Milwaukee in 1985 and 1986. It was an incredible litigation experience. I had wanted to represent people who needed my help and I was able to do it there. I am very proud of my record.

The judge went on to explain:

> I litigated landlord-tenant and fair housing cases and helped create the Legal Aid Society's housing and employment discrimination program. I probably had more courtroom experience in one and a half years as a Legal Aid Society lawyer than most attorneys in mid-size to large law firms experience in five to six, or even seven years. It was a wonderful start to my professional career. As an African American attorney from the Legal Aid Society, representing minority and poor clients, I always had to do my best to give my clients a fair chance.

(Quoted in Nicholas C. Zales, "In Chambers – Judge Paul B. Higginbotham, Court of Appeals" in *De Novo* (October 2005) 2, the newsletter of the State Bar of Wisconsin Appellate Practice Section.)

Louis Mestre, the first Latino staff attorney, joined LAS in 1968. Today, the Society has five native Spanish-speakers on staff. In 1975, Dennis Egre was hired as the first staff lawyer with a physical disability. Ty Gee became the first Asian American lawyer at the Legal Aid Society in 1988. Stephan Grochowski, a member of the Menominee Tribe, was LAS's first Native American staff attorney in 1990; Kath-

36.   Wisconsin Court of Appeals Judge Paul B. Higginbotham, former staff attorney at
the Legal Aid Society of Milwaukee. *Courtesy of Wisconsin Court of Appeals.*

leen Theimann, an enrolled member of the Oneida Nation, followed
the next year. These milestones only represent a beginning. Currently,
the Society's personnel are at their most diverse level ever – one-third
of the total staff comes from minority backgrounds. Many of them are
making important contributions to the diversification of the broader
legal and social work professions as well. For example, Carmen M.
Ortiz, supervisor of our Family Court Guardian ad Litem program,
is a past President of the Wisconsin Hispanic Lawyers Association.
Ernesto Romero, a former LAS staff attorney, served as President of

the same organization in 2001-02. Antonique Williams, a former staff attorney, continues her work as Secretary of the Wisconsin Association of African American Lawyers. Isa Gonzalez-Zayas, staff attorney in the Children's Court Guardian ad Litem office, is a director of the Puerto Rican Foundation. Staff attorney Arman Rouf currently serves as a director of the Wisconsin Asian Bar Association.

In 2007, the Society hired Rachel Arfa as a staff attorney in the Civil Division. She was born profoundly deaf. Rachel communicates by speaking and lip-reading, which she learned to do at age three. She is also fluent in American Sign Language. Rachel relies on bilateral cochlear implants to hear environmental noises (door bell, telephone ring). In the office, she employs CapTel™, an assistive technology in which an operator captions what her caller says on a small screen. To follow dialogue in the courtroom, and depending on the particular circumstances of each case, Rachel uses a sign language interpreter and/ or a court reporter who projects RealTime™ captioning onto a laptop screen. Professional Interpreting Enterprise has generously donated approximately $10,000 a year in time and services to make it possible for Rachel's low-income clients to access her legal skills in the office, thereby promoting the effective two-way communication essential to the practice of law.

After accommodating Arfa's disability at the courthouse for more than a year, the District Court Administrator and a new Chief Judge abruptly decided to reverse policy in 2009. They refused to pay for the necessary accommodation aids – effectively making it impossible for Rachel to practice law in the Milwaukee County Circuit Court. Moreover, they directed the Legal Aid Society to reimburse the County for all interpreter invoices the County had paid during the previous year. Rachel filed a motion for technical assistance with the trial court and won a favorable decision approving payment of her interpreter. *Crosby v. Williamson*, case no. 08-SC 23166 (Decision, January 9, 2009). Simultaneously, the Legal Aid Society informed the Chief Judge and District Court Administrator that it would sue them in federal court if they failed to accommodate Attorney Arfa. In a sharply worded letter to both officials, LAS's Executive Director wrote:

> We see the change in policy for what it is: invidious discrimination against the disabled – conduct that became illegal when Congress enact-

ed the Americans with Disabilities Act... It is disappointing, especially in this day and age, when those charged with enforcing laws that protect the disabled, fail to do so.

The Society also engaged outside counsel (Foley & Lardner LLP) to represent it and Rachel in litigation. After an extensive exchange of correspondence, the Chief Judge agreed to provide RealTime™ captioning for all court appearances and to consider providing an American Sign Language interpreter on a case-by-case basis.

IMMIGRANT CONNECTION

Milwaukee has long been known as a city of nations. John Gurda, *The Making of Milwaukee* (Milwaukee County Historical Society, 1999) 170. Indeed, when the Legal Aid Society was founded in 1916, Milwaukee was the most "foreign" of any major American city according to the 1910 census. Fully 78.6% of all residents were either immigrants or children of immigrants. It is not surprising, therefore, that the founding generation of the Legal Aid Society was composed predominantly of immigrants (*e.g.* Victor Berger) or children of immigrants (*e.g.* William I Iannan, John Barnes, Emmett Donnelly, Meta Schlichting Berger, William Kaumheimer). In addition, early annual reports classified the ethnicity of clients and documented the large pool of foreign-born (one-third of the total caseload) whom the Society served. This thread with America's newest residents has been a constant source of inspiration and energy throughout the organization's history.

In 1916, the United States had an essentially open immigration policy, which resulted in 31% of all Wisconsinites being foreign-born. However, a series of restrictive immigration laws enacted by Congress in the 1920s greatly reduced the flow of newcomers to America. Over time, Wisconsin has seen the number of immigrant clients decline markedly. By 2000, just 4% of state residents were foreign-born. Today, Wisconsin's newest immigrants tend to come from Latin America (35%) and Asia (32%) rather than from Western Europe, as had been the case in 1916.

The two longest serving staff members of the Legal Aid Society have been Julia (née Lebowitz) Dolan, a native of Vilnius, Lithuania, and Jim Brennan, whose father immigrated to Milwaukee from his home in Coomnakilla, County Kerry, Ireland. One of the Society's longest serving directors, Judge F. Ryan Duffy, Sr., was the son of an immigrant from Castleblaney, County Monaghan, Ireland. Today's staff includes Danuta Kurczewski, a native of Krakow, Poland; Paula Lorant, whose father was born in Kishvarda, Hungary; and Arman Rouf, whose parents came to America from Bangladesh. The organization's strong immigrant background reinforces its special obligation to make refugees from poverty or oppression feel welcome at the Legal Aid Society as newer generations of dispossessed continue to make their homes in Milwaukee.

ENLISTING VOLUNTEER LAWYERS

From the very beginning, the Legal Aid Society has relied on a dedicated corps of volunteers to expand its services to the poor. The annual report for 1918 recognized six office volunteers by name. Also from an early stage, LAS relied on an informal network of volunteer attorneys to provide assistance in cases beyond the staff's normal expertise. *Proc. NALAO* (1931) 47. In 1941, the Society developed its first formal pro bono legal services project in collaboration with the Saint Vincent de Paul Society of the Catholic Archdiocese of Milwaukee. A panel of volunteer attorneys from SVDP agreed to accept referrals on a gratis basis from the Legal Aid Society in divorce and legal separation matters. Nineteen cases were referred during that first year. In due course, the Vincentians also referred non-matrimonial matters to the Legal Aid Society.

During World War II, the Society partnered with the Miller, Mack & Fairchild law firm (today's Foley & Lardner LLP) to provide free legal services to members of the armed forces and to compile a digest of laws pertaining to their legal rights. The innovative Voluntary Defender Program, established in 1957, enlisted the services of 200 attorneys to provide free representation in misdemeanor cases [see Historical Documents Section]. The Society's Bail Bond Project, created in 1967, recruited a panel of 75 volunteer attorneys who were on call around the clock seven days per week. The Law Reform Division, which also began in 1967, enlisted six of the city's largest law firms to provide volunteer counsel to handle complex litigation, including the Society's first class action, *Ramos v. Health & Social Services Board*, 276 F. Supp. 474 (E.D. Wis. 1967). LAS Staff Attorney Bettie McJunkin successfully co-counseled that case with Foley, Sammond & Lardner attorneys Timothy C. Frautschi, Lawrence J. Bugge, and Maurice J. McSweeney.

The Volunteer Lawyer Project continues this legacy today under the supervision of Staff Attorney Karen Dardy. The Legal Aid Society trains, refers, and assists pro bono attorneys from Foley & Lardner LLP; Quarles & Brady LLP; Reinhart Boerner Van Deuren S.C.; Godfrey & Kahn S.C.; Gonzalez, Saggio & Harlan LLP; and the legal department at Northwestern Mutual Life on a wide range of civil legal matters. In addition, Quarles & Brady donates the services of a new associate half-time for an entire summer; at the end of that period, his or her clients become clients of the Quarles firm. And in 2010, LAS partnered with the Milwaukee Bar Association to recruit, train, and assign volunteer attorneys to assist elderly deaf residents at a housing project in Greenfield. In this way, the partnership between the Society and some of the city's largest and most prestigious law firms redounds to the benefit of the poor who could not otherwise obtain legal counsel. In light of the current economic crisis, one national law firm, New York's Latham & Watkins LLP, subsidized a deferred new-hire attorney to work at the Legal Aid Society of Milwaukee for the 2009-10 year.

Serving as a volunteer provides profound professional and personal satisfaction to lawyers participating in the program. Attorney Rosalie I. Gellman enrolled at Marquette University Law School just before her 70th birthday. She had decided to study law strictly as an intellectual exercise. However, after being admitted to the Wisconsin Bar in 2002, Rosalie volunteered to work in the Legal Aid Society's Civil Division where she handles Social Security disability claims. This past Mother's Day, she received an early-morning phone call from a former client at Legal Aid. "She told me how grateful she was and vowed to call me every Mother's Day for the rest of her life!" See "Rosalie Gellman" in *Marquette Lawyer* (Spring 2009) 48.

Attorney Peter W. Bruce recently retired from a distinguished 37-year career at Northwestern Mutual Life. After graduating from the University of Chicago Law School, he rose to such top positions as General Counsel, Senior Executive Vice President, and Chief Insurance Officer. Long interested in working with children in foster care,

Bruce contacted the Legal Aid Society after his retirement and generously offered his time. Chief Staff Attorney Shelia Hill-Roberts allowed him to shadow her for several months. Soon, with continued mentoring, he began handling cases on his own. Bruce writes of the experience:

> I will be forever grateful for the opportunity to "join up" with the Guardian ad Litem Office as a volunteer attorney. I had never done any kind of family or juvenile law before, and found that I was scared to death at the thought of firing live ammunition in an area where I had not previously practiced. The chance to join a group of dedicated, experienced lawyers was wonderful. People say nice things to me about doing "pro bono." Believe me, the old adage is true: I am getting a lot more as a volunteer attorney than I'm giving. It's great fun being part of such a special group and learning something new at this stage of life from a dedicated group of experts. I am very grateful to the Legal Aid Society of Milwaukee.

Bruce handles about 25 cases per year and makes it a point never to miss a monthly LAS staff meeting at the Vel R. Phillips Juvenile Justice Center.

37. First Marquette University Law School (Mackie Mansion), circa 1916.
Courtesy of Marquette University Archives.

MARQUETTE LAW SCHOOL PARTNERSHIP

The Legal Aid Society and Marquette University Law School have been partners from the very beginning, ever since Professor Stephen McMahon served as one of the original incorporators of the Society in 1916. Three years later, Marquette President Father Herbert C. Noonan, S.J., joined the Society's Advisory Board. In 1923, LAS President William Kaumheimer reported that the Society's attempt to start a legal aid clinic with Marquette law students had proven unsuccessful because the school's class schedule was limited to the afternoon hours and it was difficult to staff the office with students as a result. *Proc. NALAO* (1923) 107. Nonetheless, the relationship continued on an informal basis as students volunteered to work at the Society on their own time. In the mid-1930s, it was noted that Milwaukee was one of a handful of legal aid programs that made informal use of law students. Leon T. David, "The Value of Legal Aid Work to Law Schools" in *Annals of the American Academy of Political and Social Science* 205 (1939) 122.

In 1951, the collaboration with Marquette evolved into a formal clinic placement that has proven to be a great success. "10 MU Students Set for Internship in Law" in *Milwaukee Journal* (February 28, 1952); "MU Volunteers Help Legal Aid Program" in *Milwaukee Journal* (September 28, 1966); "Legal Aid to Honor MU Law Students" in *Milwaukee Journal* (May 5, 1968); "Legal Aid Society Joins Forces with MU Law School" in *Milwaukee Journal* (October 9, 1969). The clinic's scope of activity was considerably expanded after the Wisconsin Supreme Court promulgated its Rules for the Practical Training of Law Students. 48 Wis.2d. xix-xxii (1970); see now Wis. SCR 50.

Marquette Law School Professor Thomas J. Hammer is the longtime director of clinical education. He recently touted the program's value:

> For many, many years, the Guardian ad Litem Division of the Legal Aid Society has generously hosted Marquette University Law School students as interns at its Children's Court facilities. These students work at the elbow of Legal Aid lawyers who mentor them in their pursuit of the skills necessary to someday work as guardians ad litem themselves. In return, the students provide such assistance as they can on cases being handled by their mentors. I coordinate this internship program on be-

half of the Law School and know of its many successes. I also read each semester the comments of students who intern with the Legal Aid Society and who consistently marvel at the high quality of lawyering they observe and at the dedication of the attorneys and staff of Legal Aid's Guardian ad Litem Division. As a legal educator, I am most grateful for the wonderful example that the Legal Aid Society's lawyers provide to our future graduates.

(Letter to Milwaukee County Board of Supervisors, March 9, 2009).

These learning experiences often prove far-reaching. A case in point is that of Gary Windom (MULS, class of 1975). Gary held a student internship at the Legal Aid Society during his second and third years at Marquette. After graduation, he briefly joined the LAS staff before returning to his home state of California. Today, he is Public Defender of Riverside County where he administers an annual budget of $37 million and supervises a staff of 149 trial attorneys. Windom recently served as President of the California Public Defenders Association, and he currently holds the position of Chairman of the Board of the National Legal Aid & Defender Association.

The crucial partnership between the Society and Marquette has been cemented by the fact that a member of the Law School faculty has held a dedicated seat on the Society's board of directors since 1966. Those serving include Professor Ramon A. Klitzke, Dean Robert F. Boden, Professor Patrick K. Hetrick, Professor Lee Wells, Professor Carolyn M. Edwards, Dean Howard B. Eisenberg, Dean Janine P. Geske, and Professor Daniel D. Blinka.[3] In the early 1970s, a representative of the Marquette Student Bar Association also sat on the Society's board.

The Legal Aid Society and the Law School worked closely as partners in the development of both Milwaukee Plan Legal Services and the Public Defender Project [see Historical Documents Section]. Marquette created the Institute on Poverty and the Law to research legal issues of interest to the staff of the Legal Aid Society. That led to publication of an extremely useful deskbook reference for poverty lawyers: Ramon A. Klitzke, ed. *Legal Counseling for the Indigent* (Marquette University Institute on Poverty and the Law, 1968). The book was dedicated to Judge F. Ryan Duffy "who, for many years, has served the people well as President of the Legal Aid Society of Milwaukee."

Currently, LAS is collaborating with Marquette Law School on three projects: the Coalition for Access to Legal Resources, the Milwaukee Foreclosure Mediation Program, and the LAMP for Families Project. The relationship has also worked in the reverse direction. Various members of the Legal Aid Society staff have taught as adjunct professors on the Law School's faculty. These scholar-practitioners and their courses include Mike Guolee (Criminal Procedure), Janine Geske and Paula Lorant (Elderly Law Clinic), Katie Walsh, Rosemary Reyes Cuevas, and Hannah Dugan (Municipal Court Clinic), Christie Christie (Guardian ad Litem Workshop), Jim Walrath (Contemporary Issues in Legal Services to the Poor), Tom Zander (Mental Health Law Workshop), and Pete Koneazny (Law and Social Change).

COMMITMENT TO QUALITY REPRESENTATION

The Legal Aid Society's commitment to high quality service can be seen in the many awards won by our staff attorneys, including Lawyer of the Year Award, Pro Bono Publico Award, Leader in the Law Award, Woman in the Law Award, and Up and Coming Lawyer Award. In recent years, the Society's staff attorneys have served as President of the Milwaukee Bar Association, Chair of the Board of Governors of the State Bar of Wisconsin, Vice Chair of the State Public Defender Board, member of the Federal Judicial Nominating Commission, and member of the U.S. Senate's Committee on the Judiciary Supreme Court Task Force. Other staff attorneys have held faculty appointments at the University of Wisconsin Law School and the University of Wisconsin-Milwaukee School of Social Welfare.

In 1979, the Legal Aid Society confronted a crucial test of its commitment to the principle of effective assistance of counsel in criminal cases. The Society had previously spent many years patiently negotiating reduced caseload levels with Milwaukee County, along with an increased support staff of trained investigators and professional social workers, for its public defender office. Because of the widely acknowledged excellence of LAS's program, particularly under the highly regarded leadership of Chief Staff Attorney William U. "Chip" Burke, the State Public Defender board decided to contract with the Legal Aid Society to continue its representation in Milwaukee.[4] "State

Board OKs Legal Aid Pact" in *Milwaukee Journal* (April 22, 1978);
"Legal Aid Society Backed on Handling Poverty Cases" in *Milwaukee
Journal* (September 10, 1978); "Legal Aid Board OKs State Pact" in
Milwaukee Sentinel (October 23, 1978). A year later, however, in response to a state budget crisis, the SPD Board insisted that the Society raise its caseload per attorney by as much as 60% and concurrently
reduce its supporting complement of investigators and social workers.
The Society declined this invitation. Nonetheless, in a final bid to
persuade Legal Aid to continue the program, SPD officials asked for
and received a joint meeting of the two boards. Although the Society's
contract with the State provided 90% of its revenue, LAS did the un-
thinkable: it voluntarily turned away more than a million dollars a year
in income and ended the public defender program that it had begun
22 years earlier. "Contract Falls Through on Legal Aid for Poor" in
Milwaukee Journal (February 20, 1979). The Society felt that changes
dictated by the State's budget woes would have rendered meaning-
less the constitutional requirement to provide effective assistance of
counsel [see Historical Documents Section]. History repeated itself
in 1989 when the SPD came back to the Legal Aid Society to request
that it provide representation in misdemeanor cases, but again without offering adequate resources to fund a high-quality office. The answer was the same as it had been a decade earlier: LAS declined to
operate a guilty plea mill.

CLIENTS, CASES, AND COUNSEL

While the Legal Aid Society's essential mission has remained unchanged throughout the past century, its clientele has experienced
subtle shifts in demographic and legal trends over time. For example,
when the Society was founded in 1916, Milwaukee was the nation's
twelfth largest city with an estimated population of 118,000. After
reaching a high point of 741,000 in the 1960 census, Milwaukee's
population declined to today's level of 594,000; it now ranks 23rd in
size among all U.S. cities.

Milwaukee has historically been home to a small but vibrant African American community. Willian J. Vollmar, *The Negro in a Midwest
Frontier City: Milwaukee, 1835-1870* (Marquette University: M.A.
thesis, 1968). In the 1919-22 period, African Americans represented

less than 2% of the Society's clientele. Today, that same sector accounts for about 63% of LAS's total client base. The increase reflects the exponential growth in Milwaukee's African American population during the second half of the twentieth century and its extraordinarily high level of poverty. Patrick D. Jones, *The Selma of the North: Civil Rights Insurgency in Milwaukee* (Harvard University Press, 2009); Joe William Trotter, *Black Milwaukee: The Making of an Industrial Proletariat, 1915-45* (Urbana: University of Illinois Press, 2nd ed. 2007); Paul H. Geenan, *Milwaukee's Bronzeville, 1900-1950* (Charleston, SC: Arcadia Publishing, 2006).

This development is paralleled by a similar growth in the city's Latino population. See "Wisconsin's Latino population increases 48%" in *Milwaukee Journal Sentinel* (May 14, 2009); Joseph A. Rodriguez and Walter Sava, *Latinos in Milwaukee* (Charleston, SC: Arcadia Press, 2006). Today, more than one in four children entering Milwaukee Public Schools are of Hispanic heritage. Bilingual signs in English and Spanish are now the norm in all public buildings throughout Milwaukee County. At present, the two nations contributing the greatest number of new immigrants to Wisconsin are Mexico and Laos (mainly Hmong tribal members), whereas Germany and Poland held that distinction in 1916.

These changes reflect the fact that Milwaukee became a "majority minority" city in 1995. Paul R. Voss, et al. "Wisconsin's People: A Portrait of Wisconsin's Population on the Threshold of the 21st Century" in *Wisconsin Blue Book 2003-2004* (Madison: Wisconsin Legislature, 2003) 120. Fifteen years later, it is estimated that more than two out of every three inhabitants in the city belong to racial and ethnic minorities. They include more than a quarter million African Americans, over 115,000 Latinos, 30,000 Asian Americans (1/3 of whom are Hmong), and 8,000 Native Americans who reside in Milwaukee County. *Demographic & Economic Profile – Metro Milwaukee* (Metropolitan Milwaukee Association of Commerce, 2008) 1.

The Legal Aid Society has also seen shifts in the gender and age of its clients. In the 1920-22 period, 33% of clients were female; today that figure has risen to about 58%. This increase reflects the well-documented growth of women in poverty. Diana Pearce, "The Feminization of Poverty: Women, Work and Welfare" in *Urban and Social*

Change Review 11 (1978) 28-36; E.M. Northrop, "The Feminization of Poverty: The Demographic Factor and the Composition of Economic Growth" in *Journal of Economic Issues* 24, no. 1 (1990) 145-60. The trend has been paralleled by a steep rise in the number of children living in poverty. Milwaukee has the fourth highest percentage of poor children of any major American city. "State's poverty rate rises fastest in nation" in *Milwaukee Journal Sentinel* (August 31, 2005). While minors were rarely represented by the Society in the early years, children constitute the largest single age cohort of our clientele today. This change reflects the social disintegration of the family structure over the past generation. When this author joined the staff of the Legal Aid Society in 1971, a single judge sat in the Milwaukee County Children's Court Center; today, nine courts operate fulltime at the Vel R. Phillips Juvenile Justice Center.

Over time, the nature of cases handled by the Society has changed as well. In 1916, for example, wage claims constituted 53% of all LAS cases. As a result of the passage of Wisconsin's Wage Collection Act of 1931, based on a model law proposed by Legal Aid President William Kaumheimer, wage claims represent less than one percent of the Society's workload today. Early annual reports show a significant number of injured worker compensation claims handled by the Society; the subsequent provision of statutory attorney fees, though, has resulted in the relinquishment of this field to the private bar.

In 1916, 8% of cases involved family law matters; by 1970, an evaluation by the National Legal Aid & Defender Association found that 88% of civil cases at LAS involved family law matters (divorce, non-support, paternity, custody). Today, the Civil Division accepts family law cases only in rare circumstances, such as instances of domestic violence where no minor children are in the home. On the other hand, with the growth of the Guardian ad Litem project, about 62% of the Society's total caseload now involve representation of juveniles in matters pending in Family Court or Children's Court. Another major change involves criminal matters. At the outset, LAS eschewed such cases. From 1957 through 1979, however, the Society handled thousands of criminal cases every year; today, once again, it accepts no criminal matters.

Now in the throes of the Great Recession, the Legal Aid Society is currently flooded with housing, unemployment, disability, government benefit, and consumer cases – a further reflection of the national economic crisis shaping local trends. See "Food pantries show 40% increase in assistance" in *Milwaukee Journal Sentinel* (February 4, 2010); "2009 foreclosures top record 2008" in *Milwaukee Journal Sentinel* (January 3, 2010); "Job losses at 70-year high" in *Milwaukee Journal Sentinel* (November 20, 2009); "Food stamp use at all-time high in June" in *Milwaukee Journal Sentinel* (September 4, 2009); "Poverty rate on the rise" in *Milwaukee Journal Sentinel* (August 20, 2009); "Foreclosure filings at record high" in *Milwaukee Journal Sentinel* (August 4, 2009); "Bankruptcy filings up 30% in state at midyear; Jobless rate has nearly doubled in 12 months" in *Milwaukee Journal Sentinel* (July 22, 2009); "Evictions increase as economy drops" in *Milwaukee Journal Sentinel* (November 28, 2008).

Also evolving over the years is the way in which clients arrive at the Legal Aid Society. In the early years, only 5% were self-referred; the rest came by way of recommendations from courts, public offices, churches and synagogues, and social agencies. Today, most clients come to LAS because they have heard about the strong advocacy work the Society is doing in Milwaukee's inner city. This trend is enhanced by the fact that Legal Aid lawyers meet clients at ten conveniently located community outreach sites throughout the county. Of course, judges, social agencies, and inner-city churches continue to refer clients to the Legal Aid Society in large numbers every year, but most come because of the reputation built up over nearly a century of serving Milwaukee's poorest and most vulnerable residents.

The element of change can also be seen in the way the Society assesses new applicants for service to determine whether or not a potential conflict of interest exists with current or past clients. In the 1970s, such conflicts checks were done manually by sorting through tens of thousands of tightly-packed, 5x7-inch, index cards, some of them dating back to the 1940s, which were stored alphabetically in massive filing cabinets. These office relics were eventually discarded in favor of today's Kemps Case Management software package, which electronically scans our client database at literally the touch of a finger to disclose potential conflicts.

Another change occurred in 2004 when LAS stopped ordering bound volumes of the *Wisconsin Reports* for its small in-house law library. A new generation of lawyers have been trained to do electronic research on such legal databases as LEIXIS™, Westlaw™, Books Unbound™, and Fastcase®.

The lawyers who staff the Society's programs represent another noticeable change down through the years. In the 1970s, most attorneys were recent law school graduates who worked at LAS for two or three years before leaving for private practice or government service. Today, more staff lawyers tend to make poverty law a career. Currently, in addition to younger attorneys, the Society has a number of lawyers who have served on staff for more than twenty years. The admixture provides a blend of energy and vibrancy on the one hand, with experience and leadership on the other. The combination redounds to the benefit of our clients.

Not everything, of course, has changed. Chief Staff Attorney Catey Doyle sits in a chair and at a desk first purchased in 1971 for former Executive Director Dave Berman. And Doyle possesses the same level of dedication to the needs of the poor that past generations of Legal Aid lawyers have displayed on behalf of Milwaukee's poorest and most vulnerable residents for nearly a century.

NOTES

1. The principal difference focused on Dolan's view that individual client service should be the overriding priority while the younger generation sought systemic reform of social, political, and economic institutions through test cases, class actions, and legislative advocacy. This conflict played out in peculiar fashion. For example, Ted Seaver, head of the Milwaukee Tenants Union, engaged Freedom Through Equality to represent his organization, but he simultaneously referred all individual tenants facing eviction to the Legal Aid Society for representation in court.

   Secondly, Dolan was concerned that a staff attorney's independent legal judgment and duty of loyalty to an individual client could be compromised by representing social and political advocacy groups. An example of this occurred when an African American board member at FTE (Attorney Lloyd Barbee) accused Attorney Steve Steinglass of creating racial divisiveness by rallying members of the Wisconsin Welfare Rights Organization (an FTE client) to support his candidacy for Executive Director against an

African American candidate (Attorney Terence L. Pitts). Braun, *Policies, Programs, Politics, and the Poor* 17.

Finally, Dolan's long experience as administrator of LAS led her to avoid controversial actions that might compromise fragile public support, especially funding, for the Legal Aid Society's mission. These conflicts came to a head in legal services offices all over the country. Congress shared some of Dolan's reservations; eventually it imposed numerous restrictions designed to eliminate "social engineering" and "political advocacy" by federal legal services programs.

2. Braun's paper must be used with caution on one point. He repeatedly fails to distinguish Milwaukee Plan Legal Services as a separate organizational entity from Milwaukee Legal Services. The former, run by LAS, ended its OEO grant on September 30, 1969; the latter group succeeded as OEO grantee on October 1, 1969. Thus, much of the conflict he writes about occurred between MLS (not MPLS) and FTE.

3. When the Wisconsin Equal Justice Foundation decided to solicit funds from Milwaukee law firms, Dean Eisenberg resigned from that board so that he could continue serving on the Legal Aid Society of Milwaukee board without a conflict of interest.

4. Burke is now Deputy Federal Defender of Wisconsin.

14

A TIME OF TRANSITION

In the long history of the Legal Aid Society, four discrete periods stand out: (i) the early years (1916-29) when the organization was founded and got off to a strong start in the areas of direct client service, community education, and legislative advocacy; (ii) the middle years (1930-65) marked by the Great Depression, World War II, and the McCarthy era when the Society endured funding cuts, staff shrinkage, and a correspondingly pinched vision of its role as advocate for the poor; (iii) the turbulent transition years (1965-71) when increased funding, infusion of a younger and more dynamic staff, outside pressure from community activists, and new leadership combined to complete the evolution from social service agency to public interest law firm; and (iv) the modern era (1972 to the present) when the Society's comprehensive advocacy before administrative, judicial, and legislative tribunals enabled it to achieve the original promise envisioned by its founders. The following account represents a firsthand view of the pivotal transition year of 1971 in the Society's development.

* * *

My personal inspiration to become a poverty lawyer was rooted primarily in the legal career of my grandfather, Ray Cannon, whom newspaper obituaries had described as "a modern Robin Hood" and "a hard-fighting champion of the underdog." Education also played a major role, especially the social justice values encountered in my eight years of Jesuit education[1] and the University of Wisconsin Law School's focus on public service and its renowned law-in-action tradition, which related academic instruction to contemporary social, political, and economic conditions.[2] While studying in Madison, I clerked in the public defender program at Dane County Legal Services and actively participated in the Law Students Civil Rights Research Council.

In addition, there was a more compelling personal reason. Returning home in 1969 from thirteen months of combat in Vietnam, I was acutely conscious of having been given a rare second chance at life, one that so many fellow Marines had not been as lucky to receive. I vowed not to squander this precious gift by pursuing superficial goals like fortune, prestige, or power. It became deeply important to me that my future career in law be invested with a meaningful purpose, one that would justify my improbable survival in numerous encounters with death. Somehow, I hoped the opportunity might present itself to serve the poor and needy, and if at all possible, to do so in my own hometown of Milwaukee.

Thus, in the fall of 1970, it seemed only natural for me to make my way to the Legal Aid Society's new headquarters, located on the Marquette University campus, to drop off a resume and letter of application for a staff attorney position. After climbing up the nearly vertical flight of stairs to the second floor, I handed a letter and resume to the receptionist. She asked me to wait a moment while she delivered my envelope inside. Within seconds, the legendary Julia B. Dolan bounded out of her office and invited me back for a chat. Her diminutive stature – four feet, ten inches in height - belied her forceful (if not contentious) reputation in the city. However, she immediately disarmed me with a friendly smile and warm demeanor.

Julia announced that she would soon wind up her epic career at the Legal Aid Society, which had begun well before I was born. After having been widowed for two years, she explained that she had recently become engaged to marry Ray McClelland, then Executive Director of United Community Services, the Society's main funding source. She thought the dual relationship might create the appearance of a conflict of interest and, thus, decided to retire instead.

During a quick tour of the premises, she also told me that the Society had just moved into its new offices to be closer to the resources of Marquette University's Law Library. It was clear from her remarks that the organization was about to undergo a significant transition. For more than three decades, Julia Dolan had personified the Legal Aid Society as she guided it through a prolonged funding drought that had forced her to balance minuscule budgets against a massive need for legal services to the poor. Within the past few years, though,

38. Julia B. Dolan, Superintendent and Executive Attorney of the Legal Aid Society, 1939-71. *Courtesy of Legal Aid Society of Milwaukee.*

and for the first time in its long history, LAS had been able to deploy a significant staff with OEO and public defender funding. This allowed the Society to address some systemic issues facing our client population.

What struck me during that first visit, though, was her attention to detail. She frequently interrupted our conversation to answer the telephone herself while simultaneously typing a memo of the call for a client's file or an attorney's notes. To avoid waste, as I would later learn, she recycled all paper that had only been used on one side. Her files were a model of organization and each entry was individually typed by her on an old fashioned manual typewriter. She personally conducted each intake interview to determine client eligibility. Her management style had been largely dictated by decades of penurious budgets that forced her to economize on services and rely on volunteers and part-time staff.

Even though our views on advocacy differed quite dramatically, I always considered it an honor to be the last staff attorney hired by Julia. Six years later, when I was appointed Executive Director, my first note of congratulations came from her and it was accompanied by an invitation to lunch. When I resigned in 1981 to join the Marquette law faculty, she again sent a warm note offering her best wishes. Our final meeting occurred a year before Julia's death, when Carole Wenerowicz arranged to take a photograph of the five living executive directors of the Society who had served continuously between 1939 and 1995. The picture session was followed by a memorable lunch at the Pfister Hotel that included an affectionate sharing of stories about interesting people and events during our combined seven decades of service.

Among the former were two of the Legal Aid Society's great characters, a pair of identical twins, Clint and Roger ("Bill") Finnegan. The bachelor brothers had piercing blue eyes, a mop of sandy-colored hair, the same rumpled clothing, and a worldly look that came from having heard it all in twenty years at the Society. The Finnegans never owned a car. They weren't the kind of lawyers to tote fancy briefcases either. They walked everywhere together with a sheaf of legal files under their arms. Nobody − judges, clients, or even Legal Aid staff − could tell them apart, and they didn't make any effort to dispel the confusion. They knew intuitively that there was no point in providing an elaborate explanation that would only have to be repeated twenty times each day.

If there was one thing the Finnegans avoided, it was wasting time. Like Julia's files, theirs were models of organization. Carefully typed case chronologies on yellow, legal-size paper summarized every client matter. Taking over a case from the Finnegans involved no more than a quick scan of their concise notes. Even a newcomer like me could be brought up to date in a matter of minutes. The Finnegan brothers also had a great sense of humor, one that bordered on the sarcastic and was dryly delivered in the Irish tradition with no change in tone or facial expression. And they had an inexhaustible fund of stories. In their time, they had handled thousands of divorces, bankruptcies, evictions, small claims matters, and paternity cases. Throughout it all, they remained entirely unpretentious and consummately professional. It was a pleasure to learn the ropes from these two pioneering lawyers for the poor.

Another great character in the office was my first secretary, the aptly named Mae Looney. She had worked for Julia Dolan prior to my arrival at the Legal Aid Society. Mae was a chain-smoking, quick-typing denizen of 12th and Wisconsin. Although more than twice my age, she treated this newly minted lawyer like one of her favorite nephews. Looney loved the English language and maintained a deep interest in the precise use of words. She would have been a world champion speller had she ever taken the time to enter a spelling bee. My most frequently consulted book has always been the dictionary, but Mae was a natural born orthographer – with a great sense of humor to boot.

Like the Finnegan brothers, she seemed to have a decidedly cynical take on our part of the world and delighted in telling the most outlandish stories culled from her vast repertoire. Her eyes would roll theatrically, and her red face, brightly painted with two thick bands of lipstick, would light up during these sessions. Mae fit in well at the Legal Aid Society, perhaps because her offbeat sense of humor always struck me as being well suited for a character in one of Flannery O'Connor's short stories.

Mae's rules for young lawyers were strict. Only one preliminary draft of a document would be typed by her. I would then be given one chance to make a single set of editorial changes before she typed the second and final draft, which consisted of an original and three carbon copies (on crinkly onion-skin paper) pounded out at high speed with exceptional accuracy. She worked on an old-fashioned manual typewriter, which was set into the well of a heavy wooden secretarial desk.

The spring of 1971 marked a sea change in the history of the Legal Aid Society of Milwaukee. Julia Dolan retired on April 30 and Dave Berman took over on the following day. Prior to taking charge, he had served two years as an Assistant District Attorney and two years as Deputy Director in the Society's Public Defender Project.

Dave was in many ways the polar opposite of Julia Dolan. He was a large, gregarious man with a finely honed political instinct and a gift for telling funny stories. Julia had spent only a small portion of the first Kaumheimer bequest on the move from Jackson Street. Berman quickly blew through the remainder of those funds by purchasing air-conditioning for the new office at 12th and Wisconsin, and by buying state-of-the-art IBM Selectric typewriters, the office's first photocopier, dictaphones, fireproof filing cabinets, and new touchtone telephones to replace the older rotary dial models.

Dave was a "big-picture" manager. In contrast to Julia, he paid no attention to details. In six years as Executive Director, Berman never answered an unscreened telephone call or typed a single word. He appointed capable supervising attorneys (most of them first hired by Dolan) like Mike Guolee, Tony Karpowicz, Bill Jennaro, Jim Rudd, and Jordan Reich to lead his staff, and then he delegated broad authority to them to manage their respective divisions. As a group, these new leaders injected a large dose of energy into an organization whose outlook had atrophied. There was no doubt that the Society's old guard had been replaced by a more dynamic generation.

When I joined the staff of the Civil Division in July, on the cusp of this transition, Jordan Reich had just become the new Chief Staff Attorney.[3] Originally hired by Julia Dolan, this gifted advocate and superb mentor had only been on board for six months. A former Army Captain and Vietnam War veteran, Jordy was extroverted, brash, and funny. His work at Legal Aid was later featured in "No Help Needed in Stepping Down," *Milwaukee Sentinel* (June 15, 1974). He also wrote a valuable M.P.A. degree thesis on the management and organizational history of the Legal Aid Society. With Berman's green light, Reich was a force for change at LAS.

One of the first things the two of us did was review longtime office policies, in place since about 1940, that struck us as antiquated [see Historical Documents Section]. For example, the policy required that we could commence divorce actions "only when they serve a sound social purpose and are recommended by a family agency." Minutes from the 1940s and 1950s revealed that the board of directors individually approved acceptance of each divorce case. Similarly, in bankruptcy proceedings, the existing rule specified that the Society would only represent debtors "with a reputation for honesty" who had made "every reasonable effort" to pay their bills, and whose creditors would not allow debts to be amortized. Concluding that such rules improperly required us to make non-legal judgments about our client's personal lives, we quickly jettisoned the standing policies. From that point on, we limited our evaluation of the client to the legal merits of his or her case.

The Society's new leadership got off to a fast start. In the first few weeks of 1972, LAS won three major impact decisions in state and federal court. In the first case, U.S. District Court Judge Myron L. Gordon issued a published opinion declaring that indigents had a constitutional right to petition for bankruptcy without prepayment of the filing fees mandated by Congress (*Application of Ottman*). Within days of that decision, the Wisconsin Supreme Court reversed a criminal conviction and vacated a five-year prison sentence based on insufficient evidence (*State v. Hall*). A couple of weeks later, the same court recognized that juveniles had a due process right to disqualify a trial court judge for demonstrable prejudice (*State ex rel. Mitchell v. Bowman*). By year's end, a total of ten cases resulted in published decisions. Together, they put the Legal Aid Society of Milwaukee on the jurisprudential map in a major way for the first time since LAS had given up its OEO funding.

Staff attorneys were also making their mark on the legal landscape in the field of trial advocacy. In one sensational murder case, Berman and Mike Guolee represented an inmate at the Milwaukee County House of Correction who was charged with killing a fellow prisoner. "Workhouse Inmate Dies; Throat Was Cut" in *Milwaukee Journal* (February 24, 1972), "Inmate Charged in Slaying" in *Milwaukee Journal* (February 25, 1972). After a lengthy trial, the jury returned a verdict of not guilty. *State v. Wendell Harris*, case no. H-6435. "Jury Clears Inmate in Cell Murder" in *Milwaukee Journal* (September 16, 1972).

Another memorable homicide case was *State v. Willie Ross*, case no. H-655. Ross was convicted of murder and sentenced to up to 25 years in prison for shooting another man in a tavern brawl. Staff attorney Pat Devitt appealed the conviction on the ground that the trial judge erred in refusing to instruct the jury on manslaughter as a lesser included offense. The Supreme Court agreed with Devitt, reversed the conviction, and ordered a new trial. *Ross v. State*, 61 Wis.2d 160 (1973); "Retrial Granted In Shooting Death" in *Milwaukee Sentinel* (November 13, 1973). Devitt then represented Ross at his second jury trial and won a complete acquittal on all charges. "Suspect Found Not Guilty" in *Milwaukee Journal* (January 23, 1975). Later that year, Dave Berman reported to the Society's board that Felony Division lawyers had won not-guilty verdicts in ten of their last nineteen jury trials. The record reflected in large measure the trial skills of Chief Staff Attorney Mike Guolee and the fact that he made the time to personally observe and coach his staff of young attorneys in the courtroom.

Notwithstanding the fact that Wisconsin abolished capital punishment in 1853, I was privileged to handle the Society's only death penalty case. It involved Michiah Shobek, a Milwaukee man who had been convicted in 1974 of murder in The Bahamas. The Bahamian Supreme Court had turned down his appeal in the following year. His mother, a cleaning woman at North Division High School, called me a week before her son's scheduled execution and requested assistance. Quick research at the Marquette Law Library showed that the only legal recourse available was to lodge an appeal with the Judicial Committee of Britain's Privy Council in London. My first call, to Shobek's court-appointed counsel in The Bahamas, revealed that the barrister was not interested in a further appeal. Due to the press of time, his refusal left only one remedy – a diplomatic initiative based on the fact that Shobek was an American citizen.

I called the White House and spoke to Philip W. Buchen, President Ford's Legal Counsel. He agreed to have the State Department communicate a message through diplomatic channels to Sir Milo Butler, Governor General of the Commonwealth of The Bahamas, requesting commutation of the death sentence or a six-month delay of execution on the grounds that evidence of Shobek's untreated mental illness had not been presented to the jury. U.S. Ambassador Seymour Weiss personally delivered the appeal in Nassau just three days before the date set for hanging. On the day before the execution, the U.S. request was denied by the Governor General. Within hours, I called the White House again, this time to seek President Ford's personal intervention in the matter. I spoke for forty-five minutes to Chief of Staff Richard B. Cheney, who told me that he did not believe it was appropriate for the President to become involved in the internal court system of another country. Shobek was killed just eight hours later. The Bahamian government refused the grief-stricken family's request to return the remains for burial in Milwaukee.[4]

In dialectical terms, our generation was the antithesis to the Dolan Era's thesis. Within the space of a few years, the Legal Aid Society had morphed from an old-fashioned, almost somnolent, social service agency into an aggressive, modern public-interest law firm. That change was made possible by a combination of (i) Julia Dolan and the board winning the federal OEO grant in 1966 and the public defender contract in 1969; (ii) Dolan's hiring a complement of reform-minded younger lawyers to staff the programs, (iii) community pressure from social activists who pushed the reluctant Society into law reform mode in 1967, (iv) the critical 1970 NLADA evaluation that spurred the board in a new direction, and (v) the dynamic leadership of Dave Berman.

Taking note of the generational change in advocates for the poor, then Attorney General Nicholas deB. Katzenbach noted "that a new breed of lawyers is emerging, dedicated to using law as an instrument of orderly and constructive social change." *The Extension of Legal Services to the Poor: Conference Proceedings* (Washington, D.C.: U.S. Government Printing Office, 1964) 11. The late 1960s and early 1970s were exciting years of political and social ferment, brought about by complex forces on both local and national levels. The transition was chronicled in Earl Johnson, Jr., *Justice and Reform: The Formative Years of the American Legal Services Program* (New Brunswick, NJ: Transaction Books, 1978); Jerold S. Auerbach, *Unequal Justice: Lawyers and Social Change in Modern America* (New York: Oxford University Press, 1976); Comment, "The New Public Interest Lawyers" in *Yale Law Journal* 79 (1970) 1069-1152. It was a privilege to be part of that new breed. And as the last direct link to Julia Dolan and her era, I always felt that she was quietly proud of the changes wrought by her successors.

History has a habit of turning out in unanticipated ways. In the case of the OEO legal service funds, for example, their relinquishment was initially seen as a loss for the Legal Aid Society. Four years later, however, OEO came back to the Society and requested that it reapply for federal funding. After consulting with Milwaukee Legal Services and Freedom Through Equality, the Society's board declined the invitation [see Historical Documents Section]. Many in Congress objected to what they felt was the pursuit of political ideology and social engineering by some federal programs. Lawmakers eventually imposed a series of punitive restrictions on the use of legal services funds, which included prohibitions on welfare reform litigation, class actions, legislative advocacy, certain kinds of evictions, desegregation cases, voting rights issues, representation of prisoners and undocumented aliens, and the filing of writs of habeas corpus and bankruptcy petitions. See *e.g.* 42 U.S.C. § 2996 *et seq.*; 45 C.F.R. §§ 1615, 1617, 1626, 1633, 1637. Had the Society continued its Milwaukee Plan Legal Services project, it would not have been able to litigate many of the cases that it was able to do as a privately-funded corporation. Thus, LAS today represents more than 16,000 prisoners in the current class action suit challenging management of the Milwaukee County Jail (*Christensen v. Sullivan*), and urges passage of legislation regulating loan-sharking activities by predatory lenders, to name just two of the most recent actions engaged in by Legal Aid Society lawyers. The result is a rich irony: these were the very type of matters personally eschewed by Julia Dolan, but they were conceived and litigated by a host of Legal Aid Society lawyers ranging from Jordan Reich to Jim Walrath – both of whom were first hired by the longtime Executive Attorney.

NOTES

1. The core Jesuit principle was to educate "men (and women) for others," (*homines pro aliis*). See Pedro Arrupe, *Men for Others: Education for Social Justice and Social Action Today* (Washington, D.C.: Jesuit Secondary Education Association, 1974).

2. Paul D. Carrington and Erika King, "Law and the Wisconsin Idea" in *Journal of Legal Education* 47 (1997) 297-340; Stewart Macaulay, "Wisconsin's Legal Tradition" in *Gargoyle* 24 (1994) 6-10; John E. Conway, "The Law School: Service to the State and Nation" in 1968 *Wisconsin Law Review* 345-48.

3. The position of Chief Staff Attorney was newly created by Dave Berman in 1971. It was an outgrowth of the neighborhood office Chief Attorney

positions in the Society's Milwaukee Plan Legal Services Project (1966-69). William A. Jennaro was described in board minutes as Chief Attorney of the Children's Court office in 1970 under Julia Dolan. His successors served as Chief Staff Attorney in the Children's Court Division: James D. Rudd (1971-74), Rudolph Becker (1975-77), Charles F. Kahn, Jr. (1978-79), Carole Wenerowicz (1980-94), Julia E. Vosper (1994-2000), Michael J. Vruno, Jr. (2000-06), and Shelia Hill-Roberts (2007 to present). Chief Staff Attorneys in the Civil Division have been Jordan B. Reich (1971-74), Thomas G. Cannon (1974-77), Janine P. Geske (1977-81), James M. Brennan (1981-2007), and Catherine M. Doyle (2007 to present). In the old Criminal Division, John Lauerman held the title of Director of the Public Defender Project, 1969-71; his successors, though, were Chief Staff Attorneys Michael D. Guolee (1971-75), Martin E. Love (1976-77), and William U. Burke (1977-79).

4. The Shobek case received extensive press coverage. See, for example, "Milwaukee man to hang for murder in Bahamas" in *Chicago Tribune* (October 16, 1976); "Ford Relays Plea in Hanging" in *Milwaukee Journal* (October 17, 1976); "Ex-Milwaukeean Hanged for 1974 Bahamas Slaying" in *Milwaukee Journal* (October 19, 1976); "Milwaukee Man Is Hanged in Bahamas for Murder" in *New York Times* (October 20, 1976); "Bahamas hangs Milwaukee killer" in *Chicago Tribune* (October 20, 1976).

15

AT 12ᵀᴴ AND WISCONSIN

RAZED BUILDING HAS TWO FLOORS, BUT MANY STORIES

By

WILLIAM JANZ[1]

The workmen who tore down a building recently insisted it had only two stories, but the people who had worked there knew it had countless stories. President Kennedy was one story and Big Olive was another. Supreme Court Justice Janine Geske had been an occupant, and a stripper named X-Rated Stardust has been a much recalled visitor, of the small building on the northwest corner of N. 12th St. and W. Wisconsin Ave.

"The heat would go off and we'd work with our coats on," attorney Thomas G. Cannon said. "The windows would ice over and the ice would be on the inside."

For 10 years, until 1981, Cannon represented the Big Olives of our world, working for many of the outrageously poor and some of the shamelessly colorful, at the Legal Aid Society of Milwaukee, which had offices on the second floor. The poor have lines instead of appointments, so, often, homeless people, prostitutes, evicted people, harassed people, unemployed people and people who didn't have much of anything but misery lined up in the waiting room, down the stairs, past the bakery and out onto the street.

And then Big Olive would show up. No one knew why she called herself that, but the oddness of her name was secondary to the oddness of her fashion: She always wore a wedding dress. Sometimes, on a quiet day in the office, she'd stake out a couch and take a nap, decked out in her wedding apparel. "She was a startling sight," Cannon said.

From the window in Cannon's office, "I would see George Reedy, former press secretary to President Lyndon Johnson, walking down the Avenue, followed by a woman wearing a wedding dress, followed by the pigeon feeders." Legal Aid was across the street from one of the earth's primary feeding grounds for pigeons. And two sisters – dressed the same, exactly the same, always the same – one apparently blind, one leading the other, fed the pigeons every day.

Meanwhile, exotic dancers stood in line next to the very common homeless, waiting to get problems solved. Cannon remembered a stripper, who wanted to have her name changed to something appropriate to her work. She wanted to be called X-Rated Stardust.

On the south side of the street, Gesu Catholic Church is so huge that it has an upper church and a lower church, and Jerry Szymczak nearly drove into the lower church recently when he saw that the building across the street was missing. He recalled 1960, when Jack Kennedy's presidential primary headquarters was on the second floor. Szymczak – "I was in the fourth grade before I could spell my name" – was a volunteer assigned to Jack's brother, Bobby.

"He was a great organizer," Szymczak said. "He'd think about a problem, then boom, boom, boom, that's the way he solved it. Bobby would have been a better president than Jack."

39. Legal Aid Society headquarters at 1204 West Wisconsin Avenue, 1970-93.
Courtesy of Marquette University Archives.

But gunshots stopped both from being any better than they were.
During the 1970s, after Justice Geske graduated from the Marquette University Law School, which was a block away, she joined Legal Aid and her first job was cleaning an office.

"My predecessor didn't believe in file cases," she said. "There were 900 files on the floor."

She added that she never left her heart in San Francisco but she did leave part of it at 12th and Wisconsin: "Nothing surprises me on the Supreme Court because I heard it all at Legal Aid," she said.

Grebe's bakery was downstairs, where students, homeless people, professors and District Attorney E. Michael McCann often lined up to get a quick, and often sugary, meal after attending Mass at Gesu.

In June 1977, I wrote my first column for the Milwaukee Sentinel, about what had been the most important building on the Marquette campus. The building wasn't Gesu Church, or Johnston Hall, it was Schewe's Drugstore, which had been located in our how dear, departed building. For most of the first half of the 20th century, Schewe's, pronounced Chevy's, was where students met for Cokes when they didn't have 3,000 local beer joints to inhabit.

When he was executive director of Legal Aid, Cannon displayed the motto of his grandfather, Ray, who was one of the best trial attorneys in the state. Cannon still has his granddad's motto on his desk at O'Neil, Cannon & Hollman: "In the thousands of cases I've tried, I have represented the strong and the weak, the rich and the poor, but never the strong against the weak and never the rich against the poor."

Wonderful credo, whether it was posted at 12th and Wisconsin, or east of the Milwaukee River, where Cannon now has his office.

Cannon's old place, which was Big Olive's old place, which was Justice Geske's old place, is gone. Surrounded by the city, and some of its dismalness, Marquette needs all the grass it can grow. And it has ordered grass to grow there.

NOTE

1. Reprinted with permission of the Copyright Clearance Center from the *Milwaukee Journal Sentinel* (April 29, 1997). The 1204 West Wisconsin Avenue site is now the location of Zilber Hall, Marquette University's student services building.

16
EQUAL JUSTICE MEDAL

The Equal Justice Medal is the Legal Aid Society of Milwaukee's highest award. It was established by the board, at the suggestion of Executive Director Thomas K. Zander, in 1991 to recognize extraordinary contributions to the Society's mission of equal justice for the poor. In 2006, at the request of Mrs. Erica P. John, the board named the award the *Thomas G. Cannon Equal Justice Medal* to honor Cannon's joint contributions to the Legal Aid Society and to the Archdiocese of Milwaukee Supporting Fund. The Medal has thus far been conferred on the following:

1991

Julia Dolan McClelland, longtime Executive Attorney of the Society
Helen Bader, generous financial supporter of the Society's work (posthumously)

40. The Legal Aid Society's Equal Justice Medal.
Courtesy of Legal Aid Society of Milwaukee.

Janine P. Geske, former Chief Staff Attorney of the Society and jurist

1992

Gerald M. Elliott, Treasurer and director of the Society

1993

Robert A. Christensen, President and director of the Society
Brother Paschal (Charles W.) Stubbs, director of the Society and head of the Shalom Center

1996

Brother Booker Ashe, director of the Society and founder of Milwaukee's House of Peace
Laurence C. Hammond, President and director of the Society
Thomas K. Zander, Executive Director of the Society

1998

Professor Carolyn M. Edwards, director of the Society

2000

Olga Valcourt-Schwartz, director of the Society and leader in Milwaukee's Latino community

2001

Stephen M. Glynn, President and director of the Society
David S. Berman, Executive Director of the Society
Judge John W. Reynolds, director of the Society, former Governor of Wisconsin, and Chief Judge of the U.S. District Court

2006

Bill Janz, *Milwaukee Sentinel* courthouse reporter who chronicled the Society's work for twenty-five years
Dr. James Cameron, founder of America's Black Holocaust Museum. "Dr. James Cameron receives Equal Justice Medal for life's work" in *Milwaukee Courier* (September 16, 2006)
James A. Walrath, Executive Director of the Society

2007

Judge Vel R. Phillips, pioneer civil rights leader and first African American jurist in Wisconsin.

Meg Kissinger, reporter for the *Milwaukee Journal Sentinel* and author of a prize-winning series on the plight of the mentally ill.

Christine Neuman-Ortiz, founder of Voces de la Frontera, an emphatic advocate for immigration justice.

41. Judge Vel R. Phillips was awarded the Legal Aid Society's Equal Justice Medal in 2007. *Courtesy of Wisconsin Historical Society* (WHi-28115).

2008

Professors Keith A. Findley and John A. Pray, co-founders of the Wisconsin Innocence Project,_which works on behalf of the wrong-fully convicted.

Justice Louis B. Butler, Jr., first African American member of the Wisconsin Supreme Court.

Wendy Reed Bosworth, President and director of the Society

42. Justice Louis B. Butler, Jr. was awarded the Legal Aid Society's Equal Justice Medal in 2008. *Courtesy of Wisconsin Supreme Court.*

2009

Felmers O. Chaney, pioneer civil rights leader and longtime head of the Milwaukee branch of the NAACP and the Urban League

Jennifer A. Ortiz, Administrator of Wisconsin's Equal Rights Division

Professor Michele M. LaVigne, advocate for rights of the deaf within the legal system

2010

Dr. Earnestine Willis, founder of the Center for the Advancement of Urban Children, a voice for healthcare as a human right

Ellen Bravo, feminist, longtime activist for working women, and head of Milwaukee's 9to5 chapter

Peter Isely, advocate for victims of childhood clerical sexual abuse

17
VALUED SUPPORTERS

More than half a million clients have been helped by the Legal Aid Society of Milwaukee during the past 94 years. They could not have obtained high-quality legal representation without the generous support of our donors, large and small, who contribute nearly $4 million a year in operating revenue to provide direct client service to the poor. These gifts represent an important investment in the social and economic betterment of our community. The case for making such gifts was recently urged by an editorial in the *New York Times*. After noting that civil legal aid for the poor was "a chronically underfunded need," the editorial went on to say:

> In the real world – unlike courtroom TV – people usually get the justice they can pay for, and those who cannot afford lawyers end up bearing an unfair burden. People need decent representation when doing battle with bad landlords and employers, callous health maintenance organizations and government agencies, disgruntled business partners and grasping relatives. And in an era of predatory home loans, the legal needs of distressed homeowners are urgent and steadily rising.
>
> Advocates for the poor argue, persuasively, that outlays for civil legal services are budgetary pennies that save many dollars. A foreclosure prevented is an eviction avoided, a family kept from homelessness – and a considerable burden lifted from the government's social-service safety net. With legal help, poor people can avoid litigation, easing the load on judges and courtrooms. They can get food stamps, leveraging federal dollars in an underused program. If they avoid the poorhouse, they will have, by definition, more money to spend, increasing sales tax revenues and benefiting local businesses.

Excerpted from "A False and Unfair Economy" (January 2, 2009). A University of Southern California law professor reaffirms this point:

In the end, the cost of providing counsel must be balanced against the hidden costs of not providing representation; the social costs of displacing a frail senior, for example, can dwarf those of providing legal help to avoid the eviction ... We can no longer afford not to guarantee equal justice to the poor in civil cases.

Clare Pastore, "Rescuing Legal Aid" in *Los Angeles Times* (February 23, 2009). If there is one principle the Legal Aid Society's donors have always understood, it is the economic soundness of making a personal investment in justice.

The Society's first and most consistent donor has been the United Way of Greater Milwaukee. Starting with the first combined community fundraising drive in 1916, United Way and its predecessor organizations have assisted the Society every single year for the past 94 years. During Legal Aid's first half-century, United Way provided virtually the sole outside financial support for the Society. That commitment ensured the organization's survival through two world wars and the Great Depression when other legal aid societies around the country were closing their doors for lack of funds. To date, United Way's cumulative gifts for our mission total almost $7 million. It is a measure of how well LAS has broadened its funding base that United Way's contribution to the Society's annual budget has fallen from 99% in 1965 to about 5% today. Nonetheless, the steady yearly support has allowed LAS to leverage United Way dollars effectively to bring in additional funding sources.

By far, the biggest financial supporter of the Society has been Milwaukee County government. This close relationship, which has occasionally turned adversarial, began in 1920 when the Clerk of Civil Courts joined the Society's early board of directors. On two occasions (1932-50, 1969-78), the County Board of Supervisors generously gave the Society rent-free quarters in the Public Safety Building. Since then, Milwaukee County has purchased nearly $50 million in legal services from the Society for providing representation mandated by statute or constitution in the criminal, family, probate, and children's courts.

Various departments of the State of Wisconsin have given more than $2 million to the Society since its first contract with the State Public Defender Board in 1978. Other state agencies funding LAS include the Department of Children and Families, Wisconsin Housing and Economic Development Authority, and Department of Health Services. Beginning in 1988, the Wisconsin Trust Account Founda-

43. Philanthropist Helen Bader, a longtime supporter of the Legal Aid Society of Milwaukee. *Courtesy of Helen Bader Foundation.*

tion has provided cumulative grants of more than $1 million to support the Legal Aid Society's vital mission. These sums are derived from interest on lawyers' trust accounts and a per capita annual assessment of individual attorneys mandated by the Wisconsin Supreme Court.

In 1982-83, a mature graduate student in social work arrived at the Legal Aid Society to do a field placement. Her name was Helen Bader, and she turned out to be one of the most significant figures, and generous donors, in the history of the Society. Helen was born in Aberdeen, South Dakota, in 1927. Upon earning a degree in botany at Milwaukee Downer College, she and her husband, Alfred Bader, created a business that became one of the most successful start-up concerns of its era: Aldrich Chemical Company.

After successfully raising their children, Helen returned to school to earn a master's degree in social work. Her graduate studies field placement at the Legal Aid Society introduced her to many people in need, especially single mothers, the homeless, and adults suffering from mental illness. After graduation, she worked with elderly residents at the Milwaukee Jewish Home, many of whom suffered from dementia.

Quietly, Helen also adopted a low-key style of philanthropy that simply involved writing checks to worthwhile charities. The Legal Aid Society was one of her favorites. After her death in 1989, her family established the Helen Bader Foundation to carry on her generous legacy in the community. To date, more than a million dollars has been given to the Legal Aid Society of Milwaukee in her name. The Society honors Helen Bader by continuing our work on behalf of Milwaukee's most fragile residents – work made possible by her extraordinary compassion.

Erica P. John was born of Austrian parents in Rome, Italy, in 1932. Her father was attached to the Austrian Embassy there. Erica was educated in the city's Classical Lyceum and at the University of Rome. In 1955, she came to the United States to pursue graduate studies in art history at Columbia University. While in New York, Erica met Harry G. John, Jr., heir to the Miller Brewing Company. She eventually moved to Milwaukee and married Harry. The couple raised all nine of their children here. As the youngsters grew up, Erica gradually became more heavily involved in philanthropy.

For twenty-five years, she labored quietly as a nonprofit director in service to a variety of religious and humanitarian project in Milwaukee's inner city as well as in developing countries around the globe. In 1984, she was elected President of De Rance, Inc., then the largest Catholic charitable foundation in the world. Eight years later, she and her daughter Paula helped found the Archdiocese of Milwaukee Supporting Fund. In 2009, that organization was renamed the Erica P. John Fund.

Among Erica's many honors and awards are the Pro Ecclesia et Pontifice Cross, which was personally conferred on her by the late Pope John Paul II at the Vatican. She also received an honorary Doctor of Laws degree from Marquette University and the Charles Carroll of Carrollton Award in Catholic Philanthropy from FADICA (Foundation Donors Interested in Catholic Activities).

For more than half a century, Erica John has been deeply committed to the support of programs serving Milwaukee's and the world's poor-

44. Philanthropist Erica P. John, major donor to the Legal Aid Society of Milwaukee.
Courtesy of Erica P. John Fund.

est. In 2006, she and her co-directors (daughter Paula N. John and Archbishop Timothy M. Dolan) announced a grant of $1 million to the Legal Aid Society of Milwaukee. The gift, the largest single donation in the organization's history, recognized the Society's 90 years of advocacy on behalf of the city's most vulnerable residents. During the past few years, these visionary supporters have been joined by a variety of private-sector funding sources: Charles D. Jacobus Family Foundation, Everyday Philanthropists, Faye McBeath Foundation, Foley Family Foundation, Forest County Potawatomi Community Foundation, Gene and Ruth Posner Foundation, Gesu Parish Endowment, Greater Milwaukee Foundation, Impact Fund, Institute of Foreclosure Legal Assistance (a project of the Center for Responsible Lending, managed by the National Association of Consumer Advocates), Jane Bradley Pettit Foundation, Joseph Zilber Family Foundation, Herbert H. Kohl Charities, M&I Bank, Milwaukee Bar Association Foundation, Northwestern Mutual Foundation, Park Bank Foundation, Potawatomi Bingo Casino, Ralph Evinrude Foundation, RBC Dain Rauscher Foundation, Robert W. Baird Foundation, State Bar of Wisconsin, Towne Realty, Wauwatosa Presbyterian Church, WE Energies through the Wisconsin Energy Corporation Foundation, William Stark Jones Foundation, Wisconsin Law Journal, and the Women's Fund.

Wisconsin lawyers have an affirmative ethical obligation to render *pro bono publico* service, which may be satisfied by giving "financial support for organizations that provide legal services to persons of limited means" (Wis. SCR 20:6.1). The Comment to another provision states: "Lawyers should be encouraged to support and participate in legal service organizations" (Wis. SCR 20:6.3). The state's legal profession has responded well to its mandated responsibilities in this area.

As befits an organization co-founded by the Milwaukee Bar Association, the Legal Aid Society has been generously supported by the local legal profession throughout its history. From the very outset, Milwaukee lawyers provided individual annual donations to sustain the Society's work. The original Articles of Incorporation in 1916 authorized membership in the Legal Aid Society for a modest contribution of $1 per year. Membership reached a high point of more than 300 attorneys in the early 1960s. Today, our annual year-end fund

appeal, a mass mailing effort to 5,000 Milwaukee attorneys and supporters, takes the place of individual memberships. The annual appeal letter is traditionally co-signed by the President of the Milwaukee
Bar Association and the President of the Legal Aid Society. It raises
$60,000 a year.

LAS held an annual luncheon from 1917 until about 1974. The
event provided an opportunity to conduct the Society's annual corporate meeting and to elect officers and directors for the following
year. In light of the low membership dues, though, the event was not
considered a fundraiser. The event lapsed after the mid-1970s when
the Society abandoned its membership structure. In 2006, however, a
luncheon was held in conjunction with LAS's 90th anniversary. That
event proved so successful that the board decided to restore the tradition of an annual luncheon and make it the Society's primary fundraising event of the year. Today, the luncheon raises nearly $150,000 a year
and consistently attracts an attendance of more than 600 prominent
judges and lawyers. It has become the Milwaukee legal community's
largest such event of the year.

The Legal Aid Society's annual luncheon is sponsored primarily
by the city's major law firms. Among its most loyal donors are Foley
& Lardner, LLP, and Reinhart Boerner Van Deuren, S.C., two firms
whose early leaders were instrumental in founding the Society in
1916. Other law firm sponsors include Aiken & Scoptur, S.C.; Becker
& Hickey, S.C.; Cannon & Dunphy, S.C.; Cook & Franke, S.C.; Davis
& Kuelthau, S.C.; Emile Banks & Associates, S.C.; Friebert Finerty
& St. John, S.C.; Gillick Wicht Gillick & Graf, S.C.; Gimbel Reilly
Guerin & Brown, S.C.; Godfrey & Kahn, S.C.; Gonzalez, Saggio &
Harlan, LLP; Habush Habush & Rottier, S.C.; Hupy and Abraham
S.C.; Maistelman & Associates, LLC; Mawicke & Goisman, S.C.;
Michael Best & Friedrich LLP; O'Neil Cannon Hollman DeJong,
S.C.; Quarles & Brady, LLP; Stephen M. Fisher & Associates, LLP;
von Briesen & Roper, S.C.; and Whyte Hirschboek Dudek S.C.

"We are," noted the Legal Aid Society's first Superintendent, Alma
C. Schlesinger, "just barely scratching the surface of a great need." Annual Report (1920). That need has mushroomed dramatically within
the last generation, which has witnessed a near doubling of Milwaukee's poverty population. The enormous demand for legal representa-

tion has been documented most compellingly in *Bridging the Justice Gap: Wisconsin's Unmet Legal Needs* (Madison: State Bar of Wisconsin, 2007), the chief finding of which is that more than half a million indigents are denied access to justice, strictly on account of their poverty and the under-funding of legal aid programs, every year in the state. The study also underscores the necessity for the Legal Aid Society to cultivate its historic relationships with funding partners – an endeavor that will continue to prove essential in meeting the Society's mission during its second century of service to Milwaukee's poor.

One of the most promising recent developments in beginning to address this overwhelming need is the state appropriation for civil legal aid programs, which began in 2008 and currently totals $2.5 million per year.[1] While Wisconsin still lags well behind neighboring states, the appropriation represents a significant new source of funding from both general purpose revenues and increased court filing fees. These funds are the work product of the core legal service providers, now known collectively as the Wisconsin Alliance for Equal Justice. In 2007, John F. Ebbott and Deedee Rongstad of Alliance Legal Services, Lynn Breedlove (Executive Director of Disability Rights Wisconsin), and Catey Doyle and Tom Cannon of the Legal Aid Society met to map out a successful strategy to secure a state appropriation. Governor Jim Doyle and Department of Administration Secretary Michael L. Morgan readily agreed to place funds in their proposed biennial budget for this purpose. The three core provider programs then hired an experienced lobbyist, Pat Osborne of Hamilton Consulting Group in Madison. Together, members of the core-provider coalition developed and executed a detailed plan to (i) formulate a persuasive, research-based educational campaign, (ii) maintain tight control of the message, (iii) make repeated individual contacts with key legislators in both parties, and (iv) marshal influential judges and other prominent supporters at public hearings across the state to promote passage. In a genuine historical sense, the landmark state appropriation comes full circle to redeem the failed efforts of Socialist legislators in the 1911-1913-1915 sessions who fought unsuccessfully for enabling legislation to form the state's first free legal aid program in Milwaukee.

NOTE

1. State funding for civil legal services was first proposed by LAS Chief Staff Attorney Jordan B. Reich in 1972. He urged Governor Patrick J. Lucey's administration to provide funds for this purpose in testimony before the Governor's Task Force on Judicial Reorganization. "Statewide Legal Aid Promoted" in *Milwaukee Journal* (April 15, 1972). In 1979, another effort was made early in the administration of Governor Lee S. Dreyfus, who verbally expressed support for the idea, but was later forced to drop the initiative due to a budgetary shortfall. Governor Doyle also proposed funding for civil legal services during his first administration (2003-07), but legislators later eliminated it.

18

KEY BOARD FIGURES

Charitable organizations do not run themselves. Wisconsin law vests management responsibility for non-profit corporations squarely in the board of directors.[1] This body, which exercises ultimate corporate authority, has traditionally represented a variety of constituencies at the Legal Aid Society. As noted previously, at least one board member, usually a former President, represents the Milwaukee Bar Association. Another board seat has by longstanding custom been held by a sitting or retired judge of either the state or federal court.[2] Marquette University Law School has been represented almost since inception on the board. The city's leading law firms – most notably Foley & Lardner, Quarles & Brady, and the Reinhart law firm – have routinely contributed senior partners to board service at the Legal Aid Society. In addition, a member of the legal department at Northwestern Mutual Life has regularly held a board seat.

Lawyer-dominant organizational models were quite common in the first wave of legal aid offices founded before World War I. Reginald Heber Smith described them as a "Lawyers' Legal Aid Society" because the development and shaping of policy was almost exclusively in the hands of attorneys.[3] This type of composition had some distinct advantages. When Superintendent Alma Schlesinger announced in 1921 that the Legal Aid Society of Milwaukee advocated legislation to authorize banks to extend microcredit as a means of circumventing loan sharks, she specifically noted that members of the LAS board would meet soon to draft such legislation.[4] That kind of expertise was likely to be available only on a board controlled by lawyers. In addition, supervising the work of staff attorneys, formulating public policy relating to the administration of justice, and resolving related issues seemed most appropriately entrusted to members of the legal profession.

Although attorneys have always predominated at LAS, not all directors have been members of the bar. By tradition, one or more seats have been reserved for a representative of the community at large. Meta Berger, the prominent suffragette, pacifist, and Socialist was the first such director. Some who followed in her footsteps include Maud Swett, longtime Director of the Women's and Child Labor Department at the Wisconsin Industrial Commission; Esther Leath Ritz, President of the Milwaukee Jewish Federation and community activist, described as a "champion of the underdog [who] liked to do good and cause trouble at the same time";[5] Raymond E. Majerus, national Secretary-Treasurer of the United Auto Workers union and leader of the famous Kohler Co. strike; Dr. Howard L. Fuller, civil rights leader who later became Superintendent of Milwaukee Public Schools; and Brother Booker Ashe, O.F.M. Cap., founder and director of Milwaukee's House of Peace, which distributes food and clothing to inner-city residents. Another LAS director, community organizer Mary Lou Massignani, was deported in the mid-1970s for protesting the war in Vietnam by supporting destruction of Selective Service records. *Massignani v. Immigration and Naturalization Service*, 438 F.2d 1276 (7th Cir. 1971).[6]

The Legal Aid Society has been fortunate in attracting a number of influential board members who, at critical junctures in the organization's history, have stepped forward to demonstrate leadership. Thus, when LAS ran the public defender program here, the board relied heavily on such distinguished criminal law practitioners as Stephen M. Glynn, John D. Murray, William J. Mulligan (former United States Attorney), and David J. Cannon (former United States Attorney and former Milwaukee County District Attorney). When the Society needed entrée into the corporate or foundation world, it tapped board members like David A. Erne for access. Some board members, by virtue of their board longevity, passed along LAS's institutional memory to their successors, while others made exceptional contributions in individual ways.

The function of the board has changed over time. Initially, members like William Kaumheimer and William A. Klatte made policy on a statewide level by their support for legislation in Wisconsin to improve the lives of the poor, and on a national stage through their active engagement with the National Association of Legal Aid Organizations. In the 1940s and 1950s, however, board meetings consisted mainly of reviewing and approving individual applications for representation in divorce matters. With the availability of government funding in the 1960s – the result of the War on Poverty and Supreme Court pronouncements on the right to counsel in criminal and juvenile proceedings – the board again shifted its attention to wider policy matters. What follows are highlights of the careers of a few key directors over the years.

Charles Whitney Babcock served as a Milwaukee Bar Association representative on the Bartlett Committee that recommended establishment of the Legal Aid Society in 1915. He went on to serve as a director of the Society (1916-49) for a third of a century. His two-decade tenure as President (1929-49) is longest in the organization's history. Babcock was born at Rushville, Illinois, in 1877. He was educated at Knox College (B.S. 1901), Yale University, and Marquette University Law School. After his admission to the Wisconsin bar in 1911, Babcock joined the staff of the City Attorney's Office in Milwaukee, serving from 1913 until his retirement as First Assistant in 1947. In addition to his presidency of the Legal Aid Society, he also served as a director (1930-31) and Vice President (1940-42) of the National Association of Legal Aid Organizations. Babcock presided over his last LAS board meeting just a few months before his death of a heart attack, at age 72, in 1949. His obituary appeared in *NALAO Brief Case* vii, no. 9 (1949) 70.

William A. Klatte was another longtime board member. Born in Milwaukee in 1872, he graduated from the University of Wisconsin Law School (LL.B. 1899). Klatte served as Clerk of the Civil Courts from 1910 to 1942, overseeing the filing of nearly a million cases during his lengthy career of public service. A woman who had been evicted from her home appeared one day at the courthouse and shot Klatte three times, but, astonishingly, he survived the experience. He served on the Legal Aid Society board for nearly a quarter of a century, from 1920 until his death in 1944. Klatte took an especially strong interest in the creation of Wisconsin's first Small Claims Court in Milwaukee in 1921. He gave a lengthy account of its operation to the National Association of Legal Aid Organizations in 1924. *Proc. NALAO* (1924-25) 120-25. Klatte also served for several years on that organization's Committee on Arbitration, Conciliation, and Small Claims.

45. Edessa K. Lines, key member of the Legal Aid Society of Milwaukee board, 1918-62.
Courtesy of Marquette University Archives.

Edessa Kunz (Mrs. George) Lines served on the LAS board from 1918 until her death in 1962. She succeeded Meta S. Berger as director. Biographical notices, as well as obituaries in both the *Milwaukee Journal* and *Milwaukee Sentinel*, describe her as "one of the founders of the Legal Aid Society." Kunz was born in 1877 in Poynette and graduated from the University of Wisconsin in 1898. As Assistant Factory Inspector for the Bureau of Labor and Industrial Statistics (1903-07), she visited hundreds of factories across the state to enforce children's and women's labor laws. Even more significantly, she documented the plight of thousands of immigrants living in Milwaukee slums in 1906 by creating a compelling photographic archive to tell their story. Her collection supplemented an influential report she authored on *The Housing Problem in Wisconsin* (1906). The Kunz report led to enactment of Wisconsin's landmark tenement housing law in the following year.[7] In 1907, she married George Lines, partner in the prominent Milwaukee law firm of Lines, Spooner & Quarles.

Edessa Kunz Lines was an original board member of Milwaukee's Central Council of Social Agencies (today's United Way) and served in that position from 1909-42. During World War I, she was Secretary of the National League for Women's Service (a precursor to the Women's Army Corps) and was active in Liberty Loan drives, as well. She endowed the Edessa K. Lines Women's Athletic Scholarship, one of the first of its kind, at the University of Wisconsin. Her personal papers and photographs are preserved in the Marquette University Archives. Although neither an incorporator nor initial Legal Aid board member, Lines was the force behind the Central Council of Social Agencies' sponsorship of the new Legal Aid Society of Milwaukee in 1916. Perhaps no early board member was as critically important to the organization's success. Throughout her 44-year career on the LAS board, Lines represented the Society's vital personal link to its sole source of funding.

The longest serving director in the Society's history was Edmund B. Shea (1892-1969), who sat on the board for nearly half a century from 1922 until his death in 1969. For much of that period, he also held the position of board Vice President. Shea was born in Ashland, Wisconsin. He graduated from the University of Wisconsin (A.B. 1913) and Harvard Law School (LL.B. 1916). He was senior partner in the Milwaukee law firm of Shea, Hoyt & Green (today's Meissner, Tierney, Fisher & Nichols S.C.). Shea was elected President of the Milwaukee Bar Association in 1934 and served as President of the State Bar Association of Wisconsin in 1944-45. In these positions, he was able to maintain the Society's important relationship with state and local lawyer organizations. Shea was corporate counsel to the Journal Corporation and also served as director of the Marine National Exchange

Bank and the Northwestern National Insurance Company. In addition, he was elected President of the suburban Village of Fox Point.

Another longtime director was Charles B. Quarles (1884-1968), prominent Milwaukee lawyer and partner in the Lines, Spooner & Quarles law firm (today's Quarles & Brady LLP). He came from a

46. Attorney Edmund B. Shea, longest serving director of the Legal Aid Society of Milwaukee, 1922-69. *Courtesy of Meissner, Tierney, Fisher & Nichols S.C.*

pioneer Wisconsin family; his uncle, Joseph V. Quarles, served as U.S. Senator from Wisconsin (1899-1905) and later as U.S. District Judge in Milwaukee. Charles graduated from the University of Wisconsin (B.A. 1907); as a member of the track team there, he set a world record in the high hurdles. He read law in his father's firm before being admitted to the bar in 1909. The younger Quarles became an authority on municipal bond issues. He also served as a director of the Central Council of Social Agencies and, like Edessa Lines, helped maintain the crucial relationship with LAS's sole funding partner. In addition to his long service on the board of directors, including a lengthy tenure as President from 1949-60, Quarles was a dues-paying member of the Legal Aid Society from inception in 1916 until his death – a record period of 52 years. He also chaired the State Bar Association of Wisconsin's Committee on Legal Aid in 1930 [see Historical Documents

47. Charles B. Quarles served as President of the Legal Aid Society of Milwaukee, 1949-60. *Courtesy of Quarles & Brady LLP.*

Section]. Quarles was awarded a Founder's Certificate from the National Legal Aid & Defender's Association in recognition of his service as an original member of the Society. See *Legal Aid Brief Case* xviii, no. 1 (1959) 24.

Judge F. Ryan Duffy, Sr. was another key board member at the Legal Aid Society. He held a directorship from 1946 to 1971 (serving as

48. F. Ryan Duffy, former U.S. Senator and Chief Judge of the U.S. Court of Appeals (7th Circuit), served as President of the Legal Aid Society of Milwaukee during the turbulent 1960s. *Courtesy of Milwaukee County Historical Society.*

President in 1960-69). Duffy was born in Fond du Lac, Wisconsin, in 1888. His father immigrated to America from the family home in Castleblaney, County Monaghan; his mother's family came over from County Tipperary, Ireland. Ryan Duffy was educated at the University of Wisconsin (B.A. 1910; LL.B. 1912). He practiced law with his father in Fond du Lac for five years before resigning to accept a commission as a Lieutenant in the U.S. Army in 1917. He served 14 months with the American Expeditionary Force in France.

In the fall of 1932, Duffy was elected United States Senator from Wisconsin, only the second Democrat ever popularly elected from the state. He was a solid supporter of the New Deal, but was defeated in the 1938 Republican sweep. President Roosevelt appointed Duffy as U.S. District Court Judge in Milwaukee in 1939. Ten years later, President Truman elevated him to the U.S. Court of Appeals in Chicago. He served as Chief Judge on both courts. Duffy died in Milwaukee at the age of 91. A *Milwaukee Journal* editorial (August 18, 1979), taking note of his long record at the Legal Aid Society, described him as "a staunch proponent of the principle that the poor were entitled to free legal services, long before that idea was a popular notion." Judge Duffy felt especially strong about the professional duty of lawyers to support legal aid programs. He said:

> Many lawyers and some judges, too, do not fully understand the cause and the work to which [LAS is] devoted and dedicated. . . I think every attorney in Milwaukee County should be a paid-up member of the Legal Aid Society of Milwaukee. The dues are $2 a year. In that way, attorneys would have some personal contact with the great work being done by the Milwaukee Legal Aid Society.
>
> Practically every attorney is benefited because we have here a well-directed, smoothly-operating Legal Aid Society. Individual attorneys, no matter how well disposed or generous with their time, simply cannot adequately take care of all the poor and their legal difficulties. It cannot be denied that the primary responsibility to solve the problem rests with the Bar. Legal Aid eases the burden of lawyers who would otherwise be required to give much more time to indigent cases.

Speech to the State Bar of Wisconsin's Committee on Legal Aid (February 19, 1960); reprinted in *Legal Aid Brief Case* xviii, no. 5 (1960) 123-26.[8]

Charles L. Goldberg (1902-1975) played a crucial role in developing Milwaukee Plan Legal Services and in obtaining the first federal legal services grant for the Society in 1965-69. He was born in Milwaukee and educated at the University of Chicago (Ph.B. 1925) and Marquette University Law School (J.D. *cum laude* 1928). He established a solo practice here in the fields of real estate, probate, and corporate law in the First Wisconsin National Bank Building. Moreover, Goldberg held numerous high offices in the legal profession, including President of the Milwaukee Bar Association (1952-53), President of the State Bar of Wisconsin (1958-59), member of the American Bar Association House of Delegates (1959-67), Fellow of the American Bar Foundation, and Fellow of the American College of Trial Lawyers. Like Edmund Shea, he represented LAS's interests to its natural constituency in the private bar.

49. Attorney Charles L. Goldberg, director of the Legal Aid Society of Milwaukee, played a key role in obtaining OEO Legal Services funding in 1965.
Courtesy of State Bar of Wisconsin.

Goldberg served as a director of the Legal Aid Society of Milwaukee from 1960-75, including several terms as Vice President. Perhaps more significantly, he was President of the Board of Legal Services from 1965-69. In the latter capacity, as noted by Professor Finman's article, Goldberg was instrumental in securing OEO legal services funding for the Society's Milwaukee Plan Legal Services project [see Historical Documents Project]. Along with Julia Dolan, he was the principal architect of the unusual design of the MPLS program, which involved the services of the private bar to a greater extent that was generally found in other programs throughout the country. For example, in the first six months of MPLS's operation, 250 lawyers provided legal services to more than 4,000 low-income clients in Milwaukee.[9] Similarly, the Law Reform Division established in 1967 constituted

50. Judge John A. Decker, President of the Legal Aid Society of Milwaukee 1969-71, was prime mover behind the public defender contract with Milwaukee County.
Courtesy of Wisconsin Court of Appeals.

a unique collaboration between six private law firms and the staffed neighborhood offices run by the Legal Aid Society. As President of the Board of Legal Services, which contracted with the Society to run MPLS, Goldberg presided over many contentious meetings where he confronted, and was confronted by, community activists demanding a more aggressive approach. Undoubtedly, he also played a critical role in the decision of the Society to relinquish the OEO funding in 1969. After his death, the Wisconsin Law Foundation named its Charles L. Goldberg Distinguished Service Award in his honor to recognize lawyers' lifetime achievements in public service.

Another influential board figure in the Society's history was Judge John A. Decker. Born in Milwaukee in 1915, he was educated at the University of Wisconsin Law School (LL.B. 1939). Decker served as an Assistant City Attorney in Milwaukee, but resigned to accept a commission in the U.S. Navy during World War II. He was elected a Circuit Court judge in 1955 and taught evidence as an adjunct professor at Marquette University Law School, where students voted him the Outstanding Teacher Award. He also served on the faculty of the National Judicial College in Reno, Nevada. A profile in the *Milwaukee Sentinel* accurately described the judge as an "open, scholarly man, a hard worker with the reputation of being better prepared for a case than the attorneys involved in it."

Judge Decker joined the Legal Aid Society's board of directors in 1954. As President of the Society, Decker played a critical role in drafting the Society's application to the Ford Foundation and the National Legal Aid & Defender Association, which sought funding for a pilot project public defender program here in 1968-69 [see Historical Documents Section]. His respected stature and energetic leadership proved effective in marshaling support from fellow judges and the County Board for securing a long-term funding relationship with Milwaukee County after the initial funding ran out. In 1979, he was appointed first Chief Judge of the newly created Wisconsin Court of Appeals. Decker received the first Jurist Lifetime Achievement Award from the State Bar of Wisconsin. He retired in 1984, but pursued a successful second career as an arbitrator and mediator until his death in Milwaukee in 2006.

Wendy Reed Bosworth, a retired partner at Foley & Lardner LLP, was in many ways an ideal LAS board member. She graduated *magna cum laude* from Smith College and *cum laude* from Marquette University Law School. Over several decades, Reed Bosworth built up

51. Attorney Wendy Reed Bosworth, President of the Legal Aid Society of Milwaukee, 2003-06. *Courtesy of Foley & Lardner LLP.*

a successful tax and estate planning practice that gave her entrée to Milwaukee's tight-knit charitable community. Her board memberships constitute a veritable Who's Who of major donors: United Way of Greater Milwaukee, Foley Family Foundation, Greater Milwaukee Foundation, Family Service of Milwaukee, Visiting Nurse Association, and the Women's Fund. After joining the LAS board in 1999, she served as President 2003-06. A shrewd judge of people and donor prospects, Reed Bosworth knew every key mover and shaker in town. Deeply committed to solving the massive social and economic problems of Milwaukee's inner city, she personally raised more than $200,000 for the Legal Aid Society. She was also the main force behind establishment of the LAS Endowment Fund in 2006. Wendy Reed Bosworth was honored with the Society's Equal Justice Medal in 2008 in recognition of her significant contributions to the organization.

NOTES

1. The LAS Advisory Board, on the other hand, had no say in the management of the Society. It was established strictly for fundraising purposes and to demonstrate community support. Advisory Board members were listed on LAS stationery, along with the members of the Board of Directors, from inception in 1919 through the late 1940s. The last mention of the Advisory Board occurs in the LAS Minutes for December 6, 1946, when the Society's letterhead was revised to identify newly-named members of the Advisory Board.

2. The following jurists have served on the LAS board: retired Wisconsin Supreme Court Justice John Barnes (1916-19); U.S. Court of Appeals Chief Judge F. Ryan Duffy (1944-69); Circuit Court Judge John A. Decker (1954-71); U.S. District Court Chief Judge John W. Reynolds (1969-72); retired Chief Judge Patrick T. Sheedy (1998-2008); and retired Chief Judge Michael P. Sullivan (2008-present). A number of former board members went on to become judges after their LAS service: Wisconsin Court of Appeals Judge Joan F. Kessler, Milwaukee County Court Judge Howard G. Brown, United States Bankruptcy Judge James E. Shapiro, and United States Magistrate Judge Aaron E. Goodstein.

3. Reginald Heber Smith, "A Lawyers' Legal Aid Society" in *Case and Comment* 23 (1917) 1008-13.

4. "Draw Up Bill to Legalize Loans. The Legal Aid Society today is drawing up a bill to legalize small loans, according to Alma Schlesinger, superinten-

dent of the society. It is expected that the members of the Legal Aid Society board will hold a special meeting shortly to draw up the bill." *Milwaukee Leader* (March 14, 1921).

5. "Activist Esther Leah Ritz, Champion of the Underdog, Dies at 85" in *Jewish Daily Forward* (January 2, 2004).

6. Massignani signed a newspaper endorsement of the Milwaukee 14, a group of Catholic peace activists who broke into the Milwaukee offices of the Selective Service Administration on September 24, 1968, and burned 10,000 military draft records. She served as a director of the Legal Aid Society from January 17, 1972 to December 10, 1973, when she moved to Texas. Massignani was deported to Italy a year or two later.

7. Edessa Kunz Lines' role is discussed at length in Lawrence M. Friedman and Michael J. Spector, "Tenement House Legislation in Wisconsin: Reform and Reaction" in *American Journal of Legal History* 9, no. 1 (1965) 41-63. For her obituaries, see "Death Takes Mrs. Lines" in *Milwaukee Journal* (October 23, 1962); "Mrs. Lines Rites Set" in *Milwaukee Sentinel* (October 24, 1962).

8. For his career, see Edie Birschbach, *Fond du Lac's Forgotten Famous Son: F. Ryan Duffy* (Fond du Lac Public Library, 2007), online ed. at www.fdlpl. org.

9. Mark Braun, *Policies, Programs, Politics and the Poor in Two Milwaukee Legal Service Organizations, 1966-1972*, a paper delivered to a conference on "Historical Perspectives on Milwaukee's Urban Experience" at Marquette University (1996) 2.

19
SUPERINTENDENTS AND
EXECUTIVE DIRECTORS

The chief executive officers of the Legal Aid Society have been known by a variety of titles over the past 94 years: Superintendent (1916-43), Superintendent and Counsel (1943-53), Executive Attorney (1953-71), and Executive Director (1971 to the present). While these individuals were responsible for guiding the day-to-day operations of the Society, they also exerted the greatest single influence over the long-term institutional development of the organization. The position did not begin that way; it evolved over time. At the outset, the first two Superintendents seem to have worked closely in tandem with the Society's energetic President, William Kaumheimer. In 1930, however, the balance of power began a slow shift towards the office of Superintendent, prompted by the less hands-on style of a new President (Charles W. Babcock) and the appointment of the first lawyer-Superintendent (Margery M. Heck). The latter office emerged fully under the long leadership reign of Julia B. Dolan (1939-71). That transformation was symbolized in part by the ultimate change in her title to Executive Attorney.

Shortly after the Society celebrated its 50th anniversary, a correspondent (Attorney Clara M. Toppins) wrote the *Milwaukee Journal* (March 23, 1966):

> While it is gratifying to see the pictures and the names of those presently active in the Society (and without taking anything away from the good work done by the present executive), it would have seemed appropriate on such an auspicious occasion to have mentioned the past executive attorneys [*sic*], Mrs. George Kiewert and Mrs. Margery Heck Riffle. Had it not been for their hard and arduous years of pioneering, without too much of a pattern to follow in the earlier days, the Legal Aid [Society]

might not have come into being. When celebrating the past, it seems to me, those who contributed should be given due credit or at least honorable mention.

The Society heartily endorses the sentiments of Ms. Toppins and wishes to record its gratitude for the contributions of past leaders who made Legal Aid the strong organization it is today. The one immutable lesson of the Society's history is that each new generation has built on the legacy and successes of its predecessors.

Alma C. Schlesinger, the Society's first Superintendent, was born into a prominent Milwaukee business family in 1888. Her father, Louis, invented and patented the business machine tabulator, which he later sold to the National Cash Register Co. Alma was educated at Milwaukee-Downer Seminary and graduated from Smith College (B.A. 1910). A year-long grand tour of Europe followed. She did social work outside of Milwaukee for several years before returning home. An early news story noted Schlesinger's attendance at the annual convention of the Consumers League of Wisconsin (*Milwaukee Journal*, February 26, 1913). Three years later, she was named first head of the Legal Aid Society. The press announcement of her appointment identified Alma as "office manager and field worker." By the end of the week, she had become Superintendent. Because of her wealth, social position, and sense of noblesse oblige, she declined to accept a salary.

Alma was a trailblazer in the field of poverty law, and during her five-year tenure with the Society, she set a high standard for those who followed in her footsteps. Her sense of being a pioneer was evident in the 1918 Annual Report, which noted:

> The Legal Aid Society has grown. Last year's report was the history of the beginnings of a new social undertaking, which clearly pointed out the fact that the youngest of the twenty-two organizations included in the Centralized Budget of Philanthropies met a long standing need and had its work mapped out for it long before it existed. Its record of the year just ended presents the Legal Aid Society, its initial experimental stage concluded, firmly established as one of the recognized social service agencies of the city.

Schlesinger's concept of the Society can be seen in the first quarterly report (September 1916), which shows a penchant for hard work, a gift for public relations, cooperation with other community agencies, and detailed record keeping [see Historical Documents Section].[1] Contemporary newspaper articles consistently describe her as capable, and she certainly got the Society off to a strong start. From the beginning, she leveraged limited resources by pioneering the use of volunteers in the office. Perhaps her most important achievement was the leading role she played in helping to establish the state's first Small Claims Court in Milwaukee (1921 Wis. Laws, c. 538). What remains

52. Alma C. Schlesinger, Superintendent of the Legal Aid Society, 1916-21, set a high standard for her successors. *Courtesy of Peter C. Haensel family.*

unclear, though, is how much credit is due Schlesinger, and how much is attributable to key board members (notably William Kaumheimer and William A. Klatte) who actively promoted enactment of the Small Claims Court legislation as well.

Schlesinger also advocated legislation to make small loans available to low-income consumers as a means of nullifying the power of loan sharks. "Draw Up Bill to Legalize Loans" in *Milwaukee Leader* (March 14, 1921). That same micro-credit concept won the Nobel Peace Prize in 2006. Muhammad Yunus, *Banker to the Poor: Micro-lending and the battle against world poverty* (New York: Public Affairs, 2003). In addition, Alma launched an investigation of unbonded, out-of-state collection agencies that were dunning Milwaukee's poor for nonexistent debts. "Legal Aid Will Sift Out State Bill Collectors" in *Milwaukee Leader* (April 13, 1921). She enlisted federal postal inspectors and Justice Department officials in that effort [see Historical Documents Section]. Despite her view of LAS as a social service agency, these activities demonstrate that Schlesinger's concept of the Society's mission was remarkably modern. Her efforts went beyond individual representation to include broader challenges to systemic barriers to the poor.[2] In this respect, she anticipated the law reform movement of the War on Poverty by half a century. Her stewardship was praised by Reginald Heber Smith, who described the Milwaukee program in 1919 as a "strong organization" in his seminal book, *Justice and the Poor* (p. 148).

Three years after resigning from the Legal Aid Society, Alma married German actor Curt Haensel in 1924. The couple moved to Berlin where they lived for the next thirteen years. On one visit to her parents' home here, she gave an extensive interview about her impressions of German cultural life in the Weimar Republic. "Comment on Matters in Berlin Life" in *Milwaukee Journal* (August 1, 1926). In 1937, as the Nazis began clamping down on the country, the Haensels made a narrow, carefully-planned escape from the coming nightmare. Alma and Curt spent the next 46 years back in Milwaukee attending plays, enjoying the Milwaukee Symphony, and reading such favorite German authors as Goethe and Schiller for their book club. Their son Peter is a prominent attorney here and a partner in the Lichtsinn & Haensel

S.C. law firm. Alma Schlesinger Haensel died in Milwaukee in 1983 at the age of 94.

Agnes Campbell Kiewert, the Society's second Superintendent, was born in Milwaukee in 1894. Evidently from an upper class family, she wrote John Bradway that "I never had to work, but I did it [LAS work] simply because I loved it and it was the only hobby I had." Agnes began her professional career as a schoolteacher in her hometown, but during World War I she joined the American Red Cross and became a social worker in Ashland, Wisconsin. In 1919, she was appointed Assistant Superintendent of the Legal Aid Society; two years later, she was promoted to the top job. Her nine years at the helm built on the early success of her predecessor and set a new standard of institutional accomplishment. For example, in 1923, the Society recovered a record $14,253 in funds for clients; three years later, LAS opened a record number (4,121) of cases; and in 1927, the Society achieved record revenues of $8,526. Campbell Kiewert's work was featured in "Saving Work for the Courts" in *Milwaukee Journal* (July 20, 1924).

Conventional wisdom posits that the Progressive Era reform movement ended in 1920 with the "Return to Normalcy." See, for example, Arthur Stanley Link, "What Happened to the Progressive Movement in the 1920s?" in *American Historical Review* 64 (1959) 833-51. Such was not the case in Milwaukee, however. Kiewert, working closely with William Kaumheimer, continued the reforming spirit and legislative advocacy work begun by Alma Schlesinger. Agnes partnered with the Russell Sage Foundation to promote passage of the Small Loans Act (1927 Wis. Laws, c. 540). That anti-loan-sharking measure regulated unconventional loans and placed a 10%-ceiling on the amount of interest that lenders could charge. The statute was modeled on a national uniform act of the same name. See Otto G. Wismer, "Legal Aid Organizations: Lobbyists for the Poor" in *Annals of the American Academy of Political and Social Science* 136 (1928) 175.

During Campbell Kiewert's tenure, she worked actively on the NA-LAO Committee on Relations with Social Agencies; she completed a national survey on the subject that provides much insight into the day-to-day operations of the Legal Aid Society of Milwaukee in the 1920s [see Historical Documents Section]. Campbell Kiewert was strongly committed to the professional collaboration of social workers and lawyers in achieving the LAS mission. Also during her superintendent's term, William Kaumheimer was elected President of the National Association of Legal Aid Organizations, thus showcasing the work of the Legal Aid Society of Milwaukee before a much wider audience. Again, the precise balance of power between Kiewert and Kaumheimer is difficult to judge at this remove. A brief glimpse, though, may be gleaned from a comment she made at a national conference. Kiewert reported:

> We have a small board. We have almost no trouble in getting the board together [for meetings]. We have nine members. We discuss office policies and specific cases that come up. I ask their advice on specific cases and they like it.

Proc. NALAO (1928) 88-89. When asked if she accepted the board's input on individual cases, she gave a diplomatic reply: "Occasionally."

Kiewert spoke fondly about those she served: "I have always maintained that my clients are of a slightly higher type than the typical charity applicant; they are self-respecting and self-supporting types whose budget does not include an amount to be paid an attorney in case the family is involved in a legal tangle." *Proc. NALAO* (1923) 98-99. After announcing her resignation, Agnes' career was profiled in both the *Milwaukee Sentinel* ("Legal Aid Head to Quit; Tells of Trials and Laughs," May 5, 1930) and the *Milwaukee Journal* ("Tears and Grins Mark Pleas for Legal Help," June 1, 1930). Skeptical about the transition from a collaborative social worker-attorney model to a law firm model, she bluntly told John Bradway that she thought the LAS board was making a mistake [see Historical Documents Section]. After leaving the Society, she served a brief stint on the LAS board and also returned for a short period to her original profession as an elementary schoolteacher. Kiewert continued to reside on Milwaukee's East Side with her husband George, a manufacturer's representative, and to enjoy sailing on the *Argyle*, their yawl at the Milwaukee Yacht Club. Agnes died in 1988 in Milwaukee at the age of 93.

Margery M. Heck, the Society's third Superintendent, was born in Racine, Wisconsin, in 1900. She came to the law naturally as her father, Max, was a prominent lawyer, judge, and state senator in that city. Margery matriculated at Marquette University in 1918 and received her LL.B. degree in 1922. She was admitted to the Wisconsin bar the following year after passing the exam (there being no diploma privi-

53. Margery M. Heck, Superintendent 1930-39, was the first woman attorney hired by the Legal Aid Society of Milwaukee. She guided the organization through the Great Depression. *Courtesy of Marquette University Archives.*

lege at the time). Only 41 women in the entire history of the state had preceded her in the Supreme Court's Roll of Attorneys. Heck practiced law with her father in Racine before accepting positions as Deputy Clerk of the Circuit Court, and later as a Court Commissioner, in her hometown. She held these posts until her appointment as the new Superintendent of the Legal Aid Society in 1930.

Margery served in the head position for nine years and was the first attorney appointed to the full-time staff. Most other legal aid programs had long since shifted from outside retained counsel to a staff attorney model. The late transition here may also reflect the dominant position of William Kaumheimer as board President for the first thirteen years. During her tenure, Heck confronted daunting problems created by the Great Depression: increased demand for services in a time of diminished staff and budgets. This lethal combination closed the doors of many other legal aid programs around the country in the 1930s, but Margery was able to keep the Milwaukee program functioning. Still, the strain is evident in correspondence that shows LAS struggling to pay its annual dues to the National Association of Legal Aid Organizations. Nonetheless, Heck wrote John Bradway, "I feel we have stood up rather well under the strain of circumstances." (February 16, 1932).

Although documentation for the period is relatively scant, one gets the impression of a narrowing organizational focus, perhaps driven by the annual need to justify the Society's existence in the face of reduced budgets while at the same time trying to maintain high caseloads, sustain client recoveries, and lower the cost-per-case accounting. The Society's precarious financial situation, after more than two decades of existence, is highlighted by the fact that virtually all its funding was still provided by a single source: the Milwaukee Community Fund (successor to the Central Council of Social Agencies). LAS thus faced a major crisis when the Fund deleted the line item sum for rent in the Society's 1932 budget, forcing LAS to beg the County Board for space in the Public Safety Building [see Historical Documents Section]. In addition, regressive social and political trends (*e.g.* the growing influence of the conservative American Bar Association over the national legal aid movement) created a climate that was unreceptive to broader advocacy and litigation work. The early reforming zeal of most legal aid programs around the country, including Milwaukee's, would become dormant until the mid-1960s. See Phillip L. Merkel, "At the Crossroads of Reform: The First Fifty Years of American Legal Aid, 1876-1926" in *Houston Law Review* 27 (1990) 1-44.

National trends (both economic and political) and local funding issues combined with Heck's personal qualities to shape LAS during the Great Depression. Virtually every letter she authored begins with an apology for her delay in responding – thus furthering the impression of one who was overwhelmed by forces beyond her control [see Historical Documents Section]. She attended few NALAO conferences and, unlike her predecessor, seems to have participated very little in debates or committee work when she did attend. Heck also seems to have grappled with ill health during her tenure. Perhaps most significant, her era at the Legal Aid Society began after the departure of the pioneering generation led by such dynamic personalities as William Kaumheimer, Meta Berger, Alma Schlesinger, and Agnes Campbell Kiewert. In fact, shortly after taking over in 1930, Margery wrote John Bradway that she had never met Kaumheimer.

Early in her LAS career, Heck volunteered to serve on the NALAO committee (International Legal Aid) that dealt with immigration and refugee problems, a field she had become interested in as a result of her work in the Racine courts. In 1931, Margery saw legislative enactment of a wage collection law, which had first been promoted by William Kaumheimer in his 1924 report to NALAO. See 1931 Wis. Laws, c. 262. Later in her tenture, Heck pioneered the use of law students as a resource for the Society by establishing one of the nation's early clinical legal education programs in concert with Dean Lloyd K. Garrison's push for more practical student learning opportunities at the University of Wisconsin Law School. She was profiled for her work in the *Milwaukee Journal* ("Legal Aid Society Helps Thousands Who Fear Law," July 28, 1934).

In the summer of 1939, Heck was given a leave of absence from her position. Attorney Bernard F. Mathiowetz, a private law partner of Assistant (Staff) Attorney Melville Sell, was named Acting Superintendent for a brief period. The board declined Heck's request to extend the leave of absence. After departing from the Society, Margery married Francis Riffle, an engineer. The couple moved to California.

She did not apply for admission to that state's bar and never practiced law again. Margery Heck Riffle died in Glendale, California, in 1973.

Julia B. Dolan (née Lebowitz), fourth Superintendent of the Legal Aid Society, was born in Vilnius, Lithuania, in 1905. She came to Milwaukee as a young child. Her immigrant experience sparked a lifelong interest in advocacy for the less fortunate. Julia was educated at Marquette University Law School (LL.B. 1927). After graduation, she practiced law with her husband, John J. Dolan, raised their three sons, and served as President of the Women's Court and Civic Conference. Her ability to multitask was featured in a lengthy profile, "Energetic Woman Lawyer Is Successfully Combining Her Career With Homemaking" in *Milwaukee Journal* (April 24, 1949).

Julia Dolan took over as Superintendent of the Legal Aid Society in November 1939. She proved to be a dynamic and innovative leader. In 1943, Julia helped organize one of the first lawyer referral plans in the country. She also expanded the use of volunteers (attorneys and their spouses) to help achieve the Society's mission on a very limited budget. Fifteen years before the United States Supreme Court saw fit to require the appointment of defense counsel in misdemeanor cases, Dolan developed the Voluntary Defender Program here in conjunction with the Milwaukee Junior Bar Association (based in large part on William Kaumheimer's seminal proposal in 1926 for assigned counsel in criminal cases). She also served on committees that led to the establishment of a discrete Children's Court (1949 Wis. Laws, c. 6) and enactment of the comprehensive Wisconsin Family Code (1959 Wis. Laws, c. 595).

Although the Society's straitened finances forced her to pinch pennies for decades, when Congress created the OEO Legal Services program in 1965, Julia quickly and effectively organized a diverse coalition of the Legal Aid Society of Milwaukee, Marquette University Law School, Social Development Commission, Milwaukee Bar Association, and Milwaukee Junior Bar Association to create Milwaukee Plan Legal Services. Under Dolan's leadership, MPLS included representation from the client community, opened up the Society's first neighborhood branch offices, hired the Society's first African American and Latino attorneys, brought the first Reginald Heber Smith Fellows to Milwaukee, inaugurated a Law Reform Division to develop legislative proposals and bring test cases challenging policies and procedures that discriminated against the poor, approved filing the Society's first class action suits, and even supported a rent strike.

Despite these impressive steps, Dolan's management was criticized in the late 1960s as "conservative," "stodgy," and "part of the establishment." See Braun, *Policies, Programs, Politics, and the Poor;* "Offshoot of Legal Aid Casts Off Stodginess" in *Milwaukee Journal* (November 10, 1969). After the relinquishment of OEO funds in 1969, LAS reverted to its narrow pre-1966 focus, which an NLADA evaluation in 1970 described as "reliable, but unexciting" [see Historical Documents Section]. Even during the OEO period (1966-69), many of Dolan's initiatives were taken reluctantly or in grudging response to outside pressure from social activists, most notably the Community Action Program Residents Council (CAPRC). Each meeting of the Board of Legal Services became a pitched battle between the Dolan/Goldberg faction and community organizers. After three years, the acrimony reached a level that led the Legal Aid Society to terminate its OEO grant, thereby abandoning $425,000 in annual funding.[3]

Interestingly, after the Society ended its relationship with OEO on October 1, 1969, the successor programs at Freedom Through Equality and Milwaukee Legal Services hired their "new" staffs from the very cadre of lawyers that Julia had first appointed: Jim Walrath (who was named Acting Director of FTE), Louie Mestre, Tim Garrity, Dave Becker, Glen Ploez, Sy Pikofsky, and Jack Keese, all of whom joined the staff of MLS. Indeed, MLS took over the very neighborhood offices that Julia had first established on the city's Northside and Southside. Her career ended on another ironic note. Just as she had accelerated the push away from the social services model adopted by the founders of LAS, Dolan's successors greatly expanded her individual-client model to include broader challenges to systemic issues confronting the poor.

In the wake of the U.S. Supreme Court's declaration of the constitutional necessity of appointing counsel in juvenile and criminal proceedings, Julia and Judge John A. Decker (then President of the Society) proactively pursued and won a Ford Foundation grant to establish the first full-time Public Defender Office here in 1969. This initiative built on the success of the Voluntary Defender Project that Dolan had begun in 1957. She was also a prominent voice in the councils of the National Legal Aid & Defender Association, serving on its Executive Board for three years.

To appreciate the full range of her long career, it is only necessary to consider that Julia Dolan worked closely for more than a decade with Charles W. Babcock, a member of the Bartlett Committee in 1915 and one of the Society's original incorporators in 1916; at the other end of her tenure, the last staff attorney she hired is currently serving as Executive Director in 2010. Her influence thus encompassed the organization's entire 94-year history. Upon retiring from the Legal Aid Society in 1971, she took over as managing director of the Milwaukee Bar Association's Lawyer Referral Service where she continued to work for many years. Julia Dolan McClelland died in Milwaukee at the age of 90. The title of her obituary provided a simple, but fitting, epitaph for an extraordinary career at the Legal Aid Society: "Lawyer McClelland fought for the poor" (*Milwaukee Journal Sentinel*, October 16, 1996). Executive Director Jim Walrath and President Tom Cannon represented the Society at her funeral.

David S. Berman was born in Milwaukee in 1940. He was educated at the University of Wisconsin-Milwaukee (B.S. 1965) and Marquette University Law School (J.D. 1967). Berman served in the Army Reserve during college and was called up to active duty for a year during the Berlin Crisis (1961-62). He was appointed an Assistant District Attorney for Milwaukee County after his admission to the Wisconsin bar. Two years later, Berman was named Deputy Director of the Legal Aid Society's Public Defender Project. In 1971, he became the Society's fifth head and the first to hold the title of Executive Director.

During his six years in charge, Dave Berman guided the organization through the internecine complexities of Milwaukee County Board politics. He also adroitly managed opposition from the county's criminal and juvenile court judges whose patronage powers had been significantly diminished by the existence of the Public Defender program. "Lawyers for Poor a Big Money Issue" in *Milwaukee Journal* (November 20, 1973); "Judges Stand Too Rigid," editorial in *Milwaukee Journal* (November 22, 1973); "Duty, Not Patronage, Judges Insist" in *Milwaukee Journal* (November 23, 1973); *State ex rel. Milwaukee v. WCCJ*, 73 Wis.2d 237, 243 N.W.2d 497 (1976).

After his resignation from the Society, Dave made a commitment to offer reduced-cost legal services to low-income (but not indigent) clients who could not otherwise afford to engage private counsel at prevailing market rates. See "Legal View Changes" in *Milwaukee Sentinel* (September 15, 1977). He founded the Milwaukee Law Center toward that end. Later, he opened up a solo private law practice in Downtown that specialized in representing the elderly. Dave's real love, though, was sailing on Lake Michigan and flying his own airplane. He enjoyed nothing better, especially in good weather, than chucking work and heading out for the open water in his favorite sailboat, *Msdemeanor*. He served as president of McBoat, a nonprofit water safety educational organization, and was an active member of the Milwaukee Yacht Club. He generously spent many of his last years counseling fellow diabetic amputees before his own death in 2005. Representing the Society at his funeral were three of his successors, Tom Cannon, Tom Zander, and Jim Walrath.

54. Executive Directors of the Legal Aid Society, 1939-95 (left to right): Thomas K. Zander, David S. Berman, Julia Dolan McClelland, Thomas G. Cannon, and Carol O. Wenerowicz. *Courtesy of Legal Aid Society of Milwaukee.*

Thomas G. Cannon was born in Milwaukee in 1946. He was educated at Marquette University (A.B. 1967) and the University of Wisconsin Law School (J.D. 1971). Cannon enlisted in the U.S. Marines
and served in Vietnam during 1968-69. His 30-year association with
the Society began in 1971 as the last person hired by Julia Dolan prior
to her retirement. He worked as a staff attorney in the Civil and Felony divisions before becoming Chief Staff Attorney of Civil in 1974.
See "Underdog Lawyer Rated as Tops" in *Milwaukee Sentinel* (April
16, 1976). Three years later, he was appointed Executive Director.

Cannon's tenure saw the first million-dollar annual budget (substantially more than the accumulated revenues generated during LAS's
entire first half-century), the largest staff size (32 attorneys) in the
Society's history, establishment of a Mental Health Division, a crucial
transition from Milwaukee County to the State of Wisconsin in funding for the Society's Public Defender program, and inauguration of
the Society's Guardian ad Litem Division. He resigned in 1981 to accept an appointment as a professor of constitutional law and legal ethics at Marquette University Law School. "Poor man's lawyer to move
across the street to a new life" in *Milwaukee Sentinel* (May 18, 1981).
Four years later, he joined the O'Neil, Cannon & Hollman law firm
where he worked as a litigation partner until his retirement in 2000.

Active in the community, Cannon served as President of the Hun-
ger Task Force and as President of the Wisconsin Coalition Against
the Death Penalty. He joined the Legal Aid Society board in 1988 and
served as President in 1995-2003. Two years later, he was invited to
come out of retirement and appointed Executive Director again. "Tom
Cannon Takes Five: Back from retirement, he's still fighting for human rights" in *Milwaukee Journal Sentinel* (December 11, 2005). His
second term saw compilation of the Society's history, establishment of
a Website, creation of an endowment fund, reinstitution of the annual
luncheon, achievement of record revenue levels for four consecutive
years, and a significant upgrade in staff compensation. The current
staff level ties the previous record of 32 attorneys, while the 10 social
workers and 9 support staff represent a new record. "Cannon on target
with Legal Aid" in *Wisconsin Law Journal* (February 2010 Supplement) 11; "Cannon's career comes full circle" in *Wisconsin Law Journal*
(November 5, 2007).

Thomas K. Zander is another Milwaukee native, having been born here in 1954. He graduated with honors from the University of Wisconsin in 1975 after compiling a brilliant academic record that included Phi Beta Kappa, Iron Cross, Knapp Fellowship, and Chancellor's scholarship. Tom cruised through the University of Wisconsin Law School in two years. While there, he became the first student to have a lead article published in the *Wisconsin Law Review*. His topic was civil mental commitments, a field in which he would soon be recognized as a national expert.

His first contact with the Society came in the role of an expert witness in the *Memmel* case, a class action writ of habeas corpus that successfully challenged the constitutionality of Milwaukee County's civil mental commitment system. He testified about the findings of his study of the county's commitment process. Tom also published a pamphlet, *Your Rights in a Wisconsin Mental Hospital* (Wisconsin Civil Liberties Union Foundation, 1977). After a brief stint as an Assistant State Public Defender, Zander was appointed Chief Staff Attorney of the Legal Aid Society's Mental Health Division in 1978. Three years later, he was named Executive Director.

Tom proved to be an adept administrator who excelled at tapping into private foundations and little-known funding sources. He established the Mental Disability Law Division in 1985 to consolidate services to clients with mental health needs. Zander created an array of acronyms for numerous targeted projects delivering civil legal services to underserved segments of the inner city. Among his new programs was one of the nation's first anti-discrimination programs to represent the needs of people living with HIV/AIDS. The result of these efforts was a tripling of the Society's staff and a quadrupling of its budget from 1981 levels, thus enhancing LAS's presence in the courts and in the broader community. Zander created the position of Litigation Director in 1988 to expand the staff's law reform work and to help staff manage its growing appellate caseload. Three years later, he established the Equal Justice Medal to honor those who make a significant contribution to the Society's mission.

Tom retired from Legal Aid in 1994 after thirteen years as Executive Director, a leadership tenure exceeded only by Julia Dolan. His career was featured in a cover story in the *Wisconsin Magazine* section of the

Milwaukee Journal ("An Advocate Steps Down," September 11, 1994). Not content to rest on his laurels, he earned a doctorate in psychology from the Illinois School of Professional Psychology in 2005. Tom continues to pursue his interest in the field of forensic psychology as practitioner and consultant to members of both disciplines. He also serves as an adjunct professor at Marquette University Law School where he co-teaches the Mental Health Law Workshop. Zander currently divides his time between residences in Florida and Wisconsin.

Carole Osberg Wenerowicz was born in Auckland, New Zealand, in 1945. Her parents met while her father was stationed there with the U.S. Army during World War II. She grew up in Minneapolis and attended the University of Minnesota (B.A. 1967). After graduation, Carole traveled around the world, working for International Volunteer Services. She happened to be caught in Vietnam during the Têt Offensive in 1968. Carole also worked in Alaska for a time before deciding to become a lawyer. She graduated from the University of Wisconsin Law School in 1976.

Wenerowicz clerked a year with U.S. District Court Judge John W. Reynolds and worked mainly on the massive Milwaukee Public Schools desegregation case. *Amos v. Bd. of School Directors*, 408 F. Supp. 765 (E.D. Wis. 1976). After completing her clerkship, she joined the staff of the Legal Aid Society's Juvenile Division in 1977. When the Society relinquished the public defender contract, she transferred to the Civil Division where she handled a general civil caseload for two years.

Carole was appointed first Chief Staff Attorney of the Guardian ad Litem Division when it began in 1980. She guided the steady growth of that program for thirteen years and was active in laying the preliminary groundwork for the *Jeanine B.* case, a class action in federal court that led to state takeover of the county's foster care system. Carole was instrumental in bringing the CASA (Court Appointed Special Advocates) Project to Milwaukee. She also served as a member of various Judicial Council and Legislative Council committees dealing with children's issues.

Wenerowicz's leadership as one of the state's premier child advocates, together with her personal qualities of warmth and intelligence, led to her appointment as Executive Director in 1994. An interest in the Society's heritage led her to organize the historic photograph of the five living Executive Directors; the picture hangs in LAS's large conference room to this day. She resigned in 1995 to become President of the Wisconsin Council on Children and Families, a statewide advocacy and educational organization focusing on the needs of the poor. Carole continues to serve as a guardian ad litem in Children's Court and as appellate counsel on matters relating to the legal rights of children.

James A. Walrath, ninth head of the Legal Aid Society, is a native of Glenview, Illinois. He was educated at Lawrence University (B.A. 1965) and the University of Michigan Law School (J.D. 1968). After graduation, Jim won a prestigious Reginald Heber Smith Community Law Fellowship and was assigned to the Legal Aid Society of Milwaukee where he worked in the Southside neighborhood office. He quickly rose to a position of leadership, becoming the intellectual guru of the Society's Law Reform Division where he helped reclaim the

55. James A. Walrath, Executive Director of the Legal Aid Society, 1995-2005. *Courtesy of Legal Aid Society of Milwaukee.*

organization's original broad vision. "Young Lawyers Fight for Poor" in *Milwaukee Journal* (September 22, 1969).

Walrath's aptitude for complex litigation foreshadowed his development into one of Milwaukee's most highly regarded civil rights lawyers. He went on to work at Freedom Through Equality where he served as Acting Director, the Shellow & Shellow law firm, and the Latin American Criminal Defense Project. Walrath also developed a well-deserved reputation as an outstanding appellate and constitutional lawyer. He personally argued a First Amendment case, *City of Kenosha v. Bruno*, 412 U.S. 507 (1973), in the Supreme Court of the United States. He also appeared numerous times before the Wisconsin Supreme Court and the United States Court of Appeals in cases involving race, poverty, and civil liberties issues.

Walrath returned to the Legal Aid Society for a second tour in 1978-79 as Training Director of the Public Defender program. He came back a third time as Litigation Director in 1991; he was promoted to Executive Director in 1995. During the next decade, working with Associate Director Mary Gundrum and Litigation Director Pete Koneazny, he generated more than a million dollars in legal fee awards from statutory fee-shifting provisions in civil rights cases. He oversaw a significant expansion of the staff and grew revenue to a new record: the first $3 million budget. Jim also helped create a substantial body of new case law protecting the rights of consumers in their dealings with predatory lending institutions. In addition, he taught as an adjunct professor at Marquette University Law School where he conducted a popular course on poverty law.

After serving a decade in the post, Jim resigned to become the Federal Defender for Wisconsin. He thus holds the distinction of leading three offices devoted to serving the legal needs of the poor in Milwaukee. His work was highlighted in an extensive interview: "James Walrath Takes Five: Providing defense for a public in need" in *Milwaukee Journal Sentinel* (August 26, 2005). He is currently in private practice concentrating on criminal and consumer rights cases.

NOTES

1. The emphasis on statistical measurement of the Society's work reflected the Progressive Era belief that reform could be achieved by application of

modern management principles. Samuel Haber, *Efficiency and Uplift: Scientific Management in the Progressive Era, 1890-1920* (University of Chicago Press, 1964).

2. What later became known as "law reform" in the 1960s was dubbed "preventive law" by legal aid pioneers. See Reginald Heber Smith, "Preventive Law: The Great Opportunity of the Legal Aid Society" in *Legal Aid Review* xv, no. 2 (1917) 1-6.

3. The contentiousness did not end with the transfer of OEO funds to MLS and FTE. Both successor organizations were embroiled in charges of racism, insensitivity to the poor, internal power struggles, and external conflict. See Braun, *Policies, Programs, Politics, and the Poor* 15-18.

20

LEGAL AID SOCIETY ROSTER

1916 – 2010

PRESIDENTS

Willliam Kaumheimer, 1916-29. Charles W. Babcock, 1929-1949. Charles B. Quarles, 1949-1960. Judge F. Ryan Duffy, Sr. 1960-69. Judge John A. Decker, 1969-71. Harney B. Stover, Jr. 1971-73. Robert M. Weiss, 1973-77. Robert A. Christensen, 1977-79. Stephen M. Glynn, 1979-92. Laurence C. Hammond, Jr. 1992-95. Thomas G. Cannon, 1995-2003. Wendy Reed Bosworth, 2003-06. David A. Erne, 2006-09. Peter J. Stone, 2009-

DIRECTORS

Mrs. E.D. Adler. Nelson G. Alston. Sunella Jones Ash. Brother Booker Ashe. Charles Ashley. Charles W. Babcock. Wayne E. Babler, Jr. John F. Baker. Emile H. Banks, Jr. Pamela E. Barker. Justice John Barnes. Walter S. Bartlett. Mrs. C.R. Beck. Walter H. Bender. Meta S. Berger. Professor Daniel D. Blinka. Dean Robert F. Boden. Sean O'D Bosack. Wendy Reed Bosworth. Christy A. Brooks. Howard G. Brown. David J. Cannon, Thomas G. Cannon. David B. Carr. Timothy R. Casgar. Robert A. Christensen. Marion L. Coffey. Patrick W. Cotter. Rodney L. Cubbie. Abbie Davis. David L. DeBruin Judge John A. Decker. Frank C. DeGuire. Emmett A. Donnelly. John A. Dorney. Chief Judge F. Ryan Duffy, Sr. Robert A. Duffy. Robert A. DuPuy. Professor Caroyln M. Edwards. Dean Howard B. Eisenberg. Gerald M. Elliott. David A. Erne. David Espinoza. Mrs. E.T. Fairchild. Paul Feldner. Curry First. Morris Fox. Bernard T. Franck. Robert R. Freeman. Dr. Howard L. Fuller. Dean Janine P. Geske. Stephen M. Glynn.

Charles L. Goldberg. Socorro Gonzales. Aaron E. Goodstein. Mrs. Howard Greene. Laurence C. Hammond, Jr. Arthur J. Harrington. Father Robert Harrison. Professor Patrick K. Hetrick. Margaret W. Hickey. James Hinchey. John Hogan. Albert B. Houghton. Stephen T. Jacobs. John R. Jones. William Kaumheimer. Dr. Derek Kenner. Reginald I. Kenney. Joan F. Kessler. Agnes Campbell Kiewert. Timothy Kiley. William A. Klatte. Robert F. Klaver, Jr. Professor Ramon A. Klitzke. John A. Kluwin. Frances Krueger. William Krueger. Edessa K. Lines. Ida E. Luick. Kevin J. Lyons. Raymond E. Majerus. Mary Lou Massignani. Michael McMonigal. Alice Miller. Richard F. Mooney. Charles M. Morris. William J. Mulligan. Dr. Paul J. Mundie. John D. Murray. Daniel Wells (Neil) Norris. Brian C. O'Connor. David R. Olson. Colonel Chris J. Otjen. June M. Perry. Ernest J. Philipp. Nora M. Platt. Barbara Pleasant. Richard H. Porter. Charles B. Quarles. Larry Reed. Chief Judge John W. Reynolds. Carl L. Ricciardi. Mrs. Emmet L. Richardson. Esther Leah Ritz. Kathleen M. Rivera. Julio Rodriguez. Olga Valcourt Schwartz. Wendy Selig-Prieb. James E. Shapiro. Edmund B. Shea. Chief Judge Patrick T. Sheedy. Paul E. Sicula. Dr. Ralph P. Sproule. Perry J. Stearns. Peter J. Stone. Harney B. Stover, Jr. Brother Pascal (Charles W.) Stubbs. Chief Judge Michael P. Sullivan. Maud Swett. Paul J. Tilleman. Cecilia Valdez. Dorothy K. von Briesen. Ralph von Briesen. Benjamin S. Wagner. Robert M. Weiss. Professor Lee E. Wells. Leonard S. Zubrensky.

STAFF ATTORNEYS

Anne Marie Abell-Olson. Rachel M. Arfa. David J. Becker. Rudolph Becker. Barbara B. Berman. David S. Berman. James M. Brennan. Audrey Y. Brooks. Quentin Z. Brooks. Victor D. Brooks. Thomas E. Brown. Barbara M. Browning. Peter W. Bruce. Thomas B. Burke. William U. Burke. Stephen M. Byers. Mary B. Campbell. Thomas G. Cannon. Glenn E. Carr. Patricia M. Cavey. Christie A. Christie. William Clark. Karen G. Cobb. Lawrence J. Cofar. Rodney L. Cubbie. Rosemary Reyes Cuevas. Raymond M. Dall'Osto. Karen D. Dardy. Peggy A. Davis. Jane Davis-Weida. Francis J. Demet. Margadette M. Demet. Patrick J. Devitt. John D. Dobrowski. Thomas P. Doherty. Julia B. Dolan (McClelland). Michael Donnelly. Catherine M. Doyle. Han-

nah C. Dugan. Kevin B. Dunn. Robert J. Dvorak. Dennis W. Egre.
Jack N. Eisendrath. Ricardo F. Estrada. Michael F. Fauerbach. Clinton
J. Finnegan. Roger W. Finnegan. Curry First. Lucille T. Fitzpatrick.
Debra N. Fohr. Colleen A. Foley. Lisa Clay Foley. Rebecca A. Foley.
Daniel E. Fromstein.

56. Current Milwaukee County Courthouse, opened in 1931, is listed on the National
Register of Historic Places. *Courtesy of Milwaukee County Historical Society.*

Krista A. Gallagher. Beatrice Garrett. Timothy P. Garrity. Ty C.
Gee. Andrew I. Gehl. Rosalie I. Gellman. Horace Ray George. John
J. Germanotta. Janine P. Geske. Steven H. Glamm. William J. Gold-
schmidt. D. Byron Goltz. Isa Gonzalez-Zayas. Bonnie L. Gordon.
Lindsey C. Grady. Stephan M. Grochowski. Morton D. Grodsky.
Mary M. Gundrum. Michael D. Guolee. Kenneth Guy. Thomas G.
Halloran. Carl B. Hampton. Kay Handrick. William F. Hannan.
Margaret G. Hanrahan. Margery M. Heck (Riffle). Patricia M. Heim.
Harvey Held. Georgia L. Herrera. Paul B. Higginbotham. Shelia Hill-
Roberts. Miriam R. Horwitz. William A. Jennaro. James A. Johnson.

Richard J. Johnson. David Jorling. Jocelyn Doctura Jurva. Charles F. Kahn, Jr. Anthony K. Karpowicz. John E. Keese. Bradley J. Keith. Catherine E. Kendrigan. Arlene Kennedy. James E. Kenney. Everett King. James A. Knutson. Peter M. Koneazny. Karen Kotecki. Robert E. Kraemer. Terry R. Kraucunas. Danuta E. Kurczewski. Robert W. Landry. Jessica Roth Lasser. Robert G. LeBell. Elizabeth C. Leis. Cynthia A. Lepkowski. Micaela H. Levine. Jack D. Longert. Bonnie Lopez. Paula K. Lorant. Martin E. Love. Barbara E. Maier. Gloria Marquardt. Jess Martinez. Frederic E. Matestic. Linnea J. Matthiesen. Victoria M. McCandless. Neil C. McGinn. Richard P. McGuire. Anne S. McIntyre. Bettie McJunkin. Louis J. Mestre. Felicia S. Miller. Paul T. Miller. Candice Morgan. Janet M. Mueller.

Molly S. Nealson. Katharine A. Neugent. Lawrence E. Norton II. Carlo A. Obligato. Carmen M. Ortiz. Isaias Ortiz. Jennifer A. Ortiz. Jon J. Padgham. Michele Palmer. Nicole C. Penegor. Carol C. Petersen. Nancy A. Phelps. Seymour Pikofsky. Mary B. Pinkel. Robert W. Pledl. Glen W. Ploetz. Amanda Quester. James A. Rebholz. Mary C. Reddin. Jordan B. Reich. James C. Reiher. William G. Retert. Karl O. Rohlich. Ernesto Romero. Frederick C. Rosa. Philip J. Rosenkranz. Joel H. Rosenthal. Arman Rouf. James D. Rudd. James R. Schaefer. Frank J. Schiro. Melville H. Sell. Ellen A. Sinclair. Alexander G. Sklenarz. Sheila M. Smith. Stuart Spielman. Russell W. Stamper. James R. Stanek. E.F. Stanelle. Clifford R. Steele. Eric D. Steele. Russell L. Stewart. Randolph N. Stone. Daphne Taylor. Kathleen A. Thiemann. Angela Thundercloud. Daniel Ticcione. Nicholas Toman. Natasha L. Torry-Abate. Stephan W. Tradewell. Gerald R. Turner. Rodney J. Uphoff. Eric Van Schyndle, Dorothy K. von Briesen. Julia E. Vosper. Michael J. Vruno, Jr. Lisa D. Walker. James A. Walrath. Kathleen Walsh. Bruce R. Ware. Nancy E. Weisenberg. Deanna M. Weiss. Christine L. Wember. Carole O. Wenerowicz. Kendall K. Wick. Antonique C. Williams. Natasha M. Wilson. Gary Windom. Thomas K. Zander. Dean B. Zemel. David N. Zerwick. Andrew S. Zieve.

SOCIAL WORKERS

Edith Adelman. Mara Bach. Judith A. Ballard. Linda J. Benson-Kenneth. Agnes Campbell (Kiewert). Nancy Cecil-Mitchell. Gena L. Clark. Debbie Cornella. Collette Crowl. Sharon Dossett. Raeshann

Canady Ford. Mary Beth Geiger. Ernette Griggs. Kim Hall. Donna Hibbler. Gregory M. Hildebrand. Jocelyn Doctura Jurva. David Kachelski. Mariann Scholten Kirst. Pamela Lambach. Donna Lee. Kristin Leguizamon. Madge Loranger. Jane Moore. Tomeitha Moore. Rex Morgan. Mary Protz. Thomas Puls. Julie Rozek-Brady. Clarice Ruehl. Amy Sanchez. Alma C. Schlesinger. Todd Schroll. Wendy Schuster. Jan Shannon (Riordan). Maureen Sievers. Gregory Skibinski. Kathy L. Teague. Michelle Watts. Marie E. Wegner. Marcy R. Wichman. Nancy Doucette Wilkinson. Elsa Wilmanns. Marnie Wisniewski.

Mary Ann Czarnecki, M.S.N., worked as a client advocate for mental patients in institutional settings. Diana M. Pitkaranta, M.Ed., serves as coordinator of the GAIN project's 300 court-appointed volunteer guardians of the person.

21
DIGEST OF NOTEWORTHY CASES

Attorneys for the Legal Aid Society of Milwaukee have appeared as counsel of record, guardian ad litem, next friend, or *amicus curiae* in nearly 150 cases resulting in published decisions of state and federal courts. These opinions have created an important body of law on the constitutional rights of welfare recipients, tenants, children, prisoners, mental patients, consumers, the homeless, and the elderly. Moreover, the legal principles established by such cases serve as local and national precedent, and thus contribute to the overall development of the law. As noted above, some of these cases have been cited in decisions of the United States Supreme Court. The Society has also litigated a second group of significant matters that ended either in unpublished opinions or in consent decrees. Together, they constitute a vital part of the Society's permanent jurisprudential legacy.

It should be pointed out that some of these significant cases were co-counseled with litigation partners in private law firms or with other public interest law firms, including the AIDS Resource Center of Wisconsin, American Civil Liberties Union of Wisconsin, Center for Social Welfare Policy and the Law (Columbia University), Children's Rights, Inc. (New York), Disability Rights Wisconsin, Lamda Legal Defense & Education Fund, Legal Action of Wisconsin, and the National Association for the Advancement of Colored People. Organizations represented by LAS as *amicus curiae* have ranged from the Alzheimer's Association of Southeastern Wisconsin to the Wisconsin Defender Association; most often, though, the Society files friend of the court briefs on its own behalf. LAS's impact-litigation work carries out the Society's unique charter "to do all things necessary for the prevention of injustice."

There is some difficulty in identifying the earliest published Legal Aid case because of the fact that the Society's outside retained counsel (Hannan, Johnson & Goldschmidt) handled matters referred to it under the private law firm's name rather than the Society's banner. According to William Kaumheimer, though, the Legal Aid Society of Milwaukee litigated appeals in the 1920s and even advanced court costs to its clients for appellate matters. *Proc. NALAO* (1928) 14. Since the Hannan firm litigated more than a dozen cases in the Wisconsin Supreme Court between 1916 and 1930, any one of them could have been argued on behalf of a client of the Legal Aid Society. One matter that stands out as possibly the first Legal Aid case is *Zurich General Accident Co. v. Industrial Commission*, 203 Wis. 135, 233 N.W. 772 (1930).

In that proceeding, the Hannan firm represented Concetta Martorana, a widow whose husband died of black-lung disease as a result of inhaling lethal amounts of industrial dust in the chipping room of his employer, the Falk Corporation. A worker's compensation claim was pursued on behalf of the widow and successfully prosecuted all the way up to the Wisconsin Supreme Court. Her brief filed in the high court case contains no mention of the Legal Aid Society. *Wisconsin Briefs and Cases*, vol. 203. Nevertheless, the *Martorana* case may well have been one of the 42 worker's compensation claims that the Society opened in 1928 according to its Annual Report and one of the appellate matters mentioned above by William Kaumheimer. See, generally, Joseph Bear, "The Legal Aid Society in the Workmen's Compensation Field" in *Legal Aid Review* xxxvii, no. 3 (1939) 1-5.

In fact, Charles W. Babcock may have alluded to this very case when he informed the National Association of Legal Aid Organizations that "our part-time attorney has become an expert in securing [workers'] compensation awards in industrial T.B. [tuberculosis] cases." *Proc. NALAO* (1931) 47. The case prompted a complaint to the Community Fund from defense lawyers for the insurance companies because the LAS "attorney in question was probably not over polite to the defendant [corporation] in the industrial commission case." *Id.* [see Historical Documents Section].

It would be another thirty-seven years, however, before a published case was unequivocally brought by the Legal Aid Society's own staff. That decision was the product of the Society's Law Reform Division, a unique collaboration between LAS and the private bar [see Historical Documents Section]. Staff Attorney Bettie McJunkin served as Coordinator of the Division during its short tenure, 1967-69. As the following digest demonstrates, the Division seems to have opened a floodgate of litigation activity by the Society on behalf of its impoverished clients. LAS's debut case (*Ramos*) made the front page of both local newspapers: "Welfare Order Granted" in *Milwaukee Sentinel* (November 22, 1967); "Residency Aid Rule Unequal, Judges Say" in *Milwaukee Journal* (November 22, 1967).

In 1988, Executive Director Tom Zander established the position of Litigation Director to give more focus and attention to major impact cases and appellate matters. Noted Milwaukee civil rights attorney Curry First held the position for three years. His first major case was *Jackson v. Artison* (see below), a federal civil rights claim seeking to reduce severe overcrowding in the old Milwaukee County Jail. The case resulted in a consent decree that played a major role in prompting construction of the new Criminal Justice Facility. Curry First set a high standard for the new post. In 1991, Jim Walrath became the second Litigation Director, a position he held for four years, until his appointment as Executive Director. In 1995, he was succeeded by Mary Gundrum who, because she also did some development work, bore the title of Associate Director. Mary brought to the position a broad expertise in poverty law, consumer rights, and migrant law. In 2002, Pete Koneazny was appointed as the Society's fourth Litigation Director. His impressive background as a Root-Tilden scholar at New York University Law School, appellate attorney with the State Public Defender, staff attorney at the Legal Aid Society of Milwaukee, and Legal Director of the American Civil Liberties Union of Wisconsin represents the kind of exceptional qualifications needed to fill this important position.

In addition to planning and trying complex major cases, the Litigation Director also assists staff attorneys in all appellate cases handled by the Society. In recent years, this has worked out to about 10 or 12 appeals per term. Finally, it must be noted that the majority of the following cases were actually litigated by the Legal Aid Society's line staff attorneys. The Society's latest appeal is *In Matter of Mental Commitment of H. T-O*, case no. 2010 AP 256. That case, which may well result in a published Court of Appeals or Supreme Court opinion, challenges the trial court's denial of a Spanish-language interpreter for a monoglot

Spanish-speaking client of LAS so that English-language court documents may be translated for the client. As this book goes to press, the case is pending before the Wisconsin Court of Appeals (District I).

* * *

Ramos v. Health & Social Services Board, 276 F. Supp. 474 (E.D. Wis. 1967). Three-judge panel strikes down Wisconsin's one-year residency requirement for establishing eligibility for AFDC welfare benefits. Court finds state statute an abridgment of Equal Protection Clause. Case represents the first class action ever filed by the Legal Aid Society.

Denny v. Health & Social Services Board, 285 F. Supp. 526 (E.D. Wis. 1968). Class action case in which three-judge panel enjoins enforcement of Wisconsin's one-year residency requirement for establishing eligibility for general assistance on equal protection grounds.

Hanley v. Volpe, 305 F. Supp. 977 (E.D. Wis. 1969). Court holds that families and individuals displaced by Park Freeway project have standing to bring class action seeking declaratory and injunctive relief requiring compliance with federal statutes governing relocation assistance. 3 *Clearinghouse Rev.* (1969) 114. Other aspects of the case are reported at 48 F.R.D. 387 (E.D. Wis. 1970); and 322 F. Supp. 1306 (E.D. Wis. 1971)

Llames v. Dept. of Transportation, 320 F. Supp. 1041 (E.D. Wis. 1969). Class action federal civil rights case challenging provisions of Wisconsin's Financial Responsibility Law that automatically suspend driver's license of uninsured motorist for failure to post financial security with Motor Vehicle Department after an accident. 2 *Clearinghouse Rev.* no. 15 (1969) 15.

Dickhut v. Norton, 45 Wis.2d 389, 173 N.W.2d 297, 40 A.L.R. 3d 740 (1970). Decision recognizes the defense of retaliatory eviction on behalf of a tenant who complained to the City Health Department about housing code violations. Dissent specifically notes that appeal was litigated by the Society's Law Reform Division, which was part of Milwaukee Plan Legal Services. *Id.* at 402.

Posnanski v. Hood, 46 Wis.2d 172, 174 N.W.2d 528 (1970). Court holds that violations of city housing code do not render residential lease void and do not create an affirmative defense to eviction for nonpayment of rent.

Application of Ottman, 336 F. Supp. 746 (E.D. Wis. 1972). Petition to proceed *in forma pauperis* establishes right of equal access to justice. Decision orders that indigent debtor be permitted to file for bankruptcy without prepayment of filing fees established by Congress.

State v. Hall, 53 Wis.2d 719, 193 N.W.2d 653 (1972). Conviction for attempted burglary is reversed and 5-year prison sentence is set aside based upon insufficient evidence.

State ex rel. Mitchell v. Bowman, 54 Wis.2d 5, 194 N.W.2d 297 (1972). Decision recognizes due process right of child in juvenile delinquency proceeding to disqualify trial court judge for demonstrable bias.

57. Judge Vel R. Phillips Juvenile Justice Center, site of the Legal Aid Society's Guardian ad Litem Office. *Courtesy of Legal Aid Society of Milwaukee.*

Bennett v. State, 54 Wis.2d 727, 196 N.W.2d 704 (1972). Writ of error reviewing conviction for homicide on grounds of insufficiency of evidence and failure to exclude expert opinion.

Nelson v. State, 54 Wis.2d 758, 196 N.W.2d 710 (1972). Writ of error reviewing conviction for armed robbery on ground of systematic exclusion of African Americans from jury array.

State v. Scarbrough, 55 Wis.2d 181, 197 N.W.2d 790 (1972). Appeal of conviction for robbery on grounds of denial of right to counsel and counsel's refusal to advance alibi defense.

Hughes v. State, 55 Wis.2d 477, 198 N.W.2d 348 (1972). Writ of error reviewing conviction for statutory rape on ground of failure to instruct jury on lesser-included offense.

State ex rel. Morrow v. Lewis, 55 Wis.2d 502, 200 N.W.2d 193 (1972). Original writ of habeas corpus granted by Supreme Court requires Children's Court judges to conduct a probable cause hearing within 24 hours to review initial detention decisions made by Milwaukee County Detention Center staff.

Jung v. State, 55 Wis.2d 714, 201 N.W.2d 58 (1972). Writ of error reviewing conviction for contributing to the delinquency of minor on grounds of insufficiency of complaint and defense of lack of knowledge of fact.

Day v. State, 55 Wis.2d 756, 201 N.W.2d 42 (1972). Writ of error reviewing conviction for murder on grounds of failure to instruct jury on lesser-included offense and on reasonableness of self-defense.

State v. Fuller, 57 Wis.2d 408, 204 N.W.2d 452 (1973). Appeal of conviction for forgery and attempted theft on grounds of failure of judge to disqualify himself and failure to instruct jury on lesser-included offense.

Wilson v. State, 57 Wis.2d 508, 204 N.W.2d 508 (1973). Writ of error reviewing conviction for burglary on ground of failure to allow withdrawal of guilty plea.

Adams v. State, 57 Wis.2d 515, 204 N.W.2d 657 (1973). Writ of error reviewing conviction for attempted rape on ground of insufficiency of evidence.

State ex rel. Ahulicz v. Wolke, petition denied, 57 Wis.2d 778, cert. denied, 414 U.S. 881 (1973). Original writ of habeas corpus in Wisconsin Supreme Court to review conviction for civil contempt without benefit of counsel. Petition for certiorari filed to review denial. Justices Blackmun and Douglas voted to grant certiorari.

Taylor v. State, 59 Wis.2d 134, 207 N.W.2d 651 (1973). Writ of error reviewing conviction for burglary improvidently granted on inadequate record. Supreme Court allows case to be refiled as writ of habeas corpus.

State ex rel. Hildebrand v. Kegu, 59 Wis.2d 215, 207 N.W.2d 658 (1973) (*per curiam*). State erroneously appeals from order of dismissal in paternity action. Dismissal affirmed.

State v. Taylor, 60 Wis.2d 506, 210 N.W.2d 873 (1973). Appeal from two convictions for armed robbery on grounds of lack of probable cause for arrest, failure to exclude fruit of unconstitutional search, and absence of counsel at lineup.

State v. Kuecey, 60 Wis.2d 677, 211 N.W.2d 453 (1973). Appeal of conviction for burglary on grounds of illegality of arrest, improper admission of evidence, and tainted pretrial identification.

Schneider v. State, 60 Wis.2d 765, 211 N.W.2d 511 (1973) (*per curiam*). Writ of error reviewing conviction for theft on ground of insufficiency of evidence.

Voigt v. State, 61 Wis.2d 17, 211 N.W.2d 445 (1973). Writ of error reviewing conviction for conspiracy to commit forgery-uttering on grounds of insufficiency of evidence, judicial bias, and excessive sentence.

Ross v. State, 61 Wis.2d 160, 211 N.W.2d 827 (1973). Murder conviction is reversed due to trial judge's erroneous self-defense jury instruction. On retrial, Ross is acquitted by jury.

Hardison v. State, 61 Wis.2d 262, 212 N.W.2d 103 (1973). Writ of error reviewing convictions for murder and robbery on grounds of insufficiency of evidence, failure of state to elect between inchoate crimes, and failure to declare mistrial after witness' improper comment before jury.

Davis v. State, 61 Wis.2d 284, 212 N.W.2d 139 (1973). Writ of error reviewing conviction for armed robbery on ground of improper prosecutorial comment before jury.

Taylor v. State, 61 Wis.2d 741, 212 N.W.2d 702 (1973) (*per curiam*). Writ of error reviewing conviction for sale of unregistered securities on grounds of improper failure to allow withdrawal of guilty plea and state's breach of plea bargain.

Allison v. State, 62 Wis.2d 14, 214 N.W.2d 437 (1974). Writ of error reviewing convictions for rape and sexual perversion on grounds of insufficiency of complaint, failure to allow alibi evidence, and unconstitutionality of Wisconsin alibi statute.

Pfeifer v. Pfeifer, 62 Wis.2d 417, 215 N.W.2d 419 (1974). Appeal of custody determination in divorce on grounds of trial court's improper consideration of mother's adultery and failure to appoint guardian ad litem for minor children.

Jones v. State, 63 Wis.2d 97, 216 N.W.2d 224 (1974). Writ of error reviewing conviction for armed robbery on grounds of uncounseled lineup and tainted in-court identification.

Hall v. State, 63 Wis.2d 304, 217 N.W.2d 352 (1974). Conviction of co-defendants for strong-armed robbery reversed and their seven-year sentences vacated by the Wisconsin Supreme Court on ground that joint representation by one defense counsel constitutes an impermissible conflict of interest.

Gregory v. State, 63 Wis.2d 754, 218 N.W.2d 319 (1974). Writ of error reviewing conviction for armed robbery on grounds of improper judicial comment and abuse of discretion in sentencing.

Leahy v. State, 63 Wis.2d 785, 216 N.W.2d 47 (1974) (*per curiam*). Writ of error reviewing conviction for forgery on ground of inappropriate sentence.

Harrell v. State, 63 Wis.2d 786, 216 N.W.2d 48 (1974) (*per curiam*). Writ of error reviewing conviction for burglary on ground of insufficiency of evidence.

Patterson v. State, 63 Wis.2d 788, 216 N.W.2d 47 (1974) (*per curiam*). Writ of error reviewing conviction for burglary on ground of inappropriate sentence.

Weidenfeller v. Kidulis I, 380 F. Supp. 445 (E.D. Wis. 1974). Court holds that mentally handicapped residents of private nursing home and group home may sue under Fair Labor Standards Act and Thirteenth Amendment for being forced to perform uncompensated work for non-therapeutic purposes.

Coleman v. State, 64 Wis.2d 124, 218 N.W.2d 744 (1974). Writ of error reviewing conviction for armed robbery on grounds of tainted in-court identification, failure of state to produce discovery, and failure to exclude evidence.

Love v. State, 64 Wis.2d 432, 219 N.W.2d 294 (1974). Writ of error reviewing conviction for indecent liberties with female child on grounds of incompetency of child witness and insufficiency of evidence.

Seidler v. State, 64 Wis.2d 456, 219 N.W.2d 320 (1974). Murder conviction reversed on insufficient evidence and case remanded with directions for a new trial on lesser-included charge of homicide by reckless conduct.

State v. Frizzell, 64 Wis.2d 480, 219 N.W.2d 390 (1974). Appeal of conviction for first-degree murder on ground of failure to exclude prior criminal conviction.

State ex rel. Harris v. Larson, 64 Wis.2d 521, 219 N.W.2d 335 (1974). Supreme Court issues class-wide writs of prohibition and mandamus directing Milwaukee County Juvenile Detention Center to release children within five days of their final adjudication.

Upchurch v. State, 64 Wis.2d 553, 219 N.W.2d 363 (1974). Conviction for armed robbery reversed on ground that trial judge failed to conduct a hearing outside jury's presence on the voluntariness of defendant's statement.

Brown v. State, 64 Wis.2d 581, 219 N.W.2d 373 (1974). Writ of error reviewing conviction for robbery on ground of failure to exclude involuntary confession.

Mills v. State, 64 Wis.2d 756, 219 N.W.2d 375 (1974) (*per curiam*). Writ of error reviewing conviction for false representation to secure public assistance on grounds of failure to allow withdrawal of guilty plea and abuse of discretion at sentencing.

Dahl v. State, 64 Wis.2d 758, 218 N.W.2d 376 (1974) (*per curiam*). Writ of error reviewing conviction for armed robbery on ground of denial of constitutional right to speedy trial.

Best v. State, 64 Wis.2d 758, 218 N.W.2d 376 (1974) (*per curiam*). Writ of error reviewing conviction for forgery-uttering on grounds of denial of equal protection and inappropriate sentence.

Scaggs v. State, 64 Wis.2d 759, 218 N.W.2d 376 (1974) (*per curiam*). Writ of error reviewing conviction for receiving stolen property on ground of inappropriate sentence.

Pfrunder v. State, 64 Wis.2d 759, 218 N.W.2d 377 (1974) (*per curiam*). Writ of error reviewing conviction for armed robbery on ground of inappropriate sentence.

Cook v. State, 64 Wis.2d 760, 218 N.W.2d 377 (1974) (*per curiam*). Writ of error reviewing convictions for burglary, bail jumping, and armed robbery on ground of inappropriate sentence.

58. United States Courthouse in Milwaukee, built 1892, is listed on the National
Register of Historic Places. *Courtesy of Milwaukee County Historical Society.*

Grady v. State, 64 Wis.2d 760, 218 N.W.2d 377 (1974) (*per curiam*). Writ of error reviewing conviction for armed robbery on grounds of abuse of discretion and inappropriate sentence.

Gross v. State, 64 Wis.2d 762, 219 N.W.2d 407 (1974) (*per curiam*). Writ of error reviewing conviction for receiving stolen property on grounds of invalidity of guilty plea, failure to allow withdrawal of guilty plea, and manifest injustice.

Washington v. State, 64 Wis.2d 763, 219 N.W.2d 408 (1974) (*per curiam*). Writ of error reviewing conviction for robbery on grounds of lack of jurisdiction and lack of probable cause.

Burdick v. Miech, 385 F. Supp. 927 (E.D. Wis. 1974). Federal civil rights claim premised on violation of rights of privacy and self-incrimination in state-court paternity proceeding. Temporary restraining order denied.

Tyacke v. State, 65 Wis.2d 513, 223 N.W.2d 595 (1974). Writ of error reviewing conviction for attempted burglary on grounds of abuse of discretion, insufficiency of evidence, and exclusion of exonerating evidence.

Smith v. Burns, 65 Wis.2d 638, 223 N.W.2d 562 (1974). Constitutional challenge to Wisconsin Consumer Act provision authorizing issuance of body attachment in supplemental proceedings.

Lee v. State, 65 Wis.2d 648, 223 N.W.2d 455 (1974). Writ of error reviewing conviction for first-degree murder on ground of failure to instruct jury on intoxication as negating state of mind essential to crime.

State v. Donovan, 65 Wis.2d 786, 222 N.W.2d 708 (1974) (*per curiam*). Appeal of conviction for theft on grounds of abuse of discretion and unconstitutionality of enhanced punishment for repeater.

State v. Behling, 65 Wis.2d 788, 222 N.W.2d 708 (1974) (*per curiam*). Appeal of conviction for delivery and possession of dangerous drugs and controlled substances on ground of defendant's absence from pre-sentence conference.

Bratkowski v. State, 65 Wis.2d 789, 222 N.W.2d 707 (1974) (*per curiam*). Writ of error reviewing conviction for homicide by reckless conduct on grounds of abuse of discretion and inappropriate sentence.

Medina v. State, 65 Wis.2d 791, 222 N.W.2d 708 (1974) (*per curiam*). Writ of error reviewing conviction for forgery (uttering) on ground of abuse of discretion in rejecting plea bargain.

Galarza v. State, 66 Wis.2d 611, 225 N.W.2d 450 (1975). Writ of error reviewing conviction for commercial gambling on ground of insufficiency of evidence.

Wilkins v. State, 66 Wis.2d 628, 225 N.W.2d 492 (1975). Writ of error reviewing conviction for sexual perversion. Sentence reduced by amount of time defendant spent in pretrial detention.

La Brosse v. State, 67 Wis.2d 801, 227 N.W.2d 733 (1975) (*per curiam*). Writ of error reviewing conviction for robbery on ground of abuse of discretion in sentencing.

Clark v. State, 67 Wis.2d 801, 227 N.W.2d 731 (1975) (*per curiam*). Writ of error reviewing conviction for manslaughter on ground of abuse of discretion in sentencing.

Birts v. State, 68 Wis.2d 389, 228 N.W.2d 351 (1975). Writ of error reviewing convictions for battery and carrying a concealed weapon on grounds of manifest injustice, failure to allow withdrawal of guilty plea, and insufficiency of evidence.

Broadie v. State, 68 Wis.2d 420, 228 N.W.2d 687 (1975). Writ of error reviewing conviction for attempted rape on ground of insufficiency of evidence to support guilty plea.

In re Interest of J.K., 68 Wis.2d 426, 228 N.W.2d 713 (1975). Appeal of dispositional order in juvenile delinquency proceeding on grounds of abuse of discretion and failure to impose least restrictive alternative.

Knecht v. State, 68 Wis.2d 697, 229 N.W.2d 649 (1975). Writ of error reviewing conviction for armed robbery on ground of abuse of discretion in sentencing.

Drinkwater v. State, 69 Wis.2d 60, 230 N.W.2d 126 (1975). Writ of error reviewing conviction for operating automobile without owner's consent. Sentence modified on ground that trial judge had no authority to revoke probation and impose sentence consecutive to another prison term for separate crime.

Jones v. State, 69 Wis.2d 337, 230 N.W.2d 677 (1975). Writ of error reviewing convictions for first-degree murder and robbery on grounds of failure to exclude involuntary confession, failure to instruct on intoxication defense, and failure to disclose criminal record of prosecution witness.

Flores v. State, 69 Wis.2d 509, 230 N.W.2d 637 (1975). Writ of error reviewing conviction for sexual intercourse with child on grounds of denial of equal protection and abuse of discretion in sentencing.

Olson v. State, 69 Wis.2d 605, 230 N.W.2d 634 (1975). Writ of error reviewing conviction for delivery of a controlled substance on grounds of erroneous imposition of sentence. Sentence modified by Supreme Court.

Sykes v. State, 69 Wis.2d 616, 230 N.W.2d 760 (1975). Writ of error reviewing conviction for first-degree murder on grounds of insufficiency of evidence and failure to grant new trial in interests of justice.

Brozovich v. State, 69 Wis.2d 653, 230 N.W.2d 639 (1975). Court vacates 8-year prison sentence for burglary on ground that trial judge improperly considered pending charges in formulating sentence. Remanded for re-sentencing

Guyton v. State, 69 Wis.2d 663, 230 N.W.2d 726 (1975). Writ of error reviewing conviction for burglary on ground of erroneous imposition of sentence. Sentence modified.

Weidenfeller v. Kudulis II, 392 F. Supp. 967 (E.D. Wis. 1975). Federal civil rights claim filed on behalf of mentally handicapped nursing home residents. Motion to dismiss filed by Wisconsin Department of Health & Social Services denied.

Foster v. State, 70 Wis.2d 12, 233 N.W.2d 411 (1975). Writ of error reviewing conviction for armed robbery on ground of denial of right to speedy trial.

Jones (Hollis) v. State, 70 Wis.2d 62, 233 N.W.2d 441 (1975). Appeal of convictions for armed robbery and robbery on grounds of unreasonable search and seizure and abuse of discretion in sentencing.

Witzel v. Quatsoe, 396 F. Supp. 395 (E.D. Wis. 1975). Prison warden ordered to expunge disciplinary record, restore good time, and credit time spent in solitary confinement for prisoner punished without benefit of due process hearing.

Spannuth v. State, 70 Wis.2d 362, 234 N.W.2d 79 (1975). Writ of error reviewing conviction for forgery (uttering) on ground of erroneous imposition of sentence. Sentence modified and order for restitution vacated.

Jones v. State, 71 Wis.2d 750, 238 N.W.2d 741 (1976). Writ of error reviewing conviction for murder on ground of failure to allow withdrawal of guilty plea.

Hurst v. State, 72 Wis.2d 188, 240 N.W.2d 392 (1976). Judgment of conviction reversed, sentence vacated, and case dismissed on ground that criminal complaint failed to establish probable cause that crime of delivery of dangerous drug had been committed.

State ex rel. Milwaukee County v. Wisconsin Council on Criminal Justice, 73 Wis.2d 237, 248 N.W.2d 485 (1976) [*amicus curiae*]. Original action in Supreme Court seeking declaratory judgment on legality of Executive Branch agency (WCCJ) appointing defense counsel in criminal cases.

Cummings v. State, 73 Wis.2d 554, 243 N.W.2d 499 (1976). Writ of error reviewing conviction for delivery of controlled substance on grounds of state's refusal to reveal informant's identity, trial court's refusal to allow inquiry into prosecutorial leniency for informant's testimony, and failure to give missing witness instruction to jury.

Edwards v. State, 74 Wis.2d 79, 246 N.W.2d 109 (1976). Writ of error reviewing sentencing for theft, operating an automobile without owner's consent, and aiding escape from custody on grounds of abuse of discretion and constitutional overbreadth.

State ex rel. Memmel v. Mundy, 75 Wis.2d 276, 249 N.W.2d 573 (1977). Class action writ of habeas corpus on behalf of all patients at Milwaukee County Mental Health Center establishes right of person facing involuntary mental commitment to be represented by adversary counsel who is both zealous and competent.

In Matter of Grant, 83 Wis.2d 77, 264 N.W.2d 587 (1978). Civil contempt finding reversed on ground that constitutional right against self-incrimination applies to paternity proceedings.

State v. Cramer, 91 Wis.2d 553, 283 N.W.2d 625 (Ct. App. 1979). Appeal of order extending custody beyond mandatory release date of individual convicted of indecent behavior with child on grounds of violation of due process and failure to exclude privileged doctor-patient communications.

State ex rel. Hawkins v. DH&SS, 92 Wis.2d 420, 284 N.W.2d 680 (1979) (*per curiam*). Appeal of order revoking probation on ground that revocation was arbitrary and capricious.

In re G.G.D. v. State, 97 Wis.2d 1, 292 N.W.2d 853 (1980). Order revoking juvenile's probation is reversed on ground that constitutional right of due process was violated by the state's failure to provide notice to juvenile of his conditions of probation.

State ex rel. Lockman v. Gerhardstein, 107 Wis.2d 325, 320 N.W.2d 27 (Ct. App. 1982). Court holds that statutory time limits in civil mental commitment proceedings are mandatory and jurisdictional. If not strictly adhered to, petitions must be dismissed.

59. Milwaukee County Mental Health Center where civil mental commitment hearings are held. *Courtesy of Legal Aid Society of Milwaukee.*

In Matter of Athans, 107 Wis.2d 331, 320 N.W.2d 30 (Ct. App. 1982). Court defines "treatability" narrowly as a criterion for civil mental commitments under Chapter 51 of the Wisconsin Statutes. Consequently, a person must be shown to be incapable of rehabilitation before s/he can be involuntarily committed.

State ex rel. Watts v. Combined Community Services, 122 Wis.2d 65, 362 N.W.2d 104 (1985). Court rules that protective placement of an incompetent person must be judicially reviewed on at least an annual basis to ensure that patient is in least restrictive environment.

Guardianship and Placement of K.S., 137 Wis.2d 570, 405 N.W.2d 78 (1987). Medical and psychological records are held to be privileged in proposed guardianship and protective placement proceeding where the patient's condition is placed in issue by State.

State ex rel. Jones v. Gerhardstein, 141 Wis.2d 710, 416 N.W.2d 883 (1987). Court establishes constitutional right of an involuntarily committed mental patient to refuse psychotropic medication.

In the Interest of A.B. v. P.B. and M.W.K., 151 Wis.2d 312, 444 N.W.2d 415 (Ct. App. 1989). Termination of parental rights reversed on grounds that such rights may not be voluntarily severed for parent's convenience or financial interests, and because trial court failed to conduct adequate hearing on voluntariness of father's consent.

In the Interest of T.L.: E.H. v. Milwaukee County, 151 Wis.2d 725, 445 N.W.2d 729 (Ct. App. 1989). Dispositional order for child in need of protective services reversed on ground of inadequate competency determination.

In the Interest of H.Q. and P.Q. v. Z.Q, 152 Wis.2d 701, 449 N.W.2d 75 (Ct. App. 1989) [*amicus curiae*]. Appeal of child abuse restraining order on grounds of insufficiency of evidence and failure to appoint guardian ad litem.

City of Milwaukee v. Wroten, 160 Wis.2d 207, 466 N.W.2d 861 (1991). Court strikes down Milwaukee city ordinance prohibiting obstruction or hindering of a police officer on ground of constitutional overbreadth.

In Matter of Guardianship of R.S.: R.S. v. Milwaukee County, 162 Wis.2d 197, 470 N.W.2d 260 (1991). Guardianship for incompetent adult reversed on ground that trial court admitted written psychological report into evidence without requiring psychologist to appear in person for cross-examination.

In the Interest of K.D.J.: B.L.J. v. Polk Co. Dept. of Social Services, 163 Wis.2d 90, 470 N.W.2d 914 (1991) [*amicus curiae*]. Court rules that

60. City of Milwaukee Municipal Court Building.
Courtesy of Legal Aid Society of Milwaukee.

trial judge has the discretion to dismiss petition for termination of parental rights, even where jury finds grounds for termination exist, if judge finds conduct is not egregious.

NAACP et al. v. American Family Mutual Ins. Co., 978 F.2d 287 (7th Cir. 1992), *cert. denied*, 508 U.S. 907 (1993). Court rules that African Americans may sue under Fair Housing Act to prohibit redlining, a practice whereby insurance companies refuse to insure (or charge higher premiums) on the basis of race.

Casteel v. Vaade, 167 Wis.2d 1, 481 N.W.2d 277 (1992). Court holds that state prison inmate, in federal civil rights action, is not required to exhaust administrative remedies under Wisconsin's Inmate Complaint Review System.

In re Paternity of Joshua A. E.: State v. Jody A.E., 171 Wis.2d 327, 491 N.W.2d 136 (1992). Court determines that mother of child is necessary party to paternity proceeding and must, therefore, be served with summons and petition.

Clark v. Milwaukee County I, 172 Wis.2d. 671, 493 N.W.2d 722 (1993) (*per curiam*). Summary judgment improvidently granted in review of application for general relief where factual issues are contested.

Byrne v. Bercker, 176 Wis.2d 1037, 501 N.W.2d 402 (1993) [*amicus curiae*]. Civil action for damages in child incest case held barred by applicable statute of limitations.

Rent-A-Center v. Hall, 181 Wis.2d 243, 510 N.W.2d 789 (Ct. App. 1993). Court affirms trial court ruling rescinding high-interest, rent-to-own contract requiring consumer to pay $1,839 for household appliances worth no more than $600.

Clark v. Milwaukee County II, 188 Wis.2d 171, 524 N.W.2d 382 (1994). In class action suit filed on behalf of homeless residents, Court orders Milwaukee County to promulgate written standards establishing eligibility for housing allowance for persons on general relief.

In Matter of Mental Condition of Virgil D.: Virgil D. v. Rock Co., 189 Wis.2d 1, 524 N.W.2d 894 (1994) [*amicus curiae*]. Court holds that State must prove by clear and convincing evidence that mental patient is incapable of expressing an understanding of risks and benefits of, and alternatives to, psychotropic drugs before it may involuntarily administer such medication.

Paradinovich v. Milwaukee County, 189 Wis.2d 184, 525 N.W.2d 325 (Ct. App. 1994). Indemnification awarded to fired county employee in third-party action against employee for civil damages.

In Matter of Guardianship of Agnes T.: Agnes T. v. Milwaukee Co., 189 Wis.2d 520, 525 N.W.2d 268 (1995). Court holds trial judge must conduct protective placement hearing for incompetent resident of nursing home licensed for 16 or more beds when it appoints a guardian.

In the Interest of Tiffany W. and Myokra W.: State ex rel. Boren v. Circuit Court, 192 Wis.2d 407, 532 N.W.2d 135 (Ct. App. 1995). Concurrent jurisdiction of courts in two counties over children in need of protection or services should be resolved in favor of first court to exercise jurisdiction.

State v. Randall, 192 Wis.2d 800, 532 N.W.2d 94 (1995). Constitutional challenge to confinement of insanity acquitee, who is no longer mentally ill, solely on grounds that he is a danger to self or others.

Jeanine B. et al v. Thompson et al. 877 F. Supp. 1268 (E.D.Wis. 1995). Key pretrial ruling in class action suit against state and county officials concerning their failure to protect the interests of battered, abused, and neglected children in foster care. Legal Aid Society attorneys act in capacity of "next friend" of principal plaintiffs. See also 967 F. Supp. 1104 (E.D. Wis. 1997)

Joni B. v. State, 202 Wis.2d 1, 549 N.W.2d 411 (1996) [*amicus curiae*]. Court enumerates factors that trial judges must consider in deciding whether to appoint counsel for indigent parents when child is alleged to be in need of protective services.

City of Milwaukee v. Hampton, 204 Wis.2d 49, 553 N.W.2d 855 (Ct. App. 1996). Constitutional challenge to municipal ordinance prohibiting the carrying of a concealed weapon on grounds of equal protection and procedural due process.

In re Commitment of Louise M.: Milwaukee County v. Louise M., 205 Wis.2d 162, 555 N.W.2d 814 (1996). Court holds that trial judge has discretionary authority to review probable cause determination of court commissioner in mental commitment proceeding, and that such review, if held, must be conducted in a timely manner.

T.W. by Enk v. Brophy, 124 F.3d 893 (7th Cir. 1997). Federal jurisdiction to review state court award of child custody is barred by fact that general representative may not appear on behalf of child in litigation.

In re Paternity of Brad Michael L.: Brad Michael L. v. Lee D., 210 Wis.2d 437, 564 N.W.2d 354 (Ct. App. 1997). Court orders nonmarital father to pay 15 years of back child support for son he did not know existed.

Hartman v. Winnebago County, 216 Wis.2d 419, 574 N.W.2d 222 (1998) [*amicus curiae*]. Decision holds that attorneys' fees in federal civil rights action filed in state court are recoverable as taxable costs.

Oconomowoc Residential Programs, Inc. v. City of Greenfield, 23 F. Supp. 2d 941 (E.D. Wis. 1998). In class action lawsuit brought by Legal Aid Society and private counsel on behalf of developmentally disabled persons, Court rules that suburban zoning regulations restricting group homes violate applicable federal law by excluding people with disabilities from living in suburbs. The Society also litigates a companion case, *Vincent Z. v. Village of Greendale*, case no. 96-C-1101 (E.D. Wis. 1996). See *Opening Statements* (Winter 1998) 1 and (Summer 1999) 3.

In Matter of Delores M.: Milwaukee County v. Delores M., 217 Wis.2d 69, 577 N.W.2d 371 (Ct. App. 1998). Court rules that statutory time (72 hours) within which probable cause hearing must be held for mental patients is triggered when patient is taken into custody. Decision prevents practice of "hiding" patients in non-approved facilities.

In the Interest of Nadia S.: Sallie T. v. Milwaukee Co. DHHS, 219 Wis.2d 296, 581 N.W.2d 182 (1998). Court determines that even where biological parent complies with conditions of return home order, trial judge must assess whether such return is in child's best interests.

Paige K.B. v. Molepske, 219 Wis.2d 418, 580 N.W.2d 289 (1998) [*amicus curiae*]. Court decides that guardians ad litem are entitled to absolute quasi-judicial immunity in order to carry out their duties with necessary independence.

Roe v. City of Milwaukee, 26 F. Supp. 2d 1119 (E.D. Wis. 1998). Federal civil rights claim on behalf of HIV positive prisoner in police

lockup states sufficient claim that city failed to properly train and supervise police officers, and failed to enforce lawful policies.
    In re T.P.R. to Darryl T.-H.: State v. Margaret H., 234 Wis.2d 606, 610 N.W.2d 475 (2000). Absence of adequate findings of fact, and failure to consider all statutory criteria, require Supreme Court to remand case back to trial judge.
    In re T.P.R. to Shawn S.: State v. Frederick H, 2001 WI App 141, 246 Wis.2d 215, 630 N.W.2d 734 [*amicus curiae*]. Court rules that parents have right to present evidence of attempts to comply with visitation order, and to present evidence as to why such attempts proved unsuccessful.
    Oconomowoc Residential Programs, Inc. v. City of Milwaukee, 300 F.3d 775 (7th Cir. 2002). Denial of zoning variance to operate a group home for developmentally disabled and brain-injured individuals held to violate provisions of the Americans with Disabilities Act and the Fair Housing Amendments Act.
    Keup v. Wis. Dept. Health & Family Services, 2004 WI 16, 269 Wis.2d 59, 675 N.W.2d 755, *cert. denied* 545 U.S. 1149 (2005) [*amicus curiae*]. Court holds that private pay patient does not have federally protected right to reimbursement from provider for amount originally paid by patient in excess of medical assistance reimbursement.
    Dairyland Greyhound Park v. Doyle, 2004 WI 34, 270 Wis.2d 267, 677 N.W.2d 275 [*amicus curiae*]. When Supreme Court is equally divided, better practice is to remand case to Court of Appeals.
    Randy A.J. v. Norma I.J., 2004 WI 41, 270 Wis.2d 384, 677 N.W.2d 630 [*amicus curiae*]. Biological father of non-marital child is equitably estopped from asserting paternity when he did not have relationship with child, mother was married at time of birth, and husband supported child from inception in good faith belief that he was father.
    In re T.P.R. to Reynaldo F.: Reynaldo F. v. Christal M., 2004 WI App 106, 272 Wis.2d 816, 681 N.W.2d 289. Court reverses dismissal of petition to terminate parental rights based upon erroneous exclusion of evidence that mother was convicted of homicide of twin child.
    In re T.P.R. to Cherzon M.: State v. James P., 2005 WI 80, 281 Wis.2d 685, 698 N.W.2d 95. Biological father of non-marital child may have parental rights terminated for conduct occurring before adjudication of his paternity.

Debra F. v. Wisconsin, rev. denied, 282 Wis.2d 723 (2005), *cert. denied,* 546 U.S. 978 (2005). Petition to review trial judge's denial of tribal motion to transfer termination of parental rights petition to Chippewa Tribal Court under provisions of Indian Child Welfare Act.

In re T.P.R. to Moriah K: State v. Robert K., 2005 WI 152, 286 Wis.2d 143, 706 N.W.2d 257. Ruling holds that Children's Court judge may grant continuance of more than 45 days upon showing of good cause.

In re T.P.R. to Deannia D.: State v. Lamont D., 2005 WI App 264, 288 Wis.2d 485, 709 N.W.2d 879. Decision to set aside jury verdict is committed to discretion of trial court where jury could have reasonably concluded that state failed to prove its case.

In re T.P.R. to Idella W.: State v. Lavelle W., 2005 WI App 266, 288 Wis.2d 504, 708 N.W.2d 698. Birth parent's right to meaningful participation in termination of parental rights case was violated by sporadic and poor quality telephonic speaker.

Wisconsin Auto Title Loans v. Jones, 2006 WI 53, 290 Wis.2d 514, 714 N.W.2d 155. Statewide class action on behalf of consumers

61. Entrance to Wisconsin Supreme Court in State Capitol Building, Madison.
Courtesy of Wisconsin Supreme Court.

fleeced by predatory lenders. "Car-title loan company takes borrowers for a ride, suit says" in *Milwaukee Journal Sentinel* (July 14, 2002). Case results in holding that one-sided, mandatory arbitration clauses in consumer contracts are unenforceable on grounds of unconscionability. "Arbitration rule in auto title loan rejected" in *Milwaukee Journal Sentinel* (May 26, 2006); "Sounding the Death Knell of Forced Consumer Arbitration" in *Wisconsin Lawyer* 79, no. 12 (December 2006).

In re T.P.R. to Max G.W.: Kenosha Co. D.H.S. v. Jodie W., 2006 WI 93, 293 Wis.2d 530, 716 N.W.2d 845 [*amicus curiae*]. Court decides that parental rights may not be terminated for violation of impossible condition of child return.

In re T.P.R. to Torrance P.: State v. Shirley E., 2006 WI 129, 298 Wis.2d 1, 724 N.W.2d 623. Court rules that failure of mother to appear at termination of parental rights hearing, after being ordered to do so by trial judge, does not automatically waive her continuing right to counsel.

In re T.P.R. to Marquette S.: State v. Bobby G., 2007 WI 77, 301 Wis.2d 531, 734 N.W.2d 81. Court decides that termination of parental rights may not be ordered for failure to assume parental responsibility when non-marital biological father was unaware of existence of child until after filing of petition to terminate.

Below v. Norton, 2008 WI 77, 310 Wis.2d 713, 751 N.W.2d 351 [*amicus curiae*]. The economic loss doctrine held to bar common-law claims for intentional misrepresentation in the context of a commercial real estate transaction. Statutory claims for false advertising and plaintiff's contractual remedies, however, do survive.

Cholvin v. Wis. Dept. Health & Family Services, 2008 WI App 127, 313 Wis.2d. 749, 758 N.W.2d 118 [*amicus curiae*]. Woman disabled by multiple sclerosis and other disorders successfully challenges denial of long term care benefits under Wisconsin Medicaid program based upon application of an unpublished rule.

Christensen v. Sullivan, 2009 WI 87, 320 Wis.2d 76, 768 N.W.2d 798. Contempt proceedings against Milwaukee County to compensate class of 16,000 inmates in the new Criminal Justice Facility for blatant violations, over a period of three years, of trial court's 2001 consent decree (see below), are barred. Trial court had found it "appalling" that prisoners were held in subhuman conditions.

SIGNIFICANT UNPUBLISHED CASES

Lewis v. Housing Authority of City of Milwaukee. Case no. 67-C-355 (E.D. Wis.). Federal civil rights claim for declaratory and injunctive relief against Authority's rule requiring automatic eviction of woman with two or more children born out of wedlock. 1 *Clearinghouse Rev.* no. 3 (1967) 3-4.

Fitzgerald v. Housing Authority of City of Milwaukee. E.D. Wis. Federal civil rights claim seeking declaratory and injunctive relief against enforcement of Authority rule refusing tenancy to applicants having more than one child born out of wedlock. 2 *Clearinghouse Rev.* no. 13 (1968) 14.

Petersen v. Housing Authority of City of Milwaukee. Milwaukee County Circuit Court, case no. 359-141. Challenge to Authority rule automatically terminating month-to-month lease, without hearing, upon service of 30-day notice. 2 *Clearinghouse Rev.* no. 13 (1968) 16.

Junker v. Housing Authority of City of Milwaukee. Case no. 68-C-303 (E.D. Wis.). Court holds Authority's rule refusing tenancy to applicants related to another tenant currently in default of rent to be arbitrary and capricious as applied. 4 *Clearinghouse Rev.* (1970) 39.

Austin v. Jennaro et al. Case no. 73-C-226 (E.D. Wis.). Civil rights complaint challenging constitutionality of Wisconsin's emergency juvenile detention statute. Milwaukee County Children's Court judges and Director of Department of Public Welfare agree to establish and implement specified due process procedures involving timely written notice and meaningful opportunity to be heard.

State ex rel. R.T. v. Silverman et al. Case no. 507-431 (Milwaukee County Circuit Court, 1979). Class action writ of habeas corpus filed on behalf of children improperly detained at Child and Adolescent Treatment Center because Milwaukee County refused to pay for less restrictive care in residential treatment facilities that was in their best interests. "Suit seeks treatment for children" in *Milwaukee Journal* (December 9, 1979). County signs consent decree mandating periodic judicial review of all child placements at CATC within 48 hours of admission, after one week, and then every two weeks. County also agrees to fund and staff less restrictive placements. "Children to get court review of treatment level" in *Milwaukee Journal* (December 16, 1979).

Jackson v. Artison. Case no. 88-C-64 (E.D. Wis.). Consent decree entered in United States District Court in 1990 imposes a daily cap of 459 inmates in the Milwaukee County Jail (*i.e.* the old Safety Building jail) and appoints a Special Master to monitor population levels, release prisoners to ensure compliance with the cap, supervise staffing levels, enforce a minimum of three hours per week of exercise for all inmates, and require regular cleaning of the Jail.

Joan S. v. Gudeman. Case no. 91-C-717 (E.D. Wis.). Consent decree in United States District Court entered in 1994 against Milwaukee County, which prohibits "warehousing" of mental patients, requires meaningful treatment, and mandates adequate discharge planning for mentally ill and developmentally disabled individuals. County agrees to dedicate $3 million in new monies for community resources to comply with decree.

NAACP v. American Family Mutual Ins. Co. (E.D. Wis., 1992). Case alleging insurance redlining settles in 1995 for $14.5 million and consent to injunctive relief. "Homeowners ensure company does right thing with American Family settlement" in *Milwaukee Journal Sentinel* (November 26, 1995).

Jeanine B. et al. v. Thompson et al. Case no. 93-C-0547 (E.D. Wis.). Class action suit that leads to state takeover of Milwaukee County foster care system. Consent decree (December 2002) is issued requiring state and county to implement wide-ranging series of reforms on behalf of minors in their care and custody. "Legal Aid Attorneys Serve as Next Friends for Foster Care System Improvements" in *Opening Statements* (Spring 2003) 2.

Hinton v. ColorTyme. Case no. 94-CV-005198 (Milwaukee County Circuit Court). In class action case challenging predatory lending activities by rent-to-own industry, Legal Aid Society wins a $2.9 million settlement on behalf of 10,000 consumers. Defendant agrees to establish a $675,000 zero-interest loan fund for inner-city consumers and a $200,000 revolving fund, administered by Community Advocates, to guarantee payment of security deposits by low-income tenants. 29 *Clearinghouse Rev.* 896 (January-February 1996). See also "$2.9 million ColorTyme settlement approved" in *Milwaukee Journal Sentinel* (January 27, 1998).

Locke v. Wis. Dept. Health & Social Services. Case no. 96-CV-0621 (Dane County Circuit Court). Class action suit, brought on behalf of more than 1,000 elderly and disabled Medicaid patients, successfully challenges imposition of home healthcare caps as arbitrary. Patients' rights declared by court and DHSS enjoined from enforcing limits. State elects not to appeal.

Christensen et al. v. Sullivan. Case no. 96-CV-1835 (Milwaukee County Circuit Court). Class action filed on behalf of inmates in Milwaukee County's Criminal Justice Facility (new jail) seeking redress from overcrowding and lack of medical and mental health services. "Suit alleges terrible jail conditions" in *Milwaukee Journal Sentinel* (August 2, 1996). Consent decree issued in June 2001 imposes population caps on CJF and requires expenditure of additional $3.9 million per year to provide adequate medical services for inmates in the CJF and the House of Correction. 35 *Clearinghouse Rev.* 236 (July-Aug. 2001).

Wilson v. ATM Enterprises. Case no. 98-CV-005945 (Milwaukee County Circuit Court). Class action suit challenges out-of-state company's failure to comply with Wisconsin disclosure laws governing credit sales. Case settles when company (which changed its name to First American Rentals) agrees to rebate more than half a million dollars to 2,600 consumers. "Rent-to-own customers to get money back; First American to pay 2,600 area people in settlement" in *Milwaukee Journal Sentinel* (June 24, 2000).

Dienese v. McKenzie Check Advance. Case no. 99-C-50 (E.D. Wis.). Class action case challenging predatory activities of payday loan industry. Case results in $1.4 million settlement on behalf of 10,000 consumers. Grant of class certification reported in 2000 U.S. Dist. LEXIS 20389; 34 *Clearinghouse Rev.* 238 (July-Aug. 2000). See also "Judge approves $1.4 million payday loan company settlement" in *Milwaukee Journal Sentinel* (June 27, 2002).

State Financial Bank v. City of South Milwaukee, case no. 00-C-1530 (E.D. Wis.). After three-week trial, jury finds that municipality discriminated on basis of race and disability against low-income residents of apartment complex that city had sought to demolish. "Plan to raze South Milwaukee building would hurt minorities, jury finds" in *Milwaukee Journal Sentinel* July 30, 2009); "South Milwaukee accused of discrimination in court fight over apartments" in *Milwaukee Journal*

Sentinel (June 29, 2009). District Court enters consent decree preventing demolition and awarding attorney fees to plaintiffs' counsel.

Torzala v. McCoy. Case no. 2004-CV-002676 (Milwaukee County Circuit Court). Legal Aid Society staff attorney discovers massive fraud involving false claims of service of pleadings in hundreds of eviction cases. Court vacates more than $600,000 of judgments obtained in these matters and awards monetary damages to LAS clients.

Spera v. Orthopaedic Associates of Milwaukee, case no. 2004-CV-1063 (E.D. Wis.). A refusal-to-treat case filed in federal court on behalf of a patient whose back surgery was canceled after his physician discovered that he was HIV+. Patient asserted claims under the Americans with Disabilities Act, Rehabilitation Act, and Wisconsin's AIDS Anti-Discrimination statute. Confidential settlement reached in 2007.

In re Protective Placement of J.B. Case no. 2005-GN-000316 (Milwaukee County Circuit Court). Upon motion of the Legal Aid Society, Milwaukee County is held in contempt for repeated failure to perform court-ordered assessment of an individual in protective placement. Court orders County to draft written policies and implement procedures to ensure timely compliance in future.

In re Paternity of K.J.P.: Parrish v. Romfeldt-Mendoza, appeal no. 2006AP000243 (Wisconsin Court of Appeals, District IV) [*amicus curiae*]. Civil right-to-counsel case seeking appointment of an attorney to represent mother in custody dispute.

Crosby v. Williamson, case no. 08-SC-23166. Applying the Americans with Disabilities Act and applicable Wisconsin law, court orders Milwaukee County to pay costs of providing American Sign Language interpreter for deaf LAS staff attorney to permit representation of client.

22
HISTORICAL DOCUMENTS
SECTION
1910 – 2010

I.

LETTER FROM PROFESSOR JOHN R. COMMONS
TO VICTOR L. BERGER (EXTRACT)

THE UNIVERSITY OF WISCONSIN MADISON

April 11, 1910

Mr. Victor L. Berger
344 Sixth Street
Milwaukee, Wisconsin
Dear Sir:

Referring to your request, I send suggestions regarding a municipal survey of Milwaukee.

The object of such survey should be accurate and adequate knowledge of economic conditions leading to specific and practicable plans. The investigations should be brought to a head as promptly as possible consistent with making the recommendations absolutely safe for adoption . . .

3. **Legal Aid** – Investigations of actual conditions of litigation on the part of persons without means or knowledge of laws and courts – such as wage exemptions, mechanics' liens, loans or personal property, etc. – with the view of working out a practicable plan for free legal aid similar to that of German cities. This will be especially important after the [Wisconsin] legislature enacts a workmen's compensation law.[1]

Immigrants – could a bureau of immigration, or some agency be devised, to protect immigrants and residents – could this be connected with the Legal Aid Bureau?[2]

Sincerely yours,

J.R. Commons

NOTES

1. The signed original of this letter is preserved in the Victor Berger Correspondence at the Milwaukee County Historical Society. Socialist Party Mss. 770, Box 4, File 90. It was later reprinted in *Eighteen Months' Work* (Milwaukee Bureau of Economy and Efficiency, Bulletin no. 19, 1912), pp 31-32.

2. The Bureau of Economy and Efficiency did not publish a white paper on immigration.

2.

SENATE BILL 253

1911

INTRODUCED BY SENATOR ZOPHY.

REFERRED TO COMMITTEE ON STATE AFFAIRS. [1]

A BILL

To provide for the establishment of legal information bureaus in cities of the first class.[2]

The people of the state of Wisconsin, represented in senate and assembly, do enact as follows:

Section 1. Any city of the first class desiring to establish a legal information bureau is empowered to do so.

Section 2. The mayor of any city of the first class shall appoint a competent person to act as chief of such bureau. The chief may appoint assistants.

Section 3. The common council of any city of the first class establishing a legal information bureau under this act shall fix the compensation of the chief of the bureau and his assistants, and shall determine the fees to be collected. Such fees shall be paid into the city treasury. The council is empowered to furnish and equip an office for the bureau, and to provide suitable reference books and supplies.

Section 4. The common council of any city of the first class establishing a legal information bureau under this act, may annually levy, and cause to be collected as other general taxes are collected, a tax upon the taxable property of such city to provide a legal information bureau fund, which fund shall be kept by the city treasurer separate from other money of the city, to be used exclusively to maintain such legal information bureau.

Section 5. This act shall take effect and be in force from and after its passage and publication.

NOTES

1. This enabling legislation was introduced by Senator Zophy on February 15, 1911. Its history is set forth in *Senate Journal 1911*, pp 197, 276, 644, and 673.
2. Based on population, Milwaukee was the only city of the first class in Wisconsin.

3.
LETTER FROM PROFESSOR JOHN R. COMMONS
TO MAYOR EMIL C. SEIDEL

Milwaukee[1]
October 30, 1911

Hon. Emil C. Seidel, Mayor
City of Milwaukee
Dear Sir:

We submit herewith the report of the bureau on the question of Free Legal Aid. The report was prepared to support a bill before the legislature looking towards the creation of a municipal bureau which was to furnish free legal aid and advice to persons financially unable to hire an attorney.[2]

The bill failed of passage, but the question is considered of such prime importance that it is urged that steps be taken at once to offer free legal aid through the organization of a voluntary bureau, similar to those in New York, Chicago, and other cities.

Respectfully submitted,
John R. Commons
Director
B.M. Rastall
Associate Director

NOTES

1. Published in Fred A. King, *Free Legal Aid* (Milwaukee Bureau of Economy and Efficiency, Bulletin no. 7, 1911).

2. The reference here is to Senate Bill 253, introduced by Senator Gabriel Zophy in the 1911 legislative session.

4.

KING-COMMONS REPORT

MILWAUKEE BUREAU OF ECONOMY & EFFICIENCY
BULLETIN NO. 7
FREE LEGAL AID
BY
FRED A. KING
PREPARED UNDER THE DIRECTION OF
JOHN R. COMMONS
MILWAUKEE, WIS.

1911

METHOD OF OPERATING FREE LEGAL AID BUREAUS
IN LARGE CITIES

In spite of the fact that Milwaukee has a population of 370,000, the majority of whom are wage earners, the city has no organized free legal service for persons unable to hire an attorney. A precedent for this form of public service is found in New York, Chicago, Philadelphia, and several other cities where the "poor man's lawyer," supported by a private charitable society, has already become an established institutiuu, and in Kansas City, where the advanced step of maintaining a legal aid bureau as a regular part of its city administration has recently been taken.

The method of operating these bureaus is practically the same whether under private or public management. One or more lawyers, serving on salary, are placed in charge and are given assistants who act as paid investigators to inquire into the circumstances brought out by an office interview with the applicant. In addition, occasional legal advice is rendered by attorneys who serve without pay. In Kansas City, six city attorneys each give two hours of their time during a single week. In the work of the private societies, a small fee is charged. The Philadelphia society requires the applicant to pay 25 cents as a retainer, if possible, as well as the costs of any proceeding, and collects 10 per cent as a contingent fee in all cases where the amount recovered is over $10.

The experience of the private societies shows that their greater usefulness lies in the treatment of civil rather than criminal cases, since, in the latter, the public prosecutor ordinarily appears for the complainant and an attorney may be assigned the defendant if necessary without cost. In civil procedure, however, conditions are entirely different, as both complainant and defendant must provide their own counsel, and failure to secure a competent attorney by persons of small means often results in a miscarriage of justice. Moreover, where the dispute involves only a small sum of money, the lawyer's fee is practically prohibitive, as it would eat up the amount obtained in a successful suit.

To the objection that unnecessary litigation would be increased by giving practically free legal aid in certain cases, or that such aid would be abused by persons who are able to hire their own attorneys, it may be answered that this depends entirely upon the method of operating the bureau. All applicants in "spite" suits and those who are well able to pay for such service should be rejected at once by the attorney in

62. Wisconsin State Capitol in Madison, site of early efforts to establish a legal aid program in Milwaukee. *Courtesy of Wisconsin Historical Society* (WHi-6446).

charge or upon the report of the bureau's investigator. Moreover, the practice adopted, for example, by the New York Legal Aid Society, of settling cases without going to court, answers the former objection. From the report of this society for 1910, we find that of $64,000 collected for clients in that year, $36,000 was secured without suit.

Although a legal aid bureau renders more efficient service in civil than in criminal cases, the work of the bureau indicates certain marked abuses in present methods of defense where persons of small means are charged with crime. Two such abuses may be mentioned. First, where the prisoner tried for a petty offense, as disorderly conduct, has no counsel and is therefore entirely dependent on the police magistrate's ability to discover whatever defense he may really have; and again, where the person charged with a more serious crime is defended by an attorney provided by the court, who, to save himself extra labor, advises his client to plead guilty or conducts the case in an inefficient manner. Such failure to obtain justice makes necessary free legal aid and even calls for a radical change in court procedure, such as the frequently advocated establishment of a system of public defense conducted on lines similar to present public prosecution.

PRESENT AGENCIES IN MILWAUKEE FOR PROVIDING FREE LEGAL AID AND THEIR FAILURE TO GIVE ADEQUATE SERVICE

There is evidence of a demand for free legal aid in the city of Milwaukee. Since the coming in of the present Socialist administration, workingmen and women in increasing numbers have presented their private grievances at the City Hall, thinking that legal advice and counsel were to be had for the asking. Moreover, in recent years, several schemes have been advanced by young lawyers for providing their services to clients at a nominal rate and for a certain period, practically as doctors now give medical advice to members of workingmen's benefit societies under special agreement. Nor should we fail to note the activities of the unscrupulous claim agent who visits an injured person, the victim of an automobile accident, for example, and obtains a ready hearing when he declares he is "sent from the City Hall to look after the interests of poor people."

As for the work of the city's agencies, both public and private, which attempt to supply the present need for free legal service, the following account will be limited for the most part to their treatment of civil cases. There are two main agencies in Milwaukee through which persons with little or no money can secure advice or assistance in civil actions. These are the city and district attorneys' offices in the City Hall, and the private charitable societies. Almost any week day one will find at the City Hall working men and women applying for legal assistance who can ill afford to consult a private attorney: – wage earners in the hands of loan sharks who demand an illegal rate of interest; workmen with their wages unjustly garnished; persons who claim to have been defrauded in the purchase of goods through misrepresentation by store clerks or installment dealers; the buyer of real estate on installments seeking relief from a "cut-throat" contract, the terms of which he does not understand or has difficulty in complying with; litigants in actions growing out of "family troubles" and disputes over small property rights or personal injuries. These complaints possibly appear petty enough for the most part to persons in better circumstances, but they represent real grievances to the parties directly concerned.

With all such classes of applicants at the City Hall, a number are sent away without the prospect of securing full redress because of the inability of the city or district attorney to act in their behalf. For the chief duties of these officials and the members of their staffs lie, in the one case, in prosecuting violations of the state laws, and, in the other, in enforcing the city ordinances or attending to city litigation. In the cases already mentioned, where it is inadvisable to take legal action in the courts, both the district and city attorney attempt to secure, as far as possible, a compromise or a settlement. Such settlements may be brought about by giving office advice to applicants or by various other means, such as communicating with persons complained against by letter or telephone. For example, in handling loan shark cases, it is often difficult for the district or city attorney to prosecute loan companies for violation of the statute or city ordinance prohibiting the payment of usury, owing to the various tricks played by these companies in arranging the terms of a loan. In a certain proportion of such cases, however, and in the garnisheeing of wages as well, the district attorney is able to co-operate with the Provident Loan Society in compromising the matter. Parties referred to the latter agency by the district attorney are given new loans and their differences adjusted in this way with loan sharks or other creditors. The Provident Loan Society, organized as similar agencies in other cities for the purpose of loaning money at a moderate rate of interest, handles each month from five to twenty loan shark and ten to twelve garnishee cases referred from all sources. So, too, in wage disputes the city or district attorney may in some instances secure an immediate compromise or settlement out of court and the complainant may thus avoid the delay incident to a suit in the civil court.

The workman needs such services, for if he tries to take matters in his own hands, obtaining a remittance of the cost of summons because of his inability to pay, he is still at a disadvantage when his case finally comes to trial, as he has no attorney to oppose the lawyer for the other side. So also an adjustment out of court may be made where there is fraud in the sale of goods, for in such cases it is often very difficult to show criminal intent and it may be impossible for the complainant to start an action in the civil court, owing to his inability to secure counsel.

But in all the various classes of complaints, it is evident that the city and district attorney in attempting to make such settlements act entirely outside their official duties, and in fact may be open to criticism under strict interpretation of the law which forbids compromising a case under threat of criminal prosecution. Moreover, such settlements, if accomplished at all, depend altogether upon the personal initiative of the officials. The present district attorney declares that he is overrun with demands for his services from applicants, a considerable number of whom are not able to engage competent attorneys, and that the hearing of these complaints interferes with his regular duties. We have also the statement of a former assistant district attorney that he was able to secure good results by investigating such complaints in addition to giving office advice, but only to a limited extent, as the investigation had to be done outside of office hours.

Another place to which wage earners go for advice and help is the state factory inspector's office, which at present exceeds its regular duties in attempting to settle wage claims. Adjustments in these cases are generally made in favor of the employee, [although] it may be with the help of a friendly lawyer who charges nothing for his services. A representative of the office has even paid out of his own pocket the court fees necessary to prosecute a case. This work is restricted for the most part to minors. From sixty to one hundred wage claims are handled in a year's time.

In all the varied complaints already mentioned, the private charitable societies of the city may be called upon to render service as far as their present limited means will allow. The Associated Charities and the Hebrew Relief Association deal with a wide range of such cases. So, too, the superintendent of the Rescue Mission finds that in conducting the mission's employment bureau, one of the largest agencies in the city, he is continually obliged to attempt the settlement of disputes over wages, for example, between an unscrupulous contractor and a laborer working in a construction gang, or between a factory employer and employee. Office advice may be given by these societies, letters written, and the telephone brought into service. In some cases, the superintendent obtains advice from friendly attorneys, or advances the necessary court costs in a particular action, and engages a competent attorney to appear in court without charge. The Associated Charities and Hebrew Relief Association, however, have had difficulty in providing such lawyers. One society has found it difficult to secure an attorney without the payment of a least a small fee, and both find that, while young and inexperienced lawyers would doubtless take "any sort of a case" referred to them on a contingent basis, efficient attorneys who offer their services without pay are few in number, owing to the pressure of their private practice. As a result, satisfactory adjustment can be reached to only a limited extent. For example, investigation may show that a wife would be much better off if she could secure a divorce or separation from a husband who abuses her and fails to support his children. The ordinary lawyer's fee for such services is at the lowest from $25 to $50.

Because of the above mentioned difficulty in securing counsel, and in order to give their time to work more closely connected with their special activities, the representatives of these two societies are heartily in favor of the establishment of a legal aid bureau. So, also, is the superintendent of the Rescue Mission. In thus endeavoring to provide

free legal service, these societies have been performing their usual function of conducting a pioneer work which the community has not yet
recognized as a vital need and met accordingly in an effective manner,
but which is bound to be carried on sooner or later by a single agency.
Just as the Associated Charities' hitherto important work in instituting legal proceedings against the husband and father who refuses to

63. Carved stone detail, United States Courthouse, Milwaukee.
Courtesy of Milwaukee County Historical Society.

support his family has recently been taken over through a newly created office under supervision of the county poor commissioner, so it is justifiable that free legal assistance in other cases should be rendered by a properly conducted bureau.

NEED OF FREE LEGAL SERVICE IN MILWAUKEE IN CERTAIN IMPORTANT CIVIL ACTIONS.

Reference should be made in detail to one important class of civil actions already referred to, those resulting from personal injury, in which a legal aid bureau could check in part at least the present danger of flagrant injustice to the wage earner. In the numerous street car or shop accidents where a suit for damages may be brought, the attorney in charge of the bureau could give "first aid" by offering advice upon application made immediately following the accident, and without necessarily appearing in court later in behalf of the injured person. This is the present policy of the New York Legal Aid Society. In this way, the practices of unscrupulous claim agents and lawyers who actively solicit such business through uninvited calls and the distribution of letters and pamphlets could be checked in a measure. The writer is informed on the best of authority that such practices consist, for example, in obtaining quick settlements for small amounts and without properly considering the degree of liability of employers. The lawyer and claim agent obtain their profits from the number of cases so handled and for a contingent fee of from 40 to 50 per cent. Take the case of a Polish coal shoveler, who was rather ignorant and could speak but little English. His shoulder and leg were injured by the fall of a hatch-cover from the deck of a coal barge while he was at work in the hold. A claim agent, after repeated efforts, secured the case for a lawyer for whom he regularly solicited accident cases. The lawyer brought suit for $1,000 damages and, one month after the accident, settled for $75, one-half of which he took as his fee. In this instance, the circumstances of the accident showed that the employer was directly liable and, had the workman known of his legal rights and employed reputable counsel, he could have procured a much better settlement. Moreover, injured persons, instead of blindly accepting a small amount in settlement from employer or insurance adjuster without suit, could first secure advice from a legal aid bureau as to their rights in the matter.

Even under the state industrial compensation law, which is expected to do away with such abuses in a large measure, a legal aid bureau would still be of service. This is shown by the experience of German labor unions, which still find it necessary to provide free legal advice for their members even under the workings of an elaborate system of state compensation.

In Milwaukee, the "city of homes," the legal tangles in which the purchaser of a home and lot or land on installments finds himself may be particularly perplexing, especially to the workingman who is a foreigner and unacquainted with our procedure. Unfortunately, however, when once he is in the toils of an unscrupulous land agent, not even the best of legal advice can always free him from fulfilling to the letter the terms of a "cut-throat" contract. A recent opinion handed down by a circuit court judge in Milwaukee illustrates very well the unfair bargains which are sometimes struck with ignorant workingmen by land agents. A workingman signed the following agreement with a land company: He was to pay $100 down and $14 a month for four years for the house and lot, also to pay for repairs, insurance, and taxes. On a certain date at the expiration of the four years, he was to come into full possession of the property by making a final payment of $1,250. The agreement also provided that the monthly payments were to run for the full four years, even though the building should burn down within this time. In such an event, the land company would not be required to rebuild if the cost exceeded the amount of insurance carried. As a matter of fact, the prospective purchaser complied substantially with the terms of the agreement up to the date when the final lump sum was to be paid. This he did, as the judge's opinion states, "at great sacrifice." He was "an ignorant man, unable to speak English and of extreme poverty." As it happened, the final amount was not paid on the exact date mentioned in the agreement, and a dispute followed between land agent and purchaser over possession of the property, the agent claiming that, under the terms of contract, payment of the monthly installments gave the prospective owner no acquired rights, but simply an option on the property. However, "had the slightest forbearance been shown" by the land agent, the judge's opinion goes on to say, this money would have been paid on the day following. In deciding in favor of the workingman as complainant, the judge states further, after calling the land agent a "modern Shylock" who demands his "pound of flesh," that under a strict interpretation of the law his decision may not be upheld by a higher court, and that if so, "the law rather than justice will prevail." It is probable, however, that the complainant in this case, which has been appealed, will not be obliged finally to give up possession of the property. In this instance, as it happened, the workingman was able to secure a lawyer who, as we understand, gave services "out of charity." There is no doubt that in similar cases a legal aid bureau would be able at least to advise a client in his attempts to comply with the exact terms of a contract and so lend moral support, even though under the law the victim of trickery has no adequate redress.

THIRTY-FIVE MISCELLANEOUS CASES SHOWING THE NEED FOR FREE LEGAL SERVICE IN MILWAUKEE

The following group of thirty-five cases which suggest the present need for a legal aid bureau are taken from the files of the Associated Charities. They were selected from a total of 500 cases recorded at the main office of the society and covering a six months' period. Non-support cases were disregarded, as they are now cared for by the county poor commissioner.

Of eleven accident cases – nine industrial and two street car accidents – three of the former and one of the latter were fatal. In a majority of cases, the man injured had a wife and children dependent on him for support. One widow with children, whose husband was the victim of a street car accident, put her case in the hands of a lawyer without getting satisfactory results. When she applied to the society, she was in doubt as to her legal rights and did not know why she had received only one-half of a death benefit due from a benefit society.

Seven cases involved divorce proceedings. In one case, the husband, who was a cripple and a beggar, was abusive. In another, the husband was a drunkard. In one case where an action was especially desirable, the wife had been told by a lawyer that he must have $25 for his services, but she had no money.

There were three cases where wages were in dispute. In two of these, the workman had a wife and children to support. One of the two workmen claimed that a farmer near a neighboring town owed him $20. The remaining case was that of a nurse who had been taken ill and left her work in a hospital. The hospital superintendent had refused to pay her back wages. In this case, the wages were secured for her by the society.

There were three cases where working girls over 18 years of age had been seduced.

Two were cases where mothers complained that they were getting insufficient support from grown sons who were at work.

Two were loan shark cases, one where a man had borrowed $20 to pay for burying his baby, an only child. He had paid $2.85 for eight months on the loan, or a total of $22.80, and the loan company was demanding four additional payments, or interest at 70 per cent. The legal rate of interest is 10 per cent.

One man was refused title to a small property on which he had made payments and paid taxes.

In one case, an undertaker had levied on a widow's furniture to secure payment for her husband's funeral expenses.

A man and wife who had bought a small grocery claimed that they had been swindled. Another couple claimed that they had been deceived in buying furniture. Another applicant had been refused a barber's license.

The following additional cases, which differ somewhat from those already given, were secured from reliable sources and are all recent. In one case, a family, which was practically dependent and had applied for charitable relief, had a small amount of property involved in a legal tangle.

A family had bought a stove on installments and the dealer threatened to remove it because $2 remained unpaid. Here the society's agent arranged with the dealer for more time to make the final payment.

A man quit work and asked the society's agent to secure his wages for him, as he needed the money badly and could not wait until pay day. When the agent telephoned the employer, the agent was informed that the workman meanwhile had retained a lawyer and that, as the employer had been served with a summons, the man would have to wait until the case was decided in court. Otherwise, the employer would have granted the agent's request immediately.

A 16-year-old boy working in a foundry and the sole support of his mother was refused $20 wages due him, the employer alleging that the boy had done some damage in the shop. The boy finally won his case in court, but had to pay his lawyer a fee of $5.

A poor man, a foreigner, gave $10 as part payment for a cart and agreed to make a final payment of $10 at the end of another week. He returned in two weeks' time to find that the owner had already sold the cart to a third party and refused to return the first payment of $10.

A workman who had always borne a good reputation was arrested for stealing. The complainant, a woman, declared that he had picked up a pocketbook which she had dropped in the street. The man's wife consulted a prominent attorney, who refused to take the case for less than $100. The wife paid over this amount by obtaining a loan on the $600 which man and wife by dint of much saving had paid in part on their home. The workman was discharged in court in a few days' time and the lawyer has since demanded another $100 for his services.

A workman from Chicago came to live in Milwaukee with his wife and child. He was in debt to a Chicago loan company, and the company had placed a lien on his household goods, which were in storage in that city. A resident of Milwaukee who learned of the man's plight went to Chicago and found out that the loan company had a larger lien on the goods than they were entitled to under the law. A part of the man's goods were at once obtained for him and the case turned over to the Chicago Legal Aid Society for final adjustment.

This list of cases suggesting the need of a legal aid bureau in Milwaukee could be prolonged indefinitely. In a final analysis, however, the need for such service is best shown by the evident inability of the city and district attorneys' offices to meet the situation, and from the testimony of the representatives of the largest charitable societies who unite in demanding such a bureau. It is clear that if wage earners are expected to perform the duties of citizenship in an intelligent manner, they should at least be able to secure their rights under the law, and that as far as possible, none should find their lack of financial resources an effective barrier in obtaining these rights. Free legal service is an important means to this end.

5.

NEWS CLIPPINGS, 1915-16

THE MILWAUKEE JOURNAL

DECEMBER 12, 1915

LAWYERS FAVOR FREE LEGAL AID

BAR ASSOCIATION TAKES ACTION

Adopts Recommendation Of Committee
Which Investigated New York Plan

Robert Wild was elected president ... of the Milwaukee Bar Association at its annual meeting Saturday.

Free legal aid for the poor will be given in Milwaukee as a result of the adoption of recommendations of the legal aid committee, which reported through Walter S. Bartlett, chairman. The City Club and the Central Council of Social Agencies will be invited to co-operate with the association in organizing the legal aid society. Fifty cities in the United States have legal aid societies according to Mr. Bartlett's report.

"The movement was started by a handful of Germans in New York in 1876," said Mr. Bartlett. "The New York society now handles 39,000 cases a year. No attempt is made to give aid to indigent persons prosecuted for a crime, or in personal injury suits, the work being limited to loan shark prosecutions, wage claims, domestic relations, and collection matters. The function of the society is to secure justice for the weak and oppressed, so that they may keep securely that which is rightfully theirs, rather than have them become objects of private charity because they cannot obtain justice.

"Mr. Klatte [Clerk] of the Civil Courts reports that applications for legal aid average about 250 a month. In August, there were 250, of which 100 resulted in starting suits. No attempt is made to follow them with the attention which is necessary to bring them to a successful conclusion. The result is that the majority of applicants fail to get justice. The calls at the City Attorney's office are estimated at 300 a month. The great percentage of applicants have wage claims.

"There is no place where a poor person can to go secure legal advice in regard to his rights, and legal aid to enforce what rights he may have. It is estimated that the 1,500 to 2,000 cases which demand attention in this city are allowed to go without attention, with the result that many thousands of dollars are kept out of the pockets of that class which need it most."

THE MILWAUKEE JOURNAL

JANUARY 18, 1916

FREE LEGAL AID PLAN LAUNCHED

SOCIETY WILL BE FORMED IMMEDIATELY

Central Council of Social Agencies
Accepts Committee Recommendation.
Bar Association Active in Proposed Organization

The establishment of a legal aid society in Milwaukee was assured Monday night when the Central Council of Social Agencies indorsed the report of a joint committee of the council and the Milwaukee Bar Association, recommending that an organization be formed here to help those who have no funds to hire the services of an attorney, or who can pay only a nominal fee. This report has already been indorsed by the Milwaukee Bar Association.

President E.W. Frost of the Central Council appointed Walter S. Bartlett, head of the committee, which investigated legal aid societies as developed in other cities, as chairman of the new committee on the formation of the society. Mr. Bartlett also heads the Milwaukee Bar committee on organization. Other members of the Central council committee are Mrs. B. Rosing, Miss Alice Miller, A.C. Otto, Mrs. Susie B. Bruce, Frank Mackut, and Charles W. Babcock.

Considerable discussion arose as to whether a social worker or an attorney should be in charge of the society's office. Chairman Bartlett said reports showed that in two-thirds of the cities, which have free legal aid, a social worker is in charge. He stated that the committee estimates that from 1,500 to 1,800 cases will come before the Milwaukee society each year and that the duty of the social worker would be to establish first whether the applicant was actually in need of assistance or merely desired to avoid paying the regular fee of an attorney. No case will be handled until a complete investigation is made.

S.R. Williams, attorney, who has had considerable experience in aiding cases sent him by the Associated Charities, said that applicants fall into two classes — those who have no case, but are trying to get something they are not entitled to, and those who have just grounds for an action. He believed that only an examination of the applicant by an attorney will determine whether the case is one properly calling for free legal aid.

Reports from other cities showed that in most cases, the legal aid organizations are supported by membership dues, contributions, and the nominal fee paid by those who are not completely dependent on charity. The joint committee, including members to be appointed by the City Club, will incorporate the society here and then will take steps to finance it.

THE MILWAUKEE LEADER

MARCH 14, 1916
LEGAL AID SOCIETY
TO ELECT OFFICERS FRIDAY

Officers of the Legal Aid Society will be elected at a meeting Friday afternoon. Directors thus far are: E.D. Adler, Charles Babcock, John Barnes, Walter Bartlett, Mrs. Victor Berger, Emmett Donnelly, William Kaumheimer, Miss Alice Miller, and Neil Norris. Donnelly and Kaumheimer have been appointed to receive applications for the position of attorney and an assistant for the society.

THE MILWAUKEE LEADER

MAY 23, 1916

TO AID LEGAL AID SOCIETY

Miss Alma Schlesinger has been appointed office manager and field worker for the Milwaukee Legal Aid Society, which will begin daily work June 1. The society was organized to give free legal advice to persons involved in civil cases who are not able to engage counsel.

THE MILWAUKEE JOURNAL

JUNE 1, 1916

OPEN ROOMS OF FREE LEGAL ADVICE BUREAU

Will Act in Court for Poor Persons and Defend
Them from Unjust Prosecutions

With a sign on the door stating its mission, desk and telephone installed, and Miss Alma Schlesinger in charge, the rooms of the Free Legal Aid Bureau were opened Thursday. The bureau is ready to furnish legal advice to those who are unable to pay for the services of an attorney, and to stand between the poor and the courts when legal advice may accomplish it.

"The bureau has the united support of every member of the Milwaukee Bar Association," said William F. Hannan, who assisted in opening the offices. "It is not a bureau for bringing suits or defending suits, but it will investigate statements of persons unable to retain an attorney, and determine whether they have a cause of action. Then, in the event they cannot employ an attorney, one will be provided. It will also intervene in claims against the poor, and act as a friend and advisor in cases where it appears that a poor man or woman is being unjustly prosecuted or persecuted."

THE MILWAUKEE SENTINEL

JUNE 2, 1916

FREE LEGAL AID SOCIETY IS READY TO AID POOR

The Milwaukee Legal Aid Society opened headquarters in rooms 707-708 Merchants and Manufacturers Bank building Thursday morning. Miss Alma Schlesinger, who will have charge of the field work and investigate all applications for free legal aid, is in charge of the office. William Hannan is the legal representative of the society.

"We are ready now to give assistance to all who are unable to hire an attorney and are in need of help," said Miss Schlesinger.

THE MILWAUKEE JOURNAL

JUNE 4, 1916

LEGAL AID SOCIETY EXPECTS MANY CASES OF POOR
WHO OTHERWISE MAY LOSE RIGHTS

Each Case Will Be Investigated in Order
Not to Interfere with Regular Practitioners

Milwaukee's Legal Aid Society, which was recently established and is in active operation, is declared to be a combination of the best features of the free legal aid societies of other cities which have been pioneers in the work of securing the equal protection of the law to all, regardless of financial ability.

While primarily a charitable organization incorporated to extend aid to needy persons, the work of the Legal Aid Society has been so organized that it will in no manner conflict with nor affect the paid services of practicing attorneys. It is stated that no cases will be handled where the applicants are financially able to hire an attorney, nor will cases be accepted for prosecution or for defense where there is a reasonable certainty that such cases will be handled by attorneys on a contingent fee basis.

It is difficult to estimate the number and class of cases which will be handled. Statistics show that there are between 300 and 400 applications per month at the City Attorney's office and the office of the Clerk of the Civil Courts for advice and assistance in the prosecution and defense of actions by people who have not the means to employ counsel.

The majority of these cases involve domestic difficulties, wage claims, disputes between landlords and tenants, and similar cases. As many of these cases as can be taken care of without interference with the regular routine of the office have been handled in the past by these agencies, but as no opportunity is given for investigating the particular cases to find whether the applicant can afford an attorney, many cases are allowed to go without attention, and thousands of dollars annually are kept out of the pockets of that class of the community which is most in need of it.

The offices of the Legal Aid Society at number 707 and 708 M & M Building are open daily for clients seeking aid and advice. Miss Alma Schlesinger, a social worker of experience in Milwaukee and other cities, is in active charge. Attorney William F. Hannan is counsel for the Society and all legal work for clients will be handled by him and Attorneys William J. Goldschmidt and James A. Johnson.

THE MILWAUKEE JOURNAL

SEPTEMBER 25, 1916

FREE LEGAL AID A BOON TO POOR

SUPPORTERS SAY BUREAU DOES GOOD WORK

Nearly 300 Cases the First Three Months —
Collects Wages, Defends Unfair Garnishments
and Probes Family Troubles.

In the first three months of its work, the Legal Aid Society of Milwaukee has justified its existence, its supporters maintain. Already 297 persons have applied for aid, and $547.22 in claims have been secured for these applicants. One of the features of the work of the society is that in only twenty-nine cases was it necessary to apply to the attorneys of the society for assistance. Many of the cases are disposed of in the office of the society. The most common ones are wage claims for $3 and $4, which it would not pay an attorney to take, and divorce suits where the question of alimony is not involved.

"Although probation officers and the district attorney are willing to do everything they can," said Miss Alma Schlesinger, superintendent, "the field is so broad that it is impossible for them to study every phase of the work as thoroughly as we can go into it. Although we like to settle domestic difficulties and obtain divorces in cases where we feel it is necessary, we do not want persons to think that this is a free divorce dispensary. Every case is thoroughly investigated, and only where there is an absolute need are proper steps taken to secure a divorce.

"Many typical cases of the work which we are doing could be cited. For instance, a man was sued because he could not pay his grocery bill, and his employer was named as garnishee defendant. The man was married, had eight children, and earned a little over $60 a month. The case came into our office and was referred to our attorneys, and before the return day the matter was settled. The man is to pay his grocery bill by installments, $1 a week, through our office."

To illustrate the work that is being done, a case was cited of a man who claimed he had worked forty hours more than the company that employed him would pay for. He appealed to the Legal Aid Society, the validity of claim was established, and he got his pay. A boy who worked in a garage was discharged because a windshield in a car was found broken. His pay was held back, although there was no evidence that he was responsible for the damage. The society induced the company to pay him. Occasionally employers refuse to pay men who have worked only a part of a week or a month. Appeals to assist in collecting wages under these conditions have been successful.

6.

FIRST QUARTERLY REPORT

WHAT THE LEGAL AID SOCIETY

of Milwaukee (Inc.)

Has Done in Three Months

297 APPLICANTS

FIRST QUARTERLY REPORT
SEPTEMBER, 1916

LEGAL AID SOCIETY

of Milwaukee, (Inc.)
707-8 Merchants & Manufacturers
Bank Building
214-220 West Water Street
Phone Grand 519

———

William Kaumheimer	*President*
Mrs. Victor Berger	*Vice-President*
Emmett A. Donnelly	*Secretary-Treasurer*

DIRECTORS

Mrs. E.D. Adler
Miss Alice Miller
Hon. John Barnes
Charles W. Babcock
Neil Norris

SUPERINTENDENT

Alma Schlesinger

ATTORNEYS

Hannan, Johnson & Goldschmidt

"There is much talk today of those who through their wealth and influence are above the law. But far less is said of the infinitely greater number of persons, who, by reason of poverty or ignorance, are beneath the law. Though their rights be clear as noonday, they have not the means to enforce them in the courts. To meet this crying need, to bring justice equally to all, is the aim of the Legal Aid Society. – Robert P. Goldman.

WHAT IT DOES

1. It assists in securing legal advice for men, women, and children who are worthy but unable to employ counsel.

2. It brings about adjustment and settlement outside the courts, between litigants unable to agree and without means to pay for legal advice.

3. It takes into court cases with merit where friendly settlement cannot be effected, and where clients are without means to employ counsel.

4. In "domestic relations" cases, it makes efforts to effect reconciliation between husbands and wives and to adjust family difficulties, and gives whatever advice and assistance it deems proper after careful investigation.

5. For the sake of justice, it handles claims where the amounts involved are too small for attorneys to handle as regular business.

6. It accepts meritorious cases only, and such cases only as cannot be handled on a contingent fee basis, and are not provided for by statute.

TYPICAL CASES

A man was sued because he could not pay his grocery bill, and his employer was named as garnishee defendant. The man was married, had a family of eight children, and earned a little over $60.00 a month. The case came into our office, and was referred to our attorneys, and before the return day the matter was settled. The man is to pay his grocery bill by slow installments – $1.00 a week – through our office, and the suit and garnishment action against him has been dismissed.

What the
LEGAL AID
SOCIETY
of Milwaukee (Inc.)

Has Done in
Three Months

297 Applicants

FIRST QUARTERLY REPORT
SEPTEMBER, 1916

64. First Quarterly Report,
September 1916.
*Courtesy of Legal Aid Society
of Milwaukee.*

A very old woman who was referred to us stated that her husband was in the habit of abusing her, and spent all his earnings for drink and on himself, refusing to give her even sufficient means to buy things to eat. Her children, all of them grown up, had married away from here, leaving her at the mercy of the old man. The thought of divorce in her old age was mortifying to her, and she had been advised by someone, incorrectly informed, that due to her husband's advanced age, nothing could be done for her by the authorities. On carefully investigating the case – calling at her home and getting in touch with her neighbors – we found that the old man repeatedly struck her, locked her out, so that she was forced to spend the night with the neighbors, and raised such disturbances that the whole neighborhood knew about the case.

The chief trouble was that he no longer considered himself under obligation to support his wife because she had a small savings account of her own. This money ($200.00) she had carefully put aside out of her earnings (she does sewing now and then) over a long period of years, for a time when both he and she would be too old to earn money, and she consistently in spite of privations, refused to draw any of that money out of the bank. He was trying to force her to do so, and flatly refused to give her one cent of his earnings, although he was steadily employed at 27½ cents an hour. She, as a result, in order to keep alive, was forced to take money out of his pockets, at times, which resulted in the violent rows. We concluded that if he could be made to understand that he had to support his wife, even though she had a little money of her own saved up, we might succeed in establishing normal relations. We brought the case to the attention of the County Poor Office, and the District Attorney's Office, and the man has been put on probation. Our old lady reported to us the other day that since all has been well, and that her husband has been good to her up to the present, and we have the assurance of the Chief Probation Officer that he will carefully watch the case.

A maid servant bought a coat in a small dry goods store. The saleswoman told her it could be washed with Ivory soap. When the coat came home, she saw that it was soiled and shopworn, but, instead of returning it at once, she decided she would wash it, considering that she had been told it could be washed. She washed it with great care, so we were told by her mistress, who was present, but the coat was ruined. The girl could ill afford to lose her money in this way. We took the matter up with the concern where the coat had been bought, and were told that the saleswoman denied absolutely ever having said the coat could be washed. We believed that the girl was telling us the truth, but proving it was a different proposition, as there were no witnesses. Furthermore, as the concern was not a local corporation, suing them would have been made more difficult for us. We solved our difficulty by settling for half the value of the coat, to be taken out in merchandise from the store. We went with the girl while she made her selection, and she was very well satisfied and grateful.

A furniture company was threatening to collect some furniture on which more than half the money was still due. The woman came to us for help. We investigated the case, and found that the company was in the right, and that the woman had been taking advantage of the company's former leniency. However, we prevailed upon the company to give the woman one more chance, and we promised to take the matter up with our client and make an effort to make her pay regularly. We did this, and are still following up her payments.

B_____, who had been employed by a construction company, brought us his time slip on which 40 hours more were marked than the company wished to pay for. B_____ had refused to accept the company's paycheck. We took the matter up with the company who stated that they had offered to pay B_____ for the number of hours as recorded in their books, and that they did not believe that B_____ had worked the number of hours marked on the time slip. B_____ had witnesses to the effect that he had worked the number of hours indicated on his slip, which fact we explained to the company. Thereupon the company sent down to our office their superintendent, to verify the signature on the time slip as that of their foreman, at our suggestion, and having convinced themselves that the claim was just, they remitted the amount involved. B_____ had been trying for weeks to settle this matter himself, with no success. We collected the money due him in less than a week's time.

CLASSIFICATION OF CASES

Wage claims.. 157
Domestic relations 21
Collection 18
Advice in office 16
Recovery of personal property............................... 14
Contract 14
Installment contract... 8
Compensation 7
Landlord and tenant... 5
Wage assignment (garnishment)............................. 5
Advice by letter 5
Real estate.. 5
Alimony 4
Personal injury 3

Damage to personal property 3
Supplementary proceedings.. 2
Detention of children 2
Attorney and client... 1
Insurance... 1
Miscellaneous 6
Total 297

The above cases were referred to us from the following sources:
Civil court 103
District Attorney's office 65
City Attorney's office 29
Attorneys 14
Newspaper 29
Friends 17
Industrial commission 19
Associated charities 3
YMCA.. 1
Big Sisters and Big Brothers 1
County Poor office 4
State aid department 2
Out of town agencies 4
Police 2
Direct 4
Total 297

DISPOSITION OF CASES
(In Our Office)
Settled 61
Probably settled 15
Closed – no return 21
Refused – no subject for legal aid 29
Dismissed – case has no merit 14
Dismissed – insufficient information 5
Referred to other agencies 2
Dropped – client unworthy 3
Discontinued – no results 2

Advised 5
Dismissed at request of client 1
Total 158
Cases reported disposed of by our attorneys 18
Cases pending in our office 106
Cases pending in our attorney's office 11
Money collected for clients $546.22

MISS SCHLESINGER, MILWAUKEE, WIS.

Dear Madam:

As President of the Milwaukee Bar Association, I had occasion to appoint a committee of lawyers to co-operate with other civic organizations of Milwaukee in the organization of a legal aid bureau. I have no hesitation in saying that this society fills a public want, and that on behalf of the Milwaukee Bar Association I fully endorse its endeavors.

Yours very truly,
ROBERT WILD,
President of the Milwaukee Bar Association

From the past five years' experience as General Secretary of the Associated Charities, I am thoroughly convinced of the need of an efficient Legal Aid Society for securing justice to people with incomes too small to permit of paying lawyer's fees, particularly where the amounts involved are small but of vital importance to the lesser wage earners.

KATHERINE L. VAN WYCK

TO WHOM IT MAY CONCERN:

I take this means of expressing my firm conviction that there is a large field for a Legal Aid Society in Milwaukee, and in fact a crying demand for the same. I am brought to this conviction by seven years' experience in the City Attorney's Office, where indigent persons naturally come for some legal assistance, and by four years' intimate connection with these problems in a struggle to put the justice shops out of business in Milwaukee.

Any Legal Aid Society or Bureau which will honestly and conscientiously give assistance to poor people who are in slight difficulties should be heartily supported by the community, and I am informed by reliable persons, and I believe from my own personal investigation, that the Legal Aid Society of Milwaukee, as presently constituted, has established its usefulness even by its short career, and we are assured of its honest and business-like management. The Superintendent is profiting by a study of other bureaus of long duration, and comprehensive plans are developing for the future.

As far as the City Attorney's Office is concerned, it is really a godsend to know of some place where we can send deserving people who are unable to hire lawyers to assist them in difficulties, because the law, to say nothing of our other duties and limited force of assistants, renders it impossible for us to take care of these cases. In the past, about the only ray of hope we could hold out to these people was that they would have to see an attorney, and they had no money to employ an attorney. In some cases where litigation was necessary, the parties could be referred to the Civil Court, but an overwhelming percentage of these cases do not necessitate litigation, and a Legal Aid Society is practically the only body that can properly care for the needs of these people. Until such time as an institution of this kind may be maintained at public expense, the only alternative is to properly support the private institution.

Respectfully yours,
CLIFTON WILLIAMS
City Attorney

MISS ALMA SCHLESINGER, SUPERINTENDENT,
LEGAL AID SOCIETY

Dear Miss Schlesinger: – I desire to express to you my appreciation of the work of the Legal Aid Society of Milwaukee, and to say that the results achieved in the cases sent to you from this office in the past three months commend it highly to everyone having at heart the general welfare of Milwaukee county. I have found that the cases sent you by me are efficiently and expeditiously handled, and that they receive much better attention than I was able to give them before the formation of the society.

I trust you may be able to continue your work and enlarge its scope, and beg to remain,

Yours truly,
WM. A. KLATTE
Clerk of Civil Court of Milwaukee County

LEGAL AID BUREAU, MILWAUKEE, WIS.

We have had occasion to use your bureau in a number of cases where claims for wages were made and the amount involved being too small to warrant the issuance of a court procedure, which naturally means that the applicant would have to pay the fees of a lawyer and other expenses. In all of these cases we are pleased to say that you have taken care of them to the satisfaction of all parties concerned, and we hope that this Free Legal Aid Bureau will remain in existence for a long time to come, as it is not only a valuable aid to the man who needs legal advice and cannot afford to pay for it, but it is also a valuable aid to offices of our description

Personally speaking, I sincerely hope that you will keep up the good work you have been doing.

Yours very truly,
PUBLIC EMPLOYMENT BUREAU
Industrial Commission of Wisconsin
H.J. Beckerle, Superintendent

LEGAL AID SOCIETY OF MILWAUKEE,

Milwaukee, Wis.

Gentlemen: – There is certainly a great need for a Free Legal Aid Society in this city. This has been demonstrated to me in connection with my work of issuing labor permits to children between the ages of 14 and 16 years and also as Superintendent of the Women's Public Employment Bureau. During the past three months we have referred several cases to the society, and each one has been promptly and efficiently handled.

For the benefit of those who cannot otherwise secure legal advice, I hope that the good work already started will be carried on.

Very truly yours,
ELSIE ESSMANN,
Deputy, Industrial Commission of Wisconsin

TO THE LEGAL AID SOCIETY, CITY OF MILWAUKEE.

This Division has been in a position to direct cases to the Legal Aid Society of Milwaukee, and has obtained most satisfactory results. No doubt there is a vast field for such an organization, and, if kept at its present high standard, will continue to receive the unqualified indorsement of this Division of the Health Department for the great good it has accomplished.

GEO. R. ERNST, M.D.
Chief, Div. of Tuberculosis
Health Department

MISS ALMA SCHLESINGER, SUPERINTENDENT, LEGAL AID SOCIETY OF MILWAUKEE, MILWAUKEE, WISCONSIN

Dear Miss Schlesinger: – Your organization and your work is a very needed part of the general social work machine of a big city.

We hope that you will be able to continue the thorough work which you have started.

Very truly yours,
A.C. HEWSON
Director, Big Brother Work

Legal Aid Societies Have Been Established
in the Following Cities:

Atlanta, Ga.
Baltimore,   M.
Boston, Mass.
Buffalo, N.Y.
Chicago, Ill.
Cincinnati, O.
Cleveland, O.
Columbus,   O
Kansas City, Mo.
Milwaukee, Wis
New York City, N.Y.
   (Six branch offices)
New Rochelle, N.Y.
Philadelphia, Pa.
Pittsburgh, Pa.
Rochester, N.Y.
St. Louis, Mo.

7.

LEGAL AID SOCIETY
STATISTICAL PROFILE, 1916-66[1]

Year	New Cases	Funds Recovered for Clients	Gross Revenue
1916	297(part)	$546	$877
1917	1,174	1,892	3,017
1918	1,183	1,886	4,323
1919	1,352	5,569	5,048
1920	1,410	4,504	5,447
1921	1,411	9,157	5,594
1922	1,549	11,638	5,870
1923	2,380	14,253	6,043
1924	3,970	13,157	7,571
1925	3,970	9,177	7,948
1926	4,121	9,109	8,054
1927	3,153	11,826	8,526
1928	3,286	5,290	8,396
1929	3,184	7,236	8,367
1930	3,175	8,409	8,144
1931	3,385	9,232	7,662
1932	2,528	4,270	7,193
1933	1,828	2,506	5,613
1934	1798	1,491	5,350
1935	2,043	1,264	5,320
1936	1,844	5,739	5,282
1937	2,430	3,568	5,344
1938	2,691	4,233	5,858
1939	2,501	4,791	5,500
1940	2,939	5,256	5,955
1941	2,896	4,934	7,257
1942[2]	3,179	7,746	
1943	2,465	2,205	7,656
1944	2,105	2,767	7,741
1945	2,006	5,268	8,055
1946	2,910	9,665	9,677
1947	2,771		11,437
1948	2,800	9,902	11,772

1949	4,541		12,093
1950	5,267		17,812
1951	4,028	8,802	21,731
1952	3,238		22,236
1953	2,992		22,756
1954	3,849		23,098
1955	5,122		25,081
1956	3,881		26,980
1957	3,622		29,084
1958	4,126		36,454
1959	3,947		39,666
1960	4,213		33,701
1961	4,888		37,139
1962	4,556		38,014
1963	4,590		39,278
1964	4,801		39,493
1965	4,201		45,759
1966[3]	8,364		54,623

Total clients served, 1916-66: 160,960
Total funds raised, 1916-66: $788,641
Total funds recovered, 1916-51: $199,542 (4 years missing)

NOTES

1. Sources: Annual reports of the Legal Aid Society of Milwaukee, supplement by Reginald Heber Smith and John S. Bradway, *Growth of Legal Aid Work in the United Sates* (Washington, D.C.: Government Printing Office, 1936), tables at pp 202, 205, 208; Emery A. Brownell, *Legal Aid in the United States* (Rochester, NY: Lawyers Co-operative Publishing Co. 1951); Brownell, *Supplement to Legal Aid Work in the United States* (Rochester, NY: Lawyers' Co-operative Publishing Co 1961); *Annual Proceedings of the National Association of Legal Aid Organizations* (1923-67). These figures, compiled on the fiscal year (July 1 – June 30) occasionally vary slightly in some years from LAS's annual reports, which were compiled on an October 1 – September 30 basis.

2. The National Association of Legal Aid Organizations stopped publishing specific organizational data on funds recovered for clients after 1941 and began, instead, publishing the data only in aggregate form. Four annual

reports of the Legal Aid Society of Milwaukee from 1942-51 are missing. After 1951, data on client recoveries was no longer reported by LAS.

3. The figures for 1966 represent the first infusion of funds ($8,000) from the OEO Legal Services Program. That grant represented the Society's first new funding source since the 1932-50 period when Milwaukee County contributed rent-free quarters in the Public Safety Building.

8.

ANNUAL REPORT OF THE
LEGAL AID SOCIETY OF MILWAUKEE
1920

In the early Spring of 1916, three civic organizations, the Milwaukee Bar Association, the Central Council of Social Agencies, and the City Club, all recognizing the same urgent need in the community, appointed a joint committee to plan and establish the Legal Aid Society of Milwaukee. The purpose of this new social agency was to furnish advice and legal assistance to those in trouble who were in need of lawyers' services, but who, because of poverty, could not afford to hire counsel. On the first of June of 1916, the Society opened the door of its offices to the public, and on the very first day of its career, even before office furniture and telephone service were installed, two clients made application for relief.

Since June of 1916, the Society has been functioning in an effort to fill a long existing and clearly defined need, the extent of which is far-reaching and much greater than is generally appreciated. For it must be admitted that by comparison with our rapid industrial and economic development, progress in our legal and judicial institutions has lagged, with the result that the less fortunate of our fellow citizens are at a decided disadvantage under our judicial system. This disadvantage is caused, primarily, by the expense of counsel and by delay and complications in procedure.

A Legal Aid Society can in definite cases eliminate the first difficulty by providing counsel free of charge for indigent clients and can mitigate the second difficulty by jealously safeguarding the interests of its clients. It can, however, be of greatest service to those who need it, by effecting adjustments and compromises out of court. Therefore, until such time as our judicial and legal machinery shall have reached that advanced stage in its development, where it will enable the poor man to avail himself of its benefits to the same degree and to the same extent as the rich man, without the functionings of an outside agency, the Legal Aid Society has its work to do in the community and merits the support of public-spirited citizens.

How does the Legal Aid Society do its work? Since the first of June 1916, five thousand one hundred and twenty-one clients have made application for aid. Americans, Poles, Germans, Slavs, Scandinavians, Russians, and practically every other nationality represented in Milwaukee, have availed themselves of our services. Judges, state and county officials, organized charities, hospitals, the American Red Cross, employers, members of the bar, and the newspapers refer clients to our offices and are in close touch with our activities. Furthermore, each month the number of clients who find their way to our offices, direct, without being referred to us by a third party, increases, a fact that we report with gratification, because it indicates that, slowly but surely, the news that legal aid is available to the poor is spreading among those who need us.

The statistical report of our work that follows sets forth the different types of cases handled, and it will be noted how nearly the entire range of the civil law has been covered by our field of activity, with exception of such cases as involve big sums or property. A very large proportion of the cases handled are satisfactorily adjusted, as will be noted by the number of cases disposed of as "settled" or "probably settled" in our statistical report, and many clients apply for advice only.

Care is exercised to discriminate scrupulously between those who need our assistance and those who must be advised to seek and hire their own counsel because they are financially in position to pay for services. In a case that is dismissed as having no merit, every effort is made to convince the client that he is receiving fair treatment, so that he will not leave our offices with his sense of justice outraged. Much emphasis is put on explanation of legal procedure, especially with reference to the particular action in which the client happens to be involved.

The work of the offices of the Society is conducted by social workers, and a firm of attorneys is retained by the Society to advise and consult with the social workers and to handle the court work for the

Society. The Society is one of the organizations that is financed by the Centralized Budget of Philanthropies.

Our big problem, at the present time, is to reach large numbers of people who are entitled to and who could avail themselves of our services, if they but knew of our existence. We are, consequently, just barely scratching the surface of a great need, for although knowledge of our work among those who need us is gradually spreading, it is a slow process. It is in this respect that friends of the Society, who are interested in its work and future, can do their share to make its activities widely effective – by availing themselves of every opportunity to assist in disseminating the information that legal aid is available to those who need it.

9.

THE MILWAUKEE LEADER

APRIL 13, 1921

LEGAL AID BILL WILL SIFT OUT STATE
BILL COLLECTORS

Investigation of the practice of Chicago collection agencies operating in Milwaukee without bond will be made by the Legal Aid Society, according to Alma Schlesinger, in charge of the society's office at 216 West Water Street, today, as the result of the complaint of a number of Milwaukeeans that they have been dunned for bills they did not owe.

"Wisconsin agencies are required to put up a bond," said Miss Schlesinger. "Whether outside agencies can be restricted from operating in Milwaukee unless they comply with Wisconsin laws, I intend to determine."

Some procedure to stop irresponsible agencies from annoying Milwaukeeans is to be taken from the investigation, it is said.

The agencies, it is alleged, operate on a percentage basis. A large number of dunning letters are sent out indiscriminatingly charging the debt of small amounts. Many of the recipients, believing the debt has slipped their minds, respond after several letters, it is said. The percentage of replies received makes the game highly profitable, it is charged.

Postal inspectors and department of justice agents yesterday started an investigation into the activities of the Chicago agencies.

10.

ANNUAL REPORT OF THE
LEGAL AID SOCIETY OF MILWAUKEE

1922

The declared purpose of the Legal Aid Society of Milwaukee is to furnish legal aid to those financially unable to obtain legal counsel, to promote laws and measures, and to do all things necessary for the prevention of injustice.

CONSTITUTION OF LEGAL AID SOCIETY

The Legal Aid Society of Milwaukee was founded in the spring of 1916. Members of the Bar Association, City Club, and Central Council of Social Agencies, who realized the need in the community for "A Poor Man's Lawyer," were instrumental in the Society's organization. The Society is affiliated with the Centralized Budget of Philanthropies.

The Society does not give charity; it assists its clients to obtain full justice under the law. For the most part, the clients are self-supporting citizens whose incomes, however, are not sufficient to pay for counsel, and provide properly for their families.

Social workers at the Legal Aid Society office carefully investigate the financial condition of applicants before taking their cases. If it is felt that the applicant can afford to pay for attorneys' services, the case is not accepted by the Society. Last year the Legal Aid Society helped 1,549 clients who were too poor to hire counsel.

The cost per case for the past year was $3.61. The preceding year the cost per case was $4.25. About two-thirds of the clients during the past year were American born. The greatest proportion of the remaining third came from Poland or Germany.

$11,638.02 is the amount collected during the past year for Legal Aid clients. It is probable that double that sum was actually received by clients, but not reported to the organization.

It is the desire of the Society to maintain as friendly a feeling as possible between employer and employee, and for that reason, clients are usually referred back to their employers for an amicable adjustment.

The increase in the clientele of the office is, no doubt, largely due to the unemployment situation which existed in the early part of 1922. Irregular employment naturally means wage disputes. Some of the wage claims amounted to one or two dollars only, but they were of vital importance to the client's family budget.

No registration fee is required and no fee of any kind charged.

Nationality of clients:	1921-22	1920-21	1919-20
American	963	863	816
American, colored	33	31	19
German	151	123	132
Polish	99	137	139
Austrian	80	46	32
Hungarian	16	24	30
Russian	43	33	45
Italian	19	17	36
French	9	2	7
Irish	5	7	12
Bohemian	4	12	10
Canadian	7	4	4
Finnish	3	1	3
Scotch	3	2	2
Swiss	6	4	6
Serbian	2	3	5
Armenian	1	–	2
Spanish	1	2	1
Greek	20	19	22
Lithuanian	2	4	11
English	3	6	6
Ukranian	–	1	1
Croatian	6	4	7

Danish	3	4	–
Dutch	1	1	–
Slavonian	20	13	14
Scandinavian	12	12	18
Syrian	–	4	2
Macedonian	–	–	2
Turk	–	1	1
Albanian	–	1	1
Roumanian	–	5	1
Porto Rican	–	–	1
Belgian	–	1	1
Bulgarian	4	1	–
Egyptian	–	–	1
Unknown	33	23	20
Total	1,549	1,411	1,410

Clients referred by:

Civil Court	231	468	294
Judges	27	13	4
District Attorney, Police	425	112	150
City,County, State Officials	58	62	115
Attorneys	42	32	40
Former Clients	172	159	142
Private Individuals	218	248	112
Direct	81	93	245
Employers	29	24	37
Newspapers	31	30	43
Doctors, Hospitals, Dispensaries	15	21	12
Organized Charities	72	62	45
American Red Cross	49	88	93
Industrial Commission & Employment Office	59	47	40
Out-of-town Agencies	21	28	21
Schools	–	1	1
Rental Bureau	–	6	5
Re-opened	19	17	10

| Total | 1,549 | 1,411 | 1,410 |

Classification of cases:

Advice in General	121	133	63
Contract, Installment Contract	128	113	123
Husband and Wife	56	62	85
Wage Claims	664	449	397
Landlord and Tenant	78	106	108
Guardianship	4	3	8
Garnishment, Wage Assignment	58	43	78
Money Claims–Plaintiff	196	151	–
Money Claims–Defendant	50	67	242
Attorney and Client	12	11	3
Recovery of Personal Property	50	68	84
Workmen's Compensation	29	60	57
Insolvency	2	2	4
Criminal Matters Advised	4	–	–
Real Estate	18	21	15
Personal Injury	12	24	23
Estates of Deceased	4	12	14
Neighborhood Quarrel, Slander	8	11	6
Alimony	7	18	8
Damage to Personal Property	26	21	34
Collection of Judgment	2	11	19
Insurance	13	17	13
Miscellaneous	7	8	26
Total	1,549	1,411	1,410

Disposition:	1921-22	1920-21	1919-20
Settled	441	393	348
Probably Settled	127	215	183
Advised	148	228	178
Dismissed–No Merit	107	121	135
Dismissed–Lapsed by Client	165	178	135
Dismissed–Prohibited by Rule	38	61	57
Dismissed–Not entitled to			

Legal Aid	20	32	66
Dismissed–Client Unworthy	4	1	4
Dismissed–Insufficient Information	11	15	9
Dismissed–Referred to Appropriate Agency	160	77	16
Dismissed–No Practical Remedy	160	87	91
Total	1,381	1,408	1,222
Number of men	1,054	912	–
Number of women	495	499	–
Total	1,549	1,411	–
Cases referred to your attorney	116	93	69
Cases pending in your office	357	305	385
Cases disposed of by your attorney	119	77	90
Cases pending in office of your Attorney	44	49	33
Money collected	$11,638.08	$9,157.71	$4,504.24
Settled accounts collected for Adverse party	661.12	553.46	270.98

II.

LAS NEWSPAPER PROFILE

MILWAUKEE LEADER

January 26, 1922

Legal Aid Society Gets Many Wage Claims from Jobless

"We have had twice as many wage claim cases as any other kind during the past month," said Agnes Campbell, superintendent, Legal Aid Society, 706 M & M Bank Bldg., today. "The hard times are not yet over and we find it necessary, in some cases, to exert pressure on employers to pay wages due their employees. The employer frequently settles by agreeing to pay wages due, in installments. Our office then keeps track of payments."

"Our free legal work ranges all the way from general advice to careful examination of contracts covering payments for houses. In the past month, we refused to handle a number of cases because the client was not entitled to legal aid or because the case had no merit. Nevertheless, we look carefully into every case that is brought to our attention.

"Of the 143 new clients, 98 were American, 11 Polish, 11 German, and 6 Russian. There were three Croatians and three Frenchmen, two Swedes and two Greeks, and one each from Canada, Switzerland, Austria, Italy, Yugo-Slavia, Hungary, and Czecho-Slovakia.

"Our clients are directed to us from many quarters. Last month the civil court sent 20, other judges four. City, county, and state officials advised 46 to see us. Former clients urged 24 to come.

"The Legal Aid Society has collected, in the last 30 days, sums totaling $1,920.92 due our clients. Of this amount, $1,200 was collected through our attorneys and the rest directly or by settlement.

65. Old Milwaukee County Courthouse, 1873-1931.
Courtesy of Wisconsin Historical Society (WHi-68184).

"We have handled installment cases, husband and wife, landlord and tenant, and garnishment disputes, various money claims, attorney and client, recovery of personal property, compensation, real estate, and inheritance cases, neighborhood quarrels, slander, personal injury and damage to property cases, and have given advice on general and criminal matters.

"The slow recovery of industry doubtless will be reflected in our office by an increase of garnishments, creditors searching for the return to employment to collect claims due them by men and women who are now unable to meet their debts."

12.

LETTER FROM MAYOR DANIEL W. HOAN

November 13, 1922

Agnes Campbell
Legal Aid Society
85 Oneida Street
City
Dear Madam:

The Legal Aid Society has been of great assistance to this office in handling cases which we have referred to it. Its work was especially valuable during the industrial depression when great numbers of those thrown out of work found themselves in need of legal advice.

This society deserves the fullest support from our community.

Yours very truly,
Daniel W. Hoan
Mayor

13.

LAS BOARD RESOLUTION AUTHORIZING
CREATION OF NALAO

1923

A meeting of the Board of Directors of the Legal Aid Society of Milwaukee was held this second day of March, 1923, after due call and notice, at the Milwaukee Athletic Club, Milwaukee, Wisconsin.

The meeting was called to order at 12:15 p.m. by President William Kaumheimer. There were present Mmes. Lines and Kiewert and Messrs. Kaumheimer, Klatte, Babcock, Donnelly, and Stearns, being more than the number necessary to constitute a quorum.

The question of the formation of a new national association of legal aid organizations was considered. On this matter, the report of a special committee of the National Alliance of Legal Aid Societies, appointed by Albert F. Bigelow, President of the National Alliance, pursuant to resolutions unanimously adopted by the delegates of legal aid organization at their convention in Philadelphia on March 25, 1922, was presented.[1]

On motion duly made and seconded, it was

VOTED: That Mr. William Kaumheimer be and hereby is made the duly authorized delegate of the Legal Aid Society of Milwaukee to attend the next convention of legal aid organizations with full power, in his discretion, to constitute this Society one of the charter members of the new National Association by signing the name of this Society to the Articles of said Agreement in such form as they may finally be fixed by the said convention of legal aid organizations.

On motion duly made and seconded, it was

VOTED: That Mr. Walter S. Bartlett be and hereby is made the duly authorized alternate delegate with full powers as delegate in the event of the inability of Mr. William Kaumheimer to attend the said convention.

Emmett Donnelly
Secretary

I hereby certify that the foregoing is a true copy of the record. In witness whereof, I have hereunto set my hand this 2nd day of March, 1923, at Milwaukee in the County of Milwaukee and State of Wisconsin.

Emmett Donnelly
Secretary of the
LEGAL AID SOCIETY OF MILWAUKEE

NOTE

1. For the background to this resolution, see Reginald Heber Smith, "The First Twelve Years" in *Legal Aid Brief Case* xix, no. 5 (1961) 128-35, 171-76.

14.

KAUMHEIMER PROPOSAL RE
MODEL LAW ON COLLECTION OF WAGES

1924

The extent of the problem is shown by the fact that legal aid organizations alone collect over half a million dollars a year for their clients. The sum represents largely wages which were due the employees, but which had been collected by some outside agency. The figures for the labor organizations are not available. But they are at least as large. Wages are the lifeblood of the employee. If they are not paid promptly, poverty, crime, and illness follow rapidly. Delay in collection of money earned lowers the morale of the laborer. The effects are particularly noticeable in the poor man. The wealthy employee has recourse to the courts to assert his rights. The poor man in endeavoring to secure his due is confronted with ignorance, court costs, delay of court procedure, and expense of counsel. Ignorance is a barrier, particularly among the foreign population. The workman does not always know where to go for aid, assuming that he may be instructed on this point, [and] he again faces the barrier of court costs.

Most states require the payment of court costs as a prerequisite to a hearing by the court.[1] There is good reason for it, but if the poor man without wages cannot beg or borrow the court costs, he may not secure the aid of the court in the collection of his wages. Even if he can find the money for court costs, he is again halted by the delay of court procedure. It takes a month or two to dispose of even the simplest case in court. If the poor man cannot afford to wait that long, he may well be denied justice. Finally, how can he hope to contend successfully with the intricacies of court procedure unless he has the assistance of a lawyer? To secure legal services costs money, and the poor man cannot afford this. The denial of justice in the case of wage claims may be a very real thing.

The majority of wages are paid promptly. Of the balance, a large number yield to conciliation or arbitration. But there is a final residuum of knotty problems which require court action. All wage claims

66. Mayor Daniel W. Hoan served on the Legal Aid Society's Advisory Board 1919-44.
Courtesy of Milwaukee County Historical Society.

not paid at once require either time or money to adjust. The poor man can afford neither of these.

It is, therefore, the opportunity of this committee to consider a remedy. It is apparent that the remedy must be a piece of machinery to provide a cheap and speedy method of collection. Such a piece of machinery can only be established by a statute. So the report of this committee is substantially the presentation of a draft of a model act covering this subject. This act, when drawn, must be submitted to as many persons as possible for consideration and revision. In its final form, it should a "model" and not a "uniform" act on the subject. Speed, cheapness, and efficiency are our three aims. It would appear that the fundamentals of such a law are: (a) Someone to enforce the law for the workman so that it may be efficiently enforced without placing the burden on the workman of struggling alone and unaided with the law. (b) It should be enforceable without court costs as a prerequisite. (c) It should provide for final disposition of the case and collection of the money within a spaced time to render it of value to the worker who needs it.

Let us consider, therefore, the existing laws in this field to observe from their operation those factors which will aid us in our search. It is apparent that the failure of certain of these laws to achieve the maximum of efficiency along the lines of our search is because they do not take into account one or more of the three elements – someone to make the law work, a waiver of court costs, and a minimum of time in obtaining results. But another factor also enters in, that is, the question of constitutionality. The law may be carefully drawn, but it may conflict with the constitution of a state or nation. We are to devise a machinery for a speedy, inexpensive, and efficient collection of wage claims which will not interfere with the constitutional restrictions as to freedom of contract, due process of law, [or] special legislation.

[Here follows an extended discussion of various constitutional objections, together with the texts of various laws from Massachusetts, Utah, and California bearing on the subject of workers' claims. The committee's ultimate proposal vests the power to enforce wage claims in a state administrative official cloaked with authority to initiate civil and criminal actions as necessary].[2]

WILLIAM KAUMHEIMER, *Chairman*

NOTES

1. Prior to the adoption of Wisconsin's In Forma Pauperis statute (currently sec. 814.29, Wis. Stats.), this was the rule here as well. See *Campbell v. Chicago & Northwestern Ry. Co.*, 23 Wis. 490 (1868), affirming dismissal of plaintiff's complaint because he was too poor to provide security for court

costs. The Supreme Court remarked: "It seems almost like a hardship that a poor person should not be able to litigate." *Id.* at 491.
2. The foregoing is an abridged version of a proposal drafted and presented by Kaumheimer to the NALAO conference. See "Report of Committee on Relations with the Association of Governmental Labor Officials of the United States and Canada Re a Model Law on the Cheap and Speedy Collection of Wage Claims" in *Reports of Committees: Proc. NALAO* (1924-25) 105-20. The Kaumheimer Report became the basis of a Model Act. See Reginald Heber Smith, "First Draft of a Model Statute for Facilitating Enforcement of Wage Claims" in *Legal Aid Review* xxv, no. 3 (1927) 1-14. The Wisconsin Legislature enacted the measure in 1931 Wis. Laws, c. 262. The new law made failure to pay wage claims a misdemeanor punishable by up to a $100 fine and/or a jail term of up to 90 days, authorized the Industrial Commission to investigate claims and file suit, imposed graduated penalties from 10% to 50% of wages due for delays in payment, and provided for payment of the worker's attorney fees if successful suit was brought to enforce a wage claim.

15.

LAS RELATIONS WITH LOCAL SOCIAL AGENCIES

1926

QUESTION 1 – *Is your organization organically related to any social agency?* No.[1]

QUESTION 2a – *Is it supported by funds from a social agency at all, to what extent?* Supported by a council of social agencies or community chest.

QUESTION 2b – *Is the social agency represented on your board?* No.

QUESTION 3 – *What arrangement, if any, have you for sending cases to social agencies when more than a legal problem is involved?* There is an unwritten law among social agencies of this city that each agency will handle only the matter that it is authorized to handle by the Milwaukee Community Fund. If a problem of neglected children, relief, or a family situation comes to the attention of the legal aid worker while in contact with the legal problems, this problem is referred to the proper agency.

QUESTION 4 – *What arrangements, if any, have social agencies with you for referring cases in which legal problems are involved?* The same unwritten law requires that the social agency send their contacts with legal problems to the Legal Aid Society. May I add that there has never been any professional jealousy among the agencies of Milwaukee, and our plan works out very well. It would be hard, I believe, to find a city where the social agencies coöperate any more than here. It is my personal opinion that this is due to the fact than no two agencies are in any way responsible to each other, but we are all responsible to the Community Fund.

QUESTION 5 – *What is the limit of your responsibility as to the social factors in a legal aid case?* It is the duty of the Legal Aid Society to recognize social factors in legal aid cases and to see that these social maladjustments are properly corrected by an agency authorized to do that work.

QUESTION 6 – *How far is a legal aid society free to call upon a social agency to handle a case?* We are free to call upon a social agency to handle the social problems, and we are also free to call upon them for advice in our own problems.

QUESTION 7 – *What is the extent of the responsibility of a social agency toward a case referred by a legal aid society?* The social agencies being case working agencies must, of course, follow up any case that has been referred to the Legal Aid Society. The Legal Aid Society is not so apt to follow up cases we refer to other agencies because – (1) After the matter has been handed to them, our duty is to settle only the legal problem; (2) We know that the agency to whom the maladjustment has been referred will handle it properly.

QUESTION 8 – *How far should a legal aid society go when urging social aid on an unwilling applicant?* This is a very valuable question and one that I believe has not been thoroughly worked out by the legal aid societies of the country. I have on several occasions brought the matter up before our Central Council of Social Agencies and have come to this conclusion: When there is a moral situation at stake, or a physical situation, then that situation should be referred to the proper agency for adjustment and that agency be allowed to handle the matter as adequately as they can. However, if it is not merely a matter of relief, and a family's pride will not allow them to accept charity, I do not feel that the family should be subjected to a first interview by the Family Welfare.

QUESTION 9 – *What data should a legal aid society collect in referring a case to a social agency?* I would not feel it necessary to gather any data regarding a social problem that I am sending to a social agency as ostensibly that is not my job. I do not expect a social worker to collect legal data in turning a case over to me.[2]

QUESTION 10 – *If for any reason satisfactory to itself, a social agency refuses aid in a specific case, what should a legal aid organization do?* If a social agency refuses to give assistance in a specific case that has been handed to them by the Legal Aid Society, I feel that the Legal Aid Society should accept the agency's judgment. It is my opinion that the agency would usually have some well founded reason for the refusal. In my own work, I would rather over-assist nine clients than I would under-assist one client, but I cannot force this attitude upon the social agencies. If the social agencies do not back each other up in just this type of matter, I feel we have entirely lost track of the ideals for which we are organized.

NOTES

1. This survey, which was completed by Superintendent Agnes Campbell Kiewert, was published in the *Proceedings of the National Association of Legal Aid Organizations: Reports of Committees* (1926) 182-97, along with responses from other legal aid organizations.

2. In a later report, it was noted that the Legal Aid Society of Milwaukee shared with social agencies only such information as was not protected by the attorney-client privilege. *Proc. NALAO* (1928-29) 88.

16.

ASSIGNED COUNSEL IN CRIMINAL CASES

By William Kaumheimer
President of the Milwaukee Legal Aid Society[1]

1926

The right of a person accused of crime to be heard by himself and counsel is so well recognized by the constitutions of the various states that it would be idle at this age to trace the history of that right, and it may be safely assumed that, as one of the foundations of English jurisprudence, in all criminal prosecutions the accused shall enjoy the right to be heard by himself and counsel; to demand the nature and cause of the accusation against him; to meet the witnesses face to face; to have compulsory process to compel the attendance of witnesses in his behalf; and to a speedy public trial by an impartial jury of the county or district wherein the offense shall have been committed. The language is that of the constitution of the state of Wisconsin [Art. I, § 7].

DIRECTORS
William Kaumheimer
President
Charles W. Babcock
Vice-President
Mrs. George Lines
2d Vice-President
Perry J. Stearns
Secy.-Treas.
Charles B. Quarles
Mrs. Howard Greene
William A. Klatte
Miss Ida Luick
Edmund B. Shea

SUPERINTENDENT
Agnes Campbell Kiewert

ASST. SUPERINTENDENT
Madge Loranger

ATTORNEY
W.S. Goldschmidt

Legal Aid Society of Milwaukee

Affiliated with Centralized Budget of Philanthropies

(INCORPORATED 1916)

85 ONEIDA STREET, ROOM 411

Telephones: Broadway 1713 and 1714

Milwaukee, Wis.

ADVISORY BOARD
Hon. Daniel W. Hoan
Frank J. Weber
Most Rev. Archbishop Messmer
George A. Shaughnessy
John M. Niven
Walter Stern
Louis Kotecki
Lieut. Col. E. White
Rabbi Samuel Hirshberg
William E. McCarty
Elizabeth Marshall
Francis E. McGovern
Hon. Christian Doerfler

---

67. Legal Aid Society letterhead, 1926.

PRIMARY EFFORTS

Very early in the legal history of the country, the court laid down the rule that, although it could find no express provision of law declaring that a county shall pay for services rendered by an attorney appointed by the court in defending a person on trial for criminal offense, yet it would be a reproach upon the administration of justice if a person thus upon trial could not have the assistance of legal counsel because he was too poor to secure it. [*Carpenter v. Dane County*, 9 Wis. 249 (*274) (1859)]. After quoting from the constitution the humane and wise provision quoted above, it was argued that the right to meet the witnesses face to face and have compulsory process to compel the attendance of unwilling witnesses is no more valuable to the person in jeopardy of life and liberty than the privilege of having the benefits of the talents and assistance of counsel in examining the witness or making his defense before the jury. It would be a little like mockery to secure to the pauper these solemn constitutional guaranties for a fair and full trial of the matters with which he was charged, and yet say to him when on trial that he must employ his own counsel, who alone could render these guaranties of any real permanent value to him. [*County of Dane v. Smith*, 13 Wis. 585 (1861)]

A little later, the court took the broad ground that courts of record, having criminal jurisdiction, possess competent legal authority to appoint counsel to defend paupers and other indigent persons charged with crime. This right is placed on the basis of the common law, and the benign provisions of the Constitution by which criminal trials are in other respects governed, the right of the accused to the assistance of counsel; the just and humane results arising from the exercise of this power; the interest of the public in the correct and fair administration of the criminal laws; and the well known and constant practice of the courts from the first organization of the government. These established the right of the court to appoint counsel for the indigent and the pauper, and public justice and sound policy demanded it. To entrust the rights of the accused to the care and protection of the courts and the public prosecutor is both unsafe and hazardous. The antagonism and conflict of opposing and experienced minds, each anxious and active to detect and expose the defects and weakness in the cause of the other, are, in general, absolutely essential to the discovery and establishment of legal truth, and more particularly is this true of the investigation of extensive and complicated questions of fact such as are frequently present in the prosecution of public offenders.

The writer has quoted thus liberally from the position taken by the courts of his own state, because that state recognizes these principles and gave expression to them very early in the judicial history of the state, even going so far as to hold that a legislative enactment is void which provides that, where in a criminal proceeding an attorney shall defend a person charged with an offense, by order of the court or otherwise, the county in which the action or proceeding arises should not be held liable to pay the attorney for services in making such defense. As the writer is arguing in favor of the paid assigned counsel, it may be well to quote again what the Wisconsin Supreme Court has said in respect to such legislation:

> That the effect of the legislative enactment is that the Courts have and may exercise the power to order attorneys to defend persons charged with the commission of offenses, but that the attorney who, in obedience to that order, makes the defense, must, as a penalty for complying with the legal command of the Court, do so without compensation. The Legislature has not the power, generally, to say to the physician, the surgeon, the lawyer, the farmer, or anyone else that he shall render this or that ser-

vice, or perform this or that act in the line of his profession or business without compensation. The Legislature cannot leave with the Courts the authority to order and employ, and at the same time destroy the implied promise to pay. The latter arises immediately out of the former, and is in the law so inseparably connected with it that where the former exists, the latter exists also.

[*County of Dane*, 13 Wis. at 588-89].

VALUE OF ASSIGNED COUNSEL

The language of the court is adopted in leading text-books, stating the law almost verbatim as expressed in the opinion and based upon the same reasons set forth in the opinions from which the writer has so extensively quoted, and we may well and safely assume that it is now a settled law that courts of record having criminal jurisdiction possess competent authority to appoint counsel to defend paupers and other indigent persons charged with crime. This requires no legislative sanction, and being a part of our English jurisprudence, the question arises how best shall that function be discharged – by the election or appointment of a public defender, or by assigned counsel in individual cases. It is obvious that a public defender, to function properly, should be an appointed officer of the court, and it must be assumed that the judge, who has the power of appointment either of assigned counsel or a public defender, will conscientiously discharge his duty in that respect. We do not think it would be seriously contended that the public defender should be an elective office and that making it a political office would produce satisfactory results.

The advantage of the assigned counsel lies essentially in its adaptability to all conditions, urban and rural, while the employment of a public defender to take charge of all cases of indigent persons or paupers accused of crime can be effective only in the larger cities. Insofar as it is possible so to do, each person should be permitted to have counsel of his choice. The relation of attorney and client is one of strict confidence, and all natures are not alike, and it is quite impossible that the same individual appearing for a number of indigent or pauper clients will inspire an equal degree of confidence from them all.

Furthermore, the trial of certain classes of cases, such as are met among those whose welfare we are here considering, creates a habit

68. Original Milwaukee County Courthouse, 1836-1871.
Courtesy of Wisconsin Historical Society (WHi-53142).

of thought, resulting either in an attitude of indifference to his client, or an effort to win cases not meritorious. The effect is comparable to that of the district attorney, who is technically a quasi-judicial officer, but when the writer was discussing this with an ex-district attorney some years ago, the latter stated that after a man was in office, he lost sight of the quasi-judicial character of his office and his purpose was to secure convictions. In order to succeed and satisfy his constituency, it is necessary for a district attorney to secure convictions, and by a like token, the defender of the poor must seek acquittals or quickly lose the confidence of those he is employed to defend.

AN OBLIGATION

A few years ago in a large city, a legal aid society, acting in conjunction with the bar association and the judge of the district court of the United States (in which assigned counsel are not paid), sent to each member of the association a card asking those willing to defend indigent persons or paupers indicted by the United States Grand Jury to signify their willingness so to do, and over one hundred and forty members of the Bar indicated their willingness so to do, including leading members of the profession and lawyers who have since been elected to judicial office.[2]

This experiment has convinced the writer that, with the co-operation of the local bar association, legal aid society, and the judges having criminal jurisdiction, a method can be devised which will insure to each indigent person or pauper accused of crime the benefit of counsel able and willing to undertake his defense, without the creation of additional officers permanently employed by the political subdivision in which the trial takes place. There will always be in each community a sufficient number of capable and conscientious lawyers holding sacred that portion of the oath of an attorney under which he swears: "I will never reject, from any consideration personal to myself, the cause of the defenseless or oppressed, or delay any man's cause for lucre or malice." [Wis. SCR 40.15].

NOTES

1. This article was originally published in *Annals of the American Academy of Political and Social Science* 124 (1926) 81-83. Reginald Heber Smith, on the other hand, disagreed with Kaumheimer's thesis; he argued for a staffed public defender system in *Justice and the Poor*, pp 100-27.

2. Kaumheimer noted that Milwaukee lawyers at this time were paid to represent defendants in both felony and misdemeanor cases at the rate of $25/day for court work and $15/day for preparation. *Proc. NALAO* (1924) 36-37.

17.

MILWAUKEE COUNTY COMMUNITY FUND
STUDY REPORT

1927

THE LEGAL AID SOCIETY[1]

The Legal Aid Society, with offices at 85 E. Wells Street, is conducted to provide legal advice and service to persons with meritorious claims who appear worthy, but [are] financially unable to employ counsel.

During the fiscal year ending September 1926, the Society received 4,121 applications for legal advice or service. The majority of the cases call for advice and minor services in adjusting difficulties outside of court. Only 193 cases were handled by the attorney whose part time services are retained by the Society.

The recommendation made by the study stated the desirability for a closer search for the causes of the social maladjustment that brings the applicant to the Society with the view of rendering the social services necessary to meet the underlying problem. And the desirability of eventually placing free legal aid under the supervision of the courts.[2]

NOTES

1. This brief précis, preserved among the records of United Way of Greater Milwaukee in the Milwaukee Area Research Center at the University of Wisconsin-Milwaukee Library, is the only surviving record of the Community Fund study. The Society was one of nine organizations evaluated at this time. It is not clear what prompted the report, but it may reflect the belief that LAS was performing a public service that should be supported by governmental funds rather than a private service underwritten by relatively scarce charitable dollars.

2. The concept of court supervision was also endorsed by Reginald Heber Smith in *Justice and the Poor*, pp 246-49, both because legal aid was a public obligation and because the courts provided a hedge against political corruption found in various municipalities. Cf. the remarks of Howard G. Brown, director of the Legal Aid Society of Milwaukee, who argued against placing LAS under the control of any political authority. He believed it should be supervised by the bar association. "Report of the Seventh Annual Open

Meeting on Legal Aid Work," American Bar Association Convention, in
Legal Aid Review xli, no. 4 (1943) 5.

18.

ANNUAL REPORT OF THE
LEGAL AID SOCIETY OF MILWAUKEE

1928

"Every person is entitled to a certain remedy in the laws for all injuries
or wrongs which he may receive in his person, property or character;
he ought to obtain justice freely, and without being obliged to purchase it, completely and without denial, promptly and without delay,
conformably to the laws."

ARTICLE I, SECTION 9
CONSTITUTION OF WISCONSIN

The concern of the Legal Aid Society of Milwaukee is with the administration of justice as it affects the poor. To secure justice to the poor
and helpless has been a world plea from the beginning of time. In the
words of the late Chief Justice Winslow of our Supreme Court:

> Equal and exact justice has been the passionate demand of the human
> soul since man has wronged his fellow man; it has been the dream of
> the philosopher, the aim of the lawgiver, the endeavor of the judge, the
> ultimate test of every government and every civilization.

Our constitution has provided for the equal protection of the law to
all persons regardless of nationality, color, sex, or creed. But if the individual seeking to protect himself is without money to avail himself
of the judicial procedure to protect his rights, justice according to law
may be practically denied him.

The poor man is taught that he is entitled to justice, but he finds
that to get it he must pay for legal services for which he has no money.
Unless wrongs to the poor man are righted, he feels that justice is not
for him, and that he has not the same opportunities and protection as
his richer brother. Unless he can find redress, he nurses his grievance
until, to him, the government and the laws are a mockery. Such a condition breeds anarchy and promotes crime. *The fundamental purpose*

of the Legal Aid Society, therefore, is to see that persons who are poor and oppressed shall get justice according to law.

There is an inevitable tendency to closer co-operation between social worker and legal aid worker for it becomes readily apparent that each needs the other. The following excerpt of a letter from the General Secretary of the Family Welfare Association of Milwaukee recognizes the value of co-operation of the Legal Aid Society with the other social agencies supported by the Community Fund: "The work of the Legal Aid Society is an indispensable part of the social work of the community. Aid in legal matters is as necessary as in matters of health and others which require professional advice and service. Needless to say, there are people requiring legal help who are unable to pay for it, just as there are people in need of food, clothing, shelter, and medical attention who are unable to pay for them. The work of the Society should be well known and thoroughly appreciated, not only by the members of the bar and social workers, but by the whole community." All legal aid cases are registered with the Social Services Exchange.

No Fee Charged
No Commission Taken

19.

KIEWERT — BRADWAY LETTER
RE NALAO DUES

June 11, 1929

My dear Mr. Bradway,[1]

Enclosed you will find our check for $75 – [National Association of Legal Aid Organizations] dues for the year July 1, 1929 to June 30, 1930.

No one regrets more than I do that local conditions of our Community Fund make it impossible for us to have increased this to our allotment of $325. We hope, however, that next year things will have shaped themselves so that we can keep in step with the other organizations.

It seems to be the consensus of opinion of our board, and I share the opinion with them, that the allotment is quite unfair; judging local organizations by the population served, and not by the actual clientele, is not quite justifiable.

Our Community Fund has been in a very dangerous position in the last two years. It is most unfortunate, but it is something entirely beyond those interested in the Community Fund to remedy. In my next year's requisite from Community Fund, I asked for the $325 for the National organization. Whether or not it will be granted remains to be seen.

Originally I was through at the Legal Aid Society June 1 for a period of 3 and ½ months. The Board have persuaded me not to make up my mind definitively until after I return in the fall.

Please do not feel that my inability to get $325 is in any way due to our change in presidents. As I told you in Chicago, Mr. Babcock may need some education along national lines, but locally I become more convinced every day that he is the man for the job.

I have seen Mr. Kaumheimer since his return from Europe, and his condition is not improved. I doubt very much whether he will be with us in the fall. He is, I am sure, much too feeble to conduct our meetings.[2]

Very truly yours,
Agnes Campbell Kiewert

NOTES

1. This letter is published through the kind permission of the Duke University Archives collection of John S. Bradway Papers. It represents only the first of many occasions in the future in which the Legal Aid Society of Milwaukee had difficulty in paying its annual dues to the national organization.

2. Due to Parkinson's disease, Kaumheimer's health had deteriorated to the point where he was barely able to sign his name to documents. As Mrs. Kiewert indicates, the board had recently replaced him as President with Charles W. Babcock.

20.

KIEWERT — BRADWAY LETTER
RE NEW SUPERINDENDENT

MAY 12, 1930

Dear Mr. Bradway:[1]
    Miss Margery Heck will take over will take over the duties of the
Milwaukee office on June 1st. You are certainly right when you say that
a letter will encourage her. I, myself, am in a "blue funk" to know just
how she is going to handle the situation.
    She is a girl who graduated from Marquette law school in 1922.
Since then, she has been a stenographer in the circuit court of Racine
County. To me, the whole thing is most unfortunate, and I am thoroughly unhappy about the way the office is going to be manned.
    I have never known a city that is so conscious of its social service de-
velopments as is Milwaukee, and up to now, we have been able to keep
the Community Fund happy with the way Legal Aid work was going
because we had a social worker here; we were also able to keep the
bar happy because Mr. Goldschmidt [outside retained counsel from
the Hannan law firm] was here. Now we are going to have a peculiar
situation.[2]
    Women attorneys are not beloved by the Milwaukee bar and the
Community Fund is not happy to have a social worker removed from
the position because it says it is for the furtherance of social work.
Frankly, I think the Board used very, very poor judgment, not only
in choosing a woman lawyer, but also in taking a woman from out of
town who knows nothing of our social, industrial, or economical legal
situation.
    I do not mean to be catty, and I do not mean that I will not do every-
thing in my power to help Miss Heck get on her feet in the two weeks
that I remain with her, but it is awfully hard to see this Legal Aid child
of mine forced on a foster mother that may not be as careful of its
table manners as I have been. Milwaukee is a hard town to cope with,
and I think one of the main factors of my success was the fact that I
was born and raised here and was very well known. The attorneys all
know me as they knew my family before me, they all know that I never

had to work, but I did it simply because I loved it and it was the only hobby I have had.

A total stranger is going to find sledding hard because Milwaukee heads the list for snobbish towns. If there were no Portias in Milwaukee, it would be different, but there are about thirty-five, and many of them are very prominent and would have adored the position.[3]

We have not heard the end of the Milwaukee situation. Our board made the terrific error of not consulting the Community Fund regarding the appointment. We are, of course, under no obligation to the Community Fund to consult them regarding personnel, but we owe them the courtesy of a consultation when we are removing a social worker and putting in a lawyer whom they will be asked to support; whether or not they will is another matter. I am afraid in October when our new budget will be asked, we may have some explaining to do.

In many ways, I, too, am sorry that I am leaving Legal Aid work, Mr. Bradway, but I need a rest and am going to be very happy to have one. I will not be at the annual meeting this year, but I hope that sometime in the future I am going to meet all my good Legal Aid friends again. I am not going on the Board of Directors of the Legal Aid Society because I have sense enough to know it would be most embarrassing to Miss Heck, and I have no intentions of causing her any unhappy moments.

My home address is 536 Lake Drive, Apartment 8, and I would be very happy to hear from you at any time. I wonder if I could ever be of any assistance to you on Committee work. If so, do not hesitate to call on me. I will always be awfully loyal to Legal Aid, but at the present time I am unhappy about the local situation so I am going to quietly fold my tent and steal away.

> Very sincerely yours,
> *Agnes Campbell Kiewert*

NOTES

1. This letter appears through the kind permission of Duke University Archives collection of John S. Bradway Papers.
2. Kiewert's letter is insightful in showing that LAS felt obligated to satisfy its only two sources of funding: the Community Fund and members of the local bar. The letter also shows the professional fault line separating the

social-work model that had prevailed during the first fourteen years and the legal model that was about to replace it.
3. For the position of women in Wisconsin's legal profession at this time, see *Pioneers in the Law: The First 150 Women* (Madison: State Bar of Wisconsin, 1998). Margery M. Heck is featured at p. 24.

21.

STATE BAR ASSOCIATION REPORT ON LAS

1930

I outlined the general character of the work done by the Milwaukee Legal Aid Society and requested information as to how legal aid was handled in the cities [Madison, Green Bay, Racine] wherein the various members of the committee resided.[1] I asked whether the various members considered it advisable to organize legal aid societies in other cities similar to the Milwaukee society.

The Legal Aid Society of Milwaukee is an organization supported primarily by donations made through the Community Fund. The Society has a membership consisting mostly of lawyers, who pay nominal dues of $1 per year. The greater percentage of the expense, however, is maintained through the central charity agency.

We maintain an office with a paid Superintendent and assistants. The present Superintendent is a young woman who has been admitted to practice law. In a city of this size, the work of the Superintendent is as much of a social as of a legal nature.

All legal questions of major importance and all litigation necessary for the assistance of the clients of the Society are handled by Mr. Goldschmidt under an annual retainer paid by the Society. Mr. Goldschmidt has done this work for a great many years and has devoted very conscientious efforts to helping the Society at a compensation that certainly has been far from lucrative. Most of the members of the board of directors are lawyers. The board meets each month and also assists the Superintendent and attorney for the Society in emergency situations.

The consensus of opinion of the members of this Committee seems to be that it is not necessary to organize similar legal aid societies in the other cities of the state. Investigation carried on by the writer indicates that, excepting in rare cases, it is not considered necessary to render legal aid through societies of this kind in cities of less than 300,000 population.

It is the writer's belief that, excepting in Milwaukee and Madison, whatever charitable legal work may be necessary from time to time could be handled efficiently by having the welfare association report the cases to the president of the local Bar Association, with the understanding amongst the attorneys that, when called upon, each should be required to do his share of the work.

CHARLES B. QUARLES
Chairman

NOTE

1. Abridged report of the Committee on Legal Aid published in *Proceedings of the State Bar Association of Wisconsin*, 20 (1930) 191. Quarles took the chairmanship over from William Kaumheimer who was incapacitated with Parkinson's disease.

22.

LAS RELATIONS WITH THE MILWAUKEE BAR

1931

MR. BABCOCK (*Milwaukee*):[1] We have gone along for a great many years without having any clash with the bar, and without immediate difficulties with any member of the bar. I think the reason for it has been careful selection of the board members as to their ethical position in the bar, and possibly the fact that all members of the board have been lawyers, with the exception of the two women on the board, who have been either wives or close relatives of well known lawyers or judges interested in social work. We have always endeavored, and have nearly always succeeded in having the president of the bar association a member of the board.

And we also have a strict rule that no cases are to be taken where the client is able to afford an attorney, or where the case appears to be one on which a contingent fee could be earned. And it is also our rule that no fees of any kind and no commissions are ever charged. Even if there is a substantial recovery, as in the case of a [worker's] compensation award, no attorney gets anything out of it, and no presents or contributions are asked from the client. I don't think we ever had any contributions from clients that amounted to over a couple of dollars, no matter what the recovery was. No suggestion is made to the client that he might give something to the Society. We are very punctilious about that.

It may be ruinous to the client in his attitude of getting something for nothing, but it has kept the Society free from any criticism of commercialism whatsoever. We try to use discretion, and our personnel of the legal aid office have been able to do that judiciously and successfully in handling this delicate matter. I am not laying this down as a rule, but simply telling what our experience has been.

It has been that if a man has a case which looked as if it needed special attention, we, our volunteer lawyers, the people whom the board members know, have offered our services, and if they are not acceptable, we just put them on the list and forget about them. One very cautious and able lawyer takes real estate cases that involve some peculiar problem. We have had very little of that. Another gentleman who is an ex-referee in bankruptcy offered to take bankruptcy matters if offering any special problems.·

I understand this to be the practice if the client who is seeking help and can afford to pay for it or can pay a little, or does not know any lawyer, after being asked if knows one, and to show him some way out, showing him a list of lawyers. The applicant is referred to the president of the bar association who may send him to a lawyer, or to a clerk of a court, who is a member of our bar, who may send him to a lawyer, and in that way he gets into good hands and the case is taken care of, and nobody can say the Society is feeding anybody.

We have a legislative problem. We found our part-time attorney had become an expert in securing [worker] compensation awards in industrial T.B. cases, and that he has built up some of his own business along that line, due to his reputation, and one or two of the lawyers for insurance companies have made an objection to that practice, within the last two or three weeks, and registered it with the Community Fund from which we get our support. It is probably all fomented by the fact that the attorney in question was probably not over polite to the defendant in the industrial commission case.

That is all I have to offer. I don't think I have exaggerated the amicable relations that have always existed between the bar, the Legal Aid Society, and the Board; but it is due largely to the fact that, although we have a large bar, we are all pretty well acquainted with each other, and have each other's personal acquaintance and confidence. Whether that will change as the city grows or not, I don't know, but now we have eight hundred some-odd practicing lawyers, and are just about at the point where the practice of law is becoming more impersonal than in the past, and it may be necessary to adopt other methods in the future. I don't know whether I have said anything that may be of help to you or not.

We haven't had a complaint from any lawyer in regard to the conduct of the Legal Aid office in years, except this last one I spoke of which refers only to a part-time attorney, and not to the Superintendent's office, or anything in connection with the personnel in that office. I understand in some communities where the bar is busily engaged in high finance or something of that kind, such as in Boston, that small fees taken by the legal aid societies don't seem to matter much, but I have always felt a good many of our lawyers are jealous of taking any fees; as long as we keep out of that field and keep our general pleasant relations with the bar, that we were getting along all right.

NOTE

1. Remarks of LAS President Charles W. Babcock at the national conference. *Proc. NALAO* (1931) 46-48.

23.

HECK — BRADWAY LETTER
RE OFFICE QUARTERS

MARCH 9, 1933

Dear Mr. Bradway:[1]

Enclosed please find minimum statistics. Please accept my apology for being so late. I have just completed the annual report covering Oc-

tober 1931 to September 30, 1932. I have included these in statistics
you sent. Form 3 was compiled by the Central Council of Social Agencies for the Childrens' Bureau, and covers the year 1932, which may be
more helpful for your records.

69. Detail, Milwaukee Bar Association Building, 424 East Wells Street.
Courtesy of Legal Aid Society of Milwaukee.

We moved our offices January 1st to 502 Safety Building, 818 W.
Kilbourn Avenue, after the County Board approved our application
for space. In less than a month, the Board voted to ask us to vacate by
March 1st. We were able to postpone action until last Friday, when the
committee voted 4 to 3 to allow us to remain. We hope we shall be allowed peaceable occupation for the remainder of the year. Had we anticipated all this anxiety over quarters, we should never have appealed
to the County Board. We did so only after a drastic cut in our Budget
[by the Community Fund] of the entire rent item.[2] We wonder where
we'll go if the Board votes us out.

Do you know of Legal Aid Societies that are supported by County
or City governments, or receive support of any kind from those sources? Mr. Babcock thinks there are a few organizations of that kind. I

believe our County Board fears it will soon have to support us if we continue to occupy a public place in the community. In fact, one member of the committee who voted for us said he would be against taking over the Legal Aid Society entirely.

I will appreciate any information you can furnish that may help meet these objections, as I am certain we will be called on from time to time to defend the privilege granted to us.

With best wishes, I am
Sincerely yours,
Margery M. Heck
Superintendent

NOTES

1. This letter appears through the kind permission of Duke University Archives collection of John S. Bradway Papers. It demonstrates the precarious political and financial position of the Legal Aid Society during the Great Depression.
2. The deletion may have reflected the view expressed in the Community Fund's 1927 report (*supra*) that LAS should be placed under supervision of the courts.

24.

THE LEGAL AID SOCIETY
DURING THE GREAT DEPRESSION

1934

Thousands of bewildered Milwaukeeans turn to the Legal Aid Society every year when they find themselves in difficulties with the law that they cannot understand.[1] The Society, which is supported by the Community Fund, is not in competition with the legal profession, for only clients unable to employ a lawyer are given aid.

When necessary, the society provides attorneys to represent its "clients" in court, but every effort is made to adjust the difficulties without going to court. It is so successful in making adjustments that comparatively few of the cases in which it is interested go to trial. That is shown by the fact that its trial staff consists of one lawyer, who devotes but a part of his time to legal aid work.

Much of the credit for adjustment work goes to Margery M. Heck, superintendent of the Society. A lawyer of experience, Miss Heck is able to satisfy litigants opposing her clients of the common sense of settling their matters out of court. Miss Heck began practicing in Racine, in association with her father, Max W. Heck. Later, she became deputy clerk of the circuit court of Racine County and after that a court commissioner.

No member of the Society's staff may accept a fee of any kind for any services rendered. All members are on salary.

Matters in which the society aids persons unable to engage lawyers involve matters of general advice, affidavits, alimony, bankruptcy, workmen's compensation, contracts, collection of judgments, damages to personal property, drawing of legal documents, estates of deceased persons, garnishments, guardianships, insurance, personal injury claims not exceeding $75, and wage claims. Many of the clients, ignorant of their rights and afraid of the laws, come in despair and leave with revived courage.

An example was that of the woman who lived in a rooming house. She was out of work, in poor health, and owed her landlady for back rent. One day, while she was out looking for work, her landlady locked her room and took her trunk containing clothing and beloved keepsakes. Because she was licensed to operate a rooming house, the landlady imagined that she was within her rights. The victim was at her wits' end, knowing not which way to turn. A friend advised her to go to the Legal Aid Society. The landlady had no legal right to do what she had done, as the law forbids that method of collecting rent. The Society was able to convince the landlady without the necessity of beginning an action for replevin.

Many cases like the following one come to the Society's attention. A young married man found employment two months ago after being out of work for two years. He has many debts and immediately apportioned part of his earnings to pay creditors a small part of what was due them. He has a wife and four children. A clothing house threatened to garnishee his wages. He was frightened at the prospect, afraid he would be fired because of the action. The Society assured him that the law gave him sufficient exemption for his wife and children, and then was able to prevail upon the creditor to withhold garnishment.

A number of prominent attorneys interested in welfare make up the list of officers of the Society. Charles Babcock is president; John Dorney, vice president; C.J. Otjen, second vice president, and John Baker, secretary and treasurer. All are practicing attorneys. The board of directors consists of Mrs. George Lines and Mrs. E.L. Richardson; Perry J. Stearns, W.A. Klatte, and Charles Quarles.

NOTE

1. This article was published as "Legal Aid Society Helps Thousands Who Fear Law" in *Milwaukee Journal* (July 28, 1934).

25.

COUNCIL OF SOCIAL AGENCIES
REPORT ON THE LEGAL AID SOCIETY

MAY 3, 1940

Introduction[1]

At the request of the Family Agencies Committee of the Case Work Division of the Council of Social Agencies, the Social Planning Committee appointed three members of the Social Planning Committee to meet with a subcommittee from the Family Agencies in regard to ways and means of improving the working relationships with the Legal Aid Society so that legal services to clients of social agencies could be made more effective.

Statement of Procedure

A committee of the National Legal Aid Society [*sic*] submitted the following report in 1934 expressing the philosophy of the relationship with social agencies:

> The substance of this philosophy is that the legal aid movement is a part of the great enterprise of coordinating law with the other social sciences; that legal aid work is somewhat like a buffer state, with law on the one hand and social work on the other; that therefore, because of the nature of their support and the class of persons served, legal aid organizations are definitely charged with a relatively higher degree of social respon-

sibility in their communities than private law offices; and that legal aid work can be of tremendous value to other social agencies in furthering their purposes by becoming the medium by which the force and sanction of law can be applied to social problems and [by] initiating and promoting remedial legislation for the protection of their mutual clientele.

This philosophy allows the retention by each group of its identity and particular function in the larger field of social service and yet at the same time permits the fostering and development of effective relations between them.

Our committee accepted this as a guiding principle in discussing the relations between the Legal Aid Society and the social agencies in Milwaukee.

The committee discussed the problems as seen by social agencies in their working relationships with the Legal Aid Society; they secured available material from The Annals of September 1939, "Frontiers of Legal Aid Work," and a U.S. Department of Labor publication, "Growth of Legal Aid Work in the U.S.," as the basis for learning about legal aid work, its standards and ideals; and the Superintendent of the Legal Aid Society met with the committee several times to state their policies, the questions which they have had, and the changes which were already being effected.

Following these deliberations, the committee drew up the following suggestions which were sent to the Legal Aid Society Board and later discussed these with a committee from the Board of the Legal Aid Society.

Suggestions:

1. The Committee believes that the board of directors of any agency serving the community should be representative of community interests, including social work, and the corporate body might be enlarged to enable the board to become more representative. A board should deal with the administration of the agency and make the general policies which the staff should carry out. It is suggested that a committee composed of both board members and social workers be set up by the Legal Aid Society to discuss together individual intake cases in order to work out better relationships and establish better coordination. Such a committee should meet with sufficient frequency so that there would be delay of no more than a week in determining the acceptance

or rejection of a doubtful application. Such a committee would be accumulating case material to indicate the formation of certain definite policies by the board.

2. No private social agency should be so located as to give the appearance of being a part of a public setup, for this might limit its services. The committee believes that there is confusion in Milwaukee about the relationship of the Legal Aid Society to the courts and the District Attorney's Office because of the location of the Legal Aid Society in the Safety Building.[2]

3. It appears to the committee that the Legal Aid Society is inadequately staffed to render the legal services which a legal aid society is expected to give. The employment of a full-time attorney on the regular staff, rather than the present part-time arrangement, might remedy this situation.

4. The committee would like to see an experiment attempted some time to demonstrate whether or not a social worker to determine eligibility and to further cooperative relationships with social agencies would be a helpful adjunct.

5. There should be a small fund available to the Legal Aid Society to use for expenses of litigation, including court costs, in the cases of indigent persons so that they may not be deprived of justice.

6. The Legal Aid Society should give leadership in reviewing the laws on subjects which touch the underprivileged and stimulating action where legislation needs to be changed and improved. Social agencies which are concerned with problems affected by state statutes should turn to the Legal Aid Society for advice in regard to legislative reform. Examples include: (a) Pauper oath legislation for circuit court cases, (b) Changes in installment buying legislation, (c) Interest rates on small loans.

7. The needs for, and possibilities of, low-cost legal services outside the Legal Aid Society should be considered by the Board of the Legal Aid Society.

8. There is need for a statement for the guidance of social agencies as to the intake policies of the Legal Aid Society in reference to financial ability and the type of cases accepted.

9. It would be helpful if material could be prepared for presentation to social workers as to the courts to which they should direct clients,

the scope of legal aid services, etc. This might be done by arranging through the Council of Social Agencies for a series of lectures, as well as through printed material.[3]

Conclusions:

The Committee wishes to state that many of the questions and problems which had been raised by social agencies were already under consideration by the new superintendent, and there was mutual agreement on many points. The new superintendent's interest had already been reflected in the response which social agencies were receiving when they made contacts with the Legal Aid Society. The participation of the superintendent and the Board delegate in Council of Social Agencies activities has been further evidence of their concern and desire to establish good working relationships.

At the meeting with representatives of the Board, there was discussion of each of the suggestions which the Board had considered previously and with which they agreed to a certain extent. It was obvious from the discussion that the Legal Aid Society would need additional funds to carry out these suggestions and that they were not entirely in agreement with the second suggestion, although they would be willing to follow this if there were sufficient funds.

The committee believes that the community needs adequate legal aid services and that, if the suggestions are followed, the organization can more nearly become an adequate legal aid society. This will, of course, be largely dependent upon the ability of the Community Fund to supply more adequate funds.

It now becomes the responsibility of the Legal Aid Society Board to give further consideration to the committee's suggestions and to decide to what extent they wish to include these suggestions in their future plans.

Mr. Benjamin Glassberg
Miss Ella Hanawalt
Miss Evelyn Johnson
Mr. John Kenney
Miss Frances Price
Dr. Paul Mundie, Chairman

RESPONSE FROM LAS BOARD
(May 28, 1940 minutes)

1. Recommendation accepted to the effect that a "Coordinating Committee" will be set up to put into specific motion the method of operation which is already being carried on by our Agency.

2. Registered objection to this suggestion on the basis that the advantages to the present location outweigh the disadvantages.

3. This suggestion contains an alternative setup which we have considered from time to time; if necessary funds are allotted us to provide the necessary and experienced personnel, we will be willing to accept the suggestion.

4. Reject the proposal; we believe the Coordinating Committee will take care of the needs; the present exchange policy followed by the Legal Aid Society utilizes present social agencies and will accomplish all that is needed.

5. We are glad to accept and to utilize the revolving fund offered.

6. While we could not accept responsibility for the framing and following through of specific legislation, the Legal Aid Society would be glad to undertake leadership in calling to the attention of member agencies, social and economic abuses which exist and which we meet in the operation of our Agency, together with suggestions for reform legislation which might be followed through by the Wisconsin Conference of Social Work and similar agencies which are equipped for legislative responsibilities.

7. This covers a field which we have considered in the past, and which we will continue to study and to cooperate in the study with other groups interested along similar lines, to wit: The American and State Bar Associations, Junior Bar Association, [National] Lawyers Guild, and other civic, legal, and social service agencies.

8 & 9. The Legal Aid Society will be glad to undertake the requests and suggestions offered.[4]

NOTES

1. This study is preserved among the papers of the United Way of Greater Milwaukee in the Milwaukee Area Research Center at the University of Wisconsin-Milwaukee's Golda Meir Library.

70. Turret and arches, United States Courthouse.
Courtesy of Milwaukee County Historical Society.

2. This recommendation reverses field from the 1927 Community Fund report that suggested LAS "eventually" be placed under supervision of the courts.

3. This recommendation was followed up by publication of a widely disseminated pamphlet, *Information on Legal Procedures Commonly Requested by Social Workers* (Legal Aid Society of Milwaukee, 1942).

4. The professional differences reflected in these two documents stem from inherently conflicting approaches: the social work model envisioned by the Council of Social Agencies versus the law firm model adopted by the Legal Aid Society board. See Reginald Heber Smith and John S. Bradway, "Legal Aid and Social Service Agencies" in *The Growth of Legal Aid Work in the United States* (Washington D.C.: Government Printing Office, 1936) 140-55. The CSA report seems focused on returning LAS to its original ethos as a social service agency, while the Society's board was seeking to move toward a law firm model.

26.

LEGAL AID SOCIETY STANDING POLICIES

C.1941

Purpose and Function[1]

The Legal Aid Society provides free legal services to persons financially unable to pay private attorneys' fees. To determine eligibility if there is income, the family budget guide of the Community Welfare Council is used. Total family earnings, previous unemployment, size of the family, and health factors are also considered. Where the net income of an applicant, together with all other resources, if any, is sufficient only for basic necessities, the case can be accepted.

Clients who can pay a fee, either standard or moderate, and who do not know an attorney to consult, can be referred to an attorney on the Bar Reference Panel of the Milwaukee Bar Association. Cases that can be handled by an attorney on a contingent fee basis are not accepted.

Legal Aid Society also furnishes consultation service to Agencies affiliated with Community Welfare Council on legal problems of clients of such Agencies.

The Legal Aid Society charges no fees and does not give casework service.

Legal Aid Society Does Not Accept

Patent and copyright cases; libel, slander, and breach of promise actions, or criminal actions. Criminal actions are referred to the District Attorney's office or to a private attorney.

Actions pertaining to establishment of paternity are referred to the office of the Corporation Counsel. However, on referral from Trustee of Civil Court, Legal Aid Society does represent defendants in illegitimacy proceedings on motion for discharge following incarceration, pursuant to Section 166.15, Wis. Statutes.

Types of Cases Handled

The Legal Aid Society handles all other types of legal problems with the following qualifications:

Bankruptcies are considered only where the applicant has a reputation for honesty, has made every reasonable effort to pay his debts, and where it is impossible to work out any amortization plan.

Divorces, annulments, legal separations, and civil actions to compel support are handled only when they serve a sound social purpose and are recommended by a family agency. Cases of persons who apply directly for these types of services are referred either to the Department of Public Welfare if they are receiving relief, or to the St. Vincent de Paul Society, Family Service, or the Jewish Family & Children's Service, depending on religious affiliations, for study and evaluation.

Working Relationship with Non-Court Agencies

Legal Aid Society accepts referrals for legal advice and representation from all private and public health and welfare agencies. Persons referred are screened for financial eligibility. If ineligible for legal aid, an effort is made to assist them in working our arrangements for private legal service.

Legal Aid Society refers:

All family problems to either Family Service, Department of Public Welfare, St. Vincent de Paul Society, or Jewish Family & Children's Service. Arrangements and policies for these referrals were worked out in a conference with said agencies.

All children's problems to the appropriate child welfare agencies except cases involving dependency, neglect, or delinquency, which are referred to the Children's Court.

Relief problems to the Department of Public Welfare by telephone according to the terms of an agreement worked out with the Department.

All other problems are referred to the appropriate community resource.

NOTE

1. This document appears to have been drafted in response to points 8 and 9 in the May 3, 1940 report of the Council of Social Agencies. The file copy at the Legal Aid Society bears the notation, "Copied in the Offices of Community Welfare Council of Milwaukee County, May 21, 1952."

27.

LEGAL AID SOCIETY DURING WORLD WAR II

1943

Legal aid work springs from the eternal search for the answer to the question, Who is my neighbor? The first source of the legal aid ideal, therefore, is in the spiritual field; and it is on this premise that the legal aid program and its wartime contribution have been developed.

The position of the Legal Aid Society, in its service to the men in the armed forces and their dependents, differs in one major respect from the bar's program. Under its wartime service program, the bar cannot serve a dependent who has a claim adverse to that of the serviceman, irrespective of its merit. The Legal Aid Society has no such limitation, since any person financially unable to retain a private attorney is entitled to assistance from us.

This entire wartime program is tied up with our fighting men's morale; we recognize that it is important to free the men in the service from civilian problems. I believe, however, that maintaining the morale of the dependents of the serviceman is equally important, and wartime conditions have complicated the task.

Many of the present-day problems of the civilian are a natural byproduct of the war, for already we appreciate that along with the destruction which war brings is deterioration also in family life, induced by manifold and perplexing problems accompanying the war. Contributing to this deterioration are variegated elements. We have, for example, the families who are torn by new anxieties centering around the draft, and the inability to plan ahead. We have the mothers who are less capable of caring for their children because of their fears for the husband in the service. Then there are the emotional problems of children and adults anticipating the war horrors that are discussed in the press and over the radio. There is the overcrowding of families because of the housing shortage, a hazard alike to health and morals. There is the problem of the hasty war marriage with early separation, and we have more forced marriages and more young unmarried mothers. Practically no one is free from anxieties, fears, and general emotional disturbance, and the whole situation is a natural stimulant to the development of a host of legal and social problems.

I should like to summarize the objectives of the Legal Aid Society in its wartime role by saying this: Obviously, the deterioration of individuals and families would tend to defeat the very thing we are fighting for, our American way of life. We are fighting for the principle of human freedom, and especially we are fighting for the future of our children in a free world. But in the midst of this total war, and not unmindful of our responsibilities to the men in the service, is still the obligation to safeguard our families and our children. In such a program, several precepts are paramount: first, to protect our children from neglect, exploitation, and undue strain, especially in defense areas; and second, to safeguard and to strengthen the home life of the children whose parents are mobilized for the war.

We must bear in mind that it takes strong, secure, and hopeful men and women to be free themselves, or to build a free nation in a free world. Not one of us can afford to forget now the fundamental importance of combating the forces of deterioration in personal and family living; and the preservation of the family unit should still remain as a basic interest in our agenda.

And finally, a commentary on legal aid. Someone has said that no democracy can work if it takes a golden key to unlock the courthouse door. If we are going to preserve what we are now fighting for, we must make every citizen feel, not only that he has a stake in it, but also that his stake is protected and promoted by it. Making it possible for every person to have his day in court will strengthen our democracy, not only in the struggle in its military phases, but for the period which will follow, may we hope, in lasting peace. (Applause).

NOTE

1. This is a greatly abridged version of an address by Julia B. Dolan to the State Bar's War Legal Service Committee. She discussed a number of specific legal problems encountered by dependents of servicemen and women.

See *Proceedings of the State Bar Association of Wisconsin* 33 (1943) 72-77.
See Dolan's later reports in *Id.* 34 (1944) 80-85, and 35 (1945) 74-78.

28.

LEGAL AID IN MILWAUKEE

1954

By
Julia B. Dolan[1]

In the spring of 1916, three civic organizations – the Milwaukee Bar
Association, the Central Council of Social Agencies, and the City
Club – all recognizing the same urgent need in the community, appointed a joint committee to plan and establish the Legal Aid Society
of Milwaukee. The purpose of this new agency was to furnish advice
and legal assistance to those in trouble who were in need of lawyers'
services, but who, because of poverty, could not afford to hire counsel.
On the 1st day of June 1916, the Society opened its door to the public,
and on the very first day of its career, even before office furniture and
telephone service were installed, two clients made application for assistance.

The constitution of our LAS contains this provision: "The declared
purpose of the LAS is to furnish legal aid to those financially unable
to obtain legal counsel, to promote laws and measures, and to do all
things necessary for the prevention of injustice." And since June of
1916, legal aid in this community has been functioning to carry out
this mandate in the Society's constitution.

The agency has from its start been supported almost entirely by the
Community Chest. We have a small income from dues; any person
interested may become a voting member of the Society by paying the
annual dues of $1. And incidentally, dues paid and gifts made to the
Society are tax deductible.

Our present offices are at 757 North Water Street. Our professional
staff consists of two full-time attorneys and one half-time attorney;
the latter handles most of our court work. The agency also serves as
a clinic for Marquette University Law School; we give office training
to 20 students per year, using two students each afternoon during the
school year.

Now a word about the scope and operation of the Milwaukee agency. We find that the type and volume of work changes with economic turns. In the early days, our largest work was devoted to wage claims. During the Depression, we had a great many real estate cases, particularly in foreclosures, where we stepped in to represent the homeowner so that he could remain in the premises during the period of redemption. During the period of the war, we had the legal problems of the serviceman and his dependents. During OPA conrols, we had a very large number of landlord-tenant cases. And now our largest single classification relates to domestic cases.

When a client applies to us for service, a face sheet is filled out by the intake worker regarding income, client's property, number of dependents, and other pertinent factors, to enable us to determine whether the applicant is entitled to free legal service. The principle that we seek to keep in mind is this: A case should be accepted if the applicant would otherwise be denied justice. If his income, or other resources, or the size of his claim, are such as should reasonably enable him to retain private counsel, on a contingent fee basis or otherwise, his case is not accepted. The factors in each given case are, of course, the determining basis.

The LAS is the only agency of its kind in the metropolitan area. There is no agency, either public or private, which performs the type of service we render. We are supported by the Community Chest; we charge no fees of any kind; and staff members may accept no fees other than salary from the agency.

I might mention briefly the type of case that the agency does not handle. We do not handle patent or copyright cases. Slander, libel, or breach of promise cases are not handled. Bankruptcies are handled very occasionally, and only under exceptional circumstances; and the agency does not appear in criminal cases. We handle some divorce actions, but only where we are convinced that the divorce will serve a sound social purpose. We have an arrangement with several family agencies to do our casework in domestic cases, and before we can consider handling a divorce we must have a recommendation that the action would be desirable, from a recognized family agency.

The agency makes use of the bar reference panel, supplied by the Bar Association, for the referral of clients who can pay at least a partial fee for legal service. Our last annual report shows that in the year we handled a total of 3200 cases. First, where did the 3200 clients come from? A large proportion are referred by court officials and various departments of government; a substantial number come from social agencies; former clients, radio, and newspaper publicity furnish the remainder. What did these 3200 clients want? The typical legal aid client is a woman under 35 years of age with three or four children, several of whom she brings with her when she comes to the office. She has on no cosmetics, wears outdated clothes, and has a perpetually harassed expression. You know almost at first glance that she has a domestic problem; it is just a question of which one. Does she want support, custody of her children, help in removing her husband from the home, or all of these, plus a divorce? Or is she just finding out what the law is in case she decides to leave her husband. These domestic relations cases constitute about one-third of the cases.

A large group is concerned with money claims, in which we represent either plaintiff or defendant in such matters as collection of small debts and representation in garnishment proceedings. Another large segment involves evictions and the recovery of personal articles. It is, for example, upsetting to any one of us, personally, when we lose a bundle of laundry, or the dry cleaner ruins a dress or a suit. To a relief family, this kind of loss becomes a major catastrophe. The remaining cases include such miscellaneous problems as the preparation of affidavits, drafting of simple wills for persons of limited means, and drafting of powers of attorney for young men going into military service.

Of course, these are not the weighty matters of corporations and business law. They are the everyday problems of plain people, but as important to the total well-being of the community as are the cases which attract wide public attention and which involve large interests. While they require service of a less dramatic nature, and are not as time consuming, nevertheless they do require expert knowledge, a sympathetic understanding of people, and professional skill.

Now, what does our staff of two and one-half lawyers do, with approximately 250 cases per month? Many can be disposed of in one in-review; many have one legal problem on which they want an answer. How much notice do I have to give my landlord? If I leave my husband, am I blocking myself from alimony? Am I divorced if I haven't heard from my husband for seven years?

Then, a proportion of our cases are settled in conference with the opposing party or his lawyer. Some can afford lawyers; some do not trust lawyers or think that their services are too expensive. Here we

71. Community Chest campaign poster, circa 1953. *Courtesy of United Way of Greater Milwaukee.*

have wide opportunity for interpreting a lawyer's services, his skills, and honesty. And finally, a proportion of the applications are referred to social agencies, for frequently a matter which on the surface appears to be a legal problem is truly only symptomatic of a deeply rooted personal problem.

To conclude, whatever else one may say about legal aid work, it is certainly never dull. It has about it an air of things perpetually new and unexpected, and one who is looking for challenge and stimulation is seldom disappointed.

NOTE

1. This article was first published in the *MBA Gavel* 15, no. 4 (1954) 6-8, and appears here by kind permission of the Milwaukee Bar Association. The first paragraph is taken from the Society's Annual Report of 1920. The article provides a valuable snapshot of the Society on the eve of its fortieth anniversary. A condensed and updated version was published by Lenore Woolf, "The Legal Aid Story" in *MBA Gavel* 23, no. 1 (1962) 28.

29.

PUBLIC DEFENDER PROPOSAL

1956

Public Defense (pp 41-42)[1]

The popular belief fostered so widely by radio and television programs that the District Attorney is under a duty to defend the innocent as well as prosecute the guilty does not find any endorsement in the description of the duties of the District Attorney in Wisconsin Statutes. The accused in Wisconsin who feels himself wrongfully charged and who is without means to employ counsel may, only if charged with a felony, request the court to appoint an attorney to act in his defense. To the extent that indigence interferes with a proper defense in those cases less than felonies, the "equal justice" concept remains only partially true. In cases where the penalty for lesser crimes approaches the maximum permitted by law, the accused might conceivably consider himself more fortunate to be charged with a more serious crime and thus be able to obtain legal assistance for his defense.

The right to counsel should not be limited to felony trials only. After all, a fundamental concept of criminal justice is that the accused stands innocent before the court unless proved guilty beyond a reasonable doubt. This cloak of protection is worn thin under circumstances which expose the accused to conviction without needed assistance. The person accused of a felony is at least assured of counsel.

Whether the procedure followed in Wisconsin for providing counsel meets the requirement of "equal justice" or represents a better procedure from an administrative view than the public defender system will, and can, arouse partisan and professional feelings pro and con. Although the point should not be considered decisive, certainly relative costs of the two procedures should be kept in mind. Under the present arrangement, the cost to the county in payment for legal fees in 1954 to local attorneys for defending prisoners in Municipal Court was over $43,000. Additional legal fees in other courts representing guardian ad litem and other fees brought the total to $72,360.

(Page 59) – It is recommended, for reasons indicated in Chapter I of this report, that counsel be made available in misdemeanor as well as in felony cases where defendants lack the means to secure their own attorneys, that the present practice of employing defense attorneys on a fee basis be abandoned, and that there be established an office of Public Defender, to be filled under civil service by the Municipal and District Court Judges acting jointly.[2]

NOTES

1. Report of the Public Administration Survey of Courts and Legal Services (1956). This report and recommendation was discussed at board meetings of the Legal Aid Society on September 13 and December 11, 1956. On April 8, 1957, Mrs. Dolan reported to the board that she had met with various judges, representatives of the bar associations, and Dean Reynolds Seitz of Marquette University Law School to establish a volunteer panel of defense lawyers. That project appears to have been developed in response to the foregoing report of the Public Administration Survey.

2. Municipal Court was a specialized venue with jurisdiction over felony cases; District Court was a specialized venue with jurisdiction over misdemeanor cases. Along with the Civil Court, they were abolished in 1960 when court reorganization led to a two-tiered system of county and circuit courts. For a brief history of Milwaukee County's court system, see Karel D. Bicha, "Courts and Criminal Justice: Law Enforcement in Milwaukee County" in *Trading Post to Metropolis: Milwaukee County's First 150 Years*, ed. Ralph Aderman (Milwaukee County Historical Society, 1987) 146-73.

30.

VOLUNTEER PROGRAMS AT THE
LEGAL AID SOCIETY

1962

By

Julia B. Dolan[1]

Faced with inadequate budget allotments from United Fund, the Milwaukee Legal Aid Society has of necessity developed a highly successful program for the use of volunteers on both professional and lay levels. These programs have been in operation for five years.

The professional program involves the use of about 200 lawyers who are members of the Junior Bar Association.[2] Through the Junior Bar, volunteers are enrolled on the Voluntary Defender Panel, the first program of its kind in the country.[3] The attorney periodically gives a full day in court on his assigned day, without compensation. The volunteers serve in the misdemeanor branch of the County Court and represent approximately 3,000 individuals annually. There is no statutory provision in this court for the appointment of paid counsel (this exists only in felony cases).

Through the joint cooperation of the Junior Bar and Legal Aid Society, a statement of rules for the operation of the plan has been developed.

A volunteer (Lawyers' Wives program) has as her special project the assignment of dates for attorneys, mimeographing and mailing of the month's calendar to the attorneys and the court, record keeping, and handling the other mechanics of the plan to keep it operating smoothly and efficiently. A Legal Aid Society staff attorney fills in in emergency situations, so that a Voluntary Defender is always present in the court.

The agency and the court give periodic public recognition to the Voluntary Defenders. Once a year, there is a buffet supper and a general get-together to exchange suggestions for improvements in the operation of the program. One year, at the agency's annual meeting, each Voluntary Defender was given a certificate of appreciation suitable for framing. Last May, on USA Law Day, Judge Christ T. Seraphim (in whose court the Voluntary Defenders serve), and the Presidents of the Wisconsin, Milwaukee, and Junior Bar Associations, joined the Legal Aid Society in presenting each Voluntary Defender with a certificate of service. All of the above events received excellent newspaper, TV, and radio coverage.[4]

The lay volunteer program is operated in cooperation with the Lawyers' Wives Association. Forty women are now recruited, so that there is always a volunteer at the office, more often two at a time. Most of the volunteers give a half-day per week, some give less time, but each one has her assigned day. The volunteers register clients, handle the telephone, operate the playroom, file, and type. There is a task for each skill. The Lawyers' Wives take on the responsibility of recruitment, orientation, and setting up of the month's calendar. A special group is available to fill in during emergency situations.

A successful program of recognition for the services of the volunteers has evolved. On completion of one hundred hours, a certificate of service is presented, signed by the President of the Lawyers' Wives and the Executive Attorney of the Legal Aid Society. The certificate is encased in a small tray, which can be used on milady's dressing table – a gift that has been warmly received. After 350 hours of service, a gold bracelet charm is presented with an inscription identifying 350 hours of Legal Aid service. Five hundred hours is recognized with a gold charm replica of the Wisconsin Bar Association insignia.

The presentations are always made on occasions where good publicity can be obtained – at luncheon meetings of Lawyers' Wives; at annual meetings of the Legal Aid Society; at State Bar functions. Several times, husbands of volunteers have been invited to make the presentations. On all of the occasions, Judges and United Fund executives are invited to participate. The events are never the same and always have a "new look" to provide variance and sustain interest. The Lawyers' Wives group provided the funds for the purchase of the awards.

In addition, there is a summer picnic, and an end-of-the-year holiday cocktail party for the volunteers and their husbands. Both events have become a tradition and are highly popular.

In my opinion, both of our volunteer programs are invaluable. The service the attorneys provide in the courts cannot be measured in dollars. Without the service of Lawyer's Wives volunteers, our agency could not operate with its limited staff. We estimate that we would require the addition of two full-time clerical persons on the staff to handle the variety of services provided by the volunteers. From a public relations standpoint, both projects are tremendous and well worth the time and effort expended in the planning and operation of the programs.

NOTES

1. A slightly revised version of this untitled document, perhaps originally a speech, was later published by Julia B. Dolan, under the title, "We Honor Our Volunteers," in *Legal Aid Brief Case* xxii, no. 3 (February 1964) 130-32.

2. Those serving as Voluntary Defenders in 1966 were Attorneys Sherman S. Abrahamson, William H. Alverson, John H. Ames, Roy W. Arndt, Philip A. Atinksy, Edwin J. Bach, Albert Bahcall, Joseph P. Balistrieri, Lloyd A. Barbee, Michael J. Barron, Mary Jo Bate, Rudolph Becker, Charlotte A. Bleistein, Lawrence Bodner, James E. Boening, Leonard V. Brady, Robert J. Brady, Herbert S. Bratt, George A. Burns, Jr., Anthony V. Cadden, David J. Cannon, Royal E. Cass, Irvin B. Charne, Lawrence Clancy, Raymond M. Clark, William M. Coffey, John R. Collentine, Raymond A. Cote, Francis R. Croak, Francis J. Demet, Margadette M. Demet, Thomas G. Duggan, Karl M. Dunst, Russell A. Eisenberg, Jack N. Eisendrath, John Eppel, Paul J. Ferr, Thomas F. Finch, Richard D. Finley, J. Jerome Finn, Clinton J. Finnegan, Peter N. Flessas, John F. Foley, Sheldon D. Frank, Timothy C. Frautschi, Dominic H. Frinzi, Harry L. Garwood, William Giese, Seymour Gimbel, Thomas W. Godfrey, Daniel J. Goldman, Bernard Goldstein, Gregory Gramling, Jr., Walter F. Gregorski, Emmanuel V. Gumina, Donald C. Haberman, Laurence C. Hammond, Jr., Robert E. Hankel, David J. Hase, Richard H. Hecht, Harlow J. Hellstrom, Joseph P. House, James G. Howard, Albert M. Ilse, Thomas M. Jacobson, Harry E. Jankowitz, James F. Janz, Irving B. Kahn, John Q. Kamps, Jack E. Keyes, William J. Kiernan, Jr., Lester J. Knuese, Phillip K. Koch, William A. Korbel, Edward H. Kozlowski, Donald J. Kraemer, Henry G. Krecklow, Warren L. Kreuenen, David W. Lers, Earl D. Lillydahl, Jr., Mark G. Lipscomb, Jr., James T. Locke, Leonard L. Loeb, George G. Lorinczi, Robert J. Lowe, Ray H. MacMichael, William J. Mantyh, Albert A. Mayer, William E. McCarty, Maurice J. McSweeney, Donald J. Miller, Rudolph J. Mudroch, Mark P. Mulvanny, Wilford J. Nehmer, Jr., Edward F. Neubecker, Monroe Orman, Ronald I. Pachefsky, Robert B. Peregrine, W. Dale Phillips,

Kenneth J. Phillips, Orville E. Pitts, Terrence L. Pitts, Bernard J. Plotkin, John H. Poulos, John T. Pryor, Sidney Pump, Dennis J. Purtell, William L. Randall, Peter F. Reiske, Alvin Richman, C. James Riester, Jerome Rinzel, Daniel R. Riordan, Richard R. Robinson, Ralph K. Rosenbaum, Jr., David I. Rothstein, Emanuel N. Rotter, Merton N. Rotter, Alfred Rozran, Jerome T. Safer, David A. Saichek, Thomas Sawyer, Carl F. Schetter, E. Thomas

72. Carved stone columns, United States Courthouse.
Courtesy of Milwaukee County Historical Society.

Schilling, Matthias G. Schimenz, Jr., Walter F. Schmidt, Paul M. Schoos, Charles F. Schroeder, Fred A. Shapiro, James E. Shapiro, S.A. Shapiro, James M. Shellow, Alan P. Shrinsky, David Shute, Paul E. Sicula, Robert Silverstein, Gary B. Simon, Aaron Starobin, Martin R. Stein, Robert K. Steuer, Sherman E. Stock, Robert H. Suran, Donald S. Taitelman, Michael I. Tarnoff, Robert E. Tehan, Jr., Clifford H. Thoma, Aaron L. Tilton, David L. Walther, Phillip M. Wax, Kennard R. Weaver, Ted E. Wedemeyer, Jr., Daniel J. Weiss, John B. Werra, William S. Wiener, Ralph R. Zauner, John R. Zillmer.

3. Further details on the Voluntary Defender Project can be found in Francis J. Demet, "The Voluntary Defender Plan in Milwaukee County" in *MBA Gavel* 19, no. 2 (1958) 14-24; William L. Randall, "The Voluntary Defender Plan" in *MBA Gavel* 23, no. 3 (1962) 26-27.

4. See, for example, "High Praise Given Panel of Defenders" in *Milwaukee Journal* (March 6, 1962).

3 1 .

THE POOR MAN AND THE ROLE OF ATTORNEYS

By
Julia B. Dolan
Milwaukee Bar Association
July 19, 1965

Mr. [Curtis] Gear [Director of Milwaukee's Community Action Program] has asked me to make a few comments on that portion of the Law and Poverty Conference [held in Washington, D.C., June 23-25, 1965], which related to the role of the lawyer. While the basic overall purpose of the Conference was educational, there were, it seemed to me, some definite principles that we as participants were able to accept as conclusions.

We agreed at the outset that equal justice for every man is one of the great ideals of our society. It is the goal for which our entire system exists, and it is an integral part of that system that justice should not be withheld or denied because of an individual's race or religion, his beliefs, or his station in society. We also accepted as fundamental that the law should be the same for the rich and for the poor.

But we have long known, and our discussions at the Conference emphasized, that the actual attainment of these ideals is not an easy task. It requires sensitivity, vigilance, and also a willingness to experiment.

Our system of justice is based in large part on advocacy. However, when there is no one to provide representation for an individual, his chances of obtaining justice are greatly lessened. And if many of our fellow citizens are denied justice because of poverty, it may well be questioned how long the adversary system can survive.

The nature of the broad challenge that confronts us is therefore clear. We recognize that there often is a gap between the need for counsel and the actual availability of counsel. Until this gap is bridged, there is a partial failure of our system to serve all who need legal services. This, of course, does not mean that the system itself is a failure and should be replaced. On the contrary, in spite of its faults and shortcomings, it is a truism that the Anglo-American system of justice has preserved liberties and provided opportunities that are indeed the envy of much of mankind, and under this system, the ideal of individual liberty has been preserved realistically for more people for perhaps the longest sustained period of all history.

The War on Poverty is now an established national policy. The legal profession, long committed to working with local communities in providing legal aid service to the indigent, is now extending a like cooperation to this new program, and members of the bar, as the special guardians of our legal system, have joined in the broad effort to assure the availability of adequate counsel to the poor.

Louis Powell, a very outstanding person and the very capable president of the American Bar Association, pointed out at the Conference that so long as the new program stays within the broad framework of the legal aid concepts, there should be few serious problems. He pointed out that we can remain within this concept and still achieve significant gains, especially in broadening the scope of services rendered, by liberalizing definitions of indigency, and by making service more readily available through neighborhood centers. He also emphasized that we should build upon and benefit from the experience and know-how of the established legal aid agencies, and enlarge on these experiences in opening new frontiers for service as suggested by the guidelines of the Office of Economic Opportunity for Legal Services.

I think it might be in order also for me to add one other note, addressed particularly to those of you who are not lawyers, and that is to ask you to try to understand the reasons that underlie the bar's Canons of Ethics. These standards – against solicitation, against the use of lay intermediaries, and for the assurance of a genuine client-attorney personal relationship and responsibility – were not designed for the benefit of lawyers. The fact is that these ethical concepts were intended to safeguard the interest of clients, and to assure the fidelity and independence that are implicit in the attorney-client relationship. They were also designed to prevent the commercialization of a learned profession – a result that would indeed be as unfortunate for the public as it would be for the bar.

In summary, let me say that no subject has higher priority within the ABA agenda and the program of the Milwaukee and Junior Bar

Associations, and also the Legal Aid Society, than the assurance that legal services will in fact be made available to all who need them.

We have welcomed this opportunity to get together with you and to have the benefit of your thinking. We plan to integrate your suggestions, as far as is feasible and practical to do so, into a sound program to be submitted to the Social Development Commission.

32.

MILWAUKEE PLAN LEGAL SERVICES
November 3, 1965
THE NEED

It is recognized that there are in Milwaukee County significant areas of poverty and significant numbers of deprived persons whose needs are not being met by services available in this community. The Legal Aid Society, operating with minimum staff and budget, handles upwards of 5,000 new cases every year. In addition to this, several hundred persons are referred by the Legal Aid Society or the Milwaukee Bar Association to private attorneys for services.

The Voluntary Defender Program, the first of its kind in the country, under the auspices of the Milwaukee Junior Bar Association and the Legal Aid Society, provides representation for indigents in misdemeanor matters in the County Court in the mornings. Upwards of 150 lawyers participate in this program on a voluntary basis and approximately 3,000 individuals are served annually.

All of these services, while excellent, are insufficient to provide services to the poor within the framework of the Economic Opportunity Act of 1964. It is, therefore, proposed that the plan hereinafter outlined and designated Milwaukee Plan Legal Services be approved and made operational on January 1, 1966, under the provisions of the Economic Opportunity Act of 1964.[1]

This plan has been drafted by the Special Committee on Law and Poverty appointed by the following organizations of this community: (1) Milwaukee Bar Association, (2) Milwaukee Junior Bar Association, (3) Legal Aid Society of Milwaukee, and through it, United Community Services of Greater Milwaukee, Inc., (4) Marquette University Law School, and (5) Social Development Commission, Community Action Program.

THE MILWAUKEE PLAN

A new corporation called *The Board of Legal Services, Inc.*, has been formed and Articles of Incorporation filed with the Secretary of State on October 19, 1965, and recorded with the Office of the Register of Deeds of Milwaukee County on October 22, 1965. The incorporator is Charles Q. Kamps. The initial Board of Directors are representatives of all the sponsoring agencies as follows:

1. Mrs. Julia B. Dolan, Executive Attorney of the Legal Aid Society;
2. Bernard J. Hankin, President, Milwaukee Bar Association;
3. C. James Riester, President, Milwaukee Junior Bar Associaiton;
4. Dean Robert F. Boden, Marquette University Law School; and
5. Curt Gear, Director, Community Action Program, Social Development Commission.

They will serve until the full Board of Directors is elected and qualifies.[2] The full Board of Directors will be elected by the initial Board members and the By-laws adopted.

By-laws, as drafted, and to be approved by the Special Committee and adopted by the initial Board of Directors, contemplate a 21 member Board made up as follows:

1. Four persons selected by the Milwaukee Bar Association, one of whom shall be a lawyer who is principally engaged in the representation of persons residing in an area or areas of the community in which there is a high incidence of poverty.

2. Four persons selected by the Milwaukee Junior Bar Association, one of whom shall be a lawyer principally engaged in the representation of persons residing in an area or areas of the community in which there is a high incidence of poverty.

3. Four persons selected by the Legal Aid Society of Milwaukee, one of whom will be nominated by the United Community Services of Greater Milwaukee, Inc.

4.   Three persons selected by the Marquette University Law
      School.
5.   A number of persons, not exceeding 5, designated as di-
      rectors by the initial directors hereinbefore named, each
      of whom shall be nominated by an organization directly
      representing the impoverished of Milwaukee and each
      of whom shall himself be a member of the group to be
      benefited by the implementation of the Economic Op-
      portunity Act of 1964 or someone directly representing
      such persons.

This Board will contract with the Legal Aid Society of Milwaukee for
services to be performed in accordance with the policies and directives
laid down by the Board.

The Executive Attorney of the Legal Aid Society will be responsible
to the Board of Legal Services for the supervision of the services to
be performed by the Legal Aid Society in conjunction herewith. The
Executive Attorney of the Legal Aid Society shall also be responsible
for the supervision of liaison with Marquette University Law School,
which will organize and direct an Institute on Poverty and the Law to
be conducted in conjunction with the overall Milwaukee program and
under the supervision of the University as hereinafter set forth. The
Executive Attorney of the Legal Aid Society shall also be responsible
for the supervision of liaison with private practitioners who will furnish services under an expanded Bar Referral Program as hereinafter
detailed.

The scope of the program contemplated is as follows:

I.

[NEIGHBORHOOD OFFICES]

It is proposed that a significant first step in the development of adequate legal services would be the establishment of neighborhood offices in the two most critical areas of poverty in Milwaukee. These
offices would be located in Neighborhood Centers that are operated
as a component of the local community action program (Inner City
Development Project).

Each neighborhood office would be staffed with two full-time attorneys, one of whom would be designated the Chief Neighborhood
Attorney, secretarial and stenographic personnel, Marquette Univer-

sity Law School student interns as hereinafter detailed, and part-time indigenous sub-professional persons who would assist in various areas particularly in the education of the persons to be served as to their legal rights and duties. Further secretarial and stenographic assistance will be provided free of charge by teams of lawyers' wives working 20 hours per week in the neighborhood offices.

Types of Cases and Standards of Eligibility. (1) legal problems having broad significance to the community; (2) community contact through the use of the professional staff and also the student interns and indigenous neighborhood personnel working as teams under the supervision of the professional staff; (3) traditional legal services to a client, giving particular priority to those cases where a client's rights are in jeopardy such as debtor relief, defense of indigents in criminal matters to supplement those services now being given at state expense, family problems, tenants' rights, and other significant legal problems.

Standards of eligibility shall be as specifically laid down by the Board of Legal Services within the framework of the Economic Opportunity Act of 1964.

II.

[PRIVATE BAR REFERRALS]

It is recognized that neighborhood offices as contemplated cannot possibly serve all of the legal needs of the poor, and that it is neither practical nor desirable that they should attempt to do so. Further, it is recognized that the traditional right of the client to choose his own counsel should be preserved insofar as possible, and that the broad participation of the Bar in the War on Poverty should be actively encouraged.

At the present time, the Legal Aid Society operates, in cooperation with the Milwaukee Bar Association and the Milwaukee Junior Bar Association, a program of Bar Referral whereby a client who applies to the Legal Aid Society for service and must be refused service because he is able to pay a fee, even though it may be less than the Minimum Fee Schedule, may be referred to a private attorney.

It is proposed that clients who have qualified for service in accordance with standards of eligibility set down by the Board of Legal Services be referred to a private attorney of his choice or to any private attorney listed in the Bar Referral Plan to be set up under this program in the following cases: (1) where immediate attention to the client's legal problem is required and neither one of the attorneys in the neighborhood office is able to provide it; (2) where protracted litigation is required; (3) in all other matters in which referral is directed by the Board of Legal Services.

Attorneys would be compensated for their services from funds to be provided in the Plan and in accordance with a schedule to be agreed upon between the Milwaukee Bar Association, Milwaukee Junior Bar Association, and the Board of Legal Services taking into account the existing Minimum Fee Schedule of the Milwaukee Bar Association.

III.
[DEFENDER PROGRAM]

It is proposed that a Defender Program be set up under this Plan whereby the following services would be performed:

1. Defenders who serve under the Voluntary Program in the morning in County Court to represent indigents charged with misdemeanors will be assigned to serve as paid counsel in these courts in the afternoon

2. Payment of most attorneys fees on a per diem basis will be made to such Defenders for the service contemplated under this Plan.

3. A program of continuity of service by a Defender will be established whereby the defendant will be represented at postponed hearings by the same person who represented him in the initial hearing.

4. Investigational assistance, where needed, will be provided in the preparation of a defense.

5. The Defender will also be employed in appeal to a higher court where the interests of justice require and no other funds are available for such services.

This program will be administered under the supervision of the Legal Aid Society and in cooperation with the County Judges presiding in the above Courts and the Milwaukee Junior Bar Association.

IV.
[BAIL BOND PROGRAM]

It is proposed that a program of Bail Bond Services be provided for indigents as hereinafter set forth.

For a 30-day period in November and December of 1964, the Milwaukee Junior Bar Association and the Wisconsin Service Associa-

73. Chief Attorney Bill Stanelle and Staff Attorney Jack Keese at LAS's Southside Neighborhood Office, circa 1966. *Courtesy of Legal Aid Society of Milwaukee.*

tion conducted a Bail Bond pilot program in Branch 4 of the County Court. Its purpose was to determine whether or not defendants who could not post bail could be released "on trust." Interviews were conducted by the Wisconsin Service Association to enable the Association to advise the judge with respect to trustworthiness of individual defendants.

Within the 30-day period, 95 out of 210 defendants were released without bond (45%). Only 3 of the "trusted" defendants failed to show up for trial. A comparison with the ratio of defendants who were released on bail showed that the percentage who failed to show up was almost exactly the same.

It is proposed that a pilot program be set up for the nine months commencing January 1, 1966. This program would be conducted by the Legal Aid Society in cooperation with the Wisconsin Service Association, Milwaukee Junior Bar Association, and the courts. The purpose of the longer pilot program would be to ascertain the best method of proceeding on a permanent basis, and to consider the feasibility of further restricting or eliminating the use of bail.

V.

[MARQUETTE UNIVERSITY LAW SCHOOL]

It is proposed that the Marquette University Law School organize an Institute on Poverty and the Law designed to devote itself to the War on Poverty in five specific areas hereinafter set forth. The program would be conducted in cooperation with the Legal Aid Society of Milwaukee and the Milwaukee Bar Association, and in accordance with the policies laid down by the Board of Legal Services.

The Institute would be under the supervision of a Director who would be a full-time faculty member of the Marquette University Law School. He would be responsible for the conduct of the programs of the Institute and would work in close cooperation with liaison staff of the Legal Aid Society in the assignment of student personnel and University facilities to be employed in the Milwaukee Plan.

The five Institute programs contemplated are as follows:

[A] Continuing legal education for the Bar in the area of legal services to the poor: (1) commercial law problems of the indigent, (2) criminal law, (3) debtor relief, (4) family law problems of the indigent, (5) juvenile law, (6) labor law problems of the indigent, and (7) landlord-tenant and housing problems of the poor. Faculty will be drawn from the full and part-time faculty of the Marquette University Law School and from the practicing bench and bar of Wisconsin.

In addition to the teaching program, faculty participants will prepare for publication research work in their subject areas to be published and copyrighted by the University and used as reference material by lawyers working with the poor.

[B] A Research Project on Poverty and the Law designed primarily to discover the existing areas of legal discrimination against the indigent and to recommend legislation or other reforms that might be helpful to combat poverty.

[C] A student internship program designed to furnish assistance:

1. In neighborhood offices on a regular basis to (a) aid attorneys in counseling of clients and the preparation of legal documents, (b) brief law and prepare legal memoranda for attorneys, (c) provide limited services in filing papers in court, serving papers, and other clerical functions, and (d) assist in education of the poor as to their legal rights and duties in cooperation with part-time indigenous neighborhood staff persons and in accordance with classroom training.

2. To aid individual attorneys engaged in the Defender services as previously outlined herein. All such student services would be under the supervision of the Director of the Marquette Institute in liaison with the Legal Aid Society of Milwaukee.

[D] A Library Service Project will be provided whereby duplicating of research in neighborhood centers and by defenders will be avoided, and a properly indexed and catalogued file of legal memoranda can be provided. The Marquette Law Library would serve as a central clearinghouse for legal research for all lawyers engaged in this program.

[E] A Law Review Program will be provided to document the results of academic research in the whole area of poverty and law.

VI.
[COMMUNITY EDUCATION]

It is further proposed that a panel of legal experts of the local Bar in the various fields of law involving the indigent undertake, under supervision of the Milwaukee and Milwaukee Junior Bar Associations, and in liaison with the Legal Aid Society of Milwaukee and Marquette

University, a program of community education in this whole area of poverty and the law.

NOTES

1. The Plan had been previously announced to the local press. "Eye Unit for Indigent Legal Aid" in *Milwaukee Sentinel* (July 20, 1965). Milwaukee Plan Legal Services was approved with some modifications by the Office of Equal Opportunity on April 25, 1966 per correspondence from Congressman Clement J. Zablocki (D-Wis.). A much more detailed version of this project was published by Margadette M. Demet, "Legal Services for Urban Needs: Implementation of the Economic Opportunity Act of 1964" in *MBA Gavel* 27, no. 1 (1966) 6-16.

2. The following were elected directors of the Board of Legal Services on November 3, 1965: Honorable F. Ryan Duffy, Sr. [President, Legal Aid Society of Milwaukee], Charles L. Goldberg [LAS director], Mrs. Julia B. Dolan [LAS Executive Attorney], Ralph von Briesen [LAS director], Bernard J. Hankin [President, Milwaukee Bar Association], Harold F. Lichtsinn [MBA], Theodore W. Coggs [MBA], H.A. Kovenock [MBA], Thomas W. Godfrey [Milwaukee Junior Bar Association], William E. McCarty [MJBA], Thomas G. Hinners [MJBA], Thomas G. Duggan [MJBA], Dean Robert F. Boden [Marquette University Law School], Dr. Arthur C. Moeller [MU Academic Vice President], Louis J. Andrew [MU Student Bar Association], Mrs. Albertine Warren [NAACP], Julio Rodriguez [Spanish-American Association], Mrs. Christine Kiff [BLOCK, Inc.], Ivory Cupil [Organization Of Organizations], Ronald Padway [Allied Council of Senior Citizens], and Samuel Daniels [Northside Community Inventory Conference]. Attorney Goldberg was elected President of the Board. Julia B. Dolan and Margadette M. Demet were later named as (Executive) Director and Deputy Director respectively of Milwaukee Plan Legal Services. See "20 Directors Selected for Legal Aid Service" in *Milwaukee Journal* (November 12, 1965).

74. Old Marquette University Law School, 1924. *Courtesy of Marquette University Archives.*

33·

MPLS LAW REFORM DIVISION

By
Margadette Demet
1967

On Monday, November 20, 1967, the three-judge United States District Court, Eastern District of Wisconsin, by a preliminary injunction, ordered Wisconsin welfare officials to stop enforcing the state's one-year residency relief law, at least on a temporary basis.[1] The order in effect required welfare departments throughout the state to grant assistance to welfare applicants wherever federal funds are given on a participating basis. [*Ramos v. Health & Social Services Board*, 276 F. Supp. 474 (E.D. Wis. 1967)].

This preliminary order represents only one of the exciting successes of a program inaugurated by Milwaukee Plan Legal Services in which attorneys from six of the largest law firms in the city participate on a volunteer basis in the Legal Services Program and offer their skills and the resources of their office to the Milwaukee Plan without charge, especially in matters involving test cases, appeals, and law reform.[2] The firm participating in the welfare residency law case is Foley, Sammond & Lardner, and the attorney of record is Timothy Frautschi.

At the request of Charles L. Goldberg, president of the Board of Legal Services, six law firms agreed early in May 1967 to participate in Milwaukee Plan Legal Services on a strictly volunteer basis. Prior to approval of their participation by the Board of Legal Services, a specific plan of action was submitted by the law firms. This plan was discussed with the director [Julia B. Dolan] and deputy director [Margadette M. Demet] of the program and with members of the Board of Legal Services. In substance, the plan was as follows:

1. A standing committee of the law firms, to be known as the "Urdan Committee,"[3] was set up, having functions and membership described and composed of representatives of the six law firms involved. It was understood from the beginning that additional firms might be added as time goes on.

2. The single goal is to assist the Milwaukee OEO Legal Services Program to the attainment of its goal: "to provide a legal atmosphere conducive to the elimination of poverty."

3. Reality demands that the firms' participation be of actual assistance; efficiency demands that the firms' contribution be of talents and resources not readily available from any other source. Upon the advice of the program's director and deputy director, it was determined that the outstanding need lies in an area where the firms are uniquely endowed. It was therefore accepted as a working hypothesis that the specific task be *to supply the means whereby the program can project its efforts from legal assistance to poverty elimination.*

4. It appears that the program is effectively providing legal assistance to the poor. It equally appears that legal assistance to the poor, in and of itself, may not bring about a legal atmosphere conducive to the elimination of poverty. This was the testimony of all persons interviewed and connected with the program. (An initial task is the verification of this hypothesis.)

5. Specifically, those neighborhood attorneys interviewed testified that, because of heavy caseloads, they lack the time to generalize their experiences into permanent legal reforms. The neighborhood attorneys also observe that they might lack perspective because of their close proximity to their work and thus be blind to internal reforms that could be useful to the attainment of their ultimate goal. The firms could obviously supply the needed time and perspective, and, hopefully, the talent.

6. It seemed evident in the initial planning that, for the volunteers to be of significant assistance, they must first immerse themselves, to some extent at least, in the day-to-day operations of the program. This would give them first-hand experience of the kinds of problems with which they would deal. It would also give them incentive for the task.

7. As a practical matter, the firms plan to rotate the personnel engaged in this work. This raises a problem: How can one preserve the expertise and perspective garnered by one set of individuals for the benefit of subsequent groups? The solution seems to be a semi-permanent group to which rotating personnel would report. This semi-permanent group could also coordinate efforts and act as a moderator for them.[4]

8. It was recognized that the kinds of projects and the methods of work will probably vary widely. Some will involve a single person, some a group. Some may involve appellate litigation; some, legislative draftsmanship; some, other approaches. It was considered unwise to attempt to freeze the exact format prematurely.

It was therefore recommended:

1. that the Urdan Committee of one representative from each participating firm be maintained throughout the existence of the program;

2. that the Urdan group report to, and be responsible directly and solely to, the Board of Legal Services, Inc.;

3. that the Urdan group begin the establishment, in writing, of policy for operating the plan and covering such matters as legal ethics, conflict of interest, publicity, expenditures, and so forth;

4. that the Urdan group generally undertake a continuing process of self-evaluation: whether the plan is of any real value to the attainment of the goal; whether the organization is appropriate.

5. that the Urdan group specifically make a determination, within six months, whether the plan should be continued, wholly abandoned, or totally reconstituted;

6. that each of the firms commit itself to provide a representative to the Urdan group and an attorney, on a four-month rotating basis, who will give a minimum average of sixteen hours per month of services to the plan;

7. that the attorneys provided by the firms be volunteers; and that they be attorneys having not less than one, preferably two, years of practice;

8. that the attorneys provided first familiarize themselves with the operations and problems of the neighborhood offices. (This would not be done on any particular schedule, and the amount of time might well vary from one attorney to the next. It is likely that a certain vicarious-experience effect will develop and that later attorneys will need less time to get the feel of the offices.);

9. that the attorneys, after apprenticeship, work on a particular project or projects of their selection for the remaining period of their four-month assignment to the plan, all such projects to be approved and coordinated by the Urdan group; and

10. that all of these recommendations go into effect forthwith upon the adoption of this plan by the firms; the Board of Legal Services, Inc.; and its contracting agency, the Legal Aid Society of Milwaukee.

The plan was drafted by William J. Kiernan, Jr. of Foley, Sammond & Lardner and took effect on June 13, 1967, upon approval by the Board of Legal Services. Since then, the Urdan Committee has met regularly on a monthly basis, and each of the six law firms has an assignment in a specific area of the law.[5]

A new staff member of Legal Services, Miss Bettie McJunkin, is working with the firms' group as law-reform coordinator. She is a recent graduate of the University of Wisconsin Law School and has completed her academic work for a Master's Degree in social work.

In actual practice, there have been some modifications to the plan. For the most part, it has proved unnecessary for the participating attorneys to serve internships in the neighborhood law offices. Frequent contact with Miss McJunkin has adequately acquainted them with the types of legal problems that are involved. As the plan currently operates, Miss McJunkin goes to the neighborhood offices, at least on a weekly basis, and works with the attorneys in each office to determine what cases present particular problems that could best be tackled by members of the large law firms with their extensive resources. Miss McJunkin then meets regularly with the committee; and once an attorney has been assigned to a particular case, she works directly with him and provides whatever staff assistance may be required.

The *Ramos* case, which is presently being handled by the Foley, Sammond & Lardner firm, involves a test of the Wisconsin welfare residency law. This case provides an excellent example of the cooperation that has been developed with the firms. When it became apparent that the *Ramos* case would provide an ideal fact situation for a test of the local welfare residency law, the case was referred from the neighborhood office to the law-reform coordinator. She contacted the chairman of the committee to determine whether this was a case in which the law firms could act. The chairman of the committee indicated his approval, and, after consultation with him, the law-reform coordinator requested the firm to accept the case. Timothy C. Frautschi was assigned to handle the matter.

Recognizing that there are excellent resources now available in other parts of the country in many specialty areas of the law, attempt is being made to use those resources wherever possible and to prevent duplication of effort. In this case, Columbia University [Center for Social Welfare Policy and the Law in the School of Social Work] offered an ideal resource. The law-reform coordinator was able to obtain considerable assistance from the university in preparing initial papers and providing briefs and other materials for use by the acting attorneys. The time of the assigned attorney from the law firm is thus expended as fruitfully as possible.

The current efforts of the other five firms are as follows:

Quarles, Herriott, Clemons, Teschner & Noelke is studying a case involving several questions with respect to reaffirmation after bankruptcy. It is expected that there will be some developments in this matter shortly [See now *Hanley v Volpe*, 305 F. Supp. 977 (E.D. Wis. 1969)].

Wickham, Borgelt, Skogstad & Powell is serving as a resource in the area of trial specialty and evidentiary problems to the neighborhood offices.

Michael, Best & Friedrich is studying all cases involving questions of unconscionability of contract under the Uniform Commercial Code. Several other actions have already been taken, but details are not available at this time.

Brady, Tyrrell, Cotter & Cutler is studying the garnishment problems of the neighborhood law offices, and Michael Spector of that firm is working on a test case involving eviction of a tenant in a public housing project. The case is *Lewis v. Housing Authority of City of Milwaukee* [E.D. Wis., case no. 67-C-355; 1 *Clearinghouse Rev.* no. 3 (1967) 3-4]. Spector and Paul Miller, chief attorney in the Northside Legal Aid Society Office, are the plaintiff's attorneys. The eviction is being challenged on the grounds that Mrs. Lewis was denied due process and equal protection of the law. A motion to dismiss has been filed by the attorney for the defendant. A hearing on the motion is scheduled for December 15, 1967, in federal court for the Eastern District of Wisconsin.

Whyte, Hirschboeck, Minahan, Harding & Harland is working in the area of landlord-tenant problems. Details of their activities will be available at a later date. [See now *Petersen v. Housing Authority of City of Milwaukee*, Milwaukee County Circuit Court, case no. 359-141; 2 *Clearinghouse Rev.* no. 13 (1968) 16; and *Junker v. Housing Authority of City of Milwaukee*, E.W. Wis., case no. 68-C-303; 4 *Clearinghouse Rev.* (1970) 39].

Assisting the law-reform coordinator and the law firms is the Marquette University Institute on Poverty, through its director, Professor Ramon Klitzke.

A new aspect of assistance has become available to the Milwaukee Plan and is expected to be of great significance in the coming months. The United States Attorney for the Eastern District of Wisconsin [James B. Brennan] and his entire staff have volunteered their services as resource persons to the Milwaukee Plan. It is understood, of course, that they will not be able to participate in criminal matters, or to be involved in any activity in which the federal government is a party. It is expected, however, that the tremendous resources of their office, and

of their outstanding personnel, will be a great asset to the Milwaukee
Plan.

As is apparent in this report, the activity of the law firms is still
relatively new. Actual assignments of projects did not take place until
the latter part of August 1967; hence, the full impact of the participation is not as yet apparent. Close coordination, however, has already
produced a fine rapport between the staff and the firms. Their activities to date have met with the enthusiastic approval of the bar and of
Milwaukee Plan Legal Services.

NOTES

1. This article was written by Margadette M. Demet and published as "Law
   Firms in the Legal Services Program" in *Legal Aid Brief Case* xxvi, no. 2
   (1967) 84-87. It appears by kind permission of the National Legal Aid &
   Defender Association. See also Bettie McJunkin, "Law Reform in Milwaukee Plan Legal Services" in *MBA Gavel* 29, no. 3 (1969) 14-19.
2. The structure outlined here offered three distinct advantages from Dolan's
   perspective. First, it kept staff attorneys in the Legal Aid Society's neighborhood offices focused on individual client service, which she considered
   the primary mission. Second, it deployed significant resources to bear on
   client problems, without any cost to the Society or its clients, thus greatly
   expanding the organization's reach. Third, it provided political cover for
   the Legal Aid Society by requiring approvals from the Board of Legal Services and the Urdan Committee, which was comprised of representatives
   from the city's major law firms.
3. Attorney James A. Urdan was an associate in the Quarles, Herriott, Clemons, Teschner & Noelke law firm and a member of the Board of Legal
   Services.
4. In 1968, the Advisory Board of the Law Reform Division consisted of Mrs.
   Julia Dolan (Director of MPLS), Mrs. Margadette Demet (Deputy Director of MPLS), Lloyd A. Barbee, Michael J. Barron, Warren D. Braun, Jack
   N. Eisendrath, Timothy C. Frautschi, Harold B. Jackson, Jr., John Jackson,
   Thomas M. Jacobson, Frederick P. Kessler, Julilly W. Kohler, Mark G. Lipscomb, Jr., William E. McCarty, Louis J. Mestre, Glen W. Ploetz, Christo-
   pher M. Reuss, Ted Seaver, Robert L. Stonek, and Leonard S. Zubrensky.
   All but Jackson and Seaver were attorneys.
5. This private law firm – legal aid society model was unique in the OEO legal
   services program. *Cf.* Andrea J. Saltzman, "Private Bar Delivery of Civil
   Legal Services to the Poor: A Design for a Combined Private Attorney

and Staffed Delivery System" in *Hastings Law Journal* 34 (1983) 1165-1206; Samuel J. Brakel, *Judicare: Public Funds, Private Lawyers, and Poor People* (Chicago: American Bar Foundation, 1974); Douglas E. Rosenthal et al., *Volunteer Attorneys and Legal Services for the Poor: New York's CLO Program* (New York: Russell Sage Foundation, 1971). As events unfolded in Milwaukee, however, the private bar component receded and MPLS staff attorneys took up the laboring oar on law reform work. See the *Lewis, Junker, Dickhut,* and *Posnanski* cases, *supra.*

34.

MILWAUKEE PLAN LEGAL SERVICES
PROGRAM IDEOLOGY[1]

1965-69

By
Ted Finman

The key promoters of MPLS were Charles L. Goldberg, Mrs. Julia B. Dolan, and Mrs. Margadette M. Demet.[2] The initial impetus came from Goldberg, a member of the board of directors of the Legal Aid Society in Milwaukee and a past president of the state bar. The emerging OEO effort had been a topic of discussion at a meeting of the American Bar Association, which Goldberg attended, where local bar associations had been urged to play a role in the program's development. Goldberg asked Mrs. Dolan, the executive director of the Legal Aid Society, to assume responsibility for the development of an OEO program in Milwaukee.

Mrs. Dolan proceeded to form a committee of three representatives from the senior bar association, three from the junior bar, and three from Legal Aid itself. Mr. Goldberg served on this committee; Mrs. Dolan was its chairman; and Mrs. Demet entered the picture a few months later to take over the job of drafting a suitable proposal.

That these three individuals dominated the development of MPLS and were responsible for its ideological orientation is attributable to several factors. The influence of Dolan and Goldberg came in part from their roles as prime movers. Mrs. Dolan, moreover, as director of the Legal Aid Society, probably was perceived as an "expert" in relation to the problem at hand. Similarly, Goldberg's position as former state bar president and a member of the Legal Aid board of directors helped to make his voice an authoritative one, especially in a context in which most of the listeners were other lawyers. Though Mrs. Demet was not so prominent in her own right, she had the sponsorship of Dolan, and for some months occupied the draftsman's chair, almost always a position of considerable influence.

That the three were the most motivated of anyone involved and undertook the lion's share of the work put them in a position to formulate the proposals to be discussed and thus to set the framework of discussions. From first to final draft, in both form and substance, MPLS reflected their conception of what was needed, their attitudes toward the role of legal services in relation to poverty, and their overall ideological perspective.[3]

That perspective reflected, in Mrs. Dolan's case, many years spent as director of Legal Aid. She had seen a good deal of the poor and their personal problems, and she was not without compassion, but it was the plight of the individual that she saw and responded to, not poverty as a social phenomenon. Moreover, as director of Milwaukee's Legal Aid Society, she had been faced with the job of trying to make limited resources help many people. Given her perspective and the difficulties of her job, she had found friendly accommodation the best approach. She and the administrator of the local welfare program [Arthur Silverman] were good friends and had resolved welfare problems through informal telephone negotiations. "We usually get what we think the client should have," she said. She knew the police chief [Harold A. Brier], the judges, and she considered them her friends. Activists in the poverty community seldom view officialdom in this friendly a fashion, and Dolan, like most people, was not inclined to work with those who saw her friends as enemies.

Dolan saw the new legal service program as essentially an extension and enlargement of the Legal Aid Society, that is, as a way of serving individuals: "Now we will be able to do many things not possible under the old Legal Aid ... help people with divorces without limitation ... spend more time interviewing each individual client ... appear as representatives of plaintiffs pressing small claims." This conception of the program's role was further reflected in her notion of how MPLS could contribute to the war on poverty: "If you can help a man out of a hole, that is breaking the cycle of poverty. Also, if you can help a woman who was deserted ten years ago get a divorce now, I think that is breaking the cycle of poverty." As for law reform: "We will gain knowledge from our experience and go to the bar association and get backing for legislative change, when we have been operation long enough. We'll need about three years." On representing tenants' associations and other groups, she said: "My thought was to get us established and then go on to larger issues. I can't spring a lot of new things on the board of legal services. If I get too wild, it might jeopardize our program."

The program would be under the formal control of the [Board of] Legal Services Inc., a new corporation to be formed for that purpose, and having some members of the poverty community on its board of directors. Since this proposal called for the Legal Aid Society to administer the program, Mrs. Dolan, as executive director of Legal Aid, would be in charge of MPLS's operations. In addition, the plan called for a half-time deputy director, and it was understood that this job was to go to Mrs. Demet. Thus did the ideological orientation of the promoters become the orientation of those who were to control the day-to-day operations of MPLS.

The people who controlled general program policy also saw the program's *raison d'etre* as providing service for individuals and believed that there was little room for other work. This was the prevailing view on the board of directors and of the members of its executive committee. Moreover, in many instances, Goldberg, as president of the board, and Dolan, as program director, consulted on important questions that arose and either made the decisions themselves or framed answers for presentation to the board.

In brief, at all levels, the ideology of MPLS's promoters became the dominant ideology of its hierarchy. The most salient characteristic of this perspective was its focus on serving individual clients. Poverty was a problem of the individual, to be solved by helping him, by breaking the "cycle of poverty" he was caught in. Law reform and group representation may be all right – some doubted the propriety of the latter – but were unlikely to engage the attention of the neighborhood law offices. There was no conception of poverty as an institutional problem, at least not as an institutional problem that MPLS could do anything about. No one spoke of the lawyer as a representative of the poverty community, speaking, litigating, negotiating on behalf of community interests. And certainly no one saw legal service programs as a resource through which the poor might be helped to grow economic or political muscles of their own. As a result of pressure from OEO, the director of MPLS drew the attention of its governing board to the program's failure to promote law reform. The board took two steps to solve this problem. First, several of Milwaukee's large law firms were contacted and asked if they would contribute the services of one associate to help MPLS with law reform work; six firms agreed to participate. Second, a recent law school graduate [Bettie McJunkin] was hired to work full-time on law reform; she was to examine cases pending in the neighborhood offices to see whether any lent themselves to test case treatment, and when one came to her attention, she was to bring it to one of the large firm volunteers who would assume responsibility for the litigation.

Within eight months, the new attorney [McJunkin] had involved MPLS in several test cases. The rules denying aid to dependent children and general relief to persons who had not resided in the state for one year had been attacked [*Ramos v. Health & Social Services Board*, 276 F. Supp. 474 (E.D. Wis. 1967); *Denny v. Health & Social Services Board*, 285 F. Supp. 526 (E.D. Wis., 1968)], as had the public housing authority's rule against renting to women with illegitimate children [*Lewis v. Housing Authority of City of Milwaukee*, E.D. Wis., case no. 67-C-355, in 1 *Clearinghouse Rev.* no. 3 (1967) 3-4; *Fitzgerald v. Housing Authority of City of Milwaukee*, E.D. Wis., in 2 *Clearinghouse Rev.* no. 13 (1968) 14], and a state law on suspension of drivers' licenses [*Llamas v. Dept. of Transportation*, 320 F. Supp. 1041 (E.D. Wis. 1969)]. Two actions were being prepared, one asserting that public housing tenants could not be evicted without first being given a fair hearing [*Petersen v. Housing Authority of City of Milwaukee*, Milwaukee Co. Circuit Court, case no. 359-141, in 2 *Clearinghouse Rev.* no. 13 (1968) 16; *Junker v. Housing Authority of City of Milwaukee*, E.D. Wis., case no. 68-C-303, in 4 *Clearinghouse Rev.* (1970) 39], the other involving a retaliatory eviction [*Dickhut v. Norton*, 45 Wis.2d 289, 173 N.W.2d 297 (1970)]. A judgment obtained by a finance company had been reopened so that the underlying transaction could be challenged.

MPLS's law reform project vastly improved the program's stature as advocate for community interests. This development ran counter to program ideology, however, and there met considerable resistance from the program's hierarchy. In effect, OEO's ideological perspective had come into direct conflict with the local program's orientation. Both exerted an influence and the net result reflected both forces. MPLS developed some test cases, but other actions that should have been brought, including one involving police misconduct, never were.[4]

The lawyer in charge of law-reform coordination [McJunkin] also took an interest in organizing tenants, and met with two community groups that wished to form tenants' unions. In addition, at the behest of another antipoverty agency, she and one of its neighborhood workers investigated a small apartment house and found numerous health code violations; this led to a rent withholding action, for which she and a volunteer from one of the cooperating private law firms provided

75. Old University of Wisconsin Law School, circa 1916.
Courtesy of Wisconsin Historical Society (WHi-57821).

the legal guidance [*Posnanski v. Hood*, 46 Wis.2d 172, 174 N.W.2d 528 (1970)].

The relationship between promoter ideology and performance did not hold in MPLS after OEO began to exert pressure, for the program then developed several test cases. This episode suggests that certain forces outside a legal service program can influence its performance. The result when such force is brought to bear, however, will be a function not only of the outside pressure, but also of the manner in which a legal service program responds to it. The behavior of MPLS and other data suggest that this response will be closely related to program ideology.

NOTES

1. This is an abridged version of a lengthy paper examining five legal service programs around the country. The context of this study makes clear that it was written before October 1969 when LAS severed its ties with the OEO Legal Services program. The study was published two years later by University of Wisconsin Law School Professor Ted Finman, "OEO Legal Service Programs and the Pursuit of Social Change: The Relationship Between Program Ideology and Program Performance" in *Wisconsin Law Review* (1971) 1001-84; reprinted Chicago: American Bar Association and the Russell Sage Foundation, 1972. Copyright 1971 by The Board of Regents of the University of Wisconsin System and abridged by permission of the *Wisconsin Law Review*.

2. Professor Finman's article used letters of the alphabet to disguise the actual names of his study's subjects. Thus, Milwaukee was "City D," MPLS was "LSP-D," Attorney Goldberg was "Q," Mrs. Dolan was "J," and Mrs. Demet was "K." For the reader's convenience, I have restored the actual names throughout this abridgment.

3. Not everyone agreed with Professor Finman's assessment. Henry V. McGee, regional head of OEO Legal Services, praised the Society's MPLS project. "Praise Given to Legal Aid Setup" in *Milwaukee Journal* (November 23, 1966). In addition, MPLS was lauded by John W. Cummiskey, Chair of the American Bar Association Standing Committee on Legal Aid and the Indigent. "Law Expert Praises Aid to Poor Here" in *Milwaukee Journal* (June 8, 1966). See also "Free Legal Service Fights Variety of Battles for the Poor" in *Milwaukee Journal* (May 5, 1969).

4. An anecdote still current at the Legal Aid Society when this author joined the staff recounted that Ted Seaver, head of the Milwaukee Tenants Union, called Julia Dolan one day and demanded that she rush over to federal court and get a temporary restraining order against Police Chief Harold Brier by 5:00 p.m. that same afternoon. Dolan reportedly told Seaver that she did not take dictation from non-clients and promptly hung up the telephone. The story may be apocryphal, but it was certainly consistent with both their personalities. It may also be worth mentioning here that, apropos of LAS's changing legal culture, this author did sue Chief Brier in 1974 on behalf of a prisoner illegally detained in the City Jail.

35.

PUBLIC DEFENDER PILOT PROJECT

1968

It is proposed that the National Legal Aid & Defender Association [funded by the Ford Foundation] provide a grant to the Legal Aid Society of Milwaukee for a pilot and demonstration program in cooperation with Milwaukee County to provide administration service for an assigned counsel system in the criminal and misdemeanor branches of the Milwaukee County courts.[1]

HISTORICAL NOTE

The Legal Aid Society of Milwaukee has operated an ongoing program of legal services to the poor of Milwaukee County for more than fifty years. Since May of 1966, it has also operated an OEO-funded program of multiple legal services to the poor, which has included neighborhood law offices, a bail services program, a defender program, and an extensive community education program.

A large group of the lawyers of Milwaukee County have for many years participated as attorneys for the poor in felony and serious misdemeanor matters on appointment by the judiciary. They have rendered a high caliber of service and have been compensated by the County on a fee schedule that is below the Minimum Fee Schedule of the Milwaukee Bar Association.

The recent decisions of the United States Supreme Court, and the recent Wisconsin decision in the matter of *State ex rel. Plutshack v. State Department of Health & Social Services* [37 Wis.2d 713, 155 N.W.2d 549 (1968)], have made mandatory the appointment of counsel in an increasing number of cases. In 1967, Milwaukee County spent more than $400,000 on representation of indigent defendants in the Criminal and Misdemeanor Branches. It is anticipated that in 1968 the cost may climb to more than $500,000. There has therefore arisen in the County a desire for the examination of methods to minimize the cost of legal representation in these courts. A public defender system has been suggested as a possible means of reducing expenditures.

The Legal Aid Society and the Bar generally believe that the establishment of a public defender system may be inefficient and may not result in the alleged anticipated reduction in cost. Most important is the belief that a public defender system would not produce the caliber of service comparable to that afforded by the private Bar.

It is apparent, however, that some changes must be made in the present assigned counsel system that would produce more efficient results to aid the defendants, the courts, and the Bar, and result in some economy that would be passed on to the taxpayers of Milwaukee County.

THE PLAN

The Court will continue to use the appointive system in all cases in which there is a sentence exposure of six months or more and in such other cases as the Court may in its discretion determine to do so. However, the task of the Court in utilizing and compensating counsel can be greatly eased by the use of an administrative office.

It is proposed that the Legal Aid Society set up an administrative office in the [Public] Safety Building, adjacent to the Criminal and Misdemeanor Branches of the Court. This office would be staffed by an attorney administrator, one attorney assistant administrator, and a legal secretary. All three would be full-time employees. Additional assistance would be provided by part-time law student volunteers. Additional clerical assistance would be provided by lawyers' wives volunteers.

The administrator and his assistant could:

1. Provide such assistance as requested by the Court in expediting the appointment of counsel.
2. When requested by the Court, make the initial appearance in a case where counsel is to be appointed, make routine appear-

ances for adjournments, generally save the time of appointive counsel, and hence save some expenditure by the County.

3. Provide private counsel with assistance in procedures and preparation of pleadings when requested.

4. Develop and maintain a brief bank to which attorneys participating in the assigned counsel panel would be asked to contribute copies of their work product. Due credit would, of course, be given.

5. Work with law student volunteers in giving investigative assistance to assigned counsel and in obtaining background information to assist the Court in determining when a defendant could be released on his own recognizance.

6. Assist the assigned counsel in research on difficult or complicated tasks by putting him in touch with the proper resources at Marquette University Law School, and by maintaining, as above indicated, an up-to-date library file containing the work product of assigned counsel in all unusual cases.

7. Assist the Court when requested in reviewing vouchers of attorneys and discussing with the attorneys any questions that may arise with respect to such matters.

8. Provide such additional services in accord with the program as may be requested by the judges of the Criminal Courts and the Chief Judge.

It may be possible to make use of Milwaukee County's computer program. It is felt that data properly obtained herein and updated at regular intervals could be programmed for computer use, thus producing a further place for increased efficiency and economy.

Marquette University Law School (the resident law school in Milwaukee) and the Marquette Institute on Poverty and the Law, both located in close proximity to the Courts, will offer its extensive resources to the program in the following manner:

1. It will establish and coordinate a training program for the administrators and all members of the assigned counsel panel.

2. It will provide volunteer student participation in the research and investigative functions of the administrative office.

3. It will provide library research assistance to participating attorneys in locating particularized resource materials.

4. It will provide faculty assistance to the administrator and to assigned counsel in criminal matters of particular and special complexity.

5. It will assist in the evaluation of the system and the performance of assigned counsel.

It is recognized that this pilot and demonstration program cannot offer a solution to all needs in the area of criminal representation initially. However, the program can serve as a starting point toward an evaluation of the system of criminal representation in this community that will be useful to the defendant and to the community in the administration of justice.

In September 1968, Milwaukee Plan Legal Services will complete a two-year experimental program in the area of bail services to the indigent, aimed at releasing on his own recognizance every defendant who can be properly released. It is believed that, if such a program were extended to all defendants, it could result in a great reduction in the number being held awaiting trial in the city and county jails and in the removal of many families from the relief rolls. It is the aim of the program to assist the Court in making a decision as to whether or not bail is required, giving fair consideration to both the rights of the defendant and the general welfare of the community. It is therefore hoped that some aspect of this program may either now or in the future become a part of the work of the proposed administrative office.

NOTES

1. Beginning in 1963, the Ford Foundation made grants, which eventually totaled more than $6 million, to the National Defender Project (a collaboration with the National Legal Aid & Defender Association) for the purpose of establishing public defender programs around the country. LAS's proposal targeted these funds. For the background, see Junius L. Allison, "National Defender Project – An Introduction" in *Legal Aid Brief Case* xxvi (1968) 97-99; John J. Cleary, "National Defender Project – A Progress Report" in *Id.* at 99-105.

2. LAS's proposal represents a combination of the assigned counsel system advocated by William Kaumheimer in 1926 and some aspects of the Society's MPLS program for civil legal counsel. The proposal was soon

scrapped in favor of a staffed public defender office that Milwaukee County contracted with the Legal Aid Society to operate.

36.

NATIONAL LEGAL AID & DEFENDER

ASSOCIATION EVALUATION

November 1970

INTRODUCTION[1]

Organized legal assistance for indigents has been available in Milwaukee County continuously since 1916. Milwaukee, therefore, ranks as one of the pioneers in recognizing and implementing this much needed community service. From its inception until approximately 1966, the services were performed solely through the Legal Aid Society of Milwaukee (hereinafter referred to as LAS). In [1916], the LAS became affiliated with the Centralized Budget of Philanthropies of Milwaukee (now evolved into the United Community Services of Greater Milwaukee, Inc.). From that date to the present, the LAS has received its principal financial support from UCS. In 1964, Congress enacted the Economic Opportunity Act, under which was launched a wide expansion program for legal services through the Office of Economic Opportunity. By 1966-67, the LAS was able to expand its scope of operation with additional funding from OEO.

SUMMARY OF PROGRAM

In terms of years of service, the Legal Aid Society of Milwaukee is the elder statesman in the community. It has operated continuously since 1916. Organized as a private non-profit corporation, it is governed by a 15-member board of directors, all but two of whom are lawyers or members of the judiciary. The Society has declared that its "fundamental purpose ... is to see that persons who are poor and oppressed shall obtain justice according to law."

The Society, as presently constituted, has three divisions: the central office, handling only civil matters; the children's court defenders, representing juveniles before the juvenile court on matters of dependency, neglect, or detention; and the criminal defender branch that represents by court appointment indigent defendants in the felony courts. Staff salaries range from $19,000 annually for the executive attorney to $8,000 for an attorney-investigator on the defender staff. The executive attorney has served in that capacity for nearly 31 years. At the start of her employment in 1939, she was assisted by one parttime attorney engaged to handle the court work. One attorney in the central office is now completing 18 years of service. All of the remaining staff attorneys in all divisions have been employed in 1970.

The three divisions are housed separately, with the central office on the second floor of a building near the courthouse and in close proximity to Marquette University. The criminal defender office is in the courthouse, and the children's court defender has offices in the children's court complex in Wauwatosa. Except for the criminal defender office, the offices are adequate and well planned.

In 1940, the first full year after the present executive attorney was employed, the Society's gross budget was $5,955, subsidized primarily by UCS. In that year, nearly 3,000 cases were reported. Twenty-five years later, in 1965, the Society's gross annual budget had risen to $45,759, of which $42,291 was UCS support. New cases had risen to about 4,200 that year. The 1970 budget for the central office is $57,000, with a UCS allocation of about $52,000.

The Society's criminal divisions, recently established, are almost autonomous. Their ties to the central office are essentially administrative, such as payroll, Blue Cross arrangements, and preparation of budget. The staffs of the two criminal divisions have little understanding of what the central office does and exhibit no interest in strengthening their ties. The criminal defender has no overlap with the other legal services projects in the community.

Both criminal divisions are capably staffed with experienced, competent, and zealous lawyers. They have the confidence of the judiciary before whom they regularly appear and are respected by the bar and the community as a whole. It should be recognized that the board of LAS must be credited with the vision, persistence, and persuasiveness that led to establishing these vital community services. The study team acknowledges that both criminal programs are in their infancy. They have already proven effective and practical, although not entirely free from criticism. The nature and scope of service of the central office requires more careful review. The LAS does offer several non-budgeted services that should be mentioned. In cooperation with the Milwaukee Bar Association, it operates a lawyer referral program for persons that do not qualify for free legal assistance. For some years, it has also sponsored and coordinated a voluntary defender program of dubious value in misdemeanor court. A member of the lawyers' wives organization volunteers to handle the administrative details of this project. Marquette law students participate in a clinical experience in each of the program divisions. Most of these activities are commendable and should be retained, but do not necessarily enhance the program's primary responsibility – the delivery of quality legal services to the indigent in the community.

As standards of financial eligibility, the LAS has adopted the OEO poverty guidelines that relate family size to income – for example, a non-farm family of four with an annual income of $3,600 would qualify for free legal assistance. The LAS does take into consideration other related factors, such as recent unemployment, outstanding bills, and special needs. Fee generating cases as well as matters involving copyrights, patents, or libel and slander are automatically excluded.

The Society serves all of Milwaukee County, and also residents of Waukesha and Ozaukee Counties, only however when litigation is in the Milwaukee County court system. There has been a steady and substantial increase in intake activity after the Society terminated the OEO program on September 30, 1969. The bulk of the applications for service require only advice, are ineligible, or receive service that doesn't require litigation. Based on this general practice, it was found that of the 543 new applications for service in August 1970, 80% had only a minimal contact with the LAS. Of the remaining 20%, 4% are matters that were settled for clients and 16% represent cases that were litigated.

It should be noted that the executive attorney does very little court work except on an occasional domestic relations or adoption case. Almost exclusively, she conducts the initial interview with persons applying for service. Thus, she decides on the eligibility of almost every applicant for service. If the case is accepted and is one that she cannot dispose of by advice only, or through negotiation and compromise, she then assigns it to one of the other two full-time lawyers. The half-time lawyer does only court work on behalf of the Society.

The following [caseload] data is based on estimates made by the staff attorneys: Domestic relations 88%, Bankruptcy 7%, and miscellaneous (landlord-tenant and summary probate) 5%. The central office of the Society never appeals cases, has not had a jury trial in 10 years, performs no law reform function, and does not represent any poverty groups.[2] It is 100% oriented to individual client service. Except for family law, the staff attitude at the central office reflects a purposeful avoidance of litigation. Part of this is understandable.

They have a limited staff, a high volume of new applicants, and a relatively low budget. Their substantial domestic relations litigation requires at least one staff attorney in court all day everyday. Little time remains. Intake alone consumes most of the time of one attorney.

76. Ceremonial courtroom, United States Courthouse.
Courtesy of Milwaukee County Historical Society.

With the one full-time attorney and the half-time attorney generally in court, the LAS is left with only one attorney. Administrative responsibility, research, dictation, and the usual pedestrian duties must be fitted in somewhere.

Interviews throughout the community confirm that the LAS is best known for its help on domestic relations matters. This they do well and expeditiously. Through the years, they have developed many legal forms and shortcuts, as well as an expertise and facility for handling these cases. The public and private social agencies recognize this and generally indicate confidence and respect for the services performed by LAS. Few in the community, however, identify the LAS with anything other than family law matters. That they have the respect of the bench and bar is apparent. Again, these interests think of the LAS in terms of domestic relations. An exception are those judges who come into contact with either of the programs in the criminal divisions.

One person who had experience with all three [legal service] programs [LAS, Freedom through Equality, and Milwaukee Legal Services] categorized the LAS as the most compatible of the three. That observation sums up the LAS as a rather reliable, but unexciting, community program. The principal strengths of LAS can be summed up as the specialized services that it performs in family law and in juvenile and adult criminal representation.[3]

Principal recommendation

The LAS must be required to fulfill its own stated goal – a goal which is in complete harmony with the scope of service for a legal assistance program as required by NLADA standard #9 as follows: "Assistance furnished by the organization should encompass all legal work required by the case, including representation before administrative, judicial, and legislative bodies. Appeals should be taken in all cases where appellate review might result in a decision that would better the condition or enhance the legal rights of the persons served by the organization, and if such an appeal is in the interest of and desired by the client."

It is quite obvious that at no time in the history of the LAS has it achieved its own stated goal or that expressed in NLADA standard #9. This is the result of severe malnourishment throughout its history, as without adequate financing it has been unable to fulfill these objectives. During its early years, in an attempt to stretch its limited dollar, it opted to specialize in an area of law that appeared to require urgent assistance. This was a mistake shared by numerous other legal aid societies in the early years. Most programs, however, have revised their thinking and have aggressively sought new direction. The LAS has not. Hindsight now tells us that we were treating the effect rather than the cause. Family problems are bred by economic plight that, among others, arise out of lack of employment opportunity, education, consumer protection (easy credit/shoddy merchandise), and housing. An expanded staff with an aggressive director should immediately pursue a course of action intended to fulfill the LAS goal.

Additional Recommendations

To implement the above, the UCS should be charged with the responsibility of increasing the budget of the LAS to an amount not less than $125,000 annually. Without the infusion of additional funds, the goals of the LAS cannot be realized. The additional funds would immediately permit the LAS to expand its professional staff by from three to seven or eight attorneys with suitable clerical support. Continued UCS involvement representing the voluntary sector is both necessary and wise. Government support for the total needs of these services cannot hope to be realized. Voluntary support also means community involvement and, thus, a healthier and stronger program. Even with the proposed expansion of LAS, it would appear that Milwaukee County would not come close to realizing and meeting the total legal needs of the poor.[4]

As she [Julia Dolan] has expressed plans to retire in the near future, it is urgent that the board of directors immediately hire a new executive attorney who can begin to familiarize himself with the program's administration. That person must also have the qualifications to bring to LAS aggressive leadership in assuming the principal responsibility for expanding the program to provide a full range of legal services rather then the limited scope now available.[5]

The board of directors of LAS should be reorganized and reconstituted to comply with NLADA standard #2, which states that at least one-third (1/3) of the governing board "be residents of the areas or members of the groups eligible to be served by the organization, or their representatives."

Mayo H. Steigler
Director of NLADA Membership Services and former Chief
Counsel of the Legal Aid Society of Minneapolis
Allan Ashman
Director of NLADA Research and Special Projects

Harlan E. Smith
Chief Counsel and Executive Director of the Legal Aid Society of
Minneapolis

NOTES

1. The foregoing is a greatly abridged version of a 30-page report, much of
   which also examined Milwaukee Legal Services and Freedom Through
   Equality. The NLADA report was discussed in "Legal Society Charged
   to Expand Services" in *Milwaukee Journal* (September 19, 1970); "Urge
   Changes in Legal Aid Society" in *Milwaukee Sentinel* (February 8, 1971).
2. This statement ignores the substantial work of LAS's Law Reform Division in the 1967-70 period. It also ignores the reality that, with UCS funding just 2.5 attorneys, no significant law reform work could reasonably be
   done by the Society's central office after the relinquishment of the OEO
   grant on October 1, 1969.
3. Considerable concern was associated with the NLADA report. Some at
   LAS speculated that United Community Services commissioned the evaluation as a predicate to (a) transferring LAS's funding to Milwaukee Legal
   Services, or (b) withdrawing from funding civil legal services altogether.
4. Regrettably, UCS failed to step up to the challenge issued by the report it
   had commissioned. UCS funding of the Legal Aid Society in 1970 was
   $51,944. For 1971, UCS "increased" its grant to $55,902, but deducted
   $4,002 in moving costs it had advanced for the move from the YWCA
   Building to 12th and Wisconsin. UCS had insisted that LAS move so that
   Children's Service Society could expand its quarters in the YWCA building. The net result, therefore, was no increase in funding for 1971. UCS
   also denied the Society's appeal for an extra $12,000 in 1971. In 1972, the
   UCS grant was $58,404; once again, the Society's appeal of the allocation
   was denied.
5. It was speculated that Julia Dolan may have been nudged out by the board
   in response to this report. Jordan B. Reich, "The Legal Aid Society of Milwaukee, Inc." (University of Wisconsin-Milwaukee: unpublished M.P.A.

thesis, 1974) 25. However, her statement to the NLADA evaluators that she was already planning to retire negates that conclusion.

37.

REAPPLICATION FOR OEO FUNDS

MAY 8, 1973

Board of Directors
Legal Aid Society
Milwaukee, Wisconsin

This letter is intended as a summary of the events of the last two weeks regarding the possible funding of Legal Aid Society (LAS). The sequence of events is as follows. We received a call requesting that we send representatives to Washington to meet with O.E.O. officials. David Berman went as our agent. He was advised that O.E.O. is considering terminating the funding of MLS [Milwaukee Legal Services] and FTE [Freedom Through Equality] and transferring such funds to LAS.[1] David indicated that, subject to the approval of our Board of Directors regarding the details, we should be prepared to accept such funds. The budget was discussed in terms of some $600,000 annually. David returned to Milwaukee on Saturday, April 28, and I met with him on April 29 and he brought me up to date on his trip.

We called a board meeting as soon as possible, which turned out to be May 2, to report to our board on the status of the matter. Apparently a rumor had been circulated that that meeting was called for the purpose of ratifying certain acts such as acceptance of the funds and the meeting was attended by a large number of persons affiliated in one way or another with MLS or FTE. I attempted to assure them that we were not soliciting the funds or in any way critical of their organizations, but merely responding to overtures from OEO. The persons present at that meeting made a strong argument to the effect that if LAS was to receive such funds, it was essential that LAS become more representative of poverty groups and its Board of Directors be structured to follow the lines of the MLS and FTE boards. As chairman, I stated that I could not make such a commitment on behalf of LAS, but we would certainly consider the possibility. Mary Lou [Massignani, LAS board member] then made a motion that each of the three organizations should appoint representatives to attend a meeting to discuss changing the structure of the LAS board if LAS ended up receiving the funds.

Following that meeting, we submitted an application form to Washington, which I understood to be consistent with the original resolution authorizing David to go to Washington in our behalf.

The committee of the three organizations met on May 7. The meeting lasted about two hours and many points of view were expressed. The conclusion, however, was that MLS and FTE feel strongly that by applying for OEO funds, LAS is seriously hampering, if not destroying the possibility of MLS and FTE continuing in existence and obtaining funds themselves. They advised us that they are planning on sending representatives to Washington to persuade OEO to continue funding the merged organization, that there are some advantages in having more than one legal organization in Milwaukee representing our respective clients since there are cases where there are conflicts of interest such as divorce and others, and further, that since we received some of our funds from Milwaukee County, we are not in a position to freely pursue actions in which the County may be a party.

It became apparent to those of us representing LAS at the meeting that if we proceed on our present course of action, even if we are successful in obtaining the grant, we will arouse animosities on the part of the persons presently involved with MLS and FTE. Some of these animosities, in my judgment are not well founded, but that may be beside the point. The point is that we cannot represent poor people in this community if we do not have their confidence and respect, and we will not have their confidence and respect if they feel that we usurped their functions by forcing them out of the picture without their consent.

Accordingly, we agreed to call another meeting. You will receive notice of the time and place in the near future. At that meeting, we agreed to permit one representative of each of the organizations to appear and to state the position of their respective organizations. We further agreed to present to our board a resolution whereby we would agree to withdraw our application to OEO, thereby giving the other two organizations the opportunity to attempt to continue to receive OEO funds. Whether our withdrawal of the application would have this effect, it is, of course, impossible to say. It does seem to me, however, and I believe that the other LAS representatives at the meeting concur, that to obtain federal funds at the price of alienating the other legal service organizations in Milwaukee is self-defeating. Moreover, the point was made that our submission of the application following the May 2 meeting was not consistent with the understanding of certain persons present at that meeting. Specifically, they understood that, until the restructuring of the LAS board was considered, we would defer any further action. Since a number of persons appear to have that impression, it seems to me that for that reason alone, we should consider withdrawal of our application so that we cannot be accused of acting in bad faith.

They also requested that we endorse the MLS-FTE application for funding. This would be going one step further than merely withdrawing our application until the situation is clarified. We stated that we could give no assurance that our board members would endorse other legal service organizations with which they are not personally familiar, but we certainly would agree to present that possibility to the board.

I give you this background information for your consideration so that at the forthcoming board meeting all of us will be aware of the events to date. In view of this unsettled state of affairs, and since it is apparently impossible for us to assemble a quorum within the next few days, I suggest that David contact the officials in Washington and request that they defer acting on our application at least until our board meets, which will be within one week. Since I will be out of the city on May 8 and 9, I suggest that if any of you have a contrary view and wish the processing of the application to proceed, you contact David directly and advise him of your opinion.[2]

Sincerely yours,
Robert M. Weiss
President

NOTES

1. Contemporary news accounts described OEO's action as designed to force FTE and MLS to merge into the Legal Aid Society. See "Legal Aid Projects Near Merger Point" in *Milwaukee Journal* (May 2, 1973).

2. The LAS board met on May 14. Present were Robert M. Weiss (President), Robert A. Christensen, Patrick W. Cotter, Paul Feldner, Raymond Majerus, Mary Lou Massignani, Richard F. Mooney, William J. Mulligan, James E. Shapiro, Harney B. Stover, Brother Paschal Stubbs, and Leonard S. Zubrensky. Staff present were David S. Berman, Jordan B. Reich, and Thomas G. Cannon. Mr. Weiss reported that he had received a telephone call from Robert Kinney, Deputy Director of OEO Legal Services in Washington, D.C., requesting that LAS go forward with its application for federal funding. Steven Steinglass, Executive Director of FTE, and Robert Munro, Executive Director of MLS, were invited to speak to the board; they urged that LAS withdraw its application to OEO. Among the concerns raised was the inevitable reduction in availability of legal representation for eligible poor that would result from a combined program due to conflict of interest rules. After due discussion and debate, a motion to withdraw was passed on an 11-1 vote (Harney B. Stover dissenting). See "Legal Aid Society Drops Bid for Others' Money" in *Milwaukee Journal* (May 15, 1973).

38.

JOINT LAS-SPD BOARD MEETING

February 19, 1979

Minutes

Thomas Cannon introduced the individual members of the respective boards of the Legal Aid Society (LAS) and the State Public Defender (SPD).[1]

Mr. Cannon outlined the budget background of the SPD program. He stated that LAS would require $1.89 million in the first year of the biennium to handle a caseload of 100 felony cases per attorney per year, 250 misdemeanor cases per attorney per year, 150 mental commitment cases per attorney per year, and 125 juvenile [delinquency] cases per attorney per year. He stated that the proposed SPD budget would only provide $1.35 million with an anticipated caseload of 150 felonies/attorney/year, 350 misdemeanor cases per attorney/year, 200 mental commitments per attorney/year, and 200 juvenile cases per attorney/year.

Frank Remington [Chair, SPD Board] stated that his board had the option of instituting their own program in Milwaukee County or contracting with LAS with the understanding that there were probably inadequate funds to do so. He stated that a contract with LAS would probably be opposed by the Department of Administration and that the Legislature would not add to the budget the funds necessary to meet the contract demands stated by Mr. Cannon.

Robert Christensen [President, LAS] stated that representation of indigents should be equal to that afforded individuals represented by the private bar with the only differences in quality being those differences that are inherent among individual lawyers. He stated that the NLADA [caseload] standards are not a useful guide for discussion because those figures were developed twelve years ago, which was prior to the enormous expansion of substantive and procedural law. He stated that the Legal Aid Society would not participate in a public defender program unless it was convinced the program would provide adequate representation.

Richard Cates [Acting State Public Defender] stated that he respected Mr. Christensen's position, that he respected Mr. Cannon, and that he found the LAS staff to be inspirational.[2] However, he noted that the contracting idea was having a serious impact on the SPD budget. He stated that he respected the singular quality of the LAS staff and that he would like to enlist that staff in the event of a State takeover.

Theodore Hodan [SPD board member] stated that he felt the SPD staff was being unrealistic and that it would be a mistake for them to handle such a high caseload level. He further stated that he thought the maximum caseload should be 115 [felony] cases. He suggested contracting with LAS for one more year so that the new Public Defender would have an opportunity to become familiar with the State program.

Mr. Cannon stated that he hoped the SPD board would insist on the same level of quality that LAS was insisting on. He further stated his hope that both boards would present a united front to the Legislature.

Stephen Glynn [LAS board member] said that it would be short-sighted of the SPD board to accept from the Legislature less than that amount of money necessary to provide adequate representation. He stated his view that it would be impossible to provide adequate representation in Milwaukee County under the budget proposed by the

SPD board. He advocated that the State board advise the Governor that the budget was totally unrealistic and that the SPD board should go out of business rather than afford ineffective assistance of counsel. William Coffey [SPD board member] stated that the SPD program was locked into its budget request and that it would be impractical to push further. He pointed out that even the SPD budget proposal would not meet Mr. Cannon's contract demands.

[The meeting was adjourned for separate board conferences at this time].

Mr. Cannon advised the LAS board that it would have to balance an inability on the part of LAS to provide effective assistance of counsel under the SPD budget versus an even greater deterioration of the quality of counsel were the SPD program to take over. He advised the board not to contract with the State.

After extensive discussion, it was moved and unanimously voted not to change the LAS [caseload and budget] proposal.

[Meeting with SPD board resumed in main meeting room.]

Mr. Christensen advised the SPD board that LAS figures are the final word of the LAS board. He stated that LAS could not provide effective assistance of counsel at a caseload that exceeded the LAS proposal.

At this time, the SPD board moved and voted to not accept the LAS proposed contract. It carried on a 5-2 vote with Mr. Hodan and Mr. Sykes dissenting.

Professor Remington thanked the members of LAS for their hospitality and their demonstrated commitment to providing effective counsel to the poor. He stated that he was personally appreciative of LAS's high standards, as well as the tremendous amount of work by Thomas Cannon and the LAS board. He further stated that the SPD program would need the cooperation of the LAS and he hoped that would be forthcoming. Mr. Christensen assured him that the LAS would provide its fullest cooperation.

NOTES

1. LAS board members present were Robert A. Christensen (President), David J. Cannon, Professor Carolyn Edwards, Gerald M. Elliott, Curry First,

Stephen M. Glynn, Aaron E. Goodstein, Barbara Pleasant, and Brother Paschal Stubbs. Staff present were Thomas G. Cannon, William U. Burke, Neil C. McGinn, and Thomas K. Zander. SPD board members present were Professor Frank Remington, Eleanor Brennan, William M. Coffey, Patricia M. Heim, Anita Herrera, Theodore J. Hodan, and Donald Sykes. Staff present were Richard L. Cates (Acting State Public Defender) and Ronald L. Brandt, Deputy SPD.

2. An unusual feature of the SPD-LAS contract was that the SPD board retained the option to terminate the agreement if the LAS board removed the Society's Executive Director.

39.

TO PROTECT AND SERVE:

LEGAL AID SOCIETY CELEBRATES 90 YEARS

By
Sean Ryan[1]
2006

Thomas Cannon might not wear a cape, but he sure sounds like a superhero. The executive director of the Legal Aid Society of Milwaukee

77. Architectural detail depicting the sword and scale of Justice. Milwaukee Public Safety Building. *Courtesy of Legal Aid Society of Milwaukee.*

talks about justice for all. He recognizes the dark side of humanity that leads people to prey on those who can't protect themselves. He knows that people with power must fight villainy.

"As long as human nature is what it is, the weak and the defenseless will always need an advocate," Cannon said. "If there were no Legal Aid Society, I think it would have a catastrophic effect on the city because there'd be no place to go to right wrongs. I think there'd be an increase in violence and an increase in crimes. There would certainly be an increase in misery."

Fortunately for those in need, the Society has some deep roots in the city, a fact that the Legal Aid Society will recognize when it celebrates its 90th anniversary on September 7 at the Italian Community Center in Milwaukee.

Cannon speaks softly and deliberately, representing an unassuming approach that matches the Society's office – a short, concrete building dwarfed by the Marquette Interchange's bridges.

But the Society, with a staff of 40 people, does some heroic stuff. It represents clients who otherwise couldn't afford an attorney. Those clients include 5,000 battered and abused children a year, the Hurricane Katrina refugees who came to Milwaukee, victims of predatory lenders, the mentally disabled, and families facing unfair eviction.

"It's a tremendous privilege to work for the poor and do advocacy on their behalf," Cannon said. "It gives them an advocate for their position, whether it's a child in need of protection or an elderly person who's disabled.

The Society has a long history in the city, but Cannon said the mission is the same as it was when Milwaukee's socialists founded it in February 1916. The issues, however, are a lot different. The bulk of the Society's early work was representing workers whose employers tried to stiff them on their paychecks. These days, the group sees more predatory lending cases.

It won a decision from the Wisconsin Supreme Court in May that bars lenders from forcing borrowers into arbitration if they have a dispute. "Our victory in the (*Wisconsin Auto Title Loans Inc.*) case in the Wisconsin Supreme Court affects literally tens of thousands of consumers in the Wisconsin court system," Cannon said.

Cannon said about 80 to 95 percent of poor people who need legal help can't get an attorney, and he estimated that the Legal Aid Society has the resources to help about 5 percent of those in Milwaukee County. "We try to balance the interests of individuals in getting relief from an oppressive situation with the ramifications of other people who are similarly situated," he said.

"It does (frustrate me) because you would like to see everybody have access to justice and the opportunity to be heard." On that note, the Society filed a brief in a state Court of Appeals District 4 case arguing that all people should have a right to an attorney in civil lawsuits.

As for the future, Cannon said the Legal Aid Society will continue doing what it has always done until there are no more victims. "There's a world out there in which the strong prey on the weak and that's unfortunate, but it's part of human nature," he said. "There's always going to be a need for a Legal Aid Society."

NOTE

1. This article is reprinted, with kind permission of the editor, from *The Daily Reporter* (August 24, 2006).

40.

DELIVERING ON THE PROMISE OF

EQUAL JUSTICE

By
Thomas G. Cannon
Marquette University
March 16, 2007

In preparing my remarks for this inaugural Wisconsin Equal Justice Conference, I reread the state's pioneering legal needs study. It documents the threshold fact that existing agencies serving the poor are overwhelmed by an increased demand for civil legal services.

The report highlights some specific problems. These include: (i) loan-sharking in which the poor are charged exorbitant rates of interest on consumer loans; (ii) unjust wage garnishments, (iii) unconscionable consumer contracts, (iv) family disputes, (v) landlord-tenant problems, and many more.

The study concludes that volunteer pro bono legal services, and re-duced-fee arrangements, while helpful, are inadequate for dealing with the enormous need. It recommends that the only meaningful remedy for pervasive injustice is to provide substantial public funding for a fully-staffed legal aid program.

Lest you be misled, the seminal legal needs study I refer to is not the State Bar of Wisconsin's *Bridging the Justice Gap* report, which was released just last week. Instead, I read the King-Commons report, en-titled *Free Legal Aid*, which was compiled here in 1911. That study was the catalyst that led directly to formation of the Legal Aid Society of Milwaukee.

It must be said that in comparing the two documents – written 96 years apart – one gets the distinct impression that very little has changed with respect to the community's commitment to equal justice for the poor.

Last year, I wrote an *amicus curiae* brief in *Parrish v. Romfeldt-Men-doza* – a civil right-to-counsel case being litigated in the Wisconsin Court of Appeals by my colleague here, John Ebbott. The brief was in the Brandeis style. It cited numerous government studies and non-profit reports on the crisis facing the poor in our city and state. I'd like to share just a few of the disturbing, indeed shocking, findings cited there:

+ More than half a million Wisconsin residents are eligible for free legal services because they are too poor to hire an attorney.

+ Milwaukee is the 7th poorest city in the United States and contains the 4th highest percentage of poor children in the country.

+ In the past generation, the poverty rate in Milwaukee has nearly doubled from 1 in 7 residents to more than 1 in 4.

+ 127,000 Milwaukeeans are functionally illiterate – meaning that they would be unable to understand a summons and complaint if served upon them.

+ Milwaukee has the second-highest teen birth rate in the country.

+ By age 12, one out of every 8 Milwaukee Public School students has been raped.

+ Milwaukee's infant mortality rate is nearly double the national aver-age – and it is higher than in some Third-World countries like Costa Rica.

+ 150,000 Milwaukee County residents qualify for food stamps.

+ 89% of all Milwaukee Public School students qualify for free or reduced-price lunches.

✦ More than 1,000 people sleep every night in Milwaukee's parks, streets, alleys, and outdoor venues. Many of them suffer from mental illness.

✦ 253,000 Milwaukee County residents are on Medicaid.

✦ Eight inner-city hospitals serving the poor have shut their doors in the past 30 years; only three are left to serve this huge number of poor.

✦ The majority of the adult male population, in nearly one-third of Milwaukee's census tracts, is unemployed.

✦ An average of 10,000 Milwaukee Public School students are truant on any given school day.

✦ More than 65,000 crimes are reported each year to the Milwaukee Police Department. Most of the victims are poor.

✦ 50% of all homicides in the entire state of Wisconsin occur in just 4 Milwaukee zip codes.

✦ An epidemiologist found that murder suspects and victims had one thing in common: the overwhelming majority of both were born to teen mothers.

✦ Despite being one of the great cities in the richest nation on earth, Milwaukee's inner city increasingly has the look and feel of a Third-World community.

Lawyers – working alone – can't solve the underlying social and economic causes, which include: (i) the collapse of the heavy-manufacturing economy that once provided tens of thousands of well-paid jobs in Milwaukee; (ii) the rise of the global economy that pays slave wages in the Third World to produce consumer goods in the First World; (iii) the prevalence of regressive social attitudes that hurt the poor – especially young mothers and their children; and (iv) the culture of greed that makes it possible for the comfortable to abandon the needy.

Lawyers, however, can address the legal problems resulting from poverty. This effort has been underway in the state since the founding of the Legal Aid Society of Milwaukee in 1916. Addition of the AIDS Resource Center of Wisconsin, Catholic Charities Immigration Law Project, Disability Rights Wisconsin, Legal Action of Wisconsin, and Wisconsin Judicare has added more muscle to the cause in recent years.

Nonetheless, as the Brandeis brief demonstrates, the social and economic implosion in Wisconsin's largest city has far outstripped the limited resources of our legal service providers to respond to the growing crisis we face. In fact, the U.S. Census Bureau recently reported that, during the past two years, Wisconsin's poverty population increased the fastest of all fifty states.

It is clear, therefore, that unbundled legal services, supplemented by *pro se* training, courthouse kiosk information centers, self-help legal forms, and increased use of non-attorney specialists, while valuable for the relatively small number of well-educated litigants, only nibble at the fringes of the crisis.

Some legal service providers disagree on this point, but I do not favor charging the eligible poor a reduced fee for legal services. By definition, those attempting to survive on an income below the federal poverty guideline [45 C.F.R. § 1611.3 (2006)] cannot provide the necessities of life for themselves or their families.

The poor should not have to choose between paying rent and paying a lawyer, between feeding their family and paying a lawyer, or between heating their home in Wisconsin's winter climate and paying a lawyer. It is unconscionable to force clients, who under federal law qualify for *free legal services*, to pay up to $700 per case as they are now required to do by some providers.

Justice – and access to justice – necessarily means access to lawyers. This is the birthright of every Wisconsin resident. Justice, liberty, and equality are our most cherished ideals, but without lawyers, they're only words.

78. Stone carved pediment, United States Supreme Court Building.
Courtesy of U.S. Supreme Court.

More than half a century ago, Judge Learned Hand famously said, "If we are to keep our democracy, there must be one commandment: Thou shalt not ration justice." In discussing this topic, though, we continually hear a common refrain: "There's no money to adequately fund civil legal services for the poor."

My response? A community that spends $400 million building a baseball stadium [Miller Park] replete with a state-of-the-art retractable roof, and $295 million remodeling a football stadium [Lambeau Field], *simply to entertain itself,* has the economic wherewithal to spend a tiny fraction of those amounts on equal justice for the poor. The refusal to do so can only suggest a civic culture that values entertainment more highly than it prizes justice.

Consider this: every time an impoverished mother in Milwaukee or Green Bay buys clothing for her family, or school supplies for her children, the sales tax on those necessities goes, in part, to subsidize our court system – and, in part, to subsidize those stadiums. Unfortunately, the poor can afford access to neither courthouse nor stadium.

The State of Wisconsin currently provides zero public funding for civil legal services to the poor. This embarrassing record stands in contrast to our neighboring states. Ohio, for example, contributes $14 million per year to the cause; Minnesota appropriates more than $12 million annually, and Michigan provides $7 million a year.

Getting serious about solving the legal needs of Wisconsin's poor will inevitably require a substantial commitment of public funds. We will have made no progress during the last 96 years if we fail to understand this elementary truth. And the deliberate refusal to commit those funds will also mean that we have cynically defaulted on delivering our constitutional promise of equal justice under law.

41.

TESTIMONY BEFORE

U.S. SENATE COMMITTEE ON AGING

WASHINGTON, D.C.

By

Catherine M. Doyle

Chief Staff Attorney

February 13, 2008

Mr. Chairman [Senator Herb Kohl], Senator [Gordon] Smith, and Members of the Committee. Thank you for inviting me to testify today regarding "Foreclosure Aftermath: Preying on Senior Homeowners." Thank you also for holding this hearing to examine the issue of what are now commonly known as mortgage foreclosure "rescue" scams. I offer my testimony on behalf of the Legal Aid Society of Milwaukee's low-income clients. I appreciate the opportunity to speak about the experiences of victims of these frauds in Milwaukee County. Our experience is representative of large urban communities across the United States.

The Legal Aid Society provides legal representation to hundreds of Milwaukee County residents facing foreclosure. There were more than 5,600 mortgage foreclosures filed in Milwaukee County in 2007, an increase of 55% over 2006. With the rise in foreclosures, unfortunately, we have experienced the appearance of mortgage foreclosure "rescue" scams. Over the past two years, the Legal Aid Society has seen an increasing number of victims of these frauds, a significant percentage of whom are senior citizens.

In late 2005, an eighty-three-old woman and her daughter, Yvonne and Susan Klemund, came to our office describing a very disturbing and unusual situation. They had been served with eviction papers in an attempt to remove them from their own home of more than 30 years. These women were distraught and had great difficulty explaining what had happened to them. Fortunately, I had just returned home from a conference addressing the problem of mortgage foreclosure "rescue" frauds presented by the National Consumer Law Center. I had also read a comprehensive report issued by the NCLC, *Dreams Foreclosed:*

The Rampant Theft of American Homes Through Equity-Stripping Foreclosure "Rescue" Scams (June 2005).

Upon investigation, the Legal Aid Society discovered that, through a complex web of trusts, deeds, and power of attorney, the Klermunds had lost their home to a "rescue" fraud. The perpetrators of the scam had stolen their entire equity in the home – over $58,000. The Klermunds received nothing, not one dime, from their "rescue." The Legal Aid Society has represented the Klermunds for more than 2 years in extensive litigation over these transactions. On Christmas Day 2007, Yvonne passed away.

The Klermunds' case was our first involving mortgage foreclosure "rescue" fraud in Wisconsin. We have litigated numerous cases of fraud since then and have worked very closely with law enforcement officials and prosecutors to being these scam artists to justice. The Legal Aid Society has also worked with the Wisconsin Legislature for passage of a bill that will strictly regulate the foreclosure consultant business and the sale of properties in foreclosure.

These victims were lucky in one respect – they were able to find legal representation at the Legal Aid Society. Most victims lack the resources to retain legal counsel. Few private attorneys are experienced in recognizing and litigating this species of fraud. In Milwaukee County, state and federal prosecutors have been investigating the most egregious cases, but the scams are complicated and the resources of prosecutors are already stretched to the limit. Although we look forward to criminal prosecutions in many cases, it is often necessary to pursue civil litigation first in our effort to reclaim the stolen real or personal property within the statute of limitations.

Under the current state of the law, when representing victims, the Legal Aid Society must piece together legal claims from federal statutory law and Wisconsin common and statutory law – often dusting off old law books to bring claims for void conveyances and equitable mortgages. We bring claims of intentional misrepresentation, theft by fraud, breach of fiduciary duty, and similar claims. Where appropriate, we also bring claims under the Truth-in-Lending Act, Home Ownership Equity Protection Act, Wisconsin Consumer Act, Wisconsin Responsible High Cost Mortgage Lending Act, and Wisconsin's Unfair and Deceptive Practices Act.

In addition to the "rescuer," there may be other parties who have participated in the scam to varying degrees – straw buyers, appraisers, closing agents, mortgage brokers, and lenders. Pursuing claims against the "rescuers" and their accomplices requires intensive and lengthy litigation. Many of the claims the Legal Aid Society relies on require proof of intent or other special elements. Other claims are based on archaic common or statutory law with little, if any, recent precedent. The facts are so strange that judges have difficulty wrapping their heads around the issues. Proving damages can be very complicated.

Seeking redress for these frauds on a case-by-case basis is impossible. Clearly, a better approach is legislation that will prevent the occurrence of the scams in the first place. The testimony presented today demonstrates the need for appropriate legislation and regulation to protect vulnerable homeowners in foreclosure, many of whom are senior citizens. From my experience, many victims become paralyzed by fear and embarrassment, and thus become perfect victims for solicitations made by "rescuers." It is time to stop these scams and direct foreclosed homeowners to legitimate avenues of help.

My more detailed written presentation, filed with the Committee today, contains numerous specific suggestions that may be of assistance to the Senate in drafting the legislation necessary to protect these innocent victims. The Legal Aid Society of Milwaukee looks forward to working with Chairman Kohl and other members of this Committee to develop a strong, effective response to stop these outrageous scams. Thank you.

42.

LAS POSITION ON INDEPENDENCE OF GUARDIAN AD LITEM PROGRAM

2009

[Milwaukee County issued a Request For Proposals for guardian ad litem services in Children's Court and Family Court. The RFP contained a number of provisions that the Legal Aid Society believed would compromise the independence of its GAL program. These included (1) requiring the GAL to file a petition if the District Attorney's Office refused and the judge ordered the GAL to do so; (2)

requiring GAL staff to submit detailed hourly time records for each closed case to the Chief Judge; (3) requiring trial judges to conduct formal personnel evaluations of the GAL staff; (4) reserving to judges the right to appoint individual GALs from the Legal Aid Society staff on individual cases; (5) requiring submission of both a flat cost-per-case figure and a detailed line-item budget to the Chief Judge; (6) giving the Chief Judge power to veto GAL budget items; and (7) providing the Chief Judge with the power to resolve all disputes concerning services provided under the contract according to such vague standards as "failure to establish effective working relationships." What follows is an abstract of LAS's objections to these provisions.]

Both the Wisconsin Legislature and the Wisconsin Supreme Court guarantee the independence of guardians ad litem. Thus, Wis. Stats. ss 48.235(3)(a) [Children's Code], 54.40 [Guardianships], and 767.407(4) [Family Code] require that "the guardian ad litem shall function independently, in the same manner as an attorney for a party to the action." These statutes necessarily mean that the GAL must perform its duties as independently as the District Attorney (who represents the public), the State Public Defender (who represents the parents), and private counsel who are retained by parties to a case.

Similarly, the Supreme Court's Rules of Professional Conduct for Attorneys mandate that a lawyer must exercise independent professional judgment on a client's behalf – especially where a third party (as Milwaukee County is here) pays the lawyer's fee. Wis. SCR 20:5.4(c). The Comment to Wis.SCR 20:1.8 explains:

> Because third-party payers frequently have interests that differ from those of the client, including interests in minimizing the amount spent on the representation and in learning how the representation is progressing, lawyers are prohibited from accepting or continuing such representation unless the lawyer determines that there will be no interference with the lawyer's independent professional judgment and there is informed consent from the client.

Since LAS's wards are of tender years, they lack the legal capacity to consent to third-party payment of their legal fees – making independent judgment all the more crucial in representing the interests of vulnerable minors.

Judicial control of a GAL office also contravenes national professional benchmarks. Thus, the American Bar Association *Standards of Practice for Lawyers Who Represent Children in Abuse and Neglect Cases* (1996) insist that "[t]he child's attorney should be independent from the court, court services, the parties, and the state." *Id.* at 19.

Indeed, even the County's RFP itself, in section 7.5, makes clear that the contracting Agency is deemed to be an "Independent Agency" for all legal purposes, and that "[n]either Agency nor Agency's employees shall be deemed to be employees of Milwaukee County." The County can hardly insist on GAL independence to limit its own liability, while at the same time insist on controlling key aspects of the GAL staff and office.

The seven provisions mentioned above are objected to on a number of grounds. First, they do not apply to the District Attorney, State Public Defender, or retained private counsel. They are, therefore, an obvious violation of the statutory guarantee of GAL independence. Second, they carry with them the clear potential to chill the GAL's zealous advocacy required by Wis. SCR 20: Preamble [2]. For example, will a GAL, who knows s/he is up for a personnel review by a judge, file a writ of substitution against that judge or seek appellate review of that judge's ruling? Third, the power to appoint individual staff members to specific cases includes the power to punish some GALs for zealous representation by excluding those staff attorneys from the appointing court. In addition, the exercise of such power could wreak havoc with the efficient management of LAS's simultaneous obligations to other courts.

The provision requiring the GAL to file a petition when ordered to do so by the Court (after the refusal of the District Attorney) abrogates the GAL's independent professional judgment. If the GAL determines that such petition is (a) not in the best interest of his or her ward, or (b) is not supported by applicable facts or law, s/he cannot ethically file such a petition. Wis. SCR 20:3.1. LAS suggests that the language be changed to provide that the judge may *request* the GAL to consider filing a petition when the District Attorney declines to do so.

The proposed flat fee per case is at odds with the detailed hourly time sheets required by the RFP. Wis. SCR 20:1.0(dm) specifically warns that a flat fee is "not an advance against the lawyer's hourly rate and may not be billed against an hourly rate." The alternate forms of billing are mutually exclusive. Moreover, lacking knowledge about specific cases, neither the Chief Judge nor the Clerk of Circuit Court is in a position to evaluate whether GALs are spending too much time or too little time, and too many or too few resources on individual cases. Since the RFP calls for a fixed fee per case, it is neither necessary nor appropriate to demand itemization of time and services.

The RFP also confers on the Chief Judge the unilateral power to modify or terminate the contract under such vague standards as "inability to establish effective working relationships; inability to follow directions … and/or other performance problems." These provisions constitute a contract of adhesion that effectively converts the GALs into employees of the Chief Judge rather than the independent counsel that the Legislature, Supreme Court, and *ABA Standards of Practice* require. Such one-sided contracts have recently been invalidated by our Supreme Court as unconscionable. See *Wisconsin Auto Title Loans v. Jones,* 2006 WI 53, 290 Wis.2d 514, 714 N.W.2d 155 – a case won by the Legal Aid Society. They also conflict with Wis. SCR 20:1.15(b)(4m), which requires binding arbitration of any fee dispute.

For 40 years, the Legal Aid Society has provided full accountability for the public funds its GAL program receives by (i) undergoing daily judicial supervision of each and every GAL case presented in court, (ii) providing detailed monthly case statistics to the Clerk of Circuit Court, (iii) providing an annual independent audit to the Clerk of Circuit Court, (iv) appearing before the County Board Judiciary Committee to present testimony and answer questions about the operation of the GAL program, (v) informally soliciting judicial input into programmatic performance on an annual basis, and (vi) reporting regularly to the Legal Aid Society's independent board of directors, which includes a retired Milwaukee County Chief Judge, former Milwaukee Bar Association President, Marquette University Law School professor, and partners in the city's largest law firms. For four decades, these measures have provided taxpayers with an appropriate degree of accountability while at the same time preserving the GAL office's guaranteed independence from unwarranted judicial interference. To paraphrase an old proverb, there is no wisdom in attempting to "fix" what isn't broken.

NOTE

1. In negotiating a three-year extension of the GAL contract, Milwaukee
County agreed to drop all seven proposals for judicial control of the program.

43.

LEGISLATIVE ADVOCACY FOR CHILDREN

March 5, 2010

Honorable Russell S. Decker
Senate Majority Leader
State Capitol – Room 211 South
Madison, WI 53707-7882
Re: Senate Bill 384
Dear Senator Decker,[1]

The Legal Aid Society of Milwaukee is Wisconsin's oldest public
interest law firm. Each year it represents more than 5,500 children
in Family Court and Children's Court. In these cases, Circuit Court
judges appoint staff attorneys from the Society to serve as guardians
ad litem to advocate the best interests of our minor wards in a wide variety of cases that include child abuse and child neglect. The Legal Aid
Society represents, by far, more Wisconsin children than any other
law firm in the state.

In light of our statutory responsibility to protect the legal rights of
vulnerable children (ss. 48.235, 54.40, and 767.407, Wis. Stats.), the
Legal Aid Society of Milwaukee strongly opposes Senate Bill 384,
which seeks to create an affirmative defense in child abuse/neglect
prosecutions for parents or guardians who choose spiritual, prayer, or
religious treatment in lieu of medical treatment for minors in their
care.

Senate Bill 384, if enacted, would place Wisconsin children in grave
danger by jeopardizing their health and safety. While prayer and spiritual practices may complement sound medical care, they are no sub-
stitute for professional treatment by a licensed medical doctor. I note
that the Wisconsin Medical Society, Wisconsin District Attorneys
Association, and the Wisconsin chapters of the American Academy

79. Justice entrance to Milwaukee County Courthouse.
Courtesy of Legal Aid Society of Milwaukee.

of Pediatrics and the National Association of Social Workers join us in opposing SB 384.

Wisconsin law has long recognized that children's legal right to medical treatment overrides their parents' or guardians' religious beliefs. See Wis. Stats. ss. 48.13 (10), 48.373, 48.981 (1)(d), and 938.373. These statutes are rooted in the principle that the child's welfare and best interests must be made paramount in cases of parental neglect. *In re Stittgen*, 110 Wis. 625, 631-32, 86 N.W. 563 (1901). Furthermore, this principle has been approved by the United States Supreme Court in *Bellotti v. Baird*, 428 U.S. 132 (1976).

Given that Senate Bill 384 conflicts with these longstanding provisions of Wisconsin law, I respectfully ask that you refer it back to Committee.

We also believe that Representative Terese Berceau's AB 590 should be enacted instead. Her bill properly places children's health and safety first and eliminates any doubt about the responsibilities of adults charged with caring for minors.

Thank you for your attention to this urgent matter.

Kind personal regards.

Very truly yours,
Thomas G. Cannon
Executive Director

NOTE

1. This letter provides an example of the Society's legislative advocacy. Such representation gives a voice to otherwise voiceless wards in the halls of political power. And it fulfills LAS's original mission "to promote laws and measures" on behalf of its vulnerable clients.

44.

LETTER RE PROPOSED CLASS ACTION BAN

May 20, 2010

Honorable Willie Johnson, Jr.
Chair, Judiciary Committee
Board of Supervisors
901 North 9th Street
Milwaukee, WI 53233
Re: Resolution 10-202 (Supervisor Jursik)
Dear Chairman Johnson:

At the May 13th meeting of the Judiciary Committee, you kindly invited me to submit a written presentation explaining the Legal Aid Society of Milwaukee's opposition to Supervisor Jursik's proposed ordinance change, which would prohibit contractors from filing class action lawsuits against the County.

The resolution was prompted by the Legal Aid Society's class action suit on behalf of prisoners detained in the Milwaukee County Criminal Justice Facility on the grounds of overcrowding, unsanitary living conditions, and failure to provide adequate mental health services to inmates. *Christensen v. Sullivan*, case no. 96-CV-1835.

I want to reiterate that this case was not sought out by the Legal Aid Society. Rather, LAS was appointed to represent the prisoners by then Chief Judge Michael Skwierawski after inmates contacted the court directly. In other words, LAS was directed to represent the prisoners

by an independent, co-equal branch of Milwaukee County government, the judiciary.

Since 1970, and simultaneous with the entire *Christensen* case,
LAS has represented children as court-appointed guardians ad litem
in Milwaukee County's Family Court and Children's Court; our legal fees have been paid by contract with the County at a considerable
cost savings to local taxpayers as compared with what private counsel
would charge for the same services. The Society's representation of
children under that contract is unrelated to its court-appointed representation of prisoners.

This letter will address the public policy, constitutional, and ethical
objections LAS has to the proposed ordinance.

PUBLIC POLICY OBJECTIONS

Wisconsin law imposes a heavy stewardship responsibility upon counties for the care of the poor and vulnerable, especially children, mental
patients, the elderly, and prisoners. Over the past four decades, various
lawsuits filed by the Legal Aid Society against Milwaukee County have
led to important and necessary reforms at the Department of Public
Welfare, Juvenile Detention Center, Child and Adolescent Treatment
Center, foster care system, Mental Health Center, County Jail, and
now the Criminal Justice Facility. These lawsuits assisted Milwaukee
County in carrying out its stewardship responsibilities to care for the
vulnerable. Supervisor Jursik's proposed ordinance would remove an
important layer of accountability in the County's discharge of those
obligations by circumventing independent judicial scrutiny.

Both the Legislature and the courts have recognized a strong public
policy in encouraging efficient resolution of disputes by authorizing
class actions – cases in which multiple claims raising similar issues
can be resolved in one lawsuit. Supervisor Jursik's proposed ordinance
would require the filing of hundreds or thousands of individual suits
– all raising the same legal and factual claims – which would impose
an intolerable burden on the court system. Even if the proposed ordinance were enacted, efficiency considerations would force the judges
to convert such duplicative individual suits into a class action. See Local Rules 1.3 and 3.3. Since the County Board partially funds the Milwaukee County court system, public policies favoring efficient resolu-

tion of litigation and reduction of court congestion mandate use of class actions in appropriate circumstances.

Wisconsin law provides judges with ample authority to punish plaintiffs for filing frivolous lawsuits. This punishment includes dismissal of frivolous claims and imposition of financial sanctions against both the plaintiffs and their lawyers. See Wis. Stats. sec. 802.05. Judges are more experienced and better situated than county supervisors to determine the merits of class-action claims. Upholding the important constitutional right of access to justice, while ferreting out frivolous claims, is better handled by the judge assigned to the case than it would be by blanket legislative fiat.

It should be recalled here that the *Christensen* case was determined to be a meritorious one. In a memorandum decision dated January 2, 2006, the trial court found Milwaukee County in contempt of court for committing more than 16,000 intentional violations of the court's order implementing the Consent Decree. Specifically, it held that "conditions in the booking/open waiting area [of the Criminal Justice Facility] ... are unacceptable, if not appalling." The court went on to make specific findings of fact that included "overly crowded conditions, inmates who were forced to sit or sleep on the floor next to urinals, inmates who had to sit up for hours and hours, lack of hygiene, unsanitary conditions, inmates who were not given pillows or blankets to sleep on, cells that were infested with bugs, cold temperatures, bodily fluids on the floor, and bad odors... Some of the inmates were held in booking in excess of 100 hours." *Id.* at p. 7.

CONSTITUTIONAL OBJECTIONS

Various provisions of the Wisconsin Constitution also prohibit enactment of the proposed ordinance. Art. I, sec. 9, for example, guarantees that "Every person is entitled to a certain remedy in the laws for all injuries, or wrongs which he may receive in his person, property, or character." Our Supreme Court has interpreted this clause as guaranteeing a remedy for any "legislatively recognized right." *Aicher v. WI Patients Comp. Fund*, 237 Wis.2d 99, 122-23, 613 N.W2d 849 (2000). Wisconsin's Legislature has specifically recognized the right to file class actions by enacting Wis. Stats. sec. 803.08. Therefore, by restricting a legislatively-recognized remedy, the proposed ordinance violates a guaranteed right in the state Constitution.

Art. I, sec. 21 of the Wisconsin Constitution additionally guarantees the right of "any suitor [to] prosecute ... his suit ... by an attorney of the suitor's choice." The proposed ordinance would bar clients of the Legal Aid Society from engaging the Society to represent them in class action cases against the County – thus depriving those clients of the right to counsel of their choice. For the wealthy, this would impose no hardship; they can retain any private law firm to advocate on their behalf. The poor, however, cannot hire replacement counsel due to their poverty. Only a public-interest law firm like the Legal Aid Society, whose services are provided free of charge, can offer such representation. By banning LAS from filing class action claims against the County, the proposed ordinance violates the constitutional right of the poor (but not the wealthy) to appear by counsel of their choice. Necessarily, enactment of such an ordinance would also violate Art. I, sec. 1 of the state Constitution, which guarantees all Wisconsin citizens, rich and poor alike, the right to equal protection of the laws.

The proposed ordinance is further barred by the separation of powers doctrine in the Wisconsin Constitution, Art. VII, sec. 2. Under the contract with Milwaukee County, Legal Aid Society attorneys serve as court-appointed guardians ad litem for children. Guardians ad litem are cloaked with quasi-judicial immunity because they discharge a quasi-judicial function in ensuring the protection of minors. *Paige K.B. v. Molepske*, 219 Wis.2d 418, 580 N.W.2d 289 (1998). The legislative branch cannot restrict the role of court-appointed, quasi-judicial officers by limiting the remedies they may pursue under judicial supervision in representing their minor wards. *County of Dane v. Smith*, 13 Wis. *585 (1861). The proposed ordinance represents an impermissible interference with the functioning of an independent, co-equal, elected branch of government.

Both the Wisconsin Legislature and the Wisconsin Supreme Court have guaranteed the independent judgment of court-appointed guardians ad litem. Wis. Stats. secs. 48.235(3)(a), 54.40(3), and 767.407(4); Wis. SCR 20:5.4. Any attempt to control the remedies pursued by a guardian ad litem through passage of a local ordinance is *ultra vires* – that is beyond the constitutional power of the Board of Supervisors.

Local government cannot interfere with, or limit, state legislative and judicial mandates.[1]

ETHICS OBJECTION

In addition to its public policy and constitutional deficiencies, the proposed ordinance barring class action lawsuits against the County is itself barred by multiple provisions of the Wisconsin Supreme Court Rules of Professional Conduct for Attorneys. SCR 20:5.4 expressly prohibits this type of restriction on a lawyer's independent professional judgment. That rule mandates that "A lawyer shall not permit a person [Milwaukee County] ... who pays the lawyer [Legal Aid Society] to render legal services for another [children in Family Court and Children's Court] to direct or regulate the lawyer's professional judgment in rendering such legal services."

To similar effect, SCR 20:1.8(f)(2), governing conflicts of interest, also precludes any "interference with the lawyer's independence of professional judgment or with the client-lawyer relationship" whenever compensation is paid by one other than the client. The Comment to this rule states: "Because third-party payers [Milwaukee County] frequently have interests that differ from those of the client [LAS's child wards] ... lawyers are prohibited from accepting or continuing with such representation unless the lawyer determines that there will be no interference with the lawyer's independent professional judgment."

Since LAS's independent professional judgment may dictate that its clients' interests require the filing of a class action against Milwaukee County, an ordinance cannot direct the lawyer to refrain from doing so. Notwithstanding enactment of the proposed ordinance, no law-

---

1 . A Judiciary Committee staff memo, which attempted to draw an analogy to the Congressional ban on use of Legal Services Corporation funds for class action cases, is inapposite. That ban was (1) not imposed by a local governmental body, (2) does not address Wisconsin Constitution provisions or Supreme Court ethical rules, and (3) does not apply to court-appointed guardians ad litem discharging a quasi-judicial function. Moreover, it has been clear for more than a century and a half that Wisconsin courts have inherent judicial power under the state Constitution to order a county board to pay for court-appointed counsel. *Carpenter v. County of Dane*, 9 Wis. 249 (1859). This power cannot be limited by a county board. 63 Op. Atty. Gen. Wis. 323 (1974).

yer licensed to practice law in Wisconsin may agree to violate the Supreme Court Rules of Professional Conduct by accepting limitations on the remedies s/he will pursue on behalf of clients – especially limits imposed by a third-party payer for services provided to vulnerable children.

CONCLUSION

The proposed ordinance runs counter to sound public policy by removing independent oversight and promoting court inefficiency, strips away guaranteed constitutional rights of Milwaukee County's most vulnerable residents, and violates the Supreme Court's ethical rules for attorneys. I respectfully urge members of the Judiciary Committee to reject Resolution 10-202.

In closing, I want to thank you for affording me the opportunity to express the Legal Aid Society's views on this important matter. I will be happy to appear before the Judiciary Committee at its meeting on June 10 to answer any additional questions you or members may have.

Kind personal regards.

Very truly yours,
Thomas G. Cannon
Executive Director

45.
LETTER RE MENTAL COMMITMENT WORK

June 1, 2010

Mr. Michael L. Morgan, Secretary
Department of Administration
101 East Wilson Street – 10th Floor
Madison, WI 53702-0001
Re: RFP for fixed-fee contracts for Chapter 51 cases in Milwaukee County

Dear Secretary Morgan,

The Legal Aid Society has had a series of contracts with either the State Public Defender or Milwaukee County to provide representation of defendants in Chapter 51 mental commitment proceedings since 1977. Our current contract with the State Public Defender (SPD) expires on June 30.

80. United Way's 2010 campaign highlights Legal Aid Society on I-43 billboard.
Courtesy of Legal Aid Society of Milwaukee.

Pursuant to a directive from the Department of Administration, the SPD issued a request for proposals to do this work. The RFP, which solicited bids as of June 28, did not provide for an agency (such as the Legal Aid Society) to bid on this work. I have reviewed the RFP materials and have reluctantly concluded that its structure of parceling out Chapter 51 cases in Milwaukee County among up to ten individual attorneys would not be compatible with our agency model of providing representation. Accordingly, our individual staff attorneys will not submit a bid in response to the RFP.

Notwithstanding this decision, however, I request that the Department of Administration consider authorizing the SPD to extend its current contract with the Legal Aid Society (LAS) because of concerns that the format envisioned by the RFP would lead to a dilution of the quality of representation currently received by our clients in Chapter 51 proceedings. Extending the current contract with LAS offers three significant advantages for such clients: experience, breadth of advocacy, and leadership.

First, LAS has represented individuals facing civil mental commitments in Milwaukee County since 1944 when such proceedings were brought before the Lunacy Commission. Beginning in 1977, LAS entered into a series of contracts with both the State Public Defender and Milwaukee County to provide representation in Chapter 51 cases.

Over these many decades, the Society has developed good working relationships with the State Public Defender Office, judges, Corporation Counsel, the staff of the Mental Health Complex, Marquette University Law School, and advocacy groups such as Disability Rights Wisconsin.

Mental commitments are a highly specialized area of legal work. No private practice attorney can match either the depth of institutional experience that LAS has in this field or the network of working relationships that LAS has carefully built up over many years.

Second, the work of the Legal Aid Society in the field of mental disabilities has extended beyond individual representation to include legislative advocacy and class action litigation. Indeed, it could be said that the current statutory framework for civil commitment is largely the product of a single individual: Tom Zander, my predecessor at LAS. In addition, I offer just a few examples of LAS's ground-breaking litigation advocacy on behalf of mentally disabled clients over the past four decades:

• *State ex rel. Memmel v. Mundy*, 75 Wis.2d 276, 249 N.W.2d 573 (1977), a class action case that established the right to zealous and competent legal representation for those facing civil mental commitment.
• *State ex rel. R.T. v. Silverman*, case no. 507-431 (Milwaukee County Circuit Court, 1979), a class action case that established the right of juveniles to the most appropriate and least restrictive mental health treatment.
• *State ex rel. Watts v. Combined Community Services Bd.*, 122 Wis.2d 65, 362 N.W.2d 104 (1985), mandating annual judicial review of individuals in court-ordered protective placements.
• *Guardianship and Placement of K.S.*, 137 Wis.2d 570, 405 N.W.2d 78 (1987), which upheld the privilege of confidentiality of medical and psychological records when the patient's condition is placed in issue by the state.
• *State ex rel. Jones v. Gerhardstein*, 141 Wis.2d 710, 416 N.W.2d 883 (1987), establishing the right of an involuntarily committed patient to refuse psychotropic medication.
• *In Matter of Guardianship of R.S.*, 162 Wis.2d 197, 470 N.W.2d 260 (1991), recognizing the right to cross-examine an adverse psychologist in person in court.

• *In re Commitment of Louise M.*, 205 Wis.2d 162, 555 N.W.2d 814 (1996), holding that trial judge's review of a court commissioner's probable cause determination must be conducted in a timely manner.

• *In Matter of Delores M.*, 217 Wis.2d 69, 577 N.W.2d 371 (Ct. App. 1998), determining that the 72-hour probable cause period is triggered when the patient is taken into custody. This decision ends the practice of "hiding" patients in unapproved facilities to circumvent time constraints.

• *Christensen et al. v. Sullivan*, 2009 WI 87, 320 Wis.2d 76, 768 N.W.2d 798 (2009), a class action case that among other issues established the right of prisoners in the Milwaukee County Criminal Justice Facility to receive adequate mental health services.

• *In Matter of Mental Commitment of H.T-O.*, Appeal no. 2010-AP-256, a case challenging the denial of an interpreter to translate the commitment petition and other documents from Spanish into English for a monoglot Spanish-speaker. This case is pending.

Once again, no individual private attorney can duplicate this established record of advocacy on behalf of the mentally ill.

Third, our current supervising attorney (Karen Kotecki) has been defending individuals in mental commitment hearings continuously for the past 19 years. Her role as a leading advocate for the mentally ill can be seen in some of the numerous presentations she has made around the state. Recent examples include:

"The Ethical Considerations of Representing Mentally Ill and Retarded Individuals," Annual Poverty Law Update (December 3, 2009).

"Effective Communication Strategies for Dealing with Emotionally and Mentally Distressed Individuals," U.S. Bankruptcy Court Seminar (October 13, 2009).

"Chapter 51 from Start to Finish," Legal Aid Society of Milwaukee (November 10, 2008). This presentation included her 156-page outline.

"Addressing Elderly with Dementia and the Developmentally Disabled," at Adult GAL Training, State Bar Seminar in Madison (May 22, 2008).

The Legal Aid Society's "modern" involvement in mental commitment cases began in 1976 in response to systemic failures in legal representation that led to the *Memmel* case, *supra*. At that time, Milwaukee County Probate Court judges appointed a panel of six part-time private practitioners to handle all Chapter 51 cases. LAS brought a class action writ of habeas corpus that resulted in an order to release or retry all patients at the Mental Health Center because of inadequate legal representation.

I am deeply concerned that replacing the Legal Aid Society with a similar panel of part-time practitioners returns to a flawed model and will inevitably lead to a lower quality of representation for this very vulnerable population. Forgoing LAS's personal and institutional experience, its broad and aggressive track record of advocacy for the mentally ill, its long-established networking among community partners, and its recognized leadership in the field – and replacing these assets with a patchwork of part-time lawyers is not in the best interests of those we serve.

If you have any questions, I would be happy to meet with you to discuss the advantages of extending the SPD contract with the Legal Aid Society to continue providing highly specialized representation in Milwaukee County Chapter 51 proceedings.

Thank you for consideration of this alternative.

Kind personal regards.

Very truly yours,
Thomas G. Cannon
Executive Director

INDEX OF LEGAL CASES

GENERAL INDEX